COMPUTER EVIDENCE:

COLLECTION & PRESENTATION

LIMITED WARRANTY AND DISCLAIMER OF LIABILITY

THE CD-ROM THAT ACCOMPANIES THE BOOK MAY BE USED ON A SINGLE PC ONLY. THE LICENSE DOES NOT PERMIT THE USE ON A NETWORK (OF ANY KIND). YOU FURTHER AGREE THAT THIS LICENSE GRANTS PERMISSION TO USE THE PRODUCTS CONTAINED HEREIN, BUT DOES NOT GIVE YOU RIGHT OF OWNERSHIP TO ANY OF THE CONTENT OR PRODUCT CONTAINED ON THIS CD-ROM. USE OF THIRD-PARTY SOFTWARE CONTAINED ON THIS CD-ROM IS LIMITED TO AND SUBJECT TO LICENSING TERMS FOR THE RESPECTIVE PRODUCTS.

FIREWALL MEDIA (AN IMPRINT OF LAXMI PUBLICATIONS PVT. LTD.) AND/OR ANYONE WHO HAS BEEN INVOLVED IN THE WRITING, CREATION OR PRODUCTION OF THE ACCOMPANYING CODE ("THE SOFTWARE") OR THE THIRD-PARTY PRODUCTS CONTAINED ON THE CD-ROM OR TEXTUAL MATERIAL IN THE BOOK, CANNOT AND DO NOT WARRANT THE PERFORMANCE OR RESULTS THAT MAY BE OBTAINED BY USING THE SOFTWARE OR CONTENTS OF THE BOOK. THE AUTHOR AND PUBLISHER HAVE USED THEIR BEST EFFORTS TO ENSURE THE ACCURACY AND FUNCTIONALITY OF THE TEXTUAL MATERIAL AND PROGRAMS CONTAINED HEREIN. WE, HOWEVER, MAKE NO WARRANTY OF ANY KIND, EXPRESS OR IMPLIED, REGARDING THE PERFORMANCE OF THESE PROGRAMS OR CONTENTS. THE SOFTWARE IS SOLD "AS IS" WITHOUT WARRANTY (EXCEPT FOR DEFECTIVE MATERIALS USED IN MANUFACTURING THE DISK OR DUE TO FAULTY WORKMANSHIP).

THE AUTHOR, THE PUBLISHER, DEVELOPERS OF THIRD-PARTY SOFTWARE, AND ANYONE INVOLVED IN THE PRODUCTION AND MANUFACTURING OF THIS WORK SHALL NOT BE LIABLE FOR DAMAGES OF ANY KIND ARISING OUT OF THE USE OF (OR THE INABILITY TO USE) THE PROGRAMS, SOURCE CODE, OR TEXTUAL MATERIAL CONTAINED IN THIS PUBLICATION. THIS INCLUDES, BUT IS NOT LIMITED TO, LOSS OF REVENUE OR PROFIT, OR OTHER INCIDENTAL OR CONSEQUENTIAL DAMAGES ARISING OUT OF THE USE OF THE PRODUCT.

THE SOLE REMEDY IN THE EVENT OF A CLAIM OF ANY KIND IS EXPRESSLY LIMITED TO REPLACEMENT OF THE BOOK, AND/OR CD-ROM AND ONLY AT THE DISCRETION OF FIREWALL MEDIA (AN IMPRINT OF LAXMI PUBLICATIONS PVT. LTD.).

THE USE OF "IMPLIED WARRANTY" AND CERTAIN "EXCLUSIONS" VARIES FROM STATE TO STATE, AND MAY NOT APPLY TO THE PURCHASER OF THIS PRODUCT.

COMPUTER EVIDENCE:

COLLECTION & PRESENTATION

CHRISTOPHER L.T. BROWN

FIREWALL MEDIA

(An Imprint of Laxmi Publications Pvt. Ltd.)

BANGALORE • CHENNAI • COCHIN • GUWAHATI • HYDERABAD
JALANDHAR • KOLKATA • LUCKNOW • MUMBAI • PATNA
RANCHI • NEW DELHI

Published by :

FIREWALL MEDIA

(An Imprint of Laxmi Publications Pvt. Ltd.)
113, Golden House, Daryaganj,
New Delhi-110002

Phone : 011-43 53 25 00
Fax : 011-43 53 25 28

www.laxmipublications.com
info@laxmipublications.com

Economy Edition Price : ₹ **350.00** *Only.* *Edition* : 2012

OFFICES

✆ **Bangalore**	080-26 75 69 30	✆ **Chennai**	044-24 34 47 26
✆ **Cochin**	0484-237 70 04, 405 13 03	✆ **Guwahati**	0361-251 36 69, 251 38 81
✆ **Hyderabad**	040-24 65 23 33	✆ **Jalandhar**	0181-222 12 72
✆ **Kolkata**	033-22 27 43 84	✆ **Lucknow**	0522-220 99 16
✆ **Mumbai**	022-24 91 54 15, 24 92 78 69	✆ **Patna**	0612-230 00 97
✆ **Ranchi**	0651-221 47 64		

FCO-2871-350-COMPUTER EVIDENCE-CHR **C—3912/011/0**

Printed at : Sanjeev Offset Printers, Delh

To my life inspiration, Bobbie and Rudy & Annie

Contents

Acknowledgments

In life we hardly ever go it alone. The same holds true when taking on writing projects such as *Computer Evidence: Collection and Preservation*. Many people such as technical editors Mark Menz, Erin Kenneally, and Gary Kessler and the Charles River Media staff have contributed significantly to the creation of this book. I would like to specifically call attention to and thank members of the High-Technology Crime Investigation Association (HTCIA), High-Tech Crime Cops (HTCC), and Computer Forensics Tool Testing (CFTT) list servers for their support and mentoring over the years. This book could not have been created without their vast cumulative knowledge. Individual support that bears recognition goes to Brian Carrier for helping us all make better tools through his CFTT postings, Steven Richardson, and Ted Augustine for taking up the slack at Technology Pathways, and the staff at Tartine's in Coronado for providing a welcomed place to go at the end of the day.

Introduction

The use of computers has expanded to every part of our lives and businesses. Computers, data communications, and data-storage devices have become so ubiquitous that very few crimes or civil disputes do not involve them in some way. Many books and formal training programs have emerged to teach computer forensics to law enforcement and the private sector. The 50,000-foot view of the computer forensics process includes four phases: collection, preservation, filtering, and presentation. Because these four phases cover such a broad area, books and courses that try to address each area usually relegate evidence collection to its simplest form, disk imaging, leaving all but the most basic questions unanswered. Because of this gap, this book intends to focus on the first two phases of computer forensics, which include the critical tasks of identifying, collecting, and maintaining digital artifacts for admission as evidence. The first two phases of computer forensics are the most critical to evidence acceptance, yet they are often given narrow coverage by texts and courses to make room for the extensive coverage needed by the filtering phase. The filtering phase describes the methodologies used by computer forensics examiners to filter out unwanted information from each platform type or more accurately filter in any potential evidence. The filtering and analysis of digital evidence has been extensively covered in other sources. By focusing on the first two phases of the computer forensics process, this book allows for a more thorough coverage of the topic and sets the stage for other books that focus on the second two phases.

Evidence dynamics, which falls in the collection and preservation phases of computer forensics, can be described as any force that affects evidence in some way. An example of evidence dynamics is found in the simple act of a computer forensics investigator shutting down a suspect's computer. This seemingly innocent act changes the state of the computer as well as many of its files, which could be critical to the investigation.

NOTE

Almost 50 files are changed in some way on each boot of the Microsoft® Windows® XP operating system, and five or more new files are created.

The deterioration of backup tapes over time is also an effect of evidence dynamics. An understanding of evidence dynamics is essential when collecting evidence. This book uses evidence dynamics at the center of its approach to show the reader what forces act on data during evidence identification, collection, and storage. By placing specific focus on how the investigator and his tools are interacting with digital evidence, this book will help guide the computer forensics investigator on how to ensure case integrity during the most crucial phases of the computer forensics process.

TARGET AUDIENCE

This book is intended for use by law enforcement, system administrators, information technology security professionals, legal professionals, and students of computer forensics. Essentially anyone who could become involved in the collection and maintenance of computer evidence for court will benefit from this book.

ORGANIZATION OF THIS BOOK

Computer Evidence: Collection and Preservation is presented in five parts, containing a total of 16 chapters. Additional sections describe the accompanying CD-ROM and expansive appendixes.

Part I, Computer Forensics and Evidence Dynamics: This part includes three chapters that provide the groundwork for an understanding of what computer forensics is in the context of this book and describe our approach to the collection of digital evidence.

Chapter 1, "Computer Forensics Essentials," introduces the reader to the essential elements of computer forensics. Specific attention is paid to ensure the reader is provided with a contextual understanding of computer forensics in general as well as the specific phases of computer forensics covered in this book.

Chapter 2, "Rules of Evidence, Case Law, and Regulation," provides a discussion on rules of evidence, existing computer-related case law, and regulation as a basis of understanding the nature of computer evidence in court. In-depth discussion specifically covers the admission of computer-specific scientific evidence.

Chapter 3, "Evidence Dynamics," provides information about evidence dynamics, which is defined as anything that effects evidence in any way. Human and environmental factors that are key evidence dynamic components are explained in this chapter.

Part II, Information Systems: This part contains three chapters that explain methods through which organizations implement information technology. Understanding how organizations implement information technology solutions is a key component to identifying potential evidence.

Chapter 4, "Interview, Policy, and Audit," presents the key components to knowing where data can be found within an organization's infrastructure. This chapter explains key interview questions to ask and the importance of existing policies and auditing them.

Chapter 5, "Network Topology and Architecture," shows how an organization's information architecture can be as diverse as a city's streets. This chapter explains differing network topologies and how the topology can affect the location and accessibility of potentially critical evidence.

Chapter 6, "Volatile Data," examines the volatility of digital data in physical memory and storage. Differing types of volatile physical memory including personal devices such as PDAs and cell phones are discussed.

Part III, Data Storage Systems and Media: The primary focus of many computer forensics investigations is the extraction of digital evidence on disk. In Part III, we examine various media technologies and filesystems used to store data.

Chapter 7, "Physical Disk Technologies," explains the key components of the IDE, SIDE, and SCSI standards as they pertain to evidence collection.

Chapter 8, "SAN, NAS, and RAID," describes advanced physical storage methods in use today. This information is essential to any forensics investigator involved in the collection of digital data on corporate disks.

Chapter 9, "Removable Media," examines some of the many types and formats of removable media including flash cards and optical media.

Part IV, Artifact Collection: The methods employed for the collection of computer evidence can be one of the most highly scrutinized areas of the computer forensics process. It is essential that investigators use tested and proven methodologies. Part IV provides detailed procedures for artifact collection.

Chapter 10, "Tools, Preparation, and Documentation," describes one of the most important components of any computer forensics investigation. This chapter provides tools, methods, and forms for keeping investigations on track.

Chapter 11, "Collecting Volatile Data," shows how volatile data can be difficult to capture in a forensically sound fashion. This chapter provides proven tools and methods for capturing volatile data from systems.

Chapter 12, "Imaging Methodologies," describes how methodologies used in computer forensics can be as varied as the systems being imaged. This chapter presents the many approaches and tools used for imaging disk media. This chapter also provides discussion on which methods are indicated for specific situations.

Chapter 13, "Large System Collection," shows how the collection of evidence from large computer systems can be challenging to any investigator. In even the smallest of organizations, more than a terabyte of data is often present. This chapter examines methods for large systems collection and management.

Part V, Archiving and Maintaining Evidence: Once potential computer evidence is collected, it needs to be examined and maintained. In Part V we discuss computer forensics workstations, labs, evidence archival, and physical security.

Chapter 14, "The Forensics Workstation," reflects the peripheral diversity and unique nature of each case worked. This chapter walks readers through different design options to get the most out of their hardware configuration in the field and back at the lab.

Chapter 15, "The Forensics Lab," shows how today's computer evidence investigators rarely work from a single forensics workstation. This chapter discusses how to migrate from an individual computer forensics workstation to forensics networks within a lab environment. Additional topics include live storage, physical security, and lab certification.

Chapter 16, "What's Next," presents our final chapter in which areas for further study in computer forensics such as analysis and presentation of evidence in court are discussed. Other topics addressed include future directions in computer forensics and methods for staying informed.

Appendixes

Appendix A, "Sample Chain of Custody Form"
Appendix B, "Evidence Collection Worksheet"
Appendix C, "Evidence Access Worksheet"
Appendix D, "Forensics Field Kit"
Appendix E, "Hexadecimal Flags for Partition Types"
Appendix F, "Forensics Tools for Digital Evidence Collection"
Appendix G, "Agencies, Contacts and Resources"
Appendix H, "Investigator's Cisco Router Command Cheat Sheet"
Appendix I, "About the CD-ROM"

CONVENTIONS

This book uses several conventions to identify important information for readers as they move through the chapters. Information such as sidebars, facts, tips, notes, cautions, and warnings are identified by icons in the left margins.

Some agencies and organizations compartmentalize the profession with computer forensics investigators, technicians, examiners, and experts, all who perform some or all portions of the computer forensics process. This book makes no such distinction among these titles and refers to all computer forensics practitioners as computer forensics *investigators*.

Part I

Computer Forensics and Evidence Dynamics

Part I, "Computer Forensics and Evidence Dynamics," includes three chapters that provide the groundwork for understanding what computer forensics is in the context of this book and describes our approach to the collection of digital evidence. Part I introduces investigators to the basic crime-scene investigative principles of evidence dynamics, the legal aspects surrounding rules of evidence, and the four phases of the computer forensics process.

1 Computer Forensics Essentials

In This Chapter

- What Is Computer Forensics?
- Crime Scene Investigation
- Phases of Computer Forensics
- Formalized Computer Forensics from the Start
- Who Performs Computer Forensics?
- Seizing Computer Evidence
- Challenges to Computer Evidence

WHAT IS COMPUTER FORENSICS?

For the purposes of this text, we define *computer forensics* as the art and science of applying computer science to aid the legal process. That's right, it is both an art and a science. Although plenty of science is attributable to computer forensics, most successful investigators possess a *nose* for investigations and a skill for solving puzzles, which is where the art comes in. This subtle distinction is highlighted to encourage investigators to think outside all the structure provided in the forthcoming methodologies. That is not to say readers shouldn't follow the presented methodologies, but they should strive to use individual thought when applying methodologies, check sheets, and recommendations provided throughout the book.

With such a broad definition of the subject, our work is cut out for us. What may prove more helpful than defining the term is identifying the primary goals in computer forensics. These goals are to collect, preserve, filter, and present computer system artifacts of potential evidentiary value.

NOTE *Care is being taken to state "artifacts of potential evidentiary value" rather than say "evidence." It is important to remember that the courts will determine what is identified as evidence. Rules of evidence are discussed in great detail in Chapter 2 "Rules of Evidence, Case Law, and Regulation."*

Computer forensics for some time was considered more of a task than a profession. Most practitioners of computer forensics were people from varied backgrounds attempting to collect digital artifacts in support of a criminal or civil legal matter. Today computer forensics can be considered an emerging but true profession, or more accurately, a metaprofession comprising the skill sets of several professions and subspecialties such as law enforcement, information technology, and the legal services field.

For some time, computer forensics has been approached slightly differently when supporting criminal versus civil proceedings. The earliest computer forensics support for civil matters was usually focused only on recovering e-mail or financial data whereas criminal investigations took a more in-depth approach to identification, collection, and analysis. As the profession becomes more formalized, the distinction in methodologies used between civil, criminal, and corporate investigations is becoming less differentiated. For the purpose of this book little distinction is made—the profession's methodologies and technologies are the same.

CRIME SCENE INVESTIGATION

Basic law enforcement training in crime scene investigation has long been limited to the critical tasks of documentation and collection of physical evidence. For the purposes of this book, computer forensics investigators are performing closer to what Dr. Henry C. Lee, et al., define as scientific crime scene investigation [Lee01]. Dr. Lee describes scientific crime scene investigation as a formalized process where forensics investigators, in addition to documenting and collecting physical evidence, use scientific knowledge and forensics techniques to identify evidence and generate leads to assist in solving a crime.

NOTE *Much of scientific crime scene investigation is based on Locard's exchange principle, which states that when any two objects come into contact, there is always transference of material from each object onto the other. Operating system logs recording hacker actions and data left on hard disks in unallocated sectors are examples of Locard's principle in action.*

In many cases a computer forensics investigator may not be the first responder; rather he comes onto the scene as a supplemental expert after some time has elapsed. In other cases the computer forensics investigator may be the first or only responder. Corporate investigations are a good example where information technology security personnel serving as computer forensics investigators may be the first and only responder to a scene. Although the scene may not be a crime scene *per se*, the same principles should apply to all investigations in case they later turn into criminal or civil matters.

Responsibilities of the crime scene first responder include:

Observe and establish the parameters of the crime scene: The first responder establishes if the crime is still occurring and notes the physical characteristics of the surrounding area. For computer forensics investigators this step can be extended to data systems that are live in a network environment. In these cases, the computer may be the target of an ongoing attack such as a DoS (denial of service) attack.

Initiate safety measures: Safety should be paramount in all situations. If while observing and establishing the parameters of the crime scene, or in any subsequent step, an unsafe situation is identified, measures should be taken to mitigate the situation. Safety from electrical, chemical, and biological hazards should be considered in addition to officer safety from criminal action. An incident that highlights the need for safety occurred in August 2004, when one officer was killed and another wounded while serving a search warrant related to child pornography in Fort Lauderdale, Florida [Cnn01].

Provide emergency care: Although life-saving measures, if needed, should be considered of paramount concern, it is also important for the first responder to notify any responding emergency personnel about the importance of preserving evidence.

Physically secure the scene: This step entails removing unnecessary personnel from the scene and ensuring that personnel not involved in scene processing do not gain access to the area and thus contaminate potential evidence.

Physically secure any evidence: This step, often referred to as "bag and tag," is the key focus of this book. It is in this step that the scientific principles and methodologies for the collection of digital evidence are applied in practice. In many cases this collection may be performed by personnel who have been trained only in the "bag and tag" component of evidence collection and handling.

Release the scene: Once all other steps have been completed, the scene should be released to the proper authorities. The proper authorities can differ from case to case, but they can include law enforcement (in criminal investigations) or corporate information technology system administrators (in corporate incident response). Essentially this step is intended to ensure that it is clear to all concerned when evidence collection is completed and systems can be returned to their normal operation.

Finalize documentation: Documentation is an essential element of crime scene investigation as well as the forensics process. Throughout this book readers will be alerted to and reminded of the importance of complete narrative documentation. In this final step, documentation is reviewed, summaries are written, and documentation is finalized as reports.

NOTE

Electronic Crime Scene Investigation—A Guide for First Responders is an excellent reference for nontechnical first responders about the collection of digital evidence [Doj01]. The guide can be found online at www.ncjrs.org/pdffiles1/nij/187736.pdf.

Although this book focuses more on computer forensics methodologies and principles for collection and maintenance of digital evidence, it is recommended that all personnel involved become aware of formalized crime scene investigation methodologies. Several good references for crime scene investigation can be found in the end notes of this chapter.

PHASES OF COMPUTER FORENSICS

The primary goals in computer forensics of collecting, preserving, filtering, and presenting digital artifacts can also be used as guidelines to describe the computer forensics process. We will structure these guidelines as phases of the computer forensics process. It's no accident that these exact phases are also referred to in a phased approach of the civil discovery process. Let's discuss the four phases of computer forensics in greater detail.

Collection

The collection phase of computer forensics is when artifacts considered to be of evidentiary value are identified and collected. Normally these artifacts are digital data in the form of disk drives, flash memory drives, or other forms of digital media and data, but they can include supporting artifacts such as corporate security policies and backup procedures. Identification of which artifacts could be of evidentiary value will be discussed later in the book.

Preservation

The preservation phase of computer forensics focuses on preserving original artifacts in a way that is reliable, complete, accurate, and verifiable. Cryptographic hashing, checksums, and documentation are all key components of the preservation phase. The importance of the terms *reliable, complete, accurate,* and *verifiable* as they pertain to potential evidence will be highlighted in Chapter 2. Although preservation of evidence is certainly an identifiable phase, it can also be considered iterative throughout the computer forensics process (see Figure 1.1). The importance of preservation and its components is a key focus of this book.

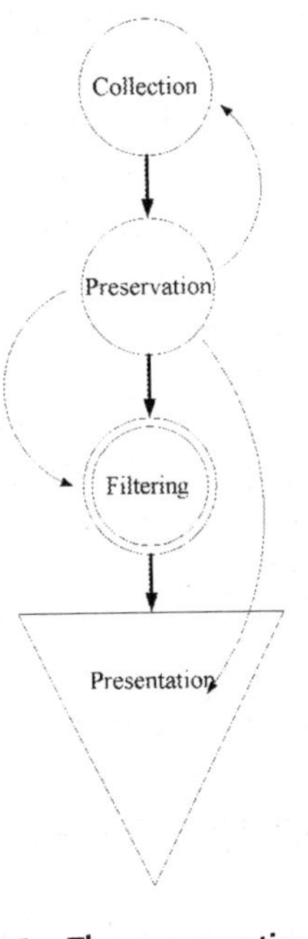

FIGURE 1.1 The preservation phase of computer forensics is iterative.

Filtering

This can also be referred to as the analysis phase of computer forensics. In this phase investigators will attempt to *filter-out* data which is determined not to contain any artifacts of evidentiary value and *filter-in* artifacts of potential evidentiary value. A wide array of tools and techniques are utilized in the filtering phase, some of which include comparing cryptographic hash values of known good and known suspect files against a known dataset. Other operating system and application specific tools used to locate and extract data are essential to the filtering phase. One such class of tool is an Internet history specific tool which will locate and extract the trail of data available left behind by Web browser activity.

Presentation

The final phase of computer forensics is when the potential artifacts of evidentiary value are presented in a variety of forms. Presentation normally starts with the investigator extracting the artifacts from the original media, and then staging and organizing them on CD-ROM or DVD-ROM. The investigator's reports, supporting documentation, declarations, depositions, and testimony in court can all be considered the presentation phase of computer forensics.

What may not be clear from the description of each phase is how time consuming the computer forensics process can be and how much attention to detail the profession requires. To perform a formalized computer forensics investigation on a single desktop computer takes an average of 25 to 35 hours to complete; it can take much more time, depending on the history of the case. It's not uncommon for keyword searches of a suspect's hard drive to take more than eight hours.

As mentioned in the introduction, this book focuses on the collection and preservation phases of computer forensics. By narrowing our focus to these preliminary phases, more detail on tools and methodologies for collection and preservation of potential evidence can be provided. Although we will discuss many automated hardware and software tools that investigators can use to accomplish their task, the understanding of individual operating systems and applications and the procedural knowledge of the investigator should never be overlooked.

The knowledge and skills needed to investigate crimes involving computers will change from case to case; nevertheless, investigators need to understand how computers operate at the component level and how each component interacts with the others. Critical components include the following:

- The central processor and how it works with the physical RAM (random access memory)
- How the physical RAM works with various operating systems, which provide virtual memory on hard disks
- How independent devices on the computer's I/O (input/output) bus interact with each other
- How all these items store and retrieve data in physical storage, such as hard disks

Investigators might consider reviewing the material for or taking a basic certification exam, such as the CompTIA A+ certification, which is designed to certify the basic PC knowledge level required for PC technicians. Investigators should also keep in mind that although certifications are certainly worthwhile, continued education and experience are essential.

In addition to knowing how the basic computing components interact, the investigator will need to understand the specific operating systems, applications, and file systems involved in the investigation. As we will see as this book progresses, this knowledge is relegated not only to the analysis phases of computer forensics but also to the collection phases. Many vendor-specific certifications may be helpful to the investigator to guide his training in operating systems and applications.

FORMALIZED COMPUTER FORENSICS FROM THE START

Sometimes the need for formalized computer forensics methodologies is not clear to investigators at the onset of an investigation. One of the best examples of this type of situation is in the commercial setting when the computer of a terminated employee is given the once-over by an internal information technology staff member. We can imagine the orders given to the IT staff: "Just take a look at the computer, and tell me if you find anything suspicious." It is assumed that IT personnel know what information is of importance to the company, such as trade secrets, business practices, and intellectual property. Unfortunately, if the IT staff member has not been trained in formalized computer forensics methodologies, artifacts of potential evidentiary value may lose their value in court and overall admissibility in court, or worse yet, evidence may be destroyed altogether. In a well-publicized trade-secret theft case, *Gates Rubber Co. v. Bando Chemical Indus., Ltd.*, nonstandard forensics procedures by the plaintiff's own expert resulted in the loss of potentially valuable artifacts to the case [Frd01]. In the *Gates* case, the computer forensics expert was criticized for making a file-by-file copy rather than a bit stream copy of the evidence disk. By not making a bit stream copy, potential evidence in unallocated or disk slack space was overlooked. The court determined that there was a mandatory legal duty on the part of the litigants to perform proper computer forensics investigations. This seminal case identifies the need for sound forensics methodologies to be used from the onset of suspicion.

NOTE

Joining various professional organizations is a great way to stay informed of developments and further refinements of accepted methodologies used in computer forensics. Two of the leading professional organizations dedicated to the education and advancement of the computer forensics profession are the IACIS (International Association of Computer Investigative Specialists) and HTCIA (High-Tech Criminal Investigative Association). Both organizations provide formalized training and serve as a conduit of information throughout the community. It is important to note that membership in IACIS is limited to law enforcement personnel; the HTCIA does allow private sector membership, but they do not accept members who conduct criminal defense work. The HTCIA stance on criminal defense representation, although often debated, is reflective of the large law enforcement constituency. The IACIS Web site can be found at www.cops.org, and the HTCIA Web site can be found at www.htcia.org.

It is essential for all computer forensics investigators involved in the collection of digital data to understand the basic nature of that data, that is, the data is very fragile and can become contaminated easily, and you often get only one chance for collection. If proper care is taken during the identification and collection of digital data—a process often referred to as "bag and tag"—a mistake in later stages of the investigation may be recoverable, but mistakes made in the initial identification and collection are rarely reversible.

NOTE

All corporate IT security personnel should be trained in formalized bag and tag procedures, even if the company has no intention of performing internal forensics investigations. This approach allows potential evidence to be collected and preserved properly for subsequent transfer to a forensics service provider or law enforcement, should the need arise. Many professional training organizations such as SANS™ (Systems Administration and Network Security) are beginning to provide computer forensics training for private industry.

The International Organization on Computer Evidence (IOCE) [Ioce01] has helped guide the computer forensics process for law enforcement personnel since its conception in 1993, at the first International Law Enforcement Conference on Computer Evidence at Quantico, Virginia. Membership in the IOCE has been somewhat limited (by design), but they have provided some very useful discussion in an international community setting for law enforcement.

Article 2 of the IOCE bylaws states: "the purpose of the organization shall be to provide an international forum for law enforcement agencies to exchange information concerning computer investigation and computer forensic issues."

Article 2 goes on to state the following organizational objectives:

- Identify and discuss issues of common interest
- Facilitate the international dissemination of information
- Develop recommendations for consideration by the member agencies

Keeping with stated objectives, several useful documents have been created by IOCE committees and are available on its Web site at *www.ioce.org*.

Two specific and very useful documents available on the IOCE Web site are:

- Best Practice Guidelines for Examination of Digital Evidence
- G8 Proposed Principles for Forensic Evidence

Though not governing in any way, both documents can be quite useful for organizations that want to set standards of practice for computer forensics. Despite the obvious law-enforcement focus of the IOCE, these documents can be useful to practitioners in law enforcement as well as private industry.

WHO PERFORMS COMPUTER FORENSICS?

Much of the early use of computers was for the storage of financial data. Hence, initial groundwork in the area of computer forensics was done by the U.S. Internal Revenue Service Criminal Investigative Division and other federal law enforcement agencies such as the FBI (Federal Bureau of Investigation). In the private sector, organizations such as Ernst & Young, Deloitte & Touche, and other large corporate auditors had an early interest in computer forensics. Today, crimes involving a computer have expanded much further than those of only financial interest. To understand who might be interested in performing computer forensics, it is helpful to break down the types of involvement the computer could have with a crime.

One type of involvement is where the computer assisted the crime, such as with fraud and child pornography. Another situation where computers commonly assist in a crime or employee malfeasance is intellectual property theft in the corporate environment. All too often a customer list or product design information is downloaded by an employee and taken to competitors. The second type of involvement is where the computer was the target of the crime, such as during a denial of service (DoS) attack against an e-commerce Web site. The last type of involvement, which is often less obvious than the previous two, is when the computer contains information that is incidental to the crime, such as a database containing the "pay and owe" list from drug traffickers. Many crimes often include more than one type of computer involvement.

NOTE

"Pay and owe" lists are documents or spreadsheets drug traffickers use to keep track of their customers and suppliers.

Investigators should also keep in mind that many crimes involve all three types of involvement and include computers that assisted a crime, were the target of a crime, and were incidental to a crime. Consider a situation where a hacker or cracker used a computer to assist him in performing a DoS attack against a company or breaking into the company's database containing credit card data. In this scenario the forensics investigator may end up investigating and seizing the hacker's computer, which assisted in the crime; the hacker's PDA (personal digital assistant) and cell phone, which contain passwords and contacts that were incidental to the crime; and the company's computer, which was the target of the crime. In the same scenario, other innocent bystanders' computers may have been used by the hacker as targets and were then subsequently used to assist the hacker.

Today's pervasive use of computers, coupled with the various types of computer involvement in crimes, has caused an explosion in practitioners of computer forensics. Arrests of almost any type today can involve collection of digital evidence. Consider the contact database in most cell phones, which can contain potentially valuable data.

Some examples of today's wide variety of practitioners of computer forensics follow:

- Federal, state and local law enforcement for criminal cases
- Legal service providers for civil discovery
- Corporate IT security personnel for criminal and civil cases
- Corporate HR investigators for workplace investigations
- Private investigators for various investigations
- Outside computer security consultants in incident response

As shown by this list, the group is indeed varied, each with his own viewpoint and skill set. In training for computer forensics, it is helpful to look beyond our own experiences in regards to computers and their place in a crime or misuse. For instance, many investigators with a law enforcement background tend to approach a computer as something that is incidental to the crime. Corporate IT security personnel tend to look at a computer as the target or instrument of a crime. By gaining a better understanding of each of the disciplines shown in the previous list and looking beyond our industry-specific approaches, we can help ensure that more potentially valuable artifacts are identified and subsequently collected. Skill sets from all the professions shown in the list are useful and make computer forensics a metaprofession.

TIP

In the corporate environment a crime is not necessarily evident from the onset of an investigation. In some cases a crime may not even exist. The investigation may involve employee misuse as defined in corporate acceptable use policies. It is important for corporate investigators to treat misuse and possible criminal activity investigations in the same manner. Many investigations may start off with the suspicion of misuse and quickly turn into a criminal or civil litigation case.

What qualifies the computer forensics investigator? Computer forensics investigator licensing and certification is a topic that can be guaranteed to spark a lively discussion among today's professionals. In the United States, some states have grouped computer forensics professionals with private investigators and require that they be licensed in accordance with the state's licensing standards. It is the belief of the author that this practice is difficult to justify without completely reworking each state's private investigator licensing standards. What is important to note is that no clear certification or licensing requirements exist today outside of a few states' attempts to regulate the profession. This inconsistency is due to the relatively new nature of this metaprofession and the definition of what to certify or license. Most technical professions have three distinctly differing areas for certification: people, places, and things. When looking at the people aspect of computer forensics, several certifications exist already through organizations such as IACIS, but none are unanimously agreed on throughout the profession. Other certifications for computer forensics investigations are product-specific certifications managed by individual computer hardware and software product vendors. Although a group of personnel certifications that are more widely accepted for differing levels of competency within computer forensics methodologies may emerge eventually, an essentially limitless array of products, operating systems, and hardware environments to gain knowledge of exists today. The collection of digital evidence from a Microsoft Windows environment would be aided by the investigator's knowledge of that environment. A wide assortment of certifications covers the multitude of Microsoft products. Several organizations, including HTCIA, IACIS, and the NIST (National Institute of Standards and Technology), are working to more clearly define certifications within computer forensics. The certification of labs and equipment, although still not universally agreed on or regulated, has moved much further due to previous work for other scientific forensic disciplines. Most disagreements surrounding computer forensics lab certifications are related to the origin of the certifications. Most of today's certifications are derived from or entirely focused on scientific forensics disciplines other than computer forensics. Despite disagreements, several certification standards for computer forensics labs have been in development, of which ISO 17025 seems to have gained the most favor due to its international focus. Three programs of interest surrounding forensics lab certifications follow:

ASCLD Forensics Lab Certification and Accreditation: This program, which has been used by the various law enforcement organizations for some time, was designed to certify forensic labs in scientific disciplines such as DNA and fingerprint analyses. ASCLD now covers digital evidence. Further information on ASCLD can be found on its Web site at *www.ascld-lab.org*.

ISO 17025 Forensics Lab Certification and Accreditation: This certification program has the support of the international community, many U.S. organizations and corporations as well as government facilities, and law enforcement agencies. ASCLD is also adopting the ISO 17025 certification process.

NIST Handbook (HB) 150 Lab Certification: This program is a baseline document that can be used as a foundation for many scientific disciplines such as ASCLD. HB 150 has been used as a foundation to validate various federal government labs.

A major player in the creation of the widely accepted ISO 17025 criteria is SWGDE (Scientific Working Group for Digital Evidence). SWDGE is a useful organization with which to keep up to date with lab certification. SWDGE can be located on the Web at *http://ncfs.org.* Lab certifications and pragmatic design principles will be discussed in greater detail in Chapter 15, "The Forensics Lab."

In the area of software certification, the NIST and NSA (National Security Agency) are working to promote and gain wider acceptance of the NIAP (National Information Assurance Partnership) product certification process [Nist01].

A vender-neutral organization with international focus that provides several tiers of computer security certifications is the ISC(2) (International Information Systems Security Certification Consortium).

The certification process will continue to be a hotly debated topic for at least the immediate future. Computer forensics investigators can follow the following steps to ensure they are accepted in the community as professionals:

- Seek out and document formalized training in computer forensics.
- Seek out and document formalized training for specific operating systems, software, and hardware for which they intend to specialize.
- Join and participate in professional organizations such as the HTCIA, IACIS, and others that will keep them abreast of the latest developments with certification and licensing in the profession.
- Use peer-accepted and peer-tested methodologies in the performance of their craft.
- Perform internal tool testing, and do not rely solely on external tests.
- Maintain a high degree of personal integrity at all times. Investigators should focus on the facts represented by the data and always present truthful and accurate statements as to the facts.

NOTE *Training is an iterative process that should never cease. This is especially true in information technology and computer science.*

The more knowledgeable a computer forensics investigator becomes, the more he will realize what a complex profession computer forensics is becoming. As corporate and consumer use of technology grows and becomes more complex, so too does the computer forensics profession. In a natural trend, computer forensics investigators already are beginning to specialize in one operating system or another. Although a broad knowledge base across technologies is a good idea, ultimately areas of specialty will emerge. In larger computer forensics shops you will find specialist in networking, Windows, UNIX, Linux, PDAs, and more.

SEIZING COMPUTER EVIDENCE

Whether your profession is law enforcement or private industry, legal guidelines will affect your rights as they pertain to seizing computer evidence. Although the legal aspects of search and seizure are beyond the scope of this book, it is helpful to understand basic concepts and references.

NOTE *This section is focused on the legal aspects of search and seizure. Subsequent chapters will outline the technical and procedural aspects of collecting evidence.*

For the purposes of this book the collection of computer evidence is intended to ultimately provide proof at trial that supports determination of some past occurrence, such as creation, deletion, or alteration of an electronic document, log, or event. Although the burden of proof is measured in different ways from country to country, the goals of limiting false convictions and false acquittals are the same. Rules of evidence used in the United States are designed to lean more toward limiting false convictions in criminal trials and, therefore, use proof beyond a reasonable doubt as the standard. Civil litigation uses a preponderance of evidence as the standard in an effort to reduce expenses caused by lengthy trials. Specific rules of evidence are covered in greater detail in Chapter 2.

Depending on the country, the collection of evidence will normally be limited and controlled by the constitution or legislation. This limitation remains true for the collection of computer evidence as well. In the United States, the most important high-level document that defines this limitation is the Fourth Amendment to the Constitution. Essentially, according to the Fourth Amendment, government agents are limited in their ability to search for evidence without a warrant, thus guaranteeing citizens a right to privacy.

An excerpt from the Fourth Amendment states: "*The right of the people to be secure in their persons, houses, papers, and effects, against unreasonable searches and seizures, shall not be violated, and no warrants shall issue, but upon probable cause, supported by oath or affirmation, and particularly describing the place to be searched, and the persons or things to be seized.*"

TIP

The United States Department of Justice document "Searching and Seizing Computers and Obtaining Electronic Evidence in Criminal Investigations" [Doj02], commonly referred to as the "Search and Seizure Manual," is one of the best references available about seizing electronic evidence. Although not regulatory, this document contains a great deal of information on warranted and warrantless searches. The document is available online at www.cybercrime.gov/s&smanual2002.htm.

Investigators can derive from the Fourth Amendment excerpt that the following two types of searches exist:

Warranted: The investigator obtained explicit authorization (the warrant) from the proper authorities, providing him with the authorization to search for and seize specific evidence.

Warrantless: The investigator has implicit authorization (warrantless) from probable cause or otherwise to conduct the search.

Furthermore, investigators must identify if the suspect has a right to privacy and, if so, they must obtain a warrant.

CAUTION

Warranted and warrantless searches are complex issues for which investigators should seek legal counsel for a complete understanding.

As outlined in the Department of Justice's "Search and Seizure Manual," it is best to think of computers as closed containers, such as a briefcase or a file cabinet. Because the Fourth Amendment generally prohibits opening, accessing, or viewing information from closed containers without a warrant, investigators should consider a warrant to be necessary. U.S. courts have examined the right-to-privacy issue as it relates to data in computers through many cases; one specific case, *U.S. v. Barth* [Barth01], found a reasonable expectation of privacy in files stored on a hard drive of a personal computer.

NOTE

In the United States, it is important to note that individuals may lose their right to privacy when transferring data to a third party, and that their right to privacy does not extend to searches conducted by private parties who are not acting on behalf of the government. For instance, if an individual had taken his personal computer into a repair facility, and the facility's technician notices contraband, such as child pornography, on the system, the facility is compelled to notify the authorities [Hall01].

The first area of interest in warrantless searches is when consent is given by the owner. Two important and governing issues related to consent in a warrantless search are the scope of the consent and who gave the consent, both of which can be complex, depending on the facts of the case. *U.S. v. Blas*, 1990, WL 265179 is an example of a case where the scope of consent was determined to be so narrow that a person's authorization to look at a pager in the back seat did not also provide consent to examine the contents of the pager. One of the most important components of third-party consent is whether the third party had "common authority" over the object involved. This point was highlighted in *U.S. v. Matlock*, 413 U.S. 164 (1974).

NOTE

Examples of private monitoring notifications can be found in the Department of Justice's "Search and Seizure Manual."

Of primary interest to corporate computer forensics investigators are warrantless workplace searches. As the provider of and the owner of the data and services, an employer normally has full authority to search corporate data systems. New case law can be expected to arise as more employers monitor employees, so policies that outline acceptable use and monitoring practices are becoming extremely important. Corporate policies are also important when it comes to warrantless workplace searches by law enforcement. Very subtle distinctions have been made in the area of warrantless workplace searches as outlined in *O'Conner v. Ortega*, 480 U.S. 709 (1987).

CAUTION

Although corporations normally have full authority over their data systems, warrantless and warranted searches within the workplace are complex legal issues for which legal counsel should always be consulted.

CHALLENGES TO COMPUTER EVIDENCE

Most challenges to computer evidence surround *authenticity* with questions such as, Was the data altered? Was the program that generated the forms or data reliable? and What was the identity of the author? Experienced practitioners of computer forensics will notice when looking back that much of what we do in our methodologies is directly focused on countering these questions. Chain of custody, documentation, and cryptographic hash verification are all components of methodologies used to counter the challenge of "was the data altered?" The second challenge surrounding the reliability of programs used to represent data is generally easier to substantiate with industry-wide acceptance, peer review, and individual testing. Legal issues surrounding acceptance of computer evidence will be covered in more detail in Chapter 2. Identity of the author is often countered with circumstantial but corroborative evidence such as suspect word usage in typed documents or online chat scripts.

> TIP
>
> *If it appears that the investigator's methodologies or integrity can be questioned easily by the defendant's attorney, they will be and to a great extent. Well-trained, confident, and methodical investigators seldom spend much time in deposition or on the witness stand.*

Another challenging area of computer forensics evidence relates to the way it is presented in reports. An investigator new to computer forensics but experienced in data processing can easily draw conclusions too quickly. It is important for forensics investigators to focus on the facts of the collected data in their reports rather than to draw conclusions too quickly or at all. In some cases the forensics investigator may not realize he was drawing a conclusion in his reports. An example of drawing a conclusion too quickly follows:

Investigator Dave is examining the corporate evidence drive taken from the desktop computer of "John A. Suspect," who is assigned the user network logon identification of "jasuspect." In investigator Dave's report, he states that "the user, John A. Suspect, performed a specified action on the computer because an event log showed that the user had accessed the file…"

In this scenario the investigator most likely did not have enough information to state that the user John A. Suspect performed any action because that statement would require that he tie the digital user id "jasuspect" with the physical person, John A. Suspect. These types of conclusions, which can be easy to make in a report, highlight the need to focus on the facts and pay attention to detail. A more correct statement on the part of the investigator would be *"the user id 'jasuspect,' which had been assigned to John A. Suspect, was used to access the file … on August 22, 2005, at 12:03 PST, as indicated by the computer workstation's event log."*

Despite the challenging and often detailed nature of computer forensics, the field can be very rewarding. In solving complex digital puzzles, computer forensics investigators are often a key component to protecting a corporation's interest and bringing criminals to justice.

SUMMARY

- *Computer forensics* is the art and science of applying computer science to aid the legal process.
- Computer forensics investigators perform components of scientific crime scene investigation, as defined by Dr. Henry C. Lee.
- Much of scientific crime scene investigation is based on Locard's exchange principle of transfer theory.

- Computer forensics investigators may not be the first responders, but they should understand the steps of first responders in crime scene investigation.
- Computer forensics can be broken down into four phases: collection, preservation, filtering, and presentation of computer system artifacts that are of potential evidentiary value.
- The case *Gates Rubber Co. v. Bando Chemical Indus., Ltd.* highlighted nonstandard forensics procedures, resulting in the destruction and loss of potentially valuable artifacts to the case.
- All computer forensics investigations (criminal, civil, and corporate misuse) should be treated with the same degree of professionalism and documentation.
- The types of involvement a computer could have with a crime include assisting in the crime, acting as the target of the crime, and being incidental to the crime, or combinations thereof.
- Warrantless and warranted searches are complex legal issues for which legal counsel should always be consulted.
- Corporate information-technology-security workers should be trained in "bag and tag" procedures.
- ISO 17025 Forensics Lab Certification and Accreditation program is one of the most widely accepted and favored certification processes today.
- Most challenges to computer evidence surround authenticity.

REFERENCES

[Barth01] *U.S. v. Barth*, 26 F. Supp. 2d 929, 936–37 (W.D. Tex. 1998).

[Cnn01] "Deputy killed serving child porn warrant," CNN Web site (Associated Press), available online at *www.cnn.com/2004/US/South/08/19/deputy.killed.ap/*, August 19, 2004.

[Doj01] U.S. Department of Justice, *Electronic Crime Scene Investigation—A Guide for First Responders*, available online at *www.ncjrs.org/pdffiles1/nij/187736.pdf*, 2002.

[Doj02] U.S. Department of Justice, *Searching and Seizing Computers and Obtaining Electronic Evidence in Criminal Investigations*, available online at *www.cybercrime.gov/s&smanual2002.htm*, 2002.

[Frd01] *Gates Rubber Co. v. Bando Chemical Indus., Ltd.* 167 F.R.D. 90 (D. Colo. 1996).

[Hall01] *U.S. v. Hall*, 142 F. 3d 988 (7th Cir. 1998).

[Ioce01] International Organization of Computer Forensics Web site, available online at *www.ioce.org*, 2004.

[Lee01] Lee, Henry, et al., *Henry Lee's Crime Scene Handbook*, Academic Press, 2001.

[Nist01] NIST, *National Information Assurance Partnership*, available online at *www.nist.gov/*, 2004.

RESOURCES

[Fisher01] Fisher, Barry A., *Techniques of Crime Scene Investigation*, CRC Press, 2003.

[Genge01] Genge, N.E., *The Science of Crime Scene Investigation, The Forensics Case Book*, Ballantine Books, 2002.

[Giannelli01] Giannelli, Paul C., *Understanding Evidence*, LexisNexis, 2003.

2 Rules of Evidence, Case Law, and Regulation

In This Chapter

- Understanding Rules of Evidence
- Expert Witness (Scientific) Acceptance
- Testifying Tips—You Are the Expert
- Computer-related Case Law
- Regulation

UNDERSTANDING RULES OF EVIDENCE

Many governing documents and case decisions describe the complex issues of evidence admissibility in court. States adopt rules of evidence, such as the *California Evidence Code of 1967* [Ca01]. The international community has documents such as the *IBA Rules of Taking Evidence in International Commercial Arbitration* [Iba01] and the *International Criminal Tribunal for Rwanda, Rules of Procedure and Evidence* [Un01]. Although the aforementioned rules do not address computer evidence specifically, the general rules of evidence are the basis of any evidence admission in court. Amendments and case law are generally used as guidance on how to apply high-level rules to the more specific computer or digital evidence. The *Federal Rules of Evidence* [Fre01] is the basis for evidence admissibility, including computer-related digital evidence, and thus the *FRE* will be utilized as a basis for this chapter.

> NOTE: *In 1961, a committee appointed by Chief Justice Earl Warren released the report "A Preliminary Report on the Advisability and Feasibility of Developing Uniform Rules of Evidence for the United States District Courts," which recommended the adoption of uniform federal rules of evidence [Warren01]. Based on the report and resulting recommendations, a committee was appointed to draft the Federal Rules of Evidence in 1965. The Federal Rules of Evidence were promulgated by the U.S. Supreme Court in 1972, and finally enacted in 1975.*

The U. S. *Federal Rules of Evidence* are structured into the following eleven articles, which have been amended many times either by Supreme Court decision or by Congress since their adoption:

- Article I: General Provisions
- Article II: Judicial Notice
- Article III: Presumptions in Civil Actions and Proceedings
- Article IV: Relevancy and Its Limits
- Article V: Privileges
- Article VI: Witnesses
- Article VII: Opinions and Expert Testimony
- Article VIII: Hearsay
- Article IX: Authentication
- Article X: Original Document Rule
- Article XI: Miscellaneous Rules

Although the overall structure of U.S. *Federal Rules of Evidence* supports both civil and criminal cases, some rules are written directly for and apply to only one or the other.

As far back as 1970, Rule 34 of the Federal Rules of Civil Procedure covering the production of documents was amended to allow discovery of electronically stored data. An excerpt from the amended rule reads:

> "to produce and permit the party making the request, or someone acting on the requester's behalf to inspect and copy, any designated documents (including writings, drawings, graphs, charts, photographs, phono records, and other data compilations from which information can be obtained, *translated, if necessary*, by the respondent through detection *devices into reasonably usable form*)..."

NOTE

A key element of the 1970 amendment to the Federal Rules of Civil Procedure's Rule 34 was that the data could be translated if necessary to a reasonably usable form such as printing out records from the collected digital data.

Translating digital data into a reasonable form brings to light the *Federal Rules of Evidence* "best evidence" rule [Fre01], which states," to prove the content of a writing, recording, or photograph, the 'original' writing, recording, or photograph is ordinarily required." Seemingly, the two components are in direct contrast. To clarify the situation, the *Federal Rules of Evidence* states that "if data are stored in a computer or similar device, any printout or other output readable by sight, shown to reflect the data accurately, is an 'original.'" This statement is the basis on which computer forensics investigators treat bit-stream images as "originals" during examination. In a recent decision in *Ohio v. Michael J. Morris* [Ohio01], the Court of Appeals of Ohio, Ninth District, upheld the evidence presented from a bit-stream "copy" of an evidence disk, even when the original no longer existed. The *Federal Rules of Evidence* go so far as to permit summaries of large volumes of evidence in the form of "a chart, summary, or calculation" in warranted situations.

In recent times federal courts have indicated that computer records can be admitted as business records if they were kept as a matter of normal day-to-day business practices, which leads to their reliability [NinthCir01] [FifthCir01], implying that businesses would not rely on records that were not considered reliable. The "Search and Seizure Manual" [Doj01] indicates a trend of moving away from blanket acceptance of computer business records because of complex distinctions between records that were computer-generated, records that were human-generated but stored on a computer, and records that were computer-generated then stored as an archived log file. Because each of these situations can invoke differing applications of hearsay rules from the *Federal Rules of Evidence* [Fre01], further case law interpretations can be expected. In one such case, *People v. Holowko*, the court distinguished between "computer-generated" and "computer-stored" data (Ill01]. The court found that the printout of results of computerized telephone-tracing equipment was not hearsay evidence because it was generated instantaneously and without assistance as the telephone call was placed. A key component of business-record acceptance under *Federal Rules of Evidence* [Fre01] Rule 801 is that the records must be authentic. It is this rule that drives the complexity, uncertainty, and ultimately, the acceptance of evidence in many cases.

CAUTION

The legal information in this section highlights subtle distinctions from a limited examination of existing case law and rules of evidence. This chapter is intended as background as to why some of today's methodologies and procedures for the collection of digital evidence exist. Legal counsel should be involved at the very earliest stage of the computer forensics process.

U.S. v. DeGeorgia [NinthCir02] highlights that the standard for authenticating computer records is exactly the same as that for authenticating other records: "if a business record is computer-generated, the basic requirements persist." A foundation for authenticity must be established for all evidence seeking to be admitted, requiring that in many cases witnesses must testify to the authenticity of computer records. What may be less clear are the qualifications needed for such testimony. The case *U.S. v. Whitaker* [SeventhCir01] highlights that the witness to authenticity need not have special qualifications or expert status, only that they must have firsthand knowledge of the relevant facts on which they testify. In *U.S. v. Whitaker*, the accepted foundation of the witness testimony was that he was present when the defendant's computer was seized and when the records were retrieved from the computer. The testimony was found to be sufficient to establish authenticity. This holding may lead many to question why there is a need for expert witnesses for digital evidence—if the *authenticity* of any particular evidence can be satisfied with the criteria mentioned, the *reliability* of evidence and testimony is another question.

EXPERT WITNESS (SCIENTIFIC) ACCEPTANCE

We've all seen those old episodes of *Perry Mason* or the newer *CSI*: *Crime Scene Investigation* television series in which the expert witness is on the stand rattling off scientific facts that wow the jury. What makes an expert an "expert," and on what criteria do judges rely to determine an expert's status? Although the answer varies in the United States from state to state, the majority of states follow the standard established in Rule 702 from the *Federal Rules of Evidence* [Fre01], which state: "*If scientific, technical or other specialized knowledge will assist the trier of fact to understand the evidence or to determine a fact in issue, a witness qualified as an expert by knowledge, skill, experience, training, or education, may testify thereto in the form of an opinion or otherwise.*"

TIP

Sometimes digital evidence that is admitted is not considered scientific evidence and never goes through the extensive acceptance review described in this section. It is always best to be prepared for the highest level of security procedures, just in case.

Since 1923, judges have used the simple test established in *Frye v. U.S.* [DcCir01], which maintained: "When the question involved is outside the range of common experience or knowledge, then [experts] are needed," based on scientific evidence challenges. *Frye* went on to establish the following two simple standards to determine whether an expert's evidence should be admitted into a trial:

- Is the evidence relevant to the case?

- Is the evidence generally accepted in the expert's community?

Although the relevancy provided by the first test and the peer review provided by the second test offer a pragmatic approach, advances and complexity in science and technology indicate the need for more comprehensive tests.

Reliability is a prerequisite for getting evidence admitted before a jury. A jury can still decide what "weight," or credibility, to assign to the evidence, even if it is deemed reliable enough to be admitted.

The U.S. Supreme Court, in a relatively recent opinion surrounding the scientific testimony regarding whether serious birth defects had been caused by the mother's prenatal ingestion of Bendectin in *Daubert v. Merrell Dow* [Us01], rejected the *Frye* test for the admissibility of scientific evidence and established that judges should be the "gatekeepers of scientific evidence," ensuring that scientific evidence is not only relevant but reliable. Although individual states are not bound by the federal *Daubert* [Us01] standard, some pattern their approach after *Daubert*, some after *Frye*, and still others apply their own reliability test (see Table 2.1).

TABLE 2.1. Reliability Tests by State [Oconnor01]

States Using *Daubert*	States Using *Frye*	States with Their Own Reliability Tests
Connecticut	Alaska	Arkansas
Indiana	Arizona	Delaware
Kentucky	California	Georgia
Louisiana	Colorado	Iowa
Massachusetts	Florida	Minnesota
New Mexico	Illinois	Montana
Oklahoma	Kansas	North Carolina
South Dakota	Maryland	Oregon
Texas	Michigan	Utah
West Virginia	Missouri	Vermont
	Nebraska	Wyoming
	New York	(Military)
	Pennsylvania	
	Washington	

Some states do not use any reliability test other than a judge or jury.

The four-part reliability test established in *Daubert* [Us01] includes the following questions:

- Has the scientific theory or technique been tested empirically?
- Has the scientific theory or technique been subjected to peer review and publication?
- What is the known or potential error rate?
- What is the expert's qualifications and stature in the scientific community?
- Does the technique rely on the special skills and equipment of one expert, or can it be replicated by other experts elsewhere?
- Can the technique and its results be explained with sufficient clarity and simplicity so that the court and the jury can understand its plain meaning?

The Daubert test is nonexhaustive; rather, it sets forth factors courts should consider in making reliability determinations.

TESTIFYING TIPS—YOU ARE THE EXPERT

Testifying in court or answering deposition questions can be an intimidating situation. Human nature works against many computer forensics investigators in these situations because most people tend to be somewhat modest as to their skill sets or knowledge level. It is important to understand that an expert in any field can be defined as one who has *special knowledge, skill, experience, training,* or *education* on a particular subject. It is this very definition that drives computer forensics investigators desire for documentation of their training. Documentation of training certainly helps establish a computer forensics investigator as an "expert," but it's not difficult for many experienced investigators to develop a special skill set from their countless hours of experience in the lab. An investigator's confidence in his abilities is the first step toward successful testimony. You know what you know.

There is a thin line between confidence and arrogance. It is important for computer forensics investigators to work closely with case attorneys to ensure they are being presented in the proper light prior to testimony or deposition.

In California, some cases have a pretrial hearing held with the judge and defense and prosecuting attorneys to establish an expert's qualifications and to determine what the judge will allow when the expert testifies in the presence of the jury.

In this type of hearing—often called a 402 hearing after the Rules of Evidence section under which it falls—the computer forensics expert is asked about his qualifications. In this type of pretrial hearing it is common for a judge to issue specific limitations on the scope of the computer forensics expert's testimony. This direction is extremely important when the expert testifies to the jury about his qualifications, any conclusions he drew from his observations, and how he arrived at his conclusions.

Because any judge, jury, or group of people gathered together will have vastly differing technical backgrounds, analogies are useful when describing technical issues in court. One of the best analogies often used to describe computer disk *slack space* to the layman is that of a video tape, for example:

"When taping over a 60-minute tape with your favorite 30-minute show, the new show is there, but the tape still contains the trailing 30 minutes from the original 60-minute tape. The area of the videotape containing the trailing 30 minutes is similar to a computer disk's slack space."

Whereas this and other analogies can be very helpful in court, be cautious to not oversimplify concepts if the distinction bears significance for the point you are trying to convey.

TIP

One tactic often used by opposing counsel is to provide an analogy to the expert, saying something like, "Isn't a computer network similar to a highway?" If the expert quickly accepts the analogy, he may become trapped by his acceptance of the broad definition. Remember, the attorney had all night to create an analogy that fits his goals.

In court, attorneys spend a great deal of time crafting questions to get the desired results. One approach is to ask, "Do you remember saying…?" In this case many people will answer with a simple, "No," when they actually mean that they had not made the statement in question. The key to any type of question along these lines is to pay close attention to the question, take time answering the question, and ask the attorney to repeat or clarify the question, if needed. Above all, forensics investigators should remember that, despite its appearance, the line of questioning is not personal. Dispassionate testimony about the facts and opinions based on the facts is the best approach to success on the stand.

COMPUTER-RELATED CASE LAW

In the technical world of computer programming, much of the buzz over the last decade or so has been about object-oriented programming and the great benefits of reusing source code. It is hard to argue with the concept of reusing source code that has already been written, if for nothing more than providing an example on which programmers can build more code. In the legal realm, attorneys take a similar approach when preparing for cases by researching previous case decisions relating to their current case. Understanding previous decisions relating to digital discovery and evidence collection can be very useful to the computer forensics investigators in refining their methodologies through each phase of the process.

TIP

The FindLaw and LexisNexis Web sites are useful resources for researching legal issues relating to computer forensics and evidence collection as well as finding services relating to digital discovery. The FindLaw Web site is available at www.findlaw.com, and the LexisNexis Web site can be found at www.lexisnexis.com.

As forensics investigators become familiar with larger numbers of existing case decisions relating to digital evidence, they will notice subtle distinctions in decisions. These subtle distinctions can open the door for various interpretations, which reinforces the need for legal counsel when reviewing case law. In addition to the subtle distinctions in decisions, investigators will have little difficulties finding conflicting guidance in similar case law. The conflicts are due partly to the relatively new presentation of digital evidence in the courtroom coupled with very specific facts of the particular case. The following case law summaries are provided as a historical reference to digital evidence issues:

> ***Kleiner v. Burns,*** **WL 1909470, (2000):** In this case the defendant had produced only limited correspondence in the original answer to discovery requests. The court in turn provided sanctions and directed the defendant to try harder to provide the requested voice mails in addition to deleted data, backup data, and history files.
>
> ***Rowe Entm't Inc. v. William Morris Agency, Inc.,*** **205 F.R.D. 241 S.D.N.Y. (2002):** This case was one of the first to tackle the distribution of costs associated with large-scale digital discovery involving backup tapes. The approach adopted a multifactor test to establish who should bear the cost of digital discovery. The factors used to weigh cost shifting follow:

- The specificity of the discovery requests
- The likelihood of a successful search
- The availability from other sources
- The purposes of retention
- The benefit to the parties
- The total cost
- The ability of each party to control costs

- The parties' resources

Zubulake v. UBS Warburg, **217 F.R.D. 309 S.D.N.Y. (2003):** This gender discrimination case was a landmark case that further examined the burden of cost and shifting of cost issues related to the previous *Rowe Entm't Inc. v. William Morris Agency, Inc.* After producing a large number of documents and e-mail messages related to the case, the plaintiff desired discovery of e-mail messages from backup archives. The defendant challenged the request and desired to shift the high cost of such discovery to the plaintiff. In reviewing *Rowe*, the court decided to use the following factors when considering cost shifting:

- The extent for which the request is specifically tailored to discover relevant information
- The availability of such information for other sources
- The total cost of production compared to the amount in controversy
- The total cost of production compared to the resources of each party
- The relative ability of each party to control cost and its incentive to do so
- The importance of the issue at stake in the litigation
- The relative benefit to the parties in obtaining the information

Based on the listed factors the court ordered the defendant to produce the requested e-mail documents from selected archives at its own expense. After discovery results from the selected archives are reviewed, cost-shifting analysis can again be performed.

***Alexander v. Fed. Bureau of Investigation*, 188 F.R.D. 111, 117 D.D.C. (1998):** This case involving the limits and scopes of large-scale digital discovery ruled that discovery would be limited to targeted and appropriately worded searches of backed-up and archived e-mail messages and hard drives of a limited number of personnel.

***Crown Life Ins. v. Craig Ltd.*, 995 F.2d 1376 7th Cir., (1993):** In this case, sanctions were made for precluding evidence and failure to comply with the discovery order. Documents were defined to include computer data and were not limited to written hard copy documents.

***Brand Name Prescription Drug Antitrust Litigation*, ND Ill., (1995):** In this early case involving who should bear the burden of discovery, e-mail messages were determined to be discoverable but at the producing party's expense.

***Simon Prop. Group v. mySimon, Inc.*, S.D.Ind., 194 F.R.D. 639 (2000):** This case highlighted that discovery of computer records included any deleted documents that were recoverable.

***Santiago v. Miles*, 121 F.R.D. 636 W.D.N.Y., (1988):** In this case, close attention was paid to how raw computer data is represented when printed out for courts. A key component in the decision was that raw computer information is obtainable under discovery rules. A specific application was created for the extraction/representation of raw data for court.

***Anti-Monopoly Inc. v. Hasbro, Inc.*, S.D.N.Y. U.S. Dist. (1995):** This case determined that even though computer-generated hard copies were provided by the producing party, the *electronic documents* were also discoverable. In addition, it was determined that the producing party can be required to design a computer program to extract the data from its computerized business records.

***Playboy Enter. v. Welles*, S.D. Cal., 60 F. Supp.2d 1050, (1999):** This case set fourth that the burden of cost factors would be the only limitation to discovery request for copying and examining a hard drive for relevant e-mail messages.

***People v. Hawkins*, 98 Cal.App.4th 1428, (2002):** This case highlighted the importance of time in computers and allowed printouts of computer access times. It was determined during the case that proper functioning of the computer clock was relevant to the case.

***U.S. v. Allen*, 106 F.3d 695, 700 6th Cir. (1997):** This case, relating to authenticity challenges to digital evidence, found that "merely raising the possibility of tampering is insufficient to render evidence inadmissible." Furthermore, without specific evidence of tampering, allegations that computer records have been altered are applied to their weight, not their admissibility.

***U.S. v. Bonallo*, 858 F.2d 1427, 1436 9th Cir. (1988):** This case is another example of court findings relating to authenticity stating that "the fact that it is possible to alter data contained in a computer is plainly insufficient to establish untrustworthiness."

***Ariz. v. Youngblood*, 488 U.S. 51 (1988):** Although this case does not relate to digital discovery directly, it is a seminal case that articulated the test for fairness requiring that the defendant demonstrate that the police acted in bad faith in failing to preserve the evidence. This can be related to digital evidence in that the failure of law enforcement to collect all evidence desired by the defense must have been in *bad faith* and, thus, violated the defendant's rights.

***Easaly, McCaleb and Assoc., Inc. v. Perry*, No. E-2663 GA Supper. Crt. (1994):** In this case the judge ruled that all deleted but recoverable files on the defendant's hard drive were discoverable. The ruling allowed the plaintiff's expert to retrieve all recoverable files. A detailed protocol for reviewing digital data was also included in the ruling.

***RKI, Inc. v. Grimes*, 177 F. Supp.2d 859 ND. Ill. (2001):** In this case the defendant was fined $100,000 in compensatory damages and $150,000 in punitive damages, attorney fees, and court cost after it was determined he conducted a disk *defrag* process the night before discovery in an effort to destroy evidence.

***State v. Cook*, WL31045293 Ohio Ct. App.** (2002): In this child pornography case, the defendant challenged analysis of a bit-stream image of the original hard disk. The court ruled that the evidence was admissible after expert testimony related to the imaging process, authenticity methods, used and possibilities of tampering.

***V Cable, Inc. v. Budnick*, 23 FED Appx. 64 Second Cir.** (2001): In this case of illegal sales and distribution of cable equipment, the police used a private agency to perform analysis of seized computer equipment. It was argued by the defense that any information retrieved from the computers after they left police custody was corrupt and, therefore, inadmissible. The court ruled that the evidence was trustworthy under rule 803(6).

REGULATION

The increased production and reliance on digital data throughout industry, as well as corporations' failure to protect sensitive public data in digital form, has caused legislators to respond with new data-focused regulations. Some regulations are industry specific, covering industries such as health care, whereas other regulations are more wide sweeping, affecting entire states or public and international companies. Although many of the newest regulatory requirements have not yet been tested, the courts will inevitably be a vehicle through which computer forensics techniques are applied.

Today's data-focused regulations can affect computer forensics investigators because the requirements for data retention, protection, and storage are tied to the potential civil and criminal enforcement. The computer forensics investigator will thus be a valued resource in assessing or disproving compliance.

Some of the current data-focused regulations are described in the following sections.

Securities and Exchange Commission (SEC) Rule 17a-4 (1947)

This rule requires that U.S. publicly traded companies must archive all customer communications and billing information for a period of six years. Failure to comply with rule 17a-4 can result in large fines or imprisonment.

National Association of Securities Dealers (NASD) Rules 3010 and 3110 (1997)

The NASD rules, which were created to work alongside SEC 17a-4, require all its members to not only retain all public communications but ensure that there was no manipulation or criminal intent on the part of the member. Amendments to Rules 3010 and 3110 approved in 1997 allow firms to develop flexible supervisory procedures for the review of correspondence with the public.

Sarbanes-Oxley Act (2002)

One of the most publicized regulatory acts of 2002 was the Sarbanes-Oxley Act, which was created to establish chief executive responsibilities in U.S. publicly traded companies. The Sarbanes-Oxley Act requires that the CEO and CFO prepare a signed statement accompanying periodic reports to the effect of "appropriateness of the financial statements and disclosures contained in the periodic report, and that those financial statements and disclosures fairly present, in all material respects, the operations and financial condition of the issuer"[SoxAct01]. One key provision of interest is section 404, "Internal Controls," which outlines requirements for accurate financial data and the information technology processes that affect the data's fidelity.

Gramm-Leach-Bliley Act (1999)

The Gramm-Leach-Bliley Act, sometimes referred to as the Financial Services Modernization Act, requires financial institutions to protect against disclosure of nonpublic personal information. This act was created as a measure to prohibit financial institutions from selling nonpublic personal information to outside agencies such as marketing companies. Gramm-Leach-Bliley requires companies that market banking, insurance, stocks, bonds, financial services, and/or investments to do the following:

- Securely store all nonpublic personal information
- Inform customers of their policy for sharing nonpublic personal information
- Provide a process for customers to "opt out" of sharing their nonpublic personal information

The Gramm-Leach-Bliley Act requires institutions to protect against any anticipated threats to the confidentially or integrity of customers' nonpublic personal data. Penalties for noncompliance can include hefty fines and/or imprisonment.

California Privacy Law–SB 1386 (2003)

SB 1386 was created in an effort to protect California residents from the growing problem of identity theft. In this new wide-sweeping law, companies that maintain personal customer information for California residents are required to disclose any breach of security of the database to all California residents that they suspect may have had their information compromised.

Although SB 1386 is a California law, it is constructed such that it affects any company that possesses the private information of a California resident.

Because SB 1386 pays close attention to the protective measures provided by the company possessing private information, any stolen or compromised data that had been encrypted is not considered to be compromised; therefore, no notification would be required. Management can use this distinction as an encouragement to encrypt sensitive data at rest in data systems. Although no specific criminal or civil penalties are outlined, SB 1386 does open the door to class-action lawsuits by the "injured" customers.

Health Insurance Portability and Accountability Act (HIPAA) (First Rule in Effect in 2002)

Another well-publicized piece of legislation is HIPAA, which was ratified by Congress in 1996, in an effort to create a "national framework for health privacy protection." Because of HIPAA's broad scope affecting the way in which health records are handled throughout the health care system, the regulation has been implemented in stages.

Just because HIPAA is health care legislation does not mean that it affects only doctors and hospitals. Insurance companies, employees, and corporations that deal with patient information are also bound by this law.

The stages and timings in which HIPAA is scheduled to be rolled out are outlined in Table 2.2.

TABLE 2.2 HIPPA Rule Rollout Schedule

Rule Area	Due Date
Transaction Rules—Affect Electronic Data Interchange (EDI) by adding eight new transactions and six new code sets	October 2002
Privacy Rules—Add record safeguards, violation sanctions, training, and designations	April 2003
Security Rules—Mandate IT safeguards for physical storage, maintenance, transmission, access, and audit of patient-related data	April 2005

Civil penalties are assessed at $100 per violation, with up to $25,000 per person per year for each requirement or prohibition violated. Congress also established criminal penalties for knowingly violating patient privacy. These criminal penalties are broken into three areas, depending on the type of violation or intended use of compromised data. The three criminal penalties areas follow:

- Up to $50,000 and one year in prison for obtaining or disclosing protected health information
- Up to $100,000 and up to five years in prison for obtaining protected health information under "false pretenses"
- Up to $250,000 and up to 10 years in prison for obtaining or disclosing protected health information with the intent to sell, transfer, or use it for commercial advantage, personal gain, or malicious harm

HIPAA is one of the most detailed and comprehensive pieces of data-security legislation enacted. HIPAA requires mandatory review of all systems, including a risk analysis to determine methods for securing patient information. Continued process improvement and audit are also components of HIPAA.

International Organization for Standardization (ISO) 17799 (2000)

ISO 17799 originated in the United Kingdom as the British Standard for Information Security 7799, often referred to as BS 7799. The international flavor of ISO 17799 makes it well suited for multinational organizations that desire a comprehensive information-technology security framework. Many insurance companies use adherence to standards set forth in ISO 17799 as a requirement for Cyber-Liability Insurance. ISO 17799 is organized into the following 10 sections:

- Business Continuity Planning
- System Access Control
- System Development and Maintenance
- Physical and Environmental Security
- Compliance
- Personnel Security
- Security Organization
- Computer and Operations Management
- Asset Classification and Control
- Security Policy

Although no penalties apply to international organizations that do not implement the ISO 17799 standard, becoming ISO 17799 certified can be a key element in a company's ability to prove it was adhering to industry standard "best practices" in regard to data security.

U.S.A. PATRIOT Act (2001)

Created as a tool to identify and stop terrorism and any source of funding for terrorism, Uniting and Strengthening America by Providing Appropriate Tools Required to Intercept and Obstruct Terrorism (U.S.A. PATRIOT) Act expands already existing acts such as the Bank Secrecy Act and the Foreign Intelligence Secrecy Act. Purely from a regulatory stance, the act requires banking institutions to report any suspicious activity, including money transfers.

NOTE *In the context of the PATRIOT Act, a financial institution can include insurance companies; investment companies; loan and finance companies; dealers in precious metals, stones, or jewels; vehicle sales; persons involved in real estate closings and settlements; and so on.*

From a compliance standpoint, financial institutions must take the following steps to assist in antimoney laundering:

- Develop internal policies, procedures, and controls
- Designate a compliance officer
- Provide ongoing employee training
- Provide an independent audit to test programs

In accordance with the PATRIOT Act, financial institutions included in the broad definition must report any suspected money laundering activity to the U.S. Department of the Treasury.

An institutionÕs failure to comply with the U.S.A. PATRIOT Act could bring civil penalties for aiding in money laundering that are not less than two times the amount of the transaction and not more than $1,000,000. The criminal penalties for aiding in money laundering are not less than two times the amount of the transaction and not more than $1,000,000.

Personal Information Protection and Electronic Documents Act (PIPED) C-6 (2001)

PIPED C-6 is a Canadian law similar to the Gramm-Leach-Bliley Act in the United States. PIPED C-6 applies to international transportation, airports, telecommunications, radio and television broadcasts, banks, or any entity that is identified as Òany work, undertaking, or business that is under the legislative authority of Parliament,Ó PIPED C-6 is simply intended to protect collected personal data from unauthorized use.

All affected entities are provided by PIPED C-6 with the following 10 responsibilities:

- Be accountable for compliance
- Identify the purpose of collecting data
- Obtain consent from the individual
- Limit collection of data to that which is needed
- Limit use, disclosure, and retention of data
- Be accurate with the data
- Use appropriate safeguards to protect the data
- Be open about your use of the data
- Give individuals access to their data
- Provide recourse when you have incorrect data or data is used incorrectly

Penalties for noncompliance with PIPED C-6 can include a fine not exceeding $10,000 or a fine not exceeding $100,000, depending on the type of offence. Table 2.3, which was adapted from the Non-Compliant Impact table available at *www.securityforensics.com*, provides a summary of computer-data-related legislation discussed in this chapter.

TABLE 2.3 Summary of Regulations [Secfor01]

Regulation	Affected Industry	Summary	Penalties for Noncompliance
SEC 17a-4	Securities	Retain customer correspondence for up to six years	Unspecified fines; fines and imprisonment

→

TABLE 2.3 Summary of Regulations [Secfor01]

Regulation	Affected Industry	Summary	Penalties for Noncompliance
NASD Rules 3010 and 3110	Securities	Retain customer correspondence for up to six years	Unspecified fines
Sarbanes-Oxley	Public corporations	Best practice to retain all documents and e-mail messages to show accountability	Fines to $5,000,000 and 20 years imprisonment for destroying e-mail messages
Gramm-Leach-Bliley	Financial institutions	Requires protection of nonpublic personal information for outside distribution	Fines and up to five years imprisonment
California Privacy Law (SB 1386)	Any company doing business with California residents	Requires protection of nonpublic personal information and notifications of compromise	Civil action allowed for any or all "injured" customers
HIPAA	Medical	Patient privacy and to ensure document confidentially and integrity	Fines to $250,000 and imprisonment up to 10 years
ISO 17799	Could be a requirement for Cyber-Liability Insurance	Guidelines to monitor and protect information infrastructure	Potential damage to corporate reputation or insurability
U.S.A. PATRIOT Act	Broad definition of of *financial institutions* within the United States	Laws require information disclosure to help protect against money laundering for terrorism	Fines and imprisonment
PIPED C-6	Any business under legislative authority of Parliament	Laws require information disclosure to help protect against terrorism or compromise of personal information	Fines up to $100,000

Although industry-specific regulation regarding information security and data handling is not completely new, regulation is increasing. Only corporate responsibility as it relates to protection of data, coupled with clearly stated industry guidelines, will reduce legislative desire to regulate. Computer forensic investigators can benefit from regulatory understanding because it relates to potential evidence availability and location.

SUMMARY

- The *Federal Rules of Evidence*, the *California Evidence Code of 1967*, and the *IBA Rules of Taking Evidence in International Commercial Arbitration* are all documents governing the acceptance of evidence in courts.
- Rule 34 of the *Federal Rules of Civil Procedure* allows for data to be translated into a reasonable form, if necessary.
- The best evidence rule states that "to prove the content of a writing, recording, or photograph, the 'original' writing, recording, or photograph is ordinarily required."
- The *Federal Rules of Evidence* state that "if data are stored in a computer or similar device, any printout or other output readable by sight, shown to reflect the data accurately, is an 'original.'"
- The *Federal Rules of Evidence* even go so far as to permit summaries of large volumes of evidence in the form of "a chart, summary, or calculation" in warranted situations.
- Since 1923, judges have used the simple scientific reliability tests established in *Frye v. U.S.* [DcCir01].
- In *Daubert v. Merrell Dow* [Us01], the U.S. Supreme Court rejected the *Frye* tests for the admissibility of scientific evidence.
- Two new tests added in the *Daubert* decision are "Has the scientific theory or technique been empirically tested?" and "What are the known or potential error rates?"
- An "expert" in any field can be defined as one who has "special knowledge, skill, experience, training, or education" on a particular subject.
- The key to any type of questioning is to pay close attention to the question, take time answering the question, and ask the attorney to repeat or clarify the question, if needed.
- The U.S.A. PATRIOT Act was created as a tool to identify and stop terrorism and any source of funding for terrorism.
- SEC Rule 17a-4 requires that U.S. publicly traded companies must archive all customer communications and billing information for a period of six years.

- The case *Simon Prop. Group v. mySimon, Inc.*, S.D.Ind., highlighted that discovery of computer records included any deleted documents that were recoverable.

REFERENCES

[Ca01] *California Evidence Code*, State of California, January 1, 1967.

[DcCir01] *Frye v. U.S.*, 293 F.1013 (D.C. Cir. 1923).

[Doj01] U. S. Department of Justice, *Searching and Seizing Computers and Obtaining Electronic Evidence in Criminal Investigations*, available online at *www.cybercrime.gov/s&smanual2002.htm*, 2002.

[FifthCir01] *Capital Marine Supply v. M/V Roland Thomas II*, 719 F.2d 104, 106 (5th Cir. 1983).

[Fre01] *Federal Rules of Evidence*, U.S. Department of Justice, 2004.

[Iba01] *IBA Rules of Taking Evidence in International Commercial Arbitration*, International Bar Association Council, 1999.

[Ill01] *People v. Holowko*, 486 N.E.2d 877, 878–79 (Ill. 1985).

[NinthCir01] *U.S. v. Catabran*, 836 F.2d 453, 457 (9th Cir. 1988).

[NinthCir02] *U.S. v. DeGeorgia*, 420 F.2d 889, 893 n.11 (9th Cir. 1969).

[Oconnor01] O'Connor, T.R., *Admissibility of Scientific Evidence under Daubert*, available online at *http://faculty.ncwc.edu/toconnor/425/425lect02.htm*, 2004.

[Ohio01] *Ohio v. Michael J. MORRIS*, Court of Appeals of Ohio, Ninth District, Wayne County, No. 04CA0036, Feb. 16, 2005.

[Secfor01] Security Forensics, Inc., available online at *www.securityforensics.com*, 2004.

[SeventhCir01] *U.S. v. Whitaker*, 127 F.3d 595, 601 (7th Cir. 1997).

[SoxAct01] One Hundred Seventh Congress of the United States of America, Sarbanes-Oxley Act of 2002, available online at *www.law.uc.edu/CCL/SOact/soact.pdf, 2002.*

[Un01] *International Criminal Tribunal for Rwanda, Rules of Procedure and Evidence*, U.N. Doc. ITR/3/REV.1, 1995.

[Us01] *Daubert v. Merrell Dow*, 509 U.S. 579 (1993).

[Warren01] *A Preliminary Report on the Advisability and Feasibility of Developing Uniform Rules of Evidence for the United States District Courts*, 30 F.R.D. 73, 1962.

RESOURCES

[Best01]Best, Richard E., *Civil Discovery Law Discovery of Electronic Data*, available online at *http://californiadiscovery.findlaw.com/electronic_data_discovery.htm*, 2004.

[Giannelli01] Giannelli, Paul C., *Understanding Evidence*, LexisNexis, 2003.

[Morgester01] Morgester, Robert M., *Survival Checklist for Forensic Experts*, unpublished, 2003.

[Sedona01] *The Sedona Principles: Best Practices Recommendations & Principles for Addressing Electronic Document Production*, Sedona Conference Working Group, available online at *www.thesedonaconference.org*, 2003.

3 Evidence Dynamics

In This Chapter

- Forces of Evidence Dynamics
- Human Forces
- Natural Forces
- Equipment Forces
- Proper Tools and Procedures

FORCES OF EVIDENCE DYNAMICS

In Chapter 1, "Computer Forensics Essentials," the importance of Locard's exchange principle was introduced in its relationship to crime scene investigation. Remembering that Locard's exchange principle is simply a way to describe two objects interacting and the resulting exchange. This basic concept can be further extended to describe the concept of evidence dynamics, covered in this chapter.

NOTE

Locard's exchange principle states that when any two objects come into contact, there is always transference of material from each object onto the other. This exchange is illustrated in Figure 3.1. Operating system logs recording hacker, investigator, or user actions and data left on hard disks in unallocated sectors are just a few examples of Locard's exchange principle in action.

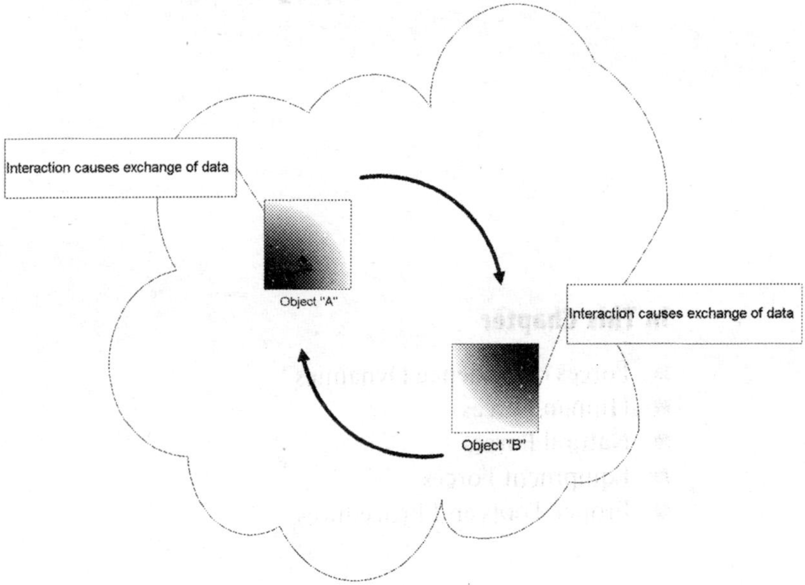

FIGURE 3.1 Locard's exchange principle.

Evidence dynamics is a way to describe and understand the forces that can act on evidence and the subsequent effects of the action. Because so many things can act on digital evidence, and as Locard's principle explains, the action will almost undoubtedly result in some effect or change on the evidence, it is essential for forensics investigators to be cognizant of evidence dynamics at all times. Evidence dynamics can be broken down into human and natural forces that may be directly involved or incidental to the crime or investigation. This chapter will explore each of these high-level forces in detail.

HUMAN FORCES

As in humans themselves, the forces that act on digital evidence from humans come in all shapes and sizes and can affect evidence in a variety of ways. As one might suspect, the forensics investigators themselves are included in the human force of evidence dynamics.

NOTE

A common scenario used to describe the human effects on evidence in crime-scene processing is that of the emergency medical technician (EMT) at the scene of a murder. The EMT attempts to save the life of a gunshot-wound victim, who later dies. The EMT most likely leaves footprints all around the victim's body. The EMT also may have moved items in the immediately surrounding area in his lifesaving efforts. In both these situations, evidence that may be vital to the case could have been destroyed or, at the very least, affected in some way.

Examples of humans who may act on digital evidence follow:

- Emergency personnel
- Forensics investigators
- Law enforcement personnel
- Victim
- Suspect
- Bystanders

Although our primary focus is computer forensics, the previously listed human forces can act on all forms of evidence in many ways. Computer forensics investigators should keep in mind that theirs may not be the only evidence being collected, and the interweaving of several forensics disciplines may be required.

CAUTION

In some situations, fingerprints or other trace evidence may need to be collected from a computer system being seized. Investigators should think of the entire crime scene and respect how there can be an evidence dynamic force acting on other forensics disciplines' evidence.

Refocusing on the human effects on digital evidence, let's take a closer look at our examples as they relate to computers.

Emergency Personnel

As previously stated, these first responders can easily affect a crime scene in many ways with their actions. Rightly so, EMTs can be very focused on their lifesaving efforts and exhibit varying levels of understanding related to evidence collection and contamination. The first way in which EMTs can affect computer evidence is usually by moving evidence to accommodate lifesaving equipment and efforts. This type of action normally will affect related forensics disciplines such as fingerprint collection, but they can directly affect digital evidence if a system or systems are turned off by any means. How a computer system is shut down can greatly affect digital evidence through the loss of volatile data in physical memory and the changing or deletion of files. The topic of computer shutdown will be discussed in greater detail later when we discuss forensics investigators as a force that acts on evidence.

Forensics Investigators

Forensic investigators are arguably the force that can have the greatest effect on digital evidence, considering they are focused directly on the computer or digital media. The major effect that forensic investigators can cause is the possible loss of volatile data in physical memory when live systems are shut down. The method of shutdown is an often-debated topic when discussing computer-forensics-related evidence dynamics, not only because of the potential loss of volatile data but because varying methods of shutdown can lead to vastly differing results in changes to digital data on disk.

The potential loss of volatile data can be mitigated through collecting a snapshot of physical memory prior to shutdown. Investigators should keep in mind the golden rule of evidence dynamics: be as least intrusive as possible.

Often investigators will use the term nonintrusive when describing their actions or tools when interacting with digital data. When looking at the basic scientific principle that "the act of observing something in fact changes it," investigators will quickly come to the understanding that least intrusive actions should be the goal. Even when hardware write-blocking devices are employed and software is proven not to write to digital media on disks, the act of turning a disk platter and friction of read heads against sectors will change the physical properties, however slightly. Again, we see Locard's principle in action.

Another way to avoid the risk of potential loss of volatile data is to accept that either there is no compelling reason for its capture or the capture process would be unacceptably intrusive and therefore do nothing.

However, once a decision has been made and after the potential loss of volatile data has been avoided, computer forensics investigators should consider how the system will be shut down. Some investigators feel that unplugging the power cord is the best alternative to a normal systematic shutdown, but each operating system and configuration interacts with the data differently, and thus, the resulting change to evidence will be different. In every case, the investigator must make an informed decision based on the evidence-changing characteristics of the shutdown method and the situational environment. Of course, the decision of which shutdown method to use is normally an easy one if the system is off; leave it that way when seizing the entire computer. Some high-level evidence-changing characteristics are displayed in Table 3.1.

TABLE 3.1 Computer Shutdown Characteristics

Action	Characteristic
Pull the plug	Volatile data is deleted if it is not collected prior to shutdown
	The file system may be damaged, although this is rare with today's file systems
	Open files or data not flushed from cache to the disk may be lost or corrupted
	Future access to data on a disk could be lost (for disks that use full disk encryption or mounted virtual encrypted disks)
	Changes to the disk during normal shutdown process are limited
Orderly shutdown process	Virtual memory space on the disk is lost; Windows operating systems offer configuration settings to clear virtual memory on disk (pagefile) during the shutdown process
	Control of evidence-destructive processes launched during shutdown is lost
	File system is likely to be intact after shutdown
	Files are likely to be intact
	Each file written to the system during shutdown can result in fewer recoverable deleted files

A common argument made for *pulling the plug* is the possibility of potentially destructive processes being launched during the shutdown process. The urban lore is that a hacker could have created and installed a script to delete evidence. The destructive script would be executed during shutdown if the person shutting down the computer does not use the proper bypass procedure known only by the owner. Although this approach is valid conceptually, permanently destroying large amounts of data on a magnetic disk can be time consuming due to the process most file systems use to delete files. When most operating systems receive a request to delete a file, the operating system simply removes the file's name from the root directory shown to users. The underlying sectors of data are still present on disk. To securely delete data from a hard disk, applications are written that repeatedly write data to the area where the file once resided. The U.S. Department of Defense has written a clearing and sanitizing standard, DOD 5220.22-M, which addresses the issues surrounding secure deletion of digital data.

Another often-discussed alternative for automated destruction of evidence is to create and install an application that would automatically delete evidence if network connections were lost. Sensing the loss of network connections is often referred to as a *dead man's switch*. Hypothetically a hacker could use the dead man's switch approach to automatically delete trace evidence of his applications and actions on a machine if someone detected their presence on a system and immediately removed the suspect system from the network.

NOTE

In cases where encryption is being utilized on a live system and the files or encrypted volumes are mounted, it is often necessary to collect evidence through a live extraction process described in later chapters.

One of the most common arguments made for an *orderly shutdown* is that investigators have a greater chance of filesystem and individual file integrity after the shutdown. Some standard operating system shutdown procedures are shown in Table 3.2.

TABLE 3.2 Operating System Shutdown Commands

Operating System	Shutdown Command
Windows 3.1	Click File, Exit
Win95/98/2000/2003/ME/XP	Click Start, Shutdown, Yes (*in classic interface mode*)
Windows NT 3.51	Click File, Shutdown
Windows NT 4.0	Click Start, Shutdown, Yes
Novell®	At server prompt, type <Alt-Esc>, then press Down
	At user/client press Syscon, then Exit
Macintosh®	Click Special, Shutdown
OS/2	Right-click, then click Shutdown
SCO UNIX	Type shutdown –y –g0
AIX UNIX	Type shutdown –f
Sun® Solaris®	Type shutdown now
Linux	Type shutdown –h now
	(also press <Ctrl-Alt-Del> in many versions)
AS-400L	Type pwrdwnsys *immed
DEC® VAX/ Alpha VMS	Type @sys$system:shutdown

The arguments for and against pulling the plug during system shutdown can both be compelling, but only the individual situation can dictate an investigator's actions. In each case it is essential that the investigator think about the results of his actions and balance the risks. Clearly the human forces acting on evidence created by investigator actions are forces over which the investigator has the most control.

Law Enforcement Personnel

All law enforcement personnel have a basic understanding of crime scene processing, but many lack technical understanding of how they are interacting with digital computer evidence.

Most investigators identify that many of the human factors of evidence dynamics can overlap. Although this fact is certainly true, the law enforcement factors of evidence dynamics usually focus on the "first responder" components of evidence dynamics, which includes incidental contact with potential digital evidence. The forensics investigator forces are closely associated with their own direct and interactive contact with potential digital evidence.

NOTE

To assist law enforcement personnel who do not have a day-to-day understanding of digital evidence collection, the National Institute of Justice produced the handbook Electronic Crime Scene Investigation—A Guide for First Responders [Nij01]. The handbook was developed in 2001 by a multiagency working group called the Technical Working Group for Electronic Crime Scene Investigation. Although the guide was developed for first responders, it provides information useful for any computer forensics investigator.

Focusing on law enforcement as first responder, the factors of evidence dynamics can be broken down into areas of preservation, identification, and collection.

Preservation

Preservation forces can include issues similar to those of emergency personnel where the interaction with potential digital evidence was incidental to serving a warrant, interviewing suspects and victims, or performing other law enforcement procedures. A key focus for law enforcement should be to gain an understanding of the fragile nature of digital evidence and how to avoid excess interaction if it is not required. Even if general law enforcement personnel will not be involved in the identification and collection, or bag and tag, of digital evidence, they should at least be trained in its identification and characterization. By understanding how to identify the potential sources of digital data, law enforcement personnel can help to preserve potential evidence. One of the cardinal rules for first responders should be "If you see a computer and it's on, leave it on; if the computer is off, leave it off." Following this rule will eliminate the many additions, deletions, and changes to a computer's filesystem during the startup and shutdown process. Other incidental interaction forces often occur when collecting evidence such as pagers, phones, and PDAs. Although many law enforcement personnel are beginning to realize the wealth of data contained in these devices, many may not realize the rather limited battery life (less than 24 hours, in some cases) in these devices. In many of these devices that store information in volatile memory, once the battery power has been expended all volatile memory contents are lost.

Identification

Identification forces are best exhibited when law enforcement personnel remember the cardinal rule for first responders: "If you see a computer and it's on, leave it on; if the computer is off, leave it off." Adherence to this rule alone eliminates the majority of issues related to law enforcement interaction with digital evidence while attempting to identify evidence. A common complaint from computer forensics investigators working in labs is that the first responder turned on a computer and searched through the hard disk looking for some form of evidence. Although this type of interaction may seem harmless enough, it can be very destructive to digital evidence by, at a minimum, changing valuable last-accessed times on files. First responders should generally focus on identifying containers (such as a computer) of digital evidence rather than the specific evidence contained in the container. Although it seems simple enough, identification of a digital container can be quite challenging. The camera shown in Figure 3.2 can hold up to 300 digital images.

FIGURE 3.2 A typical digital camera can hold up to 300 digital images.

Long gone are the simple days when identification of the computer and associated storage disk was easy. With the wide spread use of Universal Serial Bus (USB) flash memory devices, digital storage is becoming much easier to conceal. Some system administrators have begun to call USB flash memory drives (often referred to as key drives) as the Swiss army knife of the information technology worker. As seen in Figure 3.3, Victorinox, the manufacture of the Swiss army knife, took the analogy to heart.

FIGURE 3.3 Advertisement from Victorinox, the manufacturer of the Swiss army knife. ©Swissbit, Switzerland 2004

As the figures illustrate, there are many creative ways to hide a USB flash disk. Another widely distributed USB flash disk is concealed in a standard writing pen. Physical deception, however, can be much simpler than using USB key drives.

As high-grade printers become more widely available, more professional-looking CD-ROM labels can be printed to deceive first responders into thinking a CD-ROM does not contain user-stored data. CD-ROMs and other removable media can also be found in unexpected places. In San Diego, California, David Westerfield was sentenced to death on January 3, 2003, for the kidnapping and murder of seven-year-old Danielle van Dam. Although little evidence relating to the case was found in Westerfield's computers, child pornography was found on a handful of removable disks concealed behind books in a bookcase. This evidence was instrumental in convicting Westerfield's and could have been easily overlooked.

When identifying digital evidence for collection, it is best for first responders to go overboard and identify more digital evidence rather than less. An item containing digital evidence that may be overlooked, even by more experienced forensics investigators, is a printer. Experienced forensics investigators have known for some time that volatile data that could be of evidentiary value may be present in a printer's memory, but accessing the data can be difficult. What some investigators may not know is that newer printers contain a hard disk with file systems and persistent storage. The Xerox® DocuPrint® line of printers can contain hard disks as large as 10 GB.

Collection

Collection forces from law enforcement can vary greatly. Under ideal situations law enforcement first responders simply identify and bag and tag the digital evidence as found for subsequent processing by trained computer forensics investigators. It is these situations that cause many experienced investigators to recommend pulling the plug of any identified system followed by standard evidence collection procedures for bag and tag. What first responders should focus on subsequent to potential digital evidence identification relates back to standard crime scene processing. When collecting a computer system, for instance, it is helpful to know how the system was situated and interconnected. Photographing the computer system from multiple angles, showing cable connections and placement, can prove instrumental in the analysis phase by forensics investigators. Because most systems require the disconnection of an array of cables and peripheral devices, labeling each cable and its connection point can also assist forensics investigators. In some cases, forensics investigators find it helpful to test the system as it was installed by the user. Part IV of this book covers artifact collection and presents comprehensive steps for documentation, including labeling, chain of custody, and media access records.

Victim

The victim's interaction with digital evidence is normally defensive or reactive in nature. For example, in the corporate environment, a system administrator or incident-response team member reacts to a hacking event on one of their systems. In this type of case, the system administrator or incident-response team has two simple goals: confirm suspicions and restore integrity to the affected system or systems. Steps taken to achieve these two goals can be some of the most destructive effects on digital evidence because of the victim's knowledge level of the system. Confirming suspicions usually involves scanning local system-administration utilities on the suspected system and thus changing critical file last-accessed-time metadata used during analysis. The administrator may even go as far as restoring specific application files to check for system behavior changes. During this step the system administrator is more likely to suspect that something is "broken" on the system rather than that he is the victim of a hacking incident. Once confirmation that a system has been compromised has been made, the system administrator is faced with the two conflicting choices: restore services or preserve evidence. Although incident-response team members are receiving more training related to evidence preservation, restoration of services usually wins the coin toss.

A common scenario found in intellectual property theft cases is that a system administrator armed with an understanding of file recovery will offer to recover evidence from a suspected employee's computer. In these cases the computer is usually turned over to a computer forensics services provider who finds that deleted file recovery software had been installed on the suspect's computer and the last-accessed-time metadata on many files reflects a time far beyond the suspect's termination date. Control over these situations as well as many forces of evidence dynamics may be limited. Understanding the potential effects on evidence by the victim can be crucial to the investigative process.

Suspect

The suspect's effect on digital evidence usually surrounds his desire to eliminate, hide, or restrict access to any potential evidence. This desire raises the pull the plug versus proper shutdown debate once again.

CAUTION

System administrators have for some time had mechanisms in place for receiving pages of system events. It's not a far stretch to postulate that a systems owner who was not present would know someone was exercising a warrant on his computer systems, even if he is not present. With today's remote-access capabilities and persistent Internet connections, the user could remotely log in and destroy data while a limited scope warrant was being exercised.

The situation in our warning raises several questions: Should the network connection be pulled? What about a dead man's switch? Should the power plug be pulled? What about encrypted file access? Should the system be properly shut down? What about the execution of destructive scripts if the system is not shut down in a certain way? There is a counter argument for each stance. An old Navy fighter pilot phrase comes to mind, which states "situational awareness and experience will win the fight."

Bystanders

Bystanders are among the few human forces of evidence dynamics over which the forensics investigator may have the most control. Bystanders can interact with digital evidence in many of the same ways in which other human forces act. Although a bystander may not come in contact with the computers of a victim or suspect, they may be an incidental effect. In the case of public internet kiosks and terminals found in libraries, many bystanders could have come in contact with the evidence system. Another example is a cellular telephone or PDF found at a crime scene by a bystander. In both situations, how the bystander interacted with the potential evidence is ultimately important to digital evidence analysis.

As presented by this section, the human forces acting on digital evidence can vary greatly. In situations where forensics investigators do not have control over the interaction, it is important that they understand the various forces. Understanding how people in a crime scene could have acted on evidence in early stages of an investigation can only help documentation and subsequent analysis.

NATURAL FORCES

The most common natural forces that can affect evidence dynamics are fire, water, and other weather-related events. Although these forces are indisputable, time alone can be a force that affects digital evidence. In this section we will start by examining digital evidence where it rests—digital media.

A strong indication of how volatile data can be is that computer's magnetic hard disks are measured in Mean Time Between Failures (MTBF). That's right—not *if* there will be a failure but *when.* Other types of data storage devices such as USB flash disk are rated by their data-retention life. Even CD-ROMs have a data-retention life expectancy. All these indicators show that the natural force of time alone can contribute to the loss of evidence. Add to the concept of time other forces of nature such as fire, water, natural disaster, and even humidity levels (which affect electrostatic discharge), and investigators can truly begin to understand just how volatile digital data can be.

One of the first natural forces in evidence dynamics a forensics investigator can be affected by is electrostatic discharge (ESD) to open circuit boards. ESD can occur when the humidity range falls below the ideal 40 to 60 percent. When the humidity range grows higher than 60 percent, electronic components can suffer from corrosion over extended periods of time (another natural force of evidence dynamics).

TIP

The ideal humidity range of between 40 and 60 percent is the target of heating, ventilation, and air-conditioning systems (HVAC) found in data centers. Keeping the humidity level within this range protects data systems from corrosion as well as harm from ESD. Personnel involved in computer forensics lab maintenance should also consider this a target range.

Even when the humidity is within the ideal range, the presence of non-static-free carpet can contribute to ESD and thus cause damage to electronic equipment. A static charge of as little as 40 volts can damage sensitive circuits such as those found exposed on the bottom of computer hard disks. Standards such as IEC 61340-5-1 have been created to outline the requirements for electrostatic-discharge-free work environments. Protective surfaces and the use of grounding wristbands, such as that shown in Figure 3.4, are key components to protecting against ESD damage.

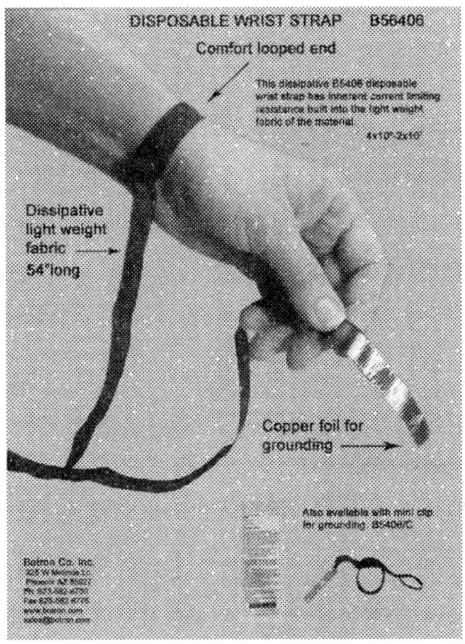

FIGURE 3.4 A grounding wristband helps protect against ESD damage [Botron01].

ESD wristbands are easy to use; the investigator wears the wristband and attaches the cable clip to the CPU being accessed. In lab work surfaces designed for ESD protection, the surface itself may include snaps for attaching ESD wristbands. Use of ESD wristbands such as that seen in Figure 3.4 is normally relegated to the lab, but they should also be used when the investigator accesses a hard disk in the field.

Using ESD wristbands and maintaining proper humidity levels through HVAC are the most common approaches to reducing ESD risks. Investigators may also choose to reduce the risk of circuit damage through the use of antistatic sprays, antistatic floor mats, and static-free bags for storage and transport.

Understanding that magnetic media is basically temporary storage is helpful over and above planning for system failures. In addition to mechanical storage devices being measured in MTBF, the media itself has an expected shelf or data-retention life. Table 3.3 shows some of the most common expected shelf lives.

TABLE 3.3 Expected Media Shelf Life

Media	Life in Years
Floppy disks	1–2
Standard hard disks	20
Removable magnetic disks	30
CDs, DVDs, and minidisks vary based on dye color	Cyanine or green tint = 10–50 Blue dye = 100 Gold dye = 100
Atomic holographic optical storage	100
DLT tapes	30
DAT tapes	30
Zip drives	10
Multimedia and secure digital cards	11
Flash key drives	10

The optimistic values for media shelf life shown in Table 3.3 are based on vendor specifications applied to optimal conditions of the operating environment. Investigators should use this table as a guide and take into account the many factors (natural forces) that can affect a reduction in shelf life. For example, a disk operating in an environment that is just a few degrees higher in temperature and humidity levels than specified by the manufacture can have its shelf life reduced drastically.

Because backup tapes, disk drives, and diskettes are vulnerable to heat, dust, humidity, and magnetic fields, they must be handled and stored in a highly protective manner. A common misunderstanding when storing magnetic media is to provide protection from fire but not heat. Standard fireproof safes will not protect the underlying data on magnetic media from destruction from exposure to heat. Most fireproof safes are intended to protect documents and are rated to keep the internal temperature below 200°C (360°F), thus preventing documents from combusting. To protect data on magnetic media from destruction due to heat, the internal safe temperature should be kept below 100°C (212°F) degrees; heatproof safes are normally rated below 52°C (93°F). Another factor to consider when choosing a fireproof safe for media storage is the rating related to the time a safe can maintain the internal temperature below a target range.

Not all is lost if magnetic media becomes unreadable in its normal environment. Although a single bit in the wrong position can prevent some file systems from being readable by an operating system, many data recovery companies are proficient in correcting these issues as well as physical problems with magnetic and optical media.

EQUIPMENT FORCES

The forces of specialized equipment used in computer forensics can be some of the most damaging to digital evidence because their underlying actions are seldom observed directly. In computer forensics the specialized equipment can be either hardware and software created specifically to support the computer forensics process or repurposed computer hardware and software. Some examples of hardware created specifically for the computer forensics process include hardware disk write-blocking and disk-imaging devices.

Hardware disk write-blocking devices are created specifically to allow an investigator to preview or collect images of digital evidence without the risk of writing to the suspect disk. Because a computer's input and output bus, basic input/output system (BIOS), operating system, and other peripheral devices can all write to a directly connected hard disk, it is essential that hardware write-blocking be used when the investigator is directly accessing an evidence hard disk. Hardware write-blocking devices are the best example of a device created specifically to mitigate the evidence dynamics effects of equipment on digital evidence.

Hardware disk-imaging devices normally provide a combination of hardware and firmware created specifically to create a disk-imaging process in a bit-stream fashion to collect sector-by-sector digital evidence. Many disk-cloning devices used by system administrators have been reengineered to provide write-blocking as well as sector-by-sector imaging to support disk imaging in support of computer forensics investigators.

In his paper on volatile memory collection, Brian Carrier proposed a hardware PCI device to reduce the destructive effects of collecting volatile memory in digital evidence collection [Carrier01]. In his paper, Carrier identifies, among other issues, many cases in which the use of software to collect volatile data from a running system can displace and damage the very data the investigator is attempting to capture. Although implementation of Carrier's device must be accomplished prior to the need for volatile evidence collection in most cases, it is an outstanding example of the need for investigators to understand the low-level effects of equipment on digital evidence.

In many cases investigators will utilize standard computer hardware in the collection and analysis of digital evidence. In such cases, specialized equipment will also be used in conjunction with the repurposed equipment to provide a forensically sound (least-intrusive) environment. An example of forensic and repurposed equipment being used in this fashion is when an investigator uses a standard USB-to-IDE conversion cable to attach to a suspect's hard disk but places a hardware write-blocking device in between the conversion cable and the suspect's hard disk.

NOTE

The specific selection and use of hardware and software equipment such as write blockers and disk imagers will be addressed in Part IV, "Artifact Collection."

Because of the many ways in which operating systems and other software can act on the underlying hard disk and filesystems, several computer-forensics-focused applications for collecting, interpreting, and viewing disk data have been developed. The creation of this software has been driven by the need for investigators to reduce the underlying evidence dynamics effects during collection and analysis of digital evidence. One of the core features of this forensics-focused software is the ability to maintain the integrity of the underlying digital evidence. To provide for digital integrity in addition to aiding analysis, computer forensics working environments provided by leading software manufactures take the approach of removing the underlying operating system's filesystem from the picture. By reassembling disk data from the bit level and implementing their own read-only file system, computer forensics software can not only ensure that no filesystem or metadata is altered but also provide deep analytical capabilities.

In some cases computer software must be repurposed to fit a computer forensics investigator's needs. Examples of repurposed software include hacking tools for cracking password-protected files and file-recovery software. There is sure to be no end of software tools that need to be repurposed from case to case, but investigators should always be aware of the following points:

- How the tool works
- If and/or what evidence data is changed by tools
- Which hardware or software tools could be used to limit changes to the data being analyzed or captured

To understand how a tool works, investigators must research published tests as well as provide their own lab analysis tests of the tool. For example, investigators can use low-level monitoring tools such as FileMon or RegMon from the Sysinternals™ Web site [sysint01] to monitor the effects of software on Windows file systems. For low-level I/O bus monitoring, investigators should investigate busTrace® [bustrace01], which offers the ability to capture and analyze all hard drive, CD/DVD, tape, jukebox, and more I/O activity. Another example would be to create a cryptographic hash baseline and then compare the baseline hashes for changes during identified test points while testing.

NOTE

A cryptographic hash is an algorithm used to produce fixed-length character sequences based on input of arbitrary length. Any given input always produces the same output, called a hash. If any input bit changes, the output hash will change significantly and in a random manner. In addition, the original input cannot be derived from the hash. Two of the most commonly used hashing algorithms are MD5 and SHA1. Cryptographic hashes essentially provide a single-sized signature of the underlying data such as a file or entire disk.

Understanding the underlying effect hardware and software equipment might have on digital evidence is paramount to providing a sound investigation. Investigators will find they need to develop and constantly utilize good lab skills to understanding their tools' interaction with digital evidence.

PROPER TOOLS AND PROCEDURES

In closing this chapter it is important to relate our understanding of evidence dynamics to the proper use of tools and procedures. Investigators should take into account the human and natural forces that can and do act on digital evidence at every stage of the investigation. As this book progresses, we will continue to discuss tools and procedures as they relate to the performance of computer forensics investigations. Many people will say investigators should seek out tools and use procedures that are "court certified." However, investigators should keep in mind that there is no court certification for tools or procedures, only past decisions or case law that helps guide judges. Investigators should rely on their own self-verified understanding of the tools and procedures. One of the first things investigators should take into account when selecting tools is how the tools will interact with digital evidence. Second, the investigator should determine if tools and procedures are available that will help reduce evidence dynamics effects.

The following list of items is useful in crime scene processing in general as well as computer forensics:

Envelopes of various sizes: For holding diskettes and loose evidence

Tamperproof tape: For labeling evidence

Tamperproof evidence bags: To hold larger disks

Static-free bags: To hold original disk wrapping

Large paper trash bags: To hold evidence

Stapler: To seal bags of evidence

Cardboard boxes: For carrying large volumes of evidence and computer components

Digital camera: For documenting the scene

Computer repair tool kit: For accessing and disassembling computer equipment

Computer forensics tool kit: Contents to be discussed in a later chapter

Electrostatic discharge wristband: To use when handling electronic components with exposed circuit boards directly

Composition notebooks: For recording a narrative log of investigator actions

Flashlight: For illuminating hard-to-see areas

Magnifying glass: For viewing really hard-to-see areas

Drawing paper: To sketch logical network topologies

Ruler and tape measure: To show item size in photos

Permanent markers: To label evidence

Chalk and/or crayons: To mark evidence in photos

Disposable latex gloves: For handling evidence

Keeping above-listed items on hand will assist forensics investigators in reducing the effects of evidence dynamics from a physical perspective. As we will see later when discussing specialized computer forensics hardware and software, evidence dynamics will again play a part in the way these tools interact with digital evidence.

SUMMARY

- Evidence dynamics can be described as any force that acts on evidence.
- The forces of evidence dynamics can be broken down into human, natural, and incidental.
- A script that senses the loss of network connections and reacts in some automated fashion is often referred to as a *dead man's switch*.
- The arguments for and against pulling the plug for system shutdown can both be compelling, but only the individual situation can dictate the investigator's actions.
- Some newer printers can contain hard disks with filesystems and persistent storage. The Xerox DocuPrint line of printers can contain hard disks as large as 10 GB.

- Understanding how people in a crime scene could have acted on evidence in early stages of an investigation will help subsequent digital evidence analysis.
- Maintaining a humidity range of between 40 and 60 percent reduces risk of electrostatic discharge and corrosion damage to circuits.
- The shelf life of CD-ROMs, DVDs, and minidisks varies based on dye color.
- Hardware disk write-blocking devices are created specifically to allow an investigator to preview or collect images of digital evidence without the risk of writing to the suspect's disk.
- Understanding the underlying effect hardware and software equipment might have on digital evidence is paramount to providing a sound investigation.

REFERENCES

[Botron01] Botron Company Web site, available online at *www.botron.com*, 2005.

[bustrace01] busTrace Web site, available online at *www.bustrace.com*, 2005.

[Carrier01] Carrier, Brian and Grand, Joe, "A Hardware-Based Memory Acquisition Procedure for Digital Investigation," *Journal of Digital Investigations*, March 2004.

[Nij01] *Electronic Crime Scene Investigation—A Guide for First Responders*, National Institute for Justice, available online at *www.ncjrs.org/pdffiles1/nij/187736.pdf*, 2001.

[Sysint01] Sysinternals Web site, available online at *www.sysinternals.com*, 2004.

RESOURCES

[Fisher01] Fisher, Barry A. J., *Techniques of Crime Scene Investigation, Seventh Edition*, CRC Press, 2003.

[Krutz01] Krutz, Ronald L. and Vines, Russell Dean, *The CISSP Prep Guide—Mastering the Ten Domains of Computer Security*, John Wiley & Sons, Inc., 2001.

Part II Information Systems

Part II, "Information Systems," contains three chapters that explain various methods through which users and organizations implement information technology. Understanding how individual users and organizations implement information technology solutions is a key component to identifying potential evidence. Part II provides detailed discussion of various network topologies in use that can act as the foundation for corporate and home networks. Additional topics of discussion include how to leverage existing corporate policies and audits to find evidence as well as interview techniques and how computer systems interact.

4 Interview, Policy, and Audit

In This Chapter

- Supporting and Corroborating Evidence
- Subject Interviews
- Policy Review
- Audit
- Statement of Work and Deliverables
- Executive Summary
- Recommendations
- Scope
- Host-Specific Findings
- War Dialing Results
- Conclusion

SUPPORTING AND CORROBORATING EVIDENCE

Computer forensics investigators often want to collect the digital evidence and rush back to the lab to start analyzing it. Unfortunately, the distributed nature of digital data doesn't provide for this approach. In this chapter we will examine what supporting evidence and information can be gained through grassroots investigative techniques. Many times the investigator will find this corroborating information instrumental in the later stages of digital analysis.

The information presented in this chapter for gaining supporting information integral to the collection of digital evidence can be considered the first step in a computer forensics investigator's case processing. Although many people consider subject interviews, policy reviews, and audits to be supplemental or nice-to-do steps, these procedures can often make or break a case. The concepts outlined in this chapter apply to corporate incident responses and civil intellectual property cases as well as criminal investigations.

Despite the seemingly local or isolated focus of the case, most computers are connected to some type of network (public or private). It's this very connection that initiates the requirement for an expanded understanding of the overall environment through interview, policy, and audit reviews. Many investigations may start off as simple e-mail discovery or document recovery, but when the system is determined to have been infected with one of the hundreds of remote-control Trojan horses, viruses, or malware, the investigation is quickly expanded beyond the single workstation. This type of case happens more often than you would expect. Even with the focus still directed at e-mail discovery or document recovery, a complete network security audit is in order to determine the effectiveness of the suspected compromise. Already, hackers have used the defense that their computer had been compromised, and therefore, any action taken on their computer could be attributed to another hacker.

SUBJECT INTERVIEWS

The subject interview component of the computer forensics process drives some states to lump computer forensics investigators with private investigators. Indeed, if a computer forensics investigator is performing all phases of an investigation including subject interviews, then a compelling argument for private investigator licensing can be made. It is the author's opinion that rather than trying to fit one profession into another's licensing requirements, a separate licensing process should be created for computer forensics investigators involved in active subject interviewing and field investigations. All licensing issues aside, it's hard to dispute that a forensics investigator benefits from information gained in subject interviews relating to the digital data collected.

What are subject interviews? The answer depends on the situation. Some examples follow:

- In a criminal case the interview could be with a suspect, victim, witness, or other person linked to the crime.
- In a civil matter the interview could be with people related to the plaintiff, defendant, or other similarly linked person in civil discovery.
- In a private corporate matter the interview is most likely focused on corporate personnel who are suspected of inappropriate activity or who may have been the victim of a cyber incident.

In each of these situations it is essential to understand that the situation could easily escalate. It is common for a situation to escalate from private to civil and ultimately to criminal. Consider a case where an incident-response team identifies that a computer system has been hacked. During the interview and investigative process the company decides to prosecute the offending hackers. Further investigation shows that the hacker had compromised the computer system to make child pornography available to others on the Internet.

When discussing subject interviews, an investigator's mind can quickly wander from simple fact finding and information gathering questions to a dramatic interrogation scene. In the real world, from a criminal-investigative perspective, subject interviews usually have two objectives:

- To determine if a person is being truthful
- To obtain confessions from guilty persons

In computer forensics, investigators can gain the most from developing an ability to spot and interpret verbal and nonverbal behaviors of deceptive and truthful people. Couple this capability with the ability to determine what information will be supportive of any digital evidence collected and the forensics investigator is well on his way to successful casework.

An interview technique referred to as the Reid Technique [Reid01] developed by John E. Reid & Associates in the 1940s and 1950s has been utilized by law enforcement and corporate and insurance investigators to get at the truth for more than half a century. The Reid Technique is a well-documented method that clearly distinguishes between interview and interrogation processes, with the interview process being less formalized. The formalized interrogation process proscribed by the Reid Technique teaches the employment of the following nine steps:

Step 1: Direct, Positive Confrontation
Step 2: Theme Development
Step 3: Handling Denials
Step 4: Overcoming Objections
Step 5: Procurement and Retention of the Suspect's Attention
Step 6: Handling the Suspect's Passive Mood
Step 7: Presenting an Alternative Question
Step 8: Having the Suspect Orally Relate Various Details of the Offense
Step 9: Converting an Oral Confession into a Written Confession

Although many of the steps seem to be focused on criminal interviews, most any interview can benefit from using the technique. The Reid Technique is even used as a basis for training in corporate employee-screening interviews.

It is important to understand the difference between an *interview* and an *interrogation*. Some investigators use the terms interchangeably, but they are actually quite different. An *interview* is nonaccusatory and can be described as a freeflowing conversation focused on information gathering and should generally be conducted first. An *interrogation* is accusatory and used by investigators to get at the truth when they are reasonably sure the suspect is guilty.

In preparing for the interview process, it is recommended that investigators first gather all relevant information pertaining to a case from the victim, then bystanders and suspects, ranging in order from least likely to most likely. This ordering allows the investigator to gain the most amount of information prior to actually interviewing the most likely suspect. Being armed with the most amount of information possible when interviewing a likely suspect allows the investigator to get the truth or, more important, understand when a suspect or interviewee is not being truthful. Even in situations where the investigator is not dealing with a suspect, the same principles may still apply. By replacing the concept of "most likely suspect" with the "person most likely to have the greatest deal of information" relating to the case, an investigator may net more information and detect the presence of someone being less than truthful during the interview process.

One of the most important factors during the interview process is the environment. Interviews are best conducted in an environment that provides the interviewee with privacy. Outside of the basic psychological factor of the appearance of confidentiality, a quiet, private room will allow the investigator and interviewee to gather their thoughts better.

While in the interview process it is helpful to focus on asking open-ended questions to generate a freeflowing conversation with the interviewee. This approach also helps make the interviewee more comfortable and helps prevent the omission of pertinent information. An example of an open-ended question is, "Can you tell me what happened tonight?" rather than "Can you tell me what you saw the hacker do to the computer tonight?" Whereas the first question may net a great deal of information not relating to the incident at hand, it may also net information pertinent to the investigation. If the interviewee was answering the first question, he would tend to be more narrative and possibly include important points. When answering the second question he may leave out information, such as the behavior of other systems throughout the network, that might be related to a hacked system on the same network.

Outside the criminal computer forensics world, many investigators performing computer forensics in support of corporate investigations and civil discovery may feel they do not need to sharpen their interviewing skills. All investigators should understand that getting at the truth does not always mean that someone was lying. Skills such as those taught in the Reid Technique can prove helpful to investigators by simply identifying the questions that need to be answered. In Chapter 3, "Evidence Dynamics," we touched on the identification process for first responders. Subject interviews, or simply asking the right questions, can help ensure investigators do not miss critical digital data or supporting data for the case. By asking the right questions and interviewing the right people, an investigator can gain a much better understanding of where the digital evidence really is. This concept can apply to small networks, but it is critical to investigating or performing digital discovery in large corporate networks because of their distributed equipment and user base. In addition, each individual user's habits may drastically affect evidence. Consider the forensics investigator who is seeking e-mail evidence. In many cases the investigator may be directed straight to the corporate mail server to collect the evidence. The more experienced investigator may even collect a few specific notebook or desktop computers, knowing that some e-mail could reside only there. An investigator who develops a comprehensive plan to understand just how the corporation communicates via e-mail and backs up data may find out through interviews that company e-mail could be found in any or all the following locations:

- Corporate mail server
- Corporate mail server backup tapes locally and off site
- Corporate notebook computers
- Corporate desktop computers
- Third-party store and forward mail server
- Third-party spam-filtering provider
- Home computers accessing corporate mail servers
- PDAs and Internet-enabled phones

Another often overlooked communications medium is public or private chat servers used by corporate support and sales personnel. Larger and more security-minded corporations may use a communications security gateway, which provides content filtering and logging.

Investigators will find that even the smallest business network can become complex, with diverse approaches to data storage and blurred borders between public and private networks. Rarely does a single corporate employee have all the answers. Investigators can use the following checklist to assist in identifying possible supporting artifact as well as to determine the data-storage habits of companies:

- Number, locations, and types of employee-used computers or data terminals (include any authorized use of personal computers)

- Number, locations, and types of PDAs or personal data-storage devices issued to employees
- Number, locations, and types of corporate servers, including their purpose
- Operating systems, versions, and patch levels in use
- Line of business applications in use (include version and patch level)
- Authorized general-purpose applications in use (include version and patch level)
- Directory taxonomy or structure in use (server-based and host-based)
- File-naming and storage standards
- Type of directory services in use (LDAP, Novel, and so on)
- Directory organization (user groupings)
- Any server-based logon scripts in use
- Network diagram specifically identifying data flow and devices that may provide log data and/or access control
- Firewall, intrusion detection system, and identity management configuration and logs
- Comprehensive antivirus, antispyware, and adware procedures addressing server and host protection
- Any documented vulnerability assessment and penetration tests conducted internally or by third parties
- Backup tapes from on-site, and off-site storage
- Data backed up in any other forms, such as network-attached storage, storage area network snapshots, or third-party network storage providers
- Copies of any internal or third-party data audit and control results
- Copies of published employee acceptable use policies
- Copies of published information technology guidelines, policies, or procedures specifically addressing the handling, retention, and storage of data

This checklist should be considered a guideline for investigators who may need to add or remove items based on the individual situation. The checklist should also be utilized with time context in mind, with the understanding that the nature of the company's network may have changed since the event in question.

POLICY REVIEW

During the interview and supporting-artifact-collection process, investigators are encouraged to collect any existing information-technology-related policies when collecting evidence in corporate environments. Although this step may seem like a daunting task, the information gathered can provide critical clues to where data can be found. Furthermore, corporate employee acceptable-use policies can prove instrumental in identifying users who were knowingly acting outside of the stated policy.

Two types of policy review can be of interest to investigators: preincident policy review and a review of policies collected as supporting artifacts in an investigation.

For corporations that are further developing their incident-response team's forensics capabilities, policy review is encouraged prior to any suspected or actual incident. Once corporate security personnel become trained in computer forensics processes, they should assemble a team to review policies, with a focus on the policies' support of forensics and incident response. As in most approaches to business it is best not to consider isolated observations from a single discipline such as corporate security personnel. Policy review teams of any type should often include personnel from several disciplines. It is recommended that corporate information technology security policy review teams consist of personnel from the following areas:

- Human relations
- Legal
- Information technology
- Security (physical and IT)
- Management
- Users

Once the forensics-focused review is scheduled, the team will want to establish which policies could directly affect better incident response and/or forensics investigations.

NOTE *User representation is essential when developing or reviewing corporate information technology security policies. User representation on policy committees allows the corporate information technology personnel who will be designing and implementing security controls to better understand users' needs. Historically, when users were not represented during the creation of policies, the resulting policies and controls frustrated end users. Frustrated users will always find a way around the policies that do not appear to support the accomplishment of their duties. An example of users circumventing controls is their using third-party e-mail services when corporate e-mail systems become too restrictive. Note, however, that some forensics investigative techniques may need to be kept classified and not disclosed to general users outside the development team.*

Several policy areas that can affect computer forensics investigations follow:

- Desktop-installation configuration policies
- Information technology acceptable-use policies
- Desktop support policies
- Data-retention policies
- HR policies (termination)

When examining specific policy areas individually, we find that by asking the following three simple questions, we will in effect be supporting any subsequent investigative actions:

- How can this policy better support the *preservation* of data?
- How can this policy better support the *authentication* of data?
- How can this policy better support the *extraction* of data?

When examining policies at the core of information technology practices, such as a desktop installation policy, we can identify that support for the computer forensics process starts when the employer issues computer systems to employees. Simply "cleaning up" a computer previously used by an employee by deleting old user data is not a sound way to prepare a computer system for redistribution. When we examine the ability to later *authenticate* any data *extracted* from a computer in this manner, many challenges come to mind surrounding just who created the data and when. Embracing a policy calls for the deployment of a fresh, forensically sound image to each employee with each new system. By doing do, we have essentially mitigated many future challenges to the originator of data contained on the system. So what do we mean by a "forensically sound image"? A forensically sound image would be a disk drive to which information technology personnel had written a known pattern (all 0s, 1s, and so on), and then installed all approved standard line-of business applications.

Specifically outlining what and how data should be accessed by each employee in acceptable-use guidelines, although not directly related to the forensics process, can certainly assist any subsequent legal action surrounding intellectually property theft and hostile workplace complaints. The Department of Justice's "Search and Seizure Manual" [Doj01] contains several examples of notifications to monitoring, which also address acceptable use.

One common issue relating to data retention and employee turnover is that the misconduct of a terminated employee is often not discovered until some time after the termination. Unfortunately, by the time the misconduct is discovered much of the digital data, such as e-mails and documents on personal computer hard disks, may have been purged when the former employee's computer was reissued to another employee. These issues have caused many larger companies to revisit data-retention policies relating to terminated employees. Should the need arise to perform an investigation and produce forensically sound evidence after employee termination, altering data-retention policies to remove and maintain any personal computer hard disks for an extended period of time could prove beneficial. This type of policy again helps support the goals of preservation, authentication, and extraction of data for evidence and could provide evidence instrumental to an investigation.

As we can see by the previous examples, future computer forensics investigations may net big results by examining and making slight adjustments to existing policies.

AUDIT

The audit of information systems has been necessary since the early days of computing. Configuration management of mainframe controls is an area where information systems audits first gained visibility as a practice needing great structure and refinement. As far back as 1969, a group of professionals formed the Information Systems Audit and Control Association (ISACA) to create a centralized source of information and guidance in the field. The ISACA Web site is available at *www.isaca.org*.

For the computer forensics investigator, there are two areas where auditing can be of great interest. The first is where information systems audits had been performed prior to the current investigation, and the second is where information systems audits are conducted as a part of the forensics investigation. In both situations a great deal of supporting information can be gained for the investigation.

Many large organizations have internal audit and control groups responsible for conducting audits affecting a wide range of areas within information technology as well as other departments. Smaller organizations, and even those with established audit and control groups, will sometimes outsource specific auditing tasks, such as those focused on information security. Although specific audits associated with other areas such as configuration management may be of interest to investigators, depending on the investigation, those focused on information technology security often net the best results. In the document *IS Standards, Guidelines, and Procedures for Auditing and Control Professionals* [ISACA01], the ISACA outlines procedures for professional auditors in many audit areas including security. The document can be of great use to investigators who want to better understand formalized audit processes. In the ISACA guidelines specific auditing procedures are provided for the following areas:

- IS risk assessment
- Digital signatures
- Intrusion detection

- Viruses and other malicious logic
- Control risk self-assessment
- Firewalls
- Irregularities and illegal acts
- Security assessment, penetration test, and vulnerability analysis

For each auditing area the procedures include procedure background, need for audit, purpose and benefits for the audit, and step-by-step procedures for review. Additional information is provided for how each audit area maps to *Control Objectives for Information and related Technology* (CobiT) published by the IT Governance Institute (*www.itgi.org/*). CobiT is high-level yet detailed framework organized into the following areas:

- Executive summary
- Framework
- Control objectives
- Audit guidelines
- Implementation tool set
- Management guidelines

After examining these frameworks, investigators will see that a great deal of information that aids in understanding the security posture of an organization can be netted from formalized audit reports. Not only can information from formalized audits be useful, the information can be essential to understanding the behavior of a single host computer after the computer has been removed from its native environment. For example, a company's regular security audits showed that a host computer under investigation was tightly secured and had been routinely patched with all currently available security patches. Examination of the host itself appeared to show the system had been recently compromised using a vulnerability for which a patch had long been available. Without the information provided by the external audit, an investigator may not have all the information necessary to correctly attest to the integrity or mechanism of the host's compromise. If nothing else, the added information may lead the investigator to look more deeply into other areas. This example illustrates the need for regular security audits prior to an investigation as well as during a forensics investigation.

One of the most common information security tests provided by consultants and information security personnel is the penetration test. When performed properly a penetration test can provide much information as to the overall security of an organization. Two of the most common types of penetration test are limited-knowledge and full-system knowledge tests. In a limited-knowledge test, the service provider is given limited knowledge of the systems and network architecture to be tested. In a full-system knowledge test, the service provider is provided with full knowledge of the network architecture, IP addressing, and systems design. These approaches to penetration testing will net different results, but both can prove beneficial to an organization's security posturing and subsequent investigations. Some say that the limited-knowledge test gives a far more accurate picture of an organization's security, whereas others stress the importance of the full-system knowledge test's thoroughness. Some organizations will perform a limited-knowledge test then follow up with a full-system knowledge test, or possibly the reverse. No matter which approach is used, the outlines are similar in that they include scanning, planning, performing the actual test, and finally creating the report.

Network scanning: During the network scanning phase, the service provider will use a variety of commercially available tools to scan a network looking for vulnerabilities. This process will typically check for open ports, patch levels, and so on.

Exploit planning: This step utilizes the information obtained from the network scanning phase to research and develop potential exploits for the penetration testing.

Penetration testing: During testing, the service provider will utilize the exploits developed in the planning phase to attempt to penetrate the target systems. Normally, comprehensive logs of all exploits attempted and results are kept. Although some of the exploits may involve altering system code, service providers should not review or alter any application data during the penetration tests and should inform the customer of any changes made as well as assist company personnel in removing any altered code at the end of the penetration testing process.

Reporting: This step is essential. Service providers should provide a complete report of all vulnerabilities uncovered, rating these vulnerabilities from low to critical. The service provider should report on exploits attempted along with the results of these exploit attempts. In many cases the service provider will also provide short-term recommendations for how to eliminate the vulnerabilities uncovered and long-term recommendations for preventing future vulnerabilities.

The following example shows a statement of work and deliverables that a company may expect to see from a penetration-testing provider.

NOTE

In the following example statement of work and resulting report, the term service provider is used as a generic term describing the consulting agency providing penetration-testing services.

STATEMENT OF WORK AND DELIVERABLES

This project is designed to exercise all components in the scope of the project in an attempt to gain unauthorized access to your internal network from three perspectives: a low-level solitary hacker, a small team of competent hackers, and an expert team of highly motivated hackers. Service Provider uses a variety of tools including scanners from CISCO, eEye, and Axent to perform the initial scanning of the IP machines. Depending on discovered vulnerabilities, we then use other custom utilities to try to determine if the vulnerability could be exploited. Service Provider requires an authorization letter (see attached) allowing us to proceed, along with a list of IP addresses and data service phone numbers to test. The scope of work also includes war dialing, to determine if a connection to the internal network could be accomplished by connecting to an installed modem at Target Company.

Service Provider will perform a review of your overall network design to determine if it effectively isolates untrusted, outside systems from gaining access to your internal, trusted networks and systems. The test concludes with a report describing the strengths and weaknesses found in the various intrusion test scenarios with recommendations for immediate and long-term improvements.

In our report to our clients, Service Provider rates the vulnerabilities found from low to critical risk. Our report will contain detailed vulnerability information, complete with solution recommendations. Service Provider typically provides two solutions: quick fix and long-term fix. The quick-fix information provides the steps needed to quickly fix the vulnerability (typically by applying a security patch). The long-term fix usually involves architecture redesign and the purchase of additional security hardware and software.

Once a company has found the statement of work and deliverables acceptable, the testing cycle will begin. Under normal conditions it is best to provide the penetration-test service provider with a window of opportunity to conduct tests. By using a window of opportunity rather than a specific date and time, a company may be able to conduct an internal test of alerting mechanisms. Most companies will also find it advisable to institute a mutually agreeable method of distinguishing actual attacks from planned penetration-test attacks. In all situations, methods should be put in place to enable corporate representatives to stop all tests at any time.

At the conclusion of all testing, the company being tested should expect to receive a briefing as well as a comprehensive report outlining the testing process, findings, and recommendations. The formal penetration-test report can be very valuable to a forensics investigator by providing an in-depth understanding to the overall environment's security posture at a specific time. The following sample Network Systems Penetration Testing Results report illustrates the detail of information regarding a company's security posture and vulnerabilities contained in such reports.

To: Company
Manager of IT Security Operations

Re: Network Systems Penetration Testing Results

Dear Customer,

Thank you for choosing Service Provider to conduct "Full-System Knowledge" network security assessment. As requested in the Security Scanning Authorization Agreement, Exhibit A, our security assessment services were conducted against the following networks and systems between START DATE and END DATE:

Los Angles 192.168.0.0/24
Boston 192.168.1.0/24
Atlanta 192.168.2.0/24
Dallas 192.168.3.0/24
New York 192.168.4.0/24
Chicago 192.168.5.0/24

EXECUTIVE SUMMARY

Security assessment services provided by *Service Provider* included Network Scanning, Exploit Planning, and Penetration Testing of *Customer Company* data networks with the ultimate goal of identifying security-related vulnerabilities on the networks. The findings in this report represent the state of the network security at the time the testing assessment was provided.

RECOMMENDATIONS

By requesting Security Assessment Services, *Customer Company* management and network administrators have demonstrated a commitment to improving network security. A continued commitment to enhanced security posture will increase *Customer Company*'s confidence in the security of its data. The following general changes are recommended to improve network security:

- Remove all desktop dial-in modems and provide users with secure, monitored, dial-in access through a centralized modem pool.
- Disable all services that are not required to perform a device's stated task.
- Implement password selection and control to minimize the hazards of poor or nonexistent passwords. Train users and system administrators on proper password usage for a secure operating environment.
- Change default configurations as appropriate for each system. See the Detailed Vulnerability Appendix for specific recommendations.
- Install appropriate tools to facilitate automation of security monitoring, intrusion detection, and recurring network vulnerability assessment.
- Use RFC 1918 private class "B" address block 172.16.0.0 for the internal networks. RFC 1918 addresses are designated as "internal only" addresses and cannot be routed across the Internet. RFC 1918 also includes private address blocks in the class "A" and "C" ranges; 10.0.0.0 and 192.168.0.0–192.168.254.0, respectively. Using the class "B" address block is often overlooked, causes less address overlap when using virtual private networking, and is somewhat less obvious to outside troublemakers.
- Experience has shown that a focused effort to address the problems outlined in this report can result in dramatic security improvements. Most of the identified problems do not require high-tech solutions, just knowledge of and commitment to good practices.
- Conduct extensive employee training in methods to limit, detect, and report social engineering.

For systems to remain secure, however, security posture must be evaluated and improved continuously. Establishing the organizational structure that will support these ongoing improvements is essential to maintain control of corporate information systems.

SCOPE

The purpose of a "Full-System Knowledge" Network Security Assessment is to identify vulnerabilities in an enterprise's network assets. The assessment can identify routers, switches, firewalls, hubs, print and file servers, and hosts. It can also identify operating systems and network services running on identified network devices. This information constitutes an effective electronic map from which the user can easily base exploitation to confirm vulnerabilities and should, therefore, be protected accordingly.

For the address spaces analyzed, the *Service Provider* discovered a total of 12 live hosts. The next section summarizes live hosts, potentially vulnerable hosts, and confirmed vulnerable hosts.

During the Host Discovery phase, *Service Provider* Network Security Assessment gathers information on all reachable hosts on the scanned address spaces, including responding ports, detected services, and operating systems. The Security Assessment uses active and passive analysis techniques, including comparing this data against a current set of rules to determine potential vulnerabilities.

The system information compiled in this section provides details on the security states on *Customer Company*'s network environment.

NOTE: Exploitation attempts can fail for a variety of reasons, including the following:

- A particular vulnerability may not be present
- Network delays
- Unforeseen equipment and software configurations
- Packet filtering and reactive firewalling anomalies

Despite risk-factor rating or failure to exploit vulnerability, the fundamental vulnerability may still exist. For this reason, *Service Provider* strongly advises that even low-risk-factor vulnerabilities be treated with the same seriousness as serious- or high-risk factor vulnerabilities.

HOST-SPECIFIC FINDINGS

Many of the vulnerabilities listed in this section will include a CVE (Common Vulnerabilities and Exposures) or BID (Bugtraq ID) reference number, which can be researched online at the following URLs:

- CVE reference numbers can be viewed online at *www.cve.mitre.org/cve/refs/refkey.html*.

- BID references can be viewed online at *www.securityfocus.com/bid/bugtraqid/.*

Host: 192.168.0.1
Service: general/udp
It was possible to crash the remote server using the Linux "zero fragment" bug. An attacker may use this flaw to prevent your network from working properly.
Solution: If the remote host is a Linux server, install a newer kernel (2.2.4). If it is not, contact your vendor for a patch.
Risk factor : High
CVE: CAN-1999-0431
BID: 2247

Service: ntp (123/udp)
It is possible to determine a lot of information about the remote host by querying the NTP variables. These variables include an OS descriptor and time settings. Theoretically, one could work out the NTP peer relationships and track back network settings from this.
Quick fix: Set NTP to restrict default access to ignore all info packets.
Risk factor: Low

Host: 192.168.0.2
Service: general/tcp
The remote host is running knfsd, a kernel NFS daemon. There is a bug in this version that may allow an attacker to disable the remote host by sending a malformed GETATTR request with an invalid length field. An attacker may exploit this flaw to prevent this host from working correctly.
Solution: Upgrade to the latest version of Linux 2.4, or do not use knfsd.
Risk Factor: High
BID : 8298

Host: 192.168.0.3
Service: general/tcp
It was possible to crash the remote host by sending a specially crafted IP packet with a null length for IP option #0xE4. An attacker may use this flaw to prevent the remote host from accomplishing its job properly.
Risk factor: High
BID: 7175

WAR DIALING RESULTS

Dialing all listed phone lines to determine network access terminals found the following lines with fax machines set to autoanswer:

- 111-555-5555
- 222-555-5555
- 333-555-5555

Network access terminals were found at:

- 111-555-5555
- 222-555-5555
- 333-555-5555

Each network access terminal displayed the following banner:

- User Access Verification
- Username:
- PASSCODE:

Due to the banner and PASSCODE prompt, *Service Provider* suspects CISCO IOS-based Terminal Server and SecureID tokens are being utilized. All login attempts were unsuccessful.

CONCLUSION

Service Provider views security as an iterative process requiring continuous improvement rather than a one-time implementation of products. Components of a corporation's continuous security process include planning, securing, monitoring, responding, testing, and process management to improve the overall security posture. Each component plays an integral role in maintaining an effective security posture. *Service Provider* Security Assessment Services fall in the Test and Management area of a corporation's continuous security process. Penetration tests help to measure security, manage risk, and eliminate vulnerabilities, which provide a foundation for overall improvement of network security.

The iterative security process includes the following seven steps:

1. Develop a comprehensive corporate security policy.
   A comprehensive corporate security policy provides the foundation for an effective security program. Corporate security policies should include coverage for design, implementation, and acceptable use as well as guidance for incident response, forensics, and the testing and review process.

2. Secure the hosts.
   Secure your hosts by using a hardware and/or software point products. Establish a host-focused configuration management and auditing process so that you can measure the state of network security.

3. Secure the network.
   Secure your network by using hardware and/or software point products. Establish a network-focused configuration management and auditing process so that you can measure the state of network security.

4. Monitor hosts and respond to attacks.
   Continuously monitor your hosts using host-based intrusion-detection and integrity-verification tools. Collect data and establish attack metrics so that you can perform trend analysis.

5. Monitor the network and respond to attacks.
   Continuously monitor your network using network-based intrusion-detection and integrity-verification tools. Collect data and establish attack metrics so that you can perform trend analysis.

6. Test existing security safeguards.
   Using manual and automated penetration tests and security-configuration management verification, regularly test the configurations of all of the components of the environment to ensure that they are secure.

7. Manage and improve corporate security.
   Use trend analysis to determine which of the host and network components are most vulnerable, and recommend methods for component and process improvement.

→

Thank you for the opportunity to provide these penetration test services for *Customer Company*. Please feel free to contact us at 888-555-5555, or via e-mail if you have any questions or comments.

Sincerely,

Service Provider, practice manager

SUMMARY

- Supporting evidence and information can be gained through grassroots investigative techniques.
- Expanding computer forensics investigative techniques helps mitigate the "hacker did it" defense.
- Computer forensics investigators who are interviewing subjects may need to be licensed as private investigators, depending on the state.
- The Reid Technique focuses on preparing for the interview and employing nine steps in the interview process.
- Users should be represented on information technology security policy review teams.
- Policy review should support goals of preservation, authentication, and extraction of data for evidence.
- One common issue relating to data retention and employee turnover is that often the misconduct of the terminated employee is not discovered until some time after the termination.
- Two types of audits associated with a computer forensics investigation are those that were conducted prior to the incident being investigated and those that are conducted as part of the computer forensics investigation.

REFERENCES

[Doj01] U.S. Department of Justice, *Searching and Seizing Computers and Obtaining Electronic Evidence in Criminal Investigations*, available online at *www.cybercrime.gov/s&smanual2002.htm*, 2002.

[ISACA01] *IS Standards, Guidelines and Procedures for Auditing and Control Professionals*, Information Systems and Control Association, July 2004.

[Reid01] Fred E. Inbau et al, *Essentials of The Reid Technique: Criminal Interrogation and Confessions*, Jones and Bartlett Publishers, 2005.

RESOURCES

[Brown01] Brown, Christopher L. T., *Developing Corporate Security Policies in Support of Computer Forensics*, available online at *www.techpathways.com*, 2002.

[Withers01] Withers, Kenneth J., *Computer-Based Discovery in Federal Civil Litigation*, Federal Courts Law Review, 2000.

5 Network Topology and Architecture

In This Chapter

- Networking Concepts
- Types of Networks
- Physical Network Topology
- Network Cabling
- Wireless Networks
- Open Systems Interconnect (OSI) Model
- TCP/IP Addressing
- Diagramming Networks

NETWORKING CONCEPTS

In years past, computer forensics investigators would often seize a single standalone computer, process the disk evidence, and write a report detailing any artifacts of evidentiary value found on disks. The majority of the investigative challenges in these cases were found in the actual disk analysis phase. In many of these situations, the only networking technology in use was a dial-up Internet service provider. Today most any computer seized will involve a network environment of some type. Even home computers seizures can involve complex LANs (local area network), WANs (wide area network), VPNs (virtual area network), WLANs (wireless local area network), and even PANs (personal area network) using Bluetooth® technologies. What may have been considered cutting edge in corporate networking design 10 years ago is now commonplace in many home networks. Walking in any national electronics store that specializes in computers these days, an investigator will see NAS (network attached storage), firewalls, Gigabit Ethernet, and other advanced networking technologies being marketed to home users. An understanding of these technologies and implementation technologies is critical to a computer forensics investigator's ability to find and collect computer evidence. Documentation of the overall network environment will also prove instrumental during the later analysis of any evidence collected.

People use networks to communicate and share data in a timely manner. The most basic computer network comprises two computers connected together to share data such as e-mail and files or to play a game with one user challenging the other.

NOTE

An example of a basic network is the telephone system, which allows two stations (telephones) to exchange voice data over telephone lines using communications protocols. In this example, the two devices (telephones) exchange data using set protocols over an established medium such as copper wire and fiber optic cable. Computer networks operate in much the same way.

In simple networks users share the following types of data and equipment, which can be of interest to investigators:

- Messages via e-mail
- Documents
- Graphics such as pictures or movies
- Music such as MP3 files
- Printers
- Fax machines
- Modems or broadband Internet connection
- Other hardware- and application-specific data

TYPES OF NETWORKS

Earlier we mentioned several types of networks with which investigators may come in contact. At a minimum, investigators should be familiar with the definition and concepts of the following networks:

LAN (Local Area Network): This setup is a network that connects computers within a given site, building, or home. Most LANs use fixed hardware media connections with fiber optic or copper cable. LANs are sometimes extended using wireless technologies in what is referred to as a wireless local area network, or WLAN.

WLAN (Wireless Local Area Network): This type of network contains computers and devices connected through wireless technologies such as 802.11b and 802.11g. The use of WLANs in homes, business, and retail facilities has exploded. WLANs are normally an extension of a hardwired LAN, but they can also exist in a wireless-only environment.

CAN (Campus Area Network): Although the name of this type of network gives the impression that it is found in an educational environment, the concept of a CAN actually applies to any situation where multiple buildings are networked together. CANs often connect LANs and WLANs. WLANs are becoming an integral component of—and some could say they are replacing—CANs.

MAN (Metropolitan Area Network): This setup is a regional group of networks connected through various technologies such as optical regional phone lines and possibly wireless technologies such as microwave. MANs often connect several CANs, which can include LANs and WLANs.

WAN (Wide Area Network): This often-used term refers to any network that connects geographically dissimilar areas or networks. WANs normally connect several LANs, CANs, or MANs. The Internet is essentially a very large WAN.

Internet: Having been available to most home owners for 15 or so years, the Internet needs little introduction. What has made the Internet so successful is not that it is the largest WAN but that it uses a standard set of protocols for communications called TCP/IP. TCP/IP, the Internet's standard protocol used to provide seamless communications across different platforms, made WANs mainstream and accessible by home users.

Intranet: Although this term originally described the use of Internet protocols and applications such as Web servers and browsers in a corporate LAN environment, today people tend to freely exchange the terms intranet and LAN or WAN. Most every corporate LAN or WAN makes wide use of Internet protocols and applications.

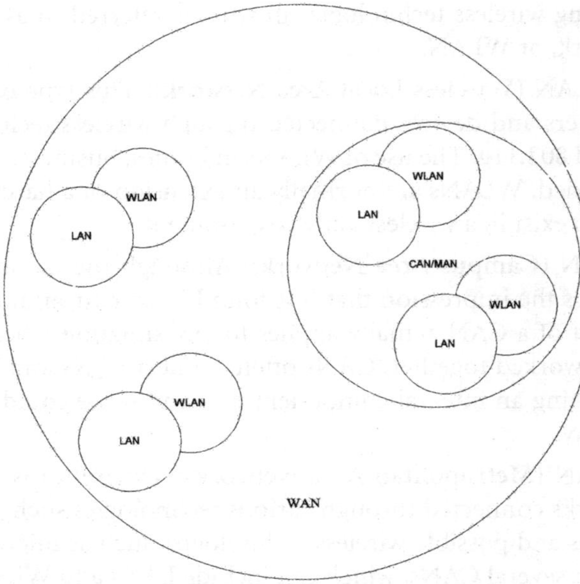

FIGURE 5.1 This networks diagram shows how differing network types can overlap and integrate.

Common networking elements are found in all types of networks that an investigator might run across (see Figure 5.1). These elements include clients, servers, media, shared data, and shared resources. How these elements interact and are accessed throughout the network is often determined by the networking category in use, whether peer-to-peer or server-based. In a peer-to-peer network, each user and system manages their own resources and configures who and how other users will access their resources on a system-by-system basis. Most home networks that an investigator encounters will be peer-to-peer networks. Server-based networks are networks in which a centralized server is used to manage which users have access to which resources. Most businesses use a server-based approach to networking because of the decreased user-management burden provided by server administration over system-by-system administration. In server-based networking, one or more dedicated servers will be found running a NOS (network operating system) such as Windows Server 2003, Unix, Linux, or Novell, which will manage users and their resource access. However, investigators should not overlook the possibilities of a small business using peer-to-peer networking or a home network using server-based networking.

PHYSICAL NETWORK TOPOLOGY

Several standard network topologies and variations are used when designing networks. Investigators who understand the basic networking topologies will not only better understand the operating environment but will be more accurate when diagramming the actual physical layout of a network system where evidence was seized.

NOTE *Some networks are designed from the start using a variety of topologies within a single LAN or WAN. Even those networks for which a given implementation used a single topology, over time the topologies will most likely morph into a hybrid topology consisting of several base topologies.*

The most common physical network topologies include the bus, star, and ring design. Each topology received its name from the physical layout, which helps in visualization. Whereas in some cases the underlying protocols and electromagnetic or electrooptical technologies in use may differ, the basic concepts remain the same for our purposes.

As seen in Figure 5.2, the topology consists of computers and network devices placed along a coaxial cable. The bus topology was one of the first topologies in use, and although not normally used in today's networks, investigators may run across this setup or a hybrid topology derived from the bus design. The basic concepts in use on a bus topology call for communications to flow in the following manner:

- When a computer or network device wants to send data, it first listens to make sure no other information is "on the wire."
- Once the computer or network device determines information can be sent, it sends the data or places the data "on the wire."
- All computers and network devices on the bus segment will see the data at the lowest level, but only the intended recipient will accept the data. The exception to this rule is when a network device such as a computer is configured to accept all traffic as a maintenance station for network traffic analysis. This type of configuration uses specialized software and places the network adapter in what is referred to as "promiscuous mode."
- To prevent the signal "on the wire" from bouncing and thus preventing other computers or network devices from sending their data, terminators are placed at each end of the bus to absorb the signal.

All bus topologies share the feature of simultaneous broadcast, that is, one station transmits and all hear at about the same time. The underlying Ethernet access method uses a logical bus topology regardless of whether it is built physically as a bus (coaxial cable) or a star (UTP).

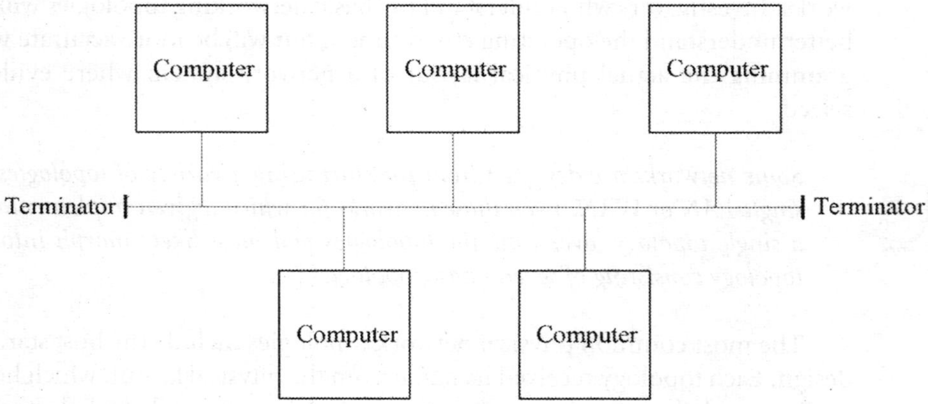

FIGURE 5.2 A network that uses bus topology.

A star topology, shown in Figure 5.3, is one of the most common topologies in use today. In a star topology, rather than all computers being connected to each other, all computers and network devices, such as network printers and firewalls, are connected to a centralized hub or switch. By placing the hub or switch in the center of a diagram, it is easy for investigators to see how this topology received its name. Although the star topology does interject the possibility of a single point of failure with the hub or switch, the benefits of centralized management as well as removing possible computer-line segmentation make the star topology more desirable. In the bus topology, a single computer can segment or bring down the network if it malfunctions or is not configured properly. Device-to-device communication in a star topology is similar to that of a bus topology, with the exception of the need for terminators to prevent data bounce. Signaling used in the star topology as well as the hub or switch design prevent any data bounce. Common types of signaling will be discussed later in this chapter. The star topology, or a hybrid topology including the star, is the most favored topology used in today's networks.

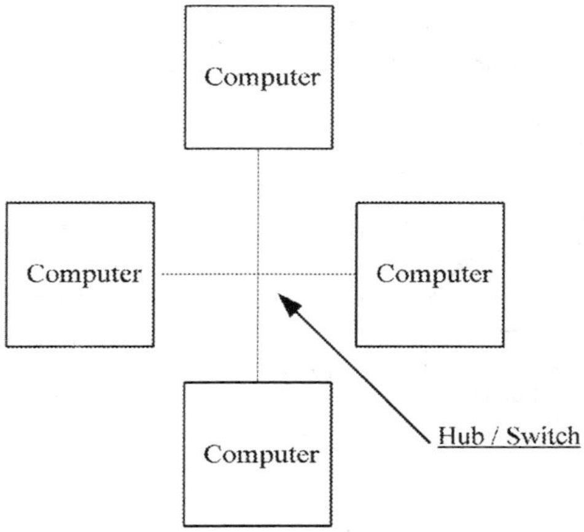

FIGURE 5.3 A network that uses star topology.

The name of the ring topology, shown in Figure 5.4, was not taken from its physical layout but from the topology's communications method. The ring topology looks similar physically to a star topology; however, the communications methods it uses cause it to send data through each computer and, thus, behaves more like a ring. Although not in favor today, the ring topology has historically been used in banking and other critical online-transaction-processing implementations where control and security over data flow were critical. Unlike the bus topology where data is passed by each computer or device, the ring uses each computer much like a repeater resending each data packet. Unfortunately, the ring topology reintroduces the reliance on all computers as well as the specially designed hubs called MAUs (multistation access unit) to function properly. Ring topologies normally use a special underlying communications method referred to as *token passing*, by where an electronic token passed from system to system acts as the system's ticket to transmit on the network.

Some common topology variations include the star bus and the star ring. The star bus, shown in Figure 5.5, was one of the first hybrid network topology designs and allowed companies to use a backbone in the bus topology that branched off to multiple star topologies in specific areas such as accounting, engineering, and so on. Advances in the underlying communications methodologies such as gigabit Ethernet and switching technologies have grayed the lines of topology designs. Most of today's implementations appear to be a star topology from a physical implementation with an underlying switch or network device. The ability to segment and group ports logically actually depicts the overall network traffic patterns.

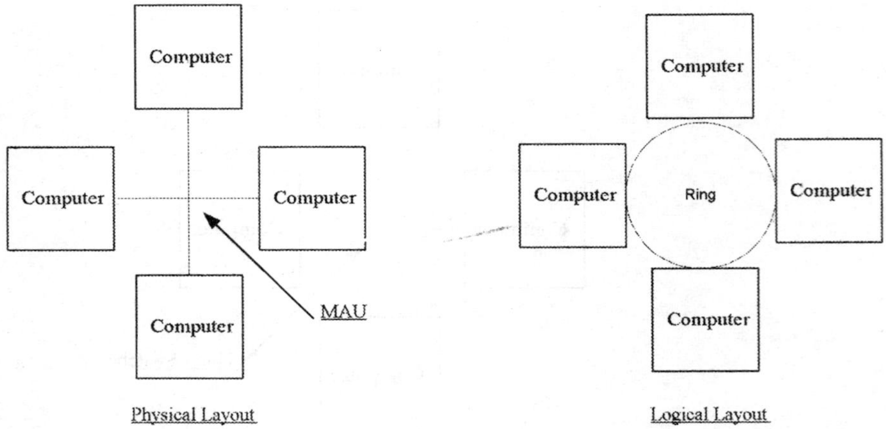

FIGURE 5.4 A network that uses ring topology.

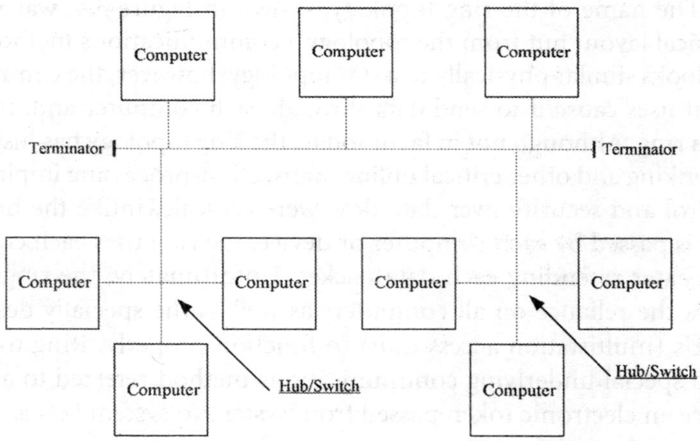

FIGURE 5.5 A network that uses a star bus topology.

NETWORK CABLING

Each networking topology can use different types of cabling. Although other factors can contribute to the selection, the type of cabling utilized in a given topology is usually based on the required communications speed and range between stations.

Bus topologies use coaxial cable, commonly referred to as *thinnet* or *thicknet*. Some common types of coaxial cable are shown in Table 5.1.

TABLE 5.1 Common Types of Coaxial Cable

Cable	Description
RG-58 /U	Solid copper core
RG-58 A/U	Stranded wire core
RG-58 C/U	Military designation and version of RG-58 A/U
RG-59	Broadband transmission such as television and broadband networking
RG-6	Higher frequency version of RG-59

Coaxial cable comes in two primary grades: polyvinyl chloride (PVC), or the standard grade, and plenum grade for use in office overhead runs. Plenum-graded cable does not give off toxic fumes when burning. Whereas older bus topologies employing thicknet may use what is called vampire taps as connectors, the most common type of coaxial connector an investigator will encounter is some variant of the BNC, or British Naval Connector.

Star or ring topologies normally use twisted-pair or fiber optic cable. Twisted-pair cable comes in many variations and ratings and is normally referred to as UTP (unshielded twisted pair) or STP (shielded twisted pair). Twisted-pair is generally good only for a maximum segment length of 100 meters (328 feet). Sometimes investigators will hear twisted-pair referred to by its EIA/TIA rating, such as CAT 5 for category 5. Table 5.2 shows several of the most common UTP ratings.

TABLE 5.2 Common UTP Ratings

Rating	Description
Category 1	Voice only
Category 2	8 wire, data at 4 Mbps early token ring cable
Category 3	Contains three twists per foot, data rated at 10 Mbps
Category 4	16 Mbps, commonly used in token ring networks
Category 5	8 wire copper, 100 Mbps
Category 5e	Enhanced version of CAT 5 intended to be able to run gigabit networks
Category 6	Rated at 250 MHz with more than twice the frequency range of CAT 5 and 5E; best for gigabit networks

Twisted-pair cables are usually connected through some type of RJ-45 connector, which looks like a phone jack but slightly larger. Phone jacks use the RJ-11 connector. A point of confusion for many network engineers is that there are two wiring schemes for RJ-45 connectors—568a and 568b. The two wiring schemes perform in a similar manner, but the same scheme should be utilized throughout an installation because each scheme places different wires to different pins on the connectors.

Star network topologies implemented with fiber optic cable take advantage of the higher speed and greater distance capability of fiber optic cable. Fiber optic networks are also considered more secure because they limit electromagnetic eavesdropping and are more difficult to tap due to highly specialized connectors. Because maximum cable runs for fiber optic cables are rated in miles rather than feet, the distance benefit alone can be compelling. The greatest disadvantage of using fiber optic cable is the higher cost and more difficult maintenance involved.

WIRELESS NETWORKS

Wireless networks were originally thought to be best suited for isolated situations in which users needed temporary and backup connections or to extend networks and provide people on the move such as doctors and nurses with connectivity. Early corporate use of wireless technologies included microwave, infrared, and even satellite. These implementations of wireless networks still exist today, but their use has greatly expanded—some would even describe this expansion as an explosion. Today wireless networks can be found in most home networking environments, companies, and even public coffee houses, hotels, and airports. Due partly by user demand for mobility and partly by the 802.11b/g, or Wi-Fi, wireless networking standards, wireless networks are everywhere. Many cities have even begun movements to provide wireless network access to citizens throughout their metropolitan areas. What this explosion in wireless network use means to the computer forensics investigator is that he can expect to have wireless networks be part of an investigation in the near future. The computer forensics investigator's concern for the use of wireless networking will normally be limited to one of the following areas:

- Was the wireless network entry point used for a direct network attack or theft of data? This concern is generally related to the accessibility of an unsecured WLAN.
- Was a third-party wireless network such as a coffee house "hot spot" used to conceal the identity of the attacker? This concern can be related to unsecured WLANs and publicly accessible WLANs.

WLANs, especially unsecured WLANs, can introduce the possibility of challenges to data authenticity and the "some hacker did it" defense. These challenges are not always unfounded. It is common for a hacker to compromise a server to provide public access to stolen software, referred to as "WAREZ," and pornography.

So many devices are now wireless enabled it is becoming hard to identify all network devices. Some of today's common data storage devices include the following:

- Wireless video cameras
- Wireless network attached storage (a disk sitting on the network anywhere within wireless range of about 122 meters (400 feet)
- PDA/phone hybrid devices with wireless access
- Wireless-enabled DVRs (digital video recorders) such as RealPlay® or Tivo®
- Wireless-enabled MP3 media centers that allow legacy stereo replay

Items one, two, and three present unique challenges to the investigation and highlight the need for an investigator to understand the LAN and any wireless network access. Item four presents a growing and unique challenge to investigators in identifying possible evidence in the local network because the local network no longer has a clearly defined or connected line. It is recommended that the computer forensics investigator use a frequency scanner to help identify the existence of any wireless storage devices. Although a standard frequency-spectrum scanner will help identify devices, tools specific to 802.11b/g are often more useful because they can identify specific wireless devices and their configuration. One such tool is the YellowJacket® from Berkeley Varitronics Systems® [BerkeleyVar01]. The normal effective range of an 802.11b/g network is about 122 meters (400 feet), but it can be extended using wireless repeaters. A less-expensive but quite capable device for locating access points is the Canary Wireless® Digital Hotspotter™ [Canarywireless01]. Many more examples exist of Wi-Fi network finders, however, and investigators should use caution and test that the system they are using has the capability of locating any Wi-Fi device rather than only the access points.

OPEN SYSTEMS INTERCONNECT (OSI) MODEL

No discussion of networks would be complete without mentioning the OSI (open systems interconnect) model. Early in their careers network engineers start hearing references about layer 2 and layer 3 devices. These terms are referring to the layer of the OSI model on which a device works or which layer of the model best describes its core functionality.

The OSI model for networking was originally designed in 1978 to set communications standards for connecting dissimilar devices. The 1984 revision has become the international guide for networking.

Although every piece of network equipment and network-enabled software do not necessarily implement every layer in the OSI seven-layer model, it has become the cornerstone of network engineer training and vocabulary. The reason for its wide spread use in describing networks and network components is that the model so clearly defined layers of communications. Table 5.3 lists each layer of the OSI model and describes how each layer interacts with a second system over a network. Investigators will note that the seven layers of the OSI model are referenced from bottom to top, and each layer communicates with the same layer on the corresponding system.

TABLE 5.3 OSI Layer Interaction

System A		System B
7. Application	→	← Application
6. Presentation	→	← Presentation
5. Session	→	← Session
4. Transport	→	← Transport
3. Network	→	← Network
2. Data Link	→	← Data Link
1. Physical	→	← Physical

Table 5.3 shows the one-to-one relationship of each layer, but the transmission is somewhat different. When information is transmitted over the network from one system to another, data is actually built one layer at a time and then stripped off one layer at a time using encapsulation. When an application on one system is sending data to another, the application layer starts by sending data down the stack, with each layer wrapping a little more data around the previous layer. When the receiving system first receives the data at layer 1, it then sends the data up the stack, with each layer unwrapping data as the data moves up the stack. Normally layers act independently and do not need information from the lower layers, allowing the receiving system to discard unwrapped data from lower levels as the data moves up the stack.

Although each layer in the OSI model has a clearly defined role in network communications, each layer may not be required in all network protocol implementations.

Layer 7 Application Layer: Describes services that directly support user applications such as file transfers, database access, and e-mail

Layer 6 Presentation Layer: Describes the format used to exchange data and is sometimes referred to as the network translator; also provides data compression and encryption

Layer 5 Session Layer: Provides name recognition, security, and user task checkpoints for data streams

Layer 4 Transport Layer: Ensures packets are delivered error free between end-communicating hosts with no loss or duplication (for example, between a client and server)

Layer 3 Network Layer: Provides addressing functions by translating logical addresses and names into physical addresses and determines the network path and priority of data; an IP header in TCP/IP is considered a network layer header

Layer 2 Data Link Layer: Provides error checking for node-to-node communication (for example, host-to-router or router-to-router)

Layer 1 Physical Layer: Describes the electrical, optical, or mechanical and functional interfaces to the cable; Layer 1 exchanges the 1s and 0s without understanding what they represent

After reviewing descriptions of each layer an investigator will realize that when someone refers to a switch that is designed to operate at layer 2 in an Ethernet network, that person is saying that network traffic is switched using MAC address headers. The same conversation may identify the switch as operating at layer 3, in which case the switch may switch traffic based on its IP routing information.

A few of the more common network communications protocol *stacks* in use today include IBM System Network Architecture (SNA), Novell Netware IPX/SPX, AppleTalk, and TCP/IP.

Each layer of a protocol stack works together to ensure that data is

- Prepared
- Transferred
- Received
- Acted on

When network communications protocols are implemented, they may not and generally do not implement each layer, but they may group layer functionality. An example of this grouping can be found in TCP/IP, which is considered a four-layer protocol. The OSI application, presentation, and session layers are all included in TCP/IP's application layer. In TCP/IP, the transport services are a one-to-one mapping with OSI network and data link combined into a single network layer. The physical layer also retains a one-to-one mapping in TCP/IP.

Common application-layer protocols on TCP/IP networks follow:

- HTTP (Hypertext Transfer Protocol)
- SMTP (Simple Mail Transfer Protocol)
- FTP (File Transfer Protocol)
- SNMP (Simple Network Management Protocol)

The two most common transport-layer protocols in use today include TCP (Transmission Control Protocol) found in TCP/IP and SPX (Sequential Packet Exchange) found in IPX/SPX. The corresponding protocol-stack network-layer protocols are IP (Internet Protocol) and IPX (Internetwork Packet Exchange). NetBEUI, used in older Microsoft networking, is also a network-layer protocol; however it is nonroutable.

When discussing the bus and star topologies, we introduced that the concept of one station listening to the cable before sending its data to ensure no other traffic was present is a characteristic of those topologies. Noting that topologies are often driven by media-access methods, this characteristic is actually dictated by the media-access method rather than the topology. Two common media-access methods include Carrier Sense Multiple Access with Collision Detection (CSMA/CD) and token passing.

In CSMA/CD each computer or network device will listen, send data, and resend data, if needed. This method is known as a Contention Method because all devices on the network contend for access to the network wire.

NOTE

In an older, less-popular network access method known as CSMA/CA (collision avoidance), each computer or network device would listen, send intent, send data, and resend, if needed.

In token passing each computer or network device will wait for the "free token," send the data, and then wait for acknowledgement.

The original version of Ethernet was a CSMA/CD media-access method and an IEEE (Institute of Electrical and Electronics Engineers) standard. Ethernet is the most common media-access method used in networking today. Investigators should note that although most people refer to the various implementations of

Ethernet in the same way, the standard has changed significantly over time. The most commonly referenced implementations include 10 Mbps, 100 Mbps, and the newer 1000 Mbps, or Gigabit. Both 10 and 100 Mbps Ethernet are CSMA/CD when implemented in half-duplex mode. Adding full-duplex network cards and switches changes the behavior of Ethernet to allow for multiple simultaneous station-to-station communications. The original Ethernet standard (Ethernet, Ethernet II) came from Xerox®, known as DIX (for DEC, Intel®, and Xerox) Ethernet. IEEE 802.3 is based on Ethernet but is slightly different.

Gigabit Ethernet can be implemented only in a full-duplex mode. Whereas early implementations of Gigabit Ethernet required fiber optic cable, newer implementations have allowed copper UTP cable to be used, allowing wider use. Some say that Gigabit Ethernet changed so much in its low-level implementation that it should no longer be referred to as Ethernet, but keeping the name the same had helped in its adoption, if nothing else. A once highly touted ATM (asynchronous transfer mode) networking access method has received many fewer adoptions partly due to its complexity and appearance as a totally new access method.

TCP/IP ADDRESSING

Addressing in TCP/IP, which falls in the OSI network layer, uses what is known as a 32-bit IP address. The phrase *32-bit* means that 4 bytes are used to hold the data. The addresses usually appear to users in dotted-decimal form, such as 123.64.12.88. Each decimal number ranges from 0 to 255. In most configurations investigators will also find what is known as a subnet mask, which may look something similar to 255.255.255.0. Although the mechanics of creating and using subnet masks involve complex math such as binary-to-decimal conversions and bit shifting, a subnet mask is simply a way of identifying on which network the IP address is located and whether the computer or network device needs to send the outgoing packet of data to a router.

This form of addressing works well for systems, but most humans would prefer a friendlier name. This is why the domain-naming system was created to map IP addresses to a friendly name and vice versa. Using the domain-naming system, each computer or network device uses a hierarchy of domain name servers to translate the numbered addresses to names and names to numbered addresses. The domain-naming system essentially allows us to refer to computer resources in a more meaningful manner, such as *www.cnn.com* and *abuse@isp.com*. In the first example, the name given is referred to as a fully qualified domain name (FQDN). Some people will also refer to this as an URL (universal resource locator) when a leading http:// is added.

The domain-naming system is a hierarchy that looks somewhat like an upside-down tree with ./ as the root leading to high-level domains such as .com, .edu, and .gov. From each of the high-level domain names, subdomains continue to branch out. Different servers become responsible, or authoritative, for each level of the domain-naming tree, giving the system great flexibility and scalability. The domain-naming system has become so popular that Microsoft started using it as the default naming system for network name resolution, beginning with the Windows 2000 Network Operating System. On internal networks Microsoft uses .local as the high-level domain. For example, an internal Web server at MyCompany might end up with a FQDN of www.*MyCompany.local.*

A few of the high-level domains in the Internet today follow:

com: Commercial businesses

net: Network-related

gov: Government agencies, branches, and departments

org: Organizations, usually nonprofit

mil: Military research facilities

edu: Universities and educational institutions

jp: Japan

de: Germany

ca: Canada

uk: United Kingdom

au: Australia

See Figure 5.6 for an illustration of the domain name hierarchy.

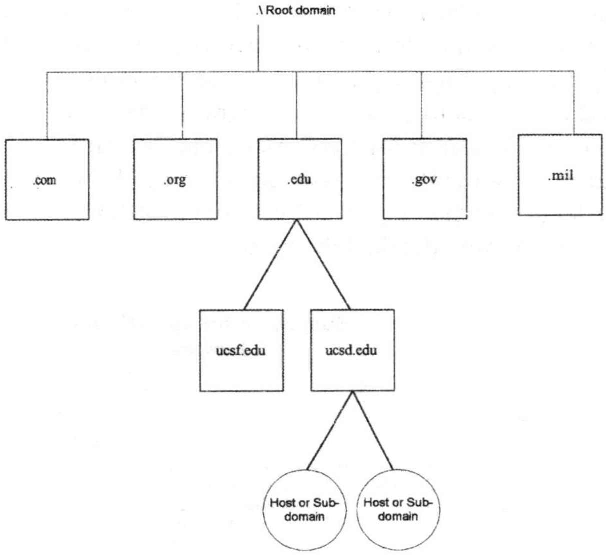

FIGURE 5.6 The hierarchy of domain names.

DIAGRAMMING NETWORKS

Networks in the corporate world have become more and more complex in recent years. The once-simple bus and star topology LANs have been complicated by new devices such as wireless access points, virtual private network access servers, network attached storage, and other specialty devices. With all these new devices entering the fold, the lines between public, private, and partner networks are becoming grayed with every new technology implemented. The aforementioned reasons, along with evidence dynamics issues relating to each system in the environment, demand that investigators accurately document the network. The increased use of networking technologies in homes, including Wi-Fi and Bluetooth wireless, has increased the likelihood of complex networks in the home and even Bluetooth PANs (personal area networks) in cars and around personal devices such as phones, PDAs, and personal audio and video players. A PAN uses the Bluetooth wireless technology to connect personal devices such as phones, headsets, and MP3 players when they are close by (normally within 9 meters [30 feet]).

With the newly found complexity of corporate and home networks, investigators frequently struggle to document networks in a timely manner. Drawing applications such as Microsoft Visio® [MS01] can offer investigators a way to create professional-quality diagrams to document networks. An array of templates, including the standard CISCO network design symbols, can be downloaded for free at the Visio downloads page at *www.mvps.org/visio/3rdparty.htm* [VisioDownload01]. Investigators may wish to invest in a tablet PC using digital pen technology to allow freehand drawing of diagrams that can later be translated to a more professional diagram using network design software.

Figure 5.7 shows how a basic diagram can be an effective tool. Of course, the level of detail shown in Figure 5.7 may not be sufficient for every project. Figure 5.8 shows a much more detailed diagram.

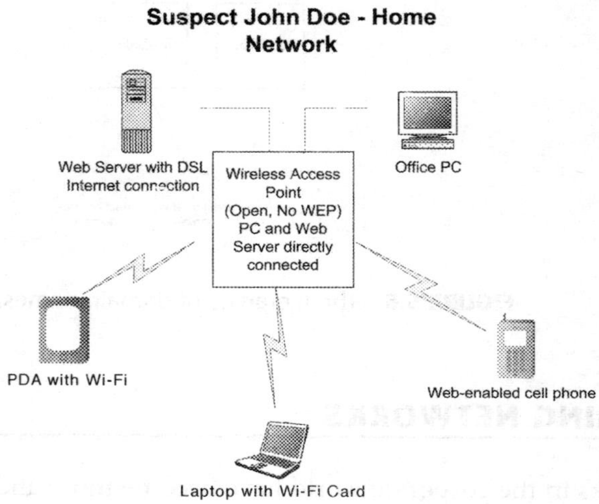

FIGURE 5.7 An example of a basic diagram.

The detail provided in Figure 5.8 may not be sufficient for every job, but it should give investigators a good idea how to start to add detail to their drawings. The important concept is that the diagram should tell a story to fill the purpose of the investigator. The detail provided in Figure 5.7 may be enough to jog the memory of an investigator as to the overall network layout. In cases where the diagram is needed for court, it may be more useful to not provide too much detail, which could confuse jurors or detract from the point being made. In the end the investigator will need to choose the level of detail in relationship to the diagram's intended purpose.

In larger seizures or installations where the interaction of devices throughout the network is complex, investigators may want to use an automated network-mapping tool to assist in creating network diagrams. Automated mapping tools, such as LANsurveyor™ from Neon Software® [Neon01], can help create very detailed network maps quickly.

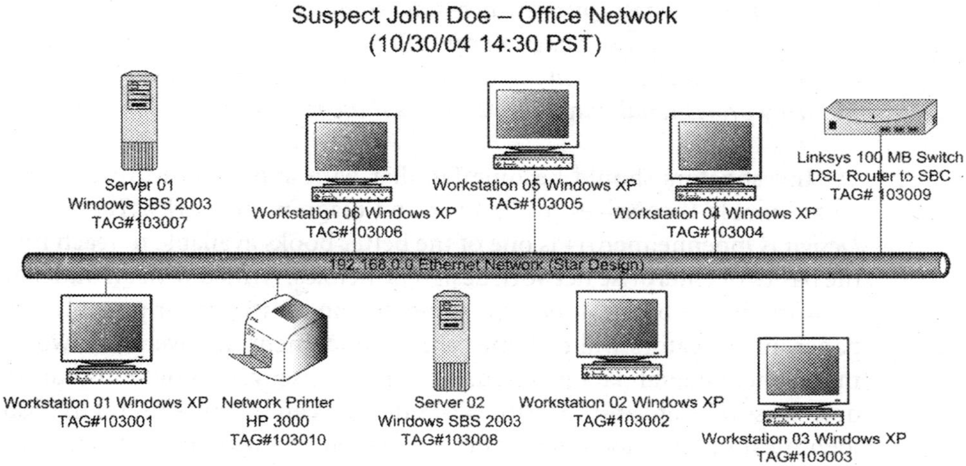

FIGURE 5.8 A detailed diagram.

CAUTION

Security concerns have caused administrators and software developers to start reducing the availability of ICMP (Internet Control Message Protocol) on devices and networks. ICMP is used by many network-identification applications to identify network devices. Firewalls, including Windows XP firewall, will automatically prohibit ICMP traffic, thereby reducing the effectiveness of many automatic node-discovery and mapping applications. For this reason investigators should use visual identification along with automated tools that use several node-identification methods as well as Wi-Fi frequency scanners when mapping a network.

The LANsurveyor network-mapping application works like many such applications by using various methods to detect and automatically generate a network map or diagram. Tools such as LANsurveyor will often employ network operating systems and other lower-level network diagnostic and management protocols such as SNMP and ICMP to identify and document network nodes or stations. In TCP/IP networks, the ICMP is used for various network management applications such as the PING application, which tests basic Internet connectivity between stations. SNMP is used as a method of managing devices such as routers, servers, and other dispersed network devices such as switches and hubs. Even with ICMP and SNMP disabled on a test network, LANsurveyor was able to correctly identify and document 9 of 14 network devices in a short period of time.

A fun place to test your network-diagramming skills as well as learn from others is www.ratemynetworkdiagram.com [Rate01]. At ratemynetworkdiagram.com users can join the site and submit diagrams for evaluation. The Web site contains some truly professional diagrams as well as those just for fun.

Investigators should become familiar with approaches to network design to better enable themselves to discover and diagram networks. *Top-Down Network Design* [Oppenheimer01] is one of the better books available to teach investigators the basics of enterprise network design principles. Armed with an understanding of network design basics, topology, some drawing software, or possibly a pencil and paper, investigators will be better able to document the overall network environment where digital data is seized. Automatic-discovery tools and radio-frequency detectors to locate and identify Wi-Fi devices can be quite useful in ensuring that identification and documentation is complete. As with any software or hardware tool used on a suspect or victim network, the investigator should consider carefully the evidence dynamics effects of the tool.

SUMMARY

- Most any computer seized today will involve a network environment of some type.
- A WLAN (wireless local area network) describes the computers and devices connected through wireless technologies such as 802.11b and 802.11g.
- A WAN (wide area network) is an often-used term to refer to any network that connects geographically dissimilar areas or networks.
- In a peer-to-peer network each user and system manages its own resources.
- Server-based networks are networks in which a centralized server is used to manage which users have access to which resources.
- Investigators who understand the basic networking topologies will be more accurate when diagramming the actual physical layout of a network system where evidence was seized.
- A star topology is one of the most common topologies in use today.
- Ring topologies normally use a special underlying communications method referred to as token passing.
- Each layer of a protocol stack works together to ensure that data is prepared, transferred, received, and acted on.
- Ethernet is the most common media-access method used in networking today.
- An example of a FQDN (fully qualified domain name) is *www.cnn.com*.

- Documenting networks from which digital data is seized is essential in todayÕs complex network environments.
- Automated tools can assist in creating detailed network diagrams.
- Visual inspection and other tools should always be used to assist in validating any automated network-discovery tool.

REFERENCES

[BerkeleyVar01] Berkeley Varitronics Systems Test Equipment Web site, available online at *www.bvsystems.com/*, 2004.

[Canarywireless01] Canary Wireless Web site, available online at *www.canary-wireless.com, 2004.*

[LanShack01] *LanShack Cat 5E Tutorial*, available online at *www.lanshack.com/cat5e-tutorial.asp*, 2004.

[MS01] Microsoft Visio Web site, available online at *http://office.microsoft.com/en-us/FX010857981033.aspx*, 2004.

[Neon01] Neon Software Web site LANsurveyor, available online at *www.neon.com/gglls.html*, 2004.

[Oppenheimer01] Priscilla Oppenheimer, *A Systems Analysis Approach to Enterprise Network Design Top-Down Network Design*, Cisco Press Macmillan Technical Publishing, 1999.

[Rate01] Rate My Network Diagram Web site, available online at *www.rate-mynetworkdiagram.com/*, 2004.

[VisioDownload01] Visio Download Sites Web page, available online at *www.mvps.org/visio/3rdparty.htm*, 2004.

RESOURCES

[Ford01] Merilee Ford et al., *Internetworking Technologies Handbook*, Cisco Press/New Riders Press, 1997.

[MSPress01] *Networking Essentials*, Microsoft Press, 1996.

[Seifert01] Seifert, Rich, *Gigabit Ethernet*, Addison Wesley Publishing Company, 1998.

[SolarWinds01] *SolarWinds Web site*, available online at *www.solarwinds.net/*, 2004.

[Stevens01] Stevens, W. Richard, *TCP/IP Illustrated Volume 1ÑThe Protocols* , Addison Wesley Publishing Company, 1993.

[Stevens02] Wright, Gary R. and Stevens, W. Richard, *TCP/IP Illustrated Volume 2—The Implementation*, Addison Wesley Publishing Company, 1995.

[Stevens03] Stevens, W. Richard, *TCP/IP Illustrated Volume 3—TCP for Transactions*, HTTP, NNTP, and the UNIX(R) Domain Protocols, Addison Wesley Publishing Company, 1996.

6 Volatile Data

In This Chapter

- Types and Nature of Volatile Data
- Operating Systems
- Volatile Data in Routers and Appliances
- Volatile Data in Personal Devices
- Traditional Incident Response of Live Systems
- Understanding Windows Rootkits in Memory
- Accessing Volatile Data

TYPES AND NATURE OF VOLATILE DATA

In the early days of computer forensics investigations in the criminal arena, investigators focused heavily on computer systems' hard disks. Today, a great deal of emphasis is still placed on the physical hard disk storage devices because of their static nature. However, corporate information-technology security personnel who are assigned responsibilities on incident-response teams tend to focus on the volatile nature of cyberattacks and intruders. Today's investigators in both the corporate and criminal realms are beginning to broaden their focus to include both static and volatile disk data, because together they can help tell a complete story. This chapter describes not only what volatile data is but also its nature as a primer to the later chapter on collecting volatile data.

Realizing that in its simplest terms *volatile data* can be defined as data in a state of change, we quickly come to the understanding that data both in physical memory as well as on hard disk can be defined as volatile data. Although this definition is certainly true, when most people refer to volatile data in computer systems, in the sense of computer forensics, they are referring only to the information or data contained in the active physical memory, such as RAM (random access memory). This limited definition occurs partly because most computer forensics investigators think of a hard disk as being a static device that is collected in an "at rest" state or offline from an active operating system. For the purposes of this chapter we will continue along the traditional tendency to consider volatile data as that data that is in an active, or changing, state in a physical memory device such as RAM, and that would be lost with the loss of power. Most criminal investigators would agree that a crime scene that could be frozen in time is the easiest to investigate. Unfortunately, a live computer system, especially one that is connected to a network, is more comparable to a crime scene in the middle of a major airport. A crime scene investigator's inclination is to partition off the crime scene; although this may be the best approach in a given situation, a great deal of information can be lost with this practice. Following along with the airport analogy, how the surrounding area was interacting with the crime scene and witnesses could be considered volatile data. In a balanced approach, the investigator does not need to make the choice of freezing the scene or not; he can choose to collect some of the volatile data and then isolate the scene and collect the rest. Following along the airport analogy once again, the investigator may observe, note, collect witnesses, collect videotape, and then isolate the scene and collect the remaining physical evidence.

In a standard PC, volatile information can be found in several places other than the RAM. By examining the boot process and the data flow through a standard PC system, we will find potentially valuable data in several locations, depending on the investigation, as follows:

1. Apply power to the main system and any peripherals.
2. Using a chip set and CPU (central processing unit), use the BIOS (basic input/output system) to conduct a POST (power-on self-test) to ensure the main unit is operating normally.
3. During the power-up process, any memory and dedicated processing units within peripherals on the system's main I/O (input/output) bus, such as network cards and video cards, will be initialized. Peripherals known as bus-mastering devices can actually share control of the main systems CPU and physical memory.
4. During POST, based on the BIOS configuration, the CPU, its control registers, and all physical memory is initialized.

5. The BIOS will read the boot block of a bootable device for which it is configured or from which it is instructed by the boot prompt to boot. This information contains boot loader code as well as physical partition and file system information.
6. The BIOS will, based on configuration, attempt to read and load into local registers as well as physical memory the boot loader section of a boot device, such as a hard disk, floppy, or bootable optical media in many of today's devices. Some of today's newer systems will also provide boot capability from devices such as USB (Universal Serial Bus) flash memory.
7. The CPU will execute the boot loader code, which will perform operating system loading and further execution of operating system code.

   At this point the operating system will keep key functions and data loaded in physical memory as well as in registers on the CPU to execute a computer system's normal user functions, such as loading applications, exchanging data over the network, and controlling peripheral devices. Keep in mind that some peripheral devices will have physical memory of their own and may share control of the CPU and main physical memory through bus mastering.

Most operating systems also provide virtual memory in the file system that is set aside as a method of extending the physical memory within the system.

As seen in Figure 6.1, a great deal of volatile data moves about "inside" the computer system, making it a live system. Although some of this data is below or out of the operating system's control, critical evidence can be controlled by the operating system, and therefore, the operating system is the key to understanding the data.

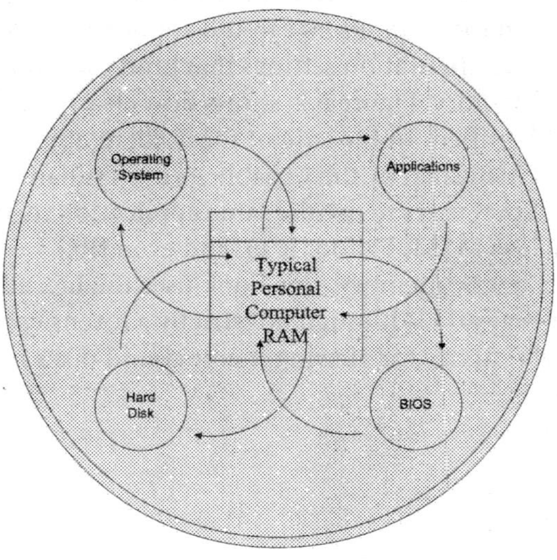

FIGURE 6.1 A typical computer system state.

OPERATING SYSTEMS

Once an operating system is up and running, what is known as a code page is loaded in memory for execution. This *code page* essentially contains the low-level functions needed for file I/O as well as the operation of other peripheral devices on the computer such as through communications ports. The code page can reside in physical memory as well as in logical page memory on disk, awaiting movement into the CPU's registers for execution. As functions are executed by the computer's CPU, the results of those functions are stored again in physical and logical page memory. Investigators now know that physical memory is volatile and will be lost on system shutdown or loss of power. Logical memory may or may not be lost, depending on the configuration of the operating system.

NOTE *Many systems allow for configuration settings to clear the contents of page memory on shutdown. This type of capability was an early requirement of the Orange Book [DOD01] to prevent the storage and possible compromise of classified information. The Windows NT operating system accomplishes this setting by enabling the following registry setting:*

HKEY_LOCAL_MACHINE\SYSTEM\CurrentControlSet\Control\SessionManager\MemoryManagement\ClearPageFileAtShutdown Value: 1 = On

If an investigator were to simply browse through the raw bits of information contained in physical and logical memory, he might find strings of information useful in an investigation, such as passwords. To prevent this type of casual sniffing of passwords in memory, users can use applications such as PGP (pretty good privacy) to allow configuration settings that limit the amount of time a passphrase will be *cached* in memory. Figure 6.2, shows how clearly a user's password kept in memory can be identified. In the case of the Trillian application, passwords are kept in memory and identified by the variable `PWD=`. Trillian is a popular chat client application that allows users to use the same application to log into all their favorite chat services, such as MSM, Yahoo, ICQ, and even IRC.

To display raw memory, this book uses the hex editor WinHex from X-Ways Software [XWays01]. Although not strictly a forensics tool, WinHex is an inexpensive and useful utility for viewing memory and disks in their raw format.

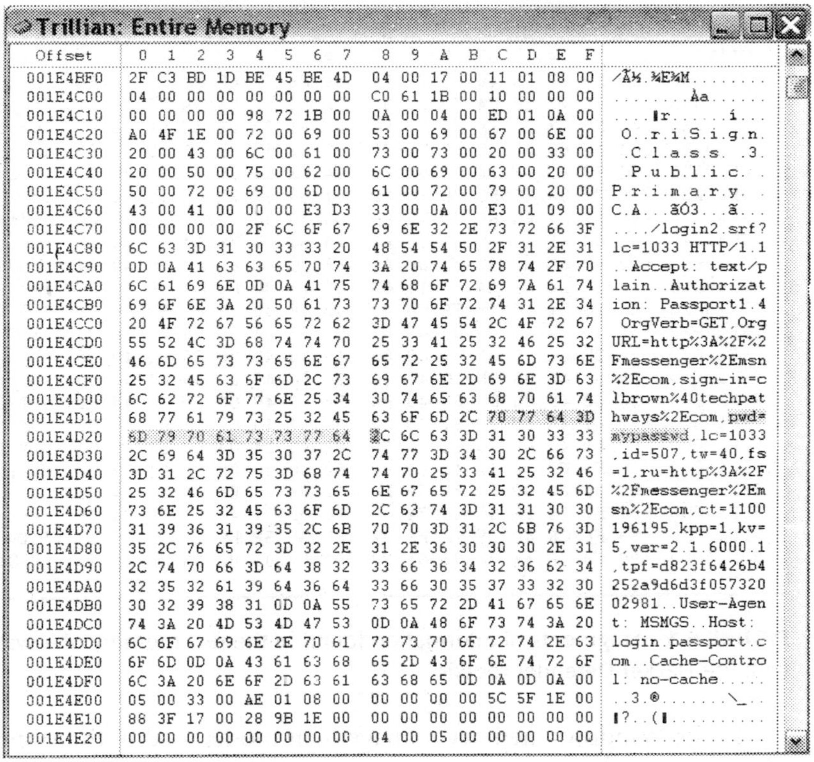

FIGURE 6.2 The Trillian password contained in the computer's memory.

Other valuable data that can be gleaned from raw memory includes indications of a system compromise. Often hackers will add messages or code names inside the code or signatures to their work. It's quite common to find hacker handles, group names, and profanity embedded in a hacker's code.

Figure 6.3 shows some identifying fragments of information in the raw memory of a system infected with the Hacker Defender rootkit. Interestingly enough, the name Hacker Defender gives the impression that this application protects users from hackers, when its actual purpose is to defend hackers by hiding files and allowing access. Rootkits are described in greater detail later in this chapter.

Investigators can easily see that even without a deep understanding of the raw memory in view, simple keyword searches and browsing of raw memory can be useful to an investigation, highlighting the need to capture such information. Much information can be obtained from in-depth analysis by investigators with a deeper understanding of the running operating system and how it manages memory.

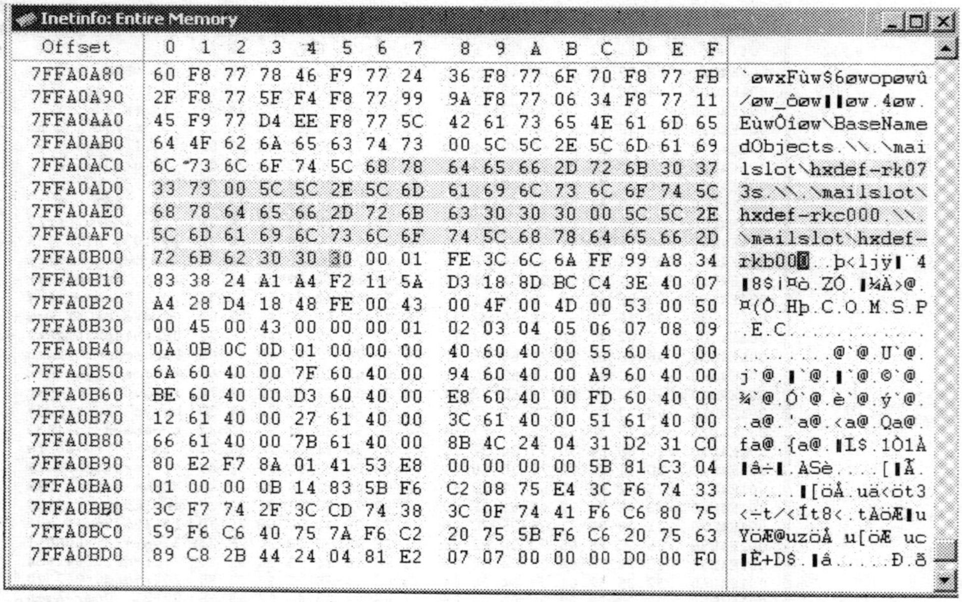

FIGURE 6.3 Fragments of information found in the raw memory of a system infected with the Hacker Defender rootkit.

In the Windows memory management model used in the Windows 2000 and XP operating systems, memory management is divided into two modes of operation, user mode and kernel mode. The user mode memory space is intended to protect a user's data in memory as well as the user's processes running in this space from adversely affecting the kernel mode processes being utilized by the operating system. The operating system manages this protection level between user mode and kernel mode by creating virtual memory address space for each user to run applications and store volatile memory. Further divisions are made within the user's virtual memory space to divide private and system memory for the needed overlap of interprocess communications.

NOTE

User Mode: This mode is where all general applications operate. General applications and subsystems for Win32, Win16, and POSIX (Portable Operating System Interface) all run in this mode.

Kernel Mode: This mode is a trusted mode of operation for system services and device operations or access. All requests by user mode applications are brokered through Windows NT Executive Services within the kernel mode. These requests include checking security ACLs (Access Control List) and allowing access to file I/O and attached devices.

Investigators should also note that Windows operating systems also manage the further "swapping" of information between physical memory and logical memory areas stored on disk in one or more memory *page*, or *swap*, files. Windows allows applications to address up to 16 page files. Though it is uncommon for more than one page file to reside on a single physical disk, administrators often create a single page file on each disk to increase performance. Both raw memory areas, which are of interest to investigators for collection, have differing volatile characteristics. The physical volatile data will be lost on loss of power, and the logical memory could be lost on orderly shutdown, depending on the system configuration.

VOLATILE DATA IN ROUTERS AND APPLIANCES

Volatile data in routers and network appliances such as dedicated firewalls is very similar to that of a personal computer with one exception—a physical hard disk may not be present. All data is likely to be located in some type of Random Access Memory (RAM) or Non-Volatile RAM (NVRAM). As an example of how many network appliances are designed, let's look at the architecture of the standard Cisco® router. Each router, depending on the model, normally contains the basic configuration an investigator would expect in a personal computer: motherboard, CPU, memory, bus, and I/O interfaces. These interfaces and expansion card slots can become complex in higher-end models.

In a network device such as a Cisco router, the key point of difference between the router and a PC is the lack of physical hard disk. The hard disk is replaced by flash memory, which can be viewed as a solid-state disk containing nonvolatile data. In Cisco routers, this flash memory is where a compressed copy of the Internetwork Operating System (IOS) image and other supporting files are kept. Volatile data such as the running IOS (operating system code pages) is kept in Dynamic RAM (DRAM) or Synchronous RAM (SRAM). In some cases the routing table or tables, statistics, local logs, and so on are also kept in DRAM/SRAM. A third memory component in Cisco routers, the Non-Volatile RAM (NVRAM), contains the startup configuration files. The BootROM, much like the Complementary Metal Oxide Semiconductor (CMOS) and BIOS of a personal computer, contains code for power-on self-test (POST), IOS loading, and so forth.

The volatile nature of data stored in devices such as Cisco routers makes collection of forensically sound artifacts difficult at best. Cisco introduced in their IOS version 12.2(18)S a feature called Router Security Audit Logs, which was intended to allow network security administrators to track changes to a router configuration via a remote syslog server. More specifically, the Secure Audit Log feature allows security administrations to create cryptographic hashes using the MD5 algorithm for the Running IOS version, hardware configuration, file system, startup configuration, and running configuration. These hash values can be recomputed at regular intervals.

Absent any floppy disk and CD-ROM access to provide the ability to get a remote agent of some type running on the "live" device, investigators are often left with few options for the collection of evidence. If the system was powered down to remove the RAM modules, all volatile RAM data is lost. With the system running, the investigator is usually limited to collecting data such as the Secure Audit Log data, which has been logged onto remote devices such as syslog servers. Most network appliance and router devices do provide a physical configuration port (usually a serial connection) from which to run a terminal session. Cisco routers call this port the *console* port. In some cases, if the AUX port has been configured, it too can be used for a terminal connection. Collection of this type of volatile data can be challenging and is limited by the attention to detail in security-related configuration of the device, that is, if the device was configured with log evidence collection in mind from the start. Three good references on router security configuration follow:

- *Hardening Cisco Routers* by Thomas Akin [Akin01]
- Cisco White Paper, "Essential IOS Features Every ISP Should Consider v 2.9" [Cisco01]
- *National Security Agency Router Security Configuration Guide* [NSA01]

Although valuable evidence can be obtained from network devices such as routers, access to volatile data in these devices is often limited and may be restricted completely. Corporate investigators should plan for the audit and evidence-collection process by ensuring that critical information is logged externally from the device in a secure and verifiable location.

VOLATILE DATA IN PERSONAL DEVICES

PDAs, cell phones, MP3 players, and even wristwatches all can contain extensive data-storage capabilities. Many of these devices maintain storage in flash cards with extended data retention rates, but not always. PDAs are particularly volatile in their design, which causes much user data to be lost with extended battery loss.

Examining PDAs closer, the investigator will find that they are much like a standard computer in that they have a CPU, RAM, and external peripheral ports such as USB ports. As mentioned, PDAs often include additional static storage, such as a Sony® Memory Stick®, Secure Digital™ (SD) card, and other flash memory media with extended data-retention capabilities. Primary storage for information such as calendars, phone numbers, and other personal information-management categories, however, is normally kept in a section of RAM. This volatile temporary storage area is kept in place by the device's power through the primary battery and, in some cases, a small internal permanent battery source that allows for data to be retained during battery changeout. One of the most common stories heard in law enforcement computer forensics labs is about a PDA that was seized from a suspect and entered into the evidence locker. A week or more goes by before the PDA makes its way to the computer forensics lab, by which time the PDA's battery has been completely drained and all volatile data has been lost. PDAs and other such personal devices have batteries that rarely last longer than a day or two. Until data can be collected, as described in Chapter 11, "Collecting Volatile Data," investigators should ensure that battery power is maintained to the device.

TRADITIONAL INCIDENT RESPONSE OF LIVE SYSTEMS

Outside the useful information contained in raw memory mentioned in the previous section, a great deal of other useful information is available. Computer forensics investigators realized early on that more important information was held in volatile memory for which only the running operating system held the key. This information from applications and the operating system itself includes users logged on, running processes, and network end points, if any. As described earlier, the running operating system manages the swapping of information fragments through physical and logical memory locations. Once the operating system is no longer running, reassembling this type of information can require heroic efforts and may not be accomplishable at all.

CAUTION

It may occur to investigators that volatile application data such as users logged onto a system, network connections made by specific applications, and running processes would be useful only in a complex cyberattack investigation. Although this type of information certainly is very useful to a cyberattack investigation, it also can be useful to any type of investigation. If a system is up and running at the time of seizure, the way in which it interacts with the native environment can be useful in all situations. Remember, once the system is shut down, most, if not all, volatile information will be lost if it is not already captured.

In the early days of incident response and cyber investigations, many corporate investigators and security consultants emerged from information technology system administration and network communications backgrounds. Certainly this type of background gave investigators a better understanding of the type of information that may be available on a given "live" system. It is for this reason, along with the relatively limited software tools available, that some early incident-response and investigative approaches were more intrusive in nature than was ultimately desired. As investigators read on, they should remember Chapter 3, "Evidence Dynamics," and always keep in mind the forces that their tools and methodologies will have on any potential evidence. Keeping these principles in mind, their goal should be to act in the least-intrusive way, which will gain the most potential evidence in a reliable manner.

TIP

Investigators will find many tools that can glean information from a running system. It is common for many older "live" incident-response tools to pull information from logs, databases, and registries. As a best practice and keeping with the least-intrusive approach, if a bit-stream disk image is being taken, there is generally no need to extract data that resides on disk and can be examined later from a "live" system. This information can be extracted and examined from the bit-stream disk image during forensics analysis.

Let's examine the type of information identified for collection by seasoned incident-response teams in greater detail.

Network information: This information includes IP connections, IP configuration, route tables, MAC address-resolution cache, and similar information from any other installed networking protocols. It is helpful to have the application or memory processes associated with IP connections listed, too.

Date and time information: This information consists of configuration settings for time zone and daylight savings time. Time settings and timeline analysis and correlation across computer systems can be one of the most tedious tasks associated with computer forensics analysis.

Processes in memory: This information concerns running processes and their dependencies or modules loaded.

User logon information: This information reports the last successful and failed logon attempts locally or from remote sources on networks.

Task management: This information describes any scheduled tasks or system jobs to be completed.

Most investigators will agree that the information listed could be valuable to any investigation involving a networked computer, and in some cases, even a stand-alone computer. In fact, this information, along with file system indexes and file signatures, was the only information collected from early incident-response teams responding to cyberattacks. In many cases a bit-stream image of the disk was not collected because the desire for or likelihood of criminal prosecution was minimal. The previously listed information was normally all that was needed to trace and understand the attack. Once an attack was understood by incident-response teams, they were better able to prevent subsequent attacks.

Over the years investigators have created batch files, shell scripts, and "trusted" binary disks to better enable timely collection of the type of information previously mentioned. Armed with the trusted binary disks loaded with the scripts and collection utilities, an investigator could insert the disk in a running system and be confident he was accessing the hard-to-get-at volatile data.

Although information gained from this type of approach is still very useful to investigations, the reliability of information gained is diminished by today's second- and third-generation rootkits. As we will see in the next section, rootkits are driving investigators to closely examine current procedures and possibly utilize newer forensics tools and techniques when collecting volatile data.

UNDERSTANDING WINDOWS ROOTKITS IN MEMORY

The war between computer users and hackers has been constant. As most computer forensics investigators know, even the most secure facility can be compromised. Firewalls, intrusion detection, and other perimeter security solutions rely on known signatures and clipping levels to detect malicious code, but it is easy for hackers to alter and recompile their exploits to get past these defenses. Computer systems may be locked down tightly, but hackers discover, develop, and deploy exploits before users and administrators can get systems patched. With automated tools, networks are scanned virtually every day by some hacker trying to find a way in. Sooner or later, someone will find a weakness and exploit it.

Just as in any type of warfare, deception and stealth are key components of success. More than 2000 years ago, Sun Tzu documented in his military essays *The Art of War* that all war is based on deception and concealment. Applying these concepts to current-day information warfare, hackers are constantly looking for a way to hide once a system has been compromised. The latest and perhaps most effective way for hackers to hide is by using a kernel-mode rootkit (or kernel-mode Trojan). These threats have been documented in several articles, including those in *Security Focus* [SecurityFocus01].

Earlier, less-stealthy versions of rootkits have been used over the past several years to compromise systems. Worms such as the TK Worm have even been found to install rootkits as part of their infection. This type of worm allows the system to be used in DoS attacks and can host warez servers. A recent report by iDefense [iDefense01] stated that authorities estimate 50,000 servers are infected with the TK Worm, and this number is still growing. Though this form of rootkit does not hide all the files and processes, it nevertheless ran unchecked for well over a year. Imagine the damage a newer kernel-mode rootkit could do if delivered in a worm.

NOTE

A rootkit is an application or group of applications that are installed on a system with the main purpose of hiding itself and other files and processes. Rootkits may be installed after a compromise has taken place or as a part of the compromise.

Because the threat of kernel-mode rootkits is larger than ever, all forensics investigators should become familiar with their operation and effects on an operating system's volatile memory. At the Defcon security and hacking conference held in Las Vegas in July 2003, the classes teaching people how to create kernel-mode rootkits were filled. Many rootkits are available on the Internet to anyone who is interested. Although examples used in this section focus on Windows systems, the concepts outlined in this book will pertain to all of today's popular operating systems.

To better understand rootkits and their effects on Windows platforms, let's take a look at their history.

The first generation of Windows rootkits are called file system rootkits. These original rootkits essentially replaced Trojan applications such as "netstat" and "dir." By replacing "dir," a hacker could control the "dir" application output (set to not display certain files). Although originally quite effective at allowing hackers to hide in the system, new Trojan-detection software and improved virus-protection software were able to find these rootkits and alert the system administrator to their presence. File system rootkits can be categorized as user-mode rootkits.

The second-generation of Windows rootkits, which affect volatile memory, are called library rootkits (also referred to as *DLL injection rootkits*). These rootkits take a lower-level approach by replacing existing system DLLs with new Trojan versions, which lie to applications requesting information. In this approach the hacker needs only to change the system DLLs used by several applications to gather information from the system and achieve a wider effect. This improved rootkit was effective in hiding from Trojan and virus scanners; the first generation of Trojan scanners, which use hash signatures, were effective in finding only this first-generation rootkit. However, the relative difficulty in executing DLL injection has limited the overall number of these rootkits. Library rootkits can also be categorized as user-mode rootkits. Hacker Defender is one of the more successful and widely available second-generation rootkits.

Kernel-mode rootkits are the third-generation rootkit, and as indicated by their name, they operate in kernel mode. These rootkits take the library rootkit approach one deadly step further. If the goal is to hide a file or process rather than replace "dir" or "netstat," why not replace the command that all applications would call for information from within the kernel? In the case of file I/O, we need to replace the kernel mode I/O routine "ZWQUERYDIRECTORYFILE." In this approach, not only will "dir" be able to hide the hacker's files, but any other applications such as today's virus scanners, Trojan scanners, and integrity checkers, which make calls to the kernel mode I/O routine "ZWQUERYDIRECTORYFILE," will receive compromised information. Hackers accomplish this task by writing a Windows device driver that, through a process called *hooking*, replaces trusted kernel-mode I/O routines with their own. Of course, the hacker's routine provides only information they want users to see. By hooking "ZWQUERYDIRECTORYFILE," the hacker can hide any file he wants. By the same process, hackers can and do just as easily hook process and registry query routines to hide running processes and changes to the registry. Doing so gives them a complete cloak of secrecy to do whatever they want in a user's system and remain undetected.

Vanquish and HE4Hook are older and more widely known precompiled kernel-mode rootkits. Newer development and open discussions have been taking place online to improve these and other kernel-mode rootkits. A basic kernel-mode rootkit is available in source code and has been steadily improved by a talented group of contributors. As of the time of this writing, the basic kernel-mode rootkit was up to version 8 and now includes network functionality. Greg Hoglund is no stranger to kernel-mode rootkits; he was the original author of NTROOT, a concept kernel-mode rootkit made available in early 2001. The NTROOT kernel-mode rootkit was unique in that it included its own rudimentary TCP/IP stack within the device driver that accepts connections on any port of a spoofed IP address. The known development and suspected deployment of kernel-mode rootkits is growing at an alarming rate. A relatively new Web site, appropriately called *www.rootkit.com*, has become a proving ground for kernel-mode rootkits. The site contains a development discussion list and precompiled rootkits as well as source code for several different rootkits, including the basic rootkit. It's not hard to extrapolate that many new and innovative kernel-mode rootkits have been created and deployed from the thousands of kernel-mode rootkits that have already been downloaded from *www.rootkit.com*.

In an attack on a scale similar to Code Red and Nimda, hackers created a worm dubbed Lovsan, or Blaster, which took advantage of the recent Microsoft RPC/DCOM buffer overflow [SecurityFocus02]. Lovsan is reported to have infected more than 250,000 computers in a matter of days. Not long after the initial Lovsan worm was released, a modified version was released that installed a remote-access Trojan. The remote-access Trojan version of Lovsan could have easily included a Windows kernel-mode rootkit to cover its tracks.

Although the kernel-mode rootkit is a major threat to live investigations involving volatile memory, effective computer forensics tools are available to detect them. Over the years savvy system administrators, incident-response teams, and investigators have developed the following two methods to help detect file system and library rootkits as well as other Trojan files on systems:

- Create cryptographic hashes of important files on the file system. In this approach the investigator who suspects a compromised host can create new hash values and compare the new hash values to a set of "known good" values.
- Use a set of known good applications, sometimes referred to as "trusted binaries," to investigate the suspected host running from a CD-ROM or remote disk.

A cryptographic hash is an algorithm used to produce fixed-length character sequences based on input of arbitrary length. Any given input always produces the same output, called a hash. If any input bit changes, the output hash will change significantly and in a random manner. In addition, there is no way the original input can be derived from the hash. Two of the most commonly used hashing algorithms are MD5 and SHA1.

When using these techniques, an important issue to consider is that the investigation on the suspect system, even when using trusted binaries from a CD-ROM, changes almost every file's last-accessed time. If it turns out the system has been compromised, tracking hackers' actions becomes more difficult and can raise authenticity issues in legal proceedings, thus violating sound computer forensics principles.

The implication of kernel-mode rootkits is that comparing hash values of files on the system is useless because any hashes created through file I/O on the system can't be trusted. The newly created local hashes would use local system I/O, and the files seen by user-mode applications most likely didn't change anyway. Using trusted binaries running locally will not help for the same reasons.

One accepted way to detect a kernel-mode rootkit is to reboot the suspected system in safe mode, and then look around for anything that's been hiding. Another way is to connect to the suspect system's file shares from a trusted remote system (using the trusted remote system's I/O and trusted binaries), and then explore as before. In the first case, taking the server offline for mere suspicion is rarely an option. In both cases, files' last-access times will be changed, and the question may still remain whether the trusted system in use is truly trusted. How do investigators find kernel-mode rootkits on a live system and not destroy valuable tracking data? Today, many investigators and corporate security professionals are turning to the growing selection of network-enabled computer forensics and incident-response tools such as ProDiscover® from Technology Pathways (*www.techpathways.com*) and EnCase® Enterprise Edition from Guidance Software® (*www.guidancesoftware.com*). These tools are based on core capabilities of the company's original professional-grade computer forensics workstation products. These new tools read disks sector by sector, and then implement a read-only file system for analysis of the suspect system. By reading the data at the sector level, they avoid the code modified in volatile memory by the kernel-mode rootkit and uncover the real data on the disk. Both of the products mentioned also offer features that provide the ability to investigate suspected systems in a least-intrusive manor, leaving vital metadata such as last-time accessed times intact and preserving evidence for possible criminal or civil litigation if a compromised system is found.

By selecting a network-enabled computer forensics product, investigators can search remotely for known-bad-file hash values, compare file hash values to known-good-file hash values to ensure there have been no changes, recover deleted files, or search files and disks for keywords, all without being affected by the compromised volatile or kernel memory. Figure 6.4 shows the Hacker Defender rootkit being detected in volatile memory.

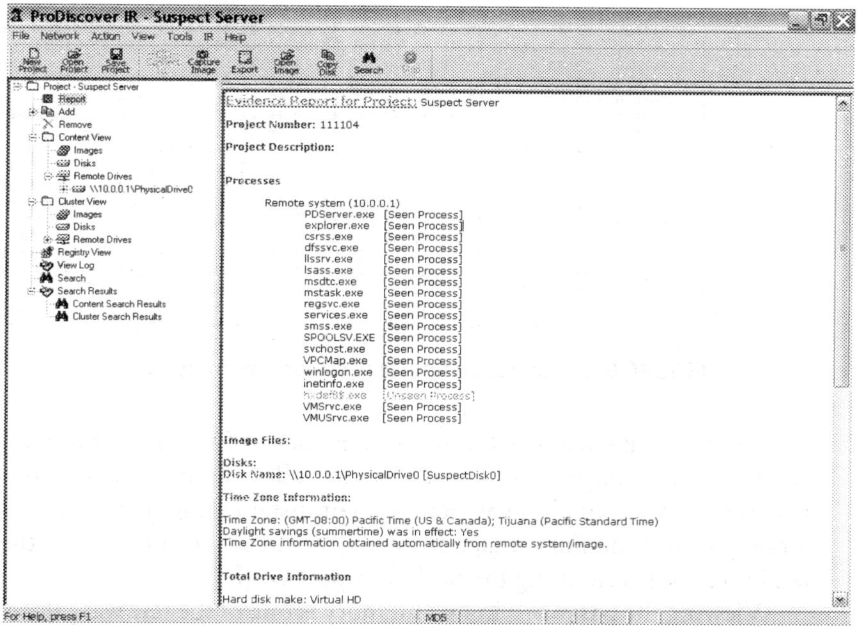

FIGURE 6.4 The Hacker Defender rootkit detected by ProDiscover.

NOTE

Some investigators believe that if a rootkit could hook (replace) a file I/O request, the rootkit could simply hook the sector-level read commands and foil the approach that applications such as ProDiscover and EnCase use. Although this is theoretically possible, hooking kernel-sector read commands would require a complete real-to-Trojan sector mapping and/or specific sector placement for the rootkit and supporting files. This undertaking would be major and would require extensive knowledge of the particular system's current sector map prior to the creation of such a rootkit; therefore, it is highly unlikely.

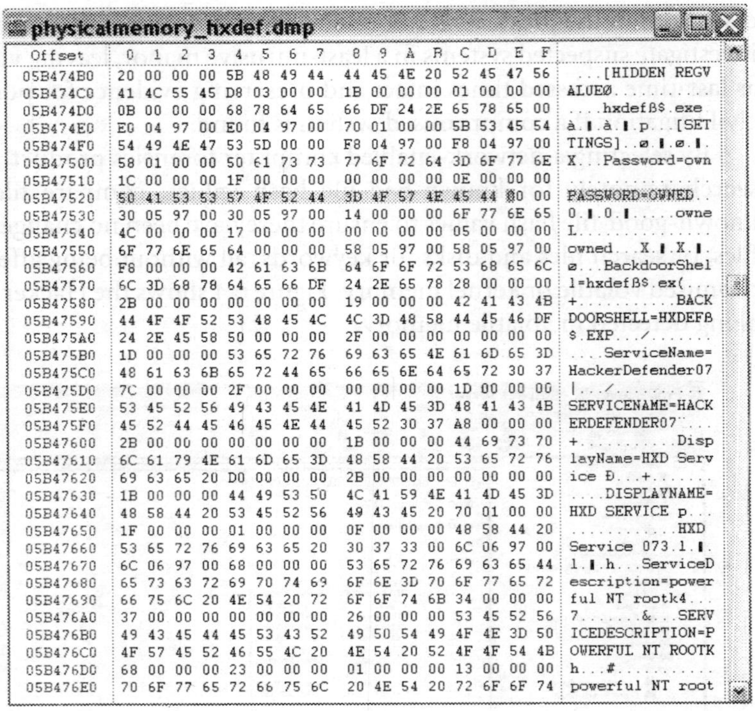

FIGURE 6.5 Hacker Defender password memory.

Network-enabled disk forensics tools such as ProDiscover are now able to create bit-stream images of physical memory, allowing investigators to conduct near real-time analysis of physical memory. For instance, Figure 6.5 shows the section of a raw physical memory image from a system compromised with the Hacker Defender rootkit containing the backdoor password.

Viewing the password in raw memory is one of the few ways this rootkit can be detected, because any standard file I/O, registry, or system information calls have been compromised and will not return accurate information.

When conducting full-scale investigations of cyberattacks, investigators should employ network-enabled forensics products as a key component of their toolbox. A comprehensive investigation, by its very nature, should include collection of volatile memory. With the proper tools and methodologies in place, the investigator's goal of minimal victim impact can be achieved while also preserving the evidence.

ACCESSING VOLATILE DATA

When accessing volatile memory one of the first things a computer forensics investigator may recall is the basic scientific principle that *the very act of observing something changes it.* Certainly there is no exception to this principle in the case of accessing volatile memory. The evidence dynamics effects of loading program code in memory, or even moving the mouse in a Windows-based operating system, needs to be understood. As described earlier in this chapter, starting an application will load some or all of the programs' code pages into physical, and possibly virtual, page memory on disk. The loading of code pages in memory alters the memory data structures, if in physical memory only, and alters the system's disk if any code is loaded into logical page memory. In each case, not only is a change being made but valuable evidence could quite possibly be displaced by the actions. In Windows-based operating systems, the simple act of moving a mouse accesses dynamic registry hives.

As an interesting exercise, investigators can download and run Regmon and Filemon from Mark Russinovich's and Bryce Cogswell's Sysinternals Web site [Sysinternals01] located at www.sysinternals.com. The two real-time utility applications are useful in helping investigators understand when and what files or registry keys are being accessed by their actions. Once at the Sysinternals Web site, investigators can check out all of the free utilities available. This is not the last time we will reference one of this site's useful utility programs.

Brian D. Carrier and Joe Grand presented their paper, "A Hardware-based Memory Acquisition Procedure for Digital Investigations" in the February 2004 *Digital Forensics Investigation Journal* [Carrier01]. In this paper the authors describe Tribble, a hardware expansion card design to reliably acquire the volatile memory of a live system. Acquired memory is captured and extracted to a removable storage system. The hardware device accesses memory directly, and because it does not require software to be loaded, it overwrites possible evidence. Although the Tribble system presents a compelling solution to the problem of live memory access, the device would most likely require preinstallation, causing difficulties in incident-response situations where system engineers had not planned for this type of investigation. As the need for forensically clean extraction increases, system manufactures may be compelled to offer integrated memory access such as that offered by Tribble. For some time now manufactures have offered monitoring ports, or taps, on network switches. The need for this type of access has even shown up in recent U.S. legislation through the Communications Assistance for Law Enforcement Act (CALEA) [fcc01], which outlines requirements for communications carriers to provide access to law enforcement agencies.

The reduced ability to access physical memory without making some changes by displacing or changing content does not immediately negate the value of the content's capture. Computer forensics investigators must make the determination whether the value of potential evidence in physical memory justifies collection. This type of determination often needs to be made on-site based on the parameters of the case. Key questions investigators must ask themselves include: Given the situation, will the case investigation benefit from the capture of physical memory? and Can I capture this information in a least-intrusive manner? Armed with the answers to these questions and an understanding of the effects on the evidence made by their action and tools, investigators can easily justify if their approach was a reasonable one. As we discussed in earlier chapters on evidence dynamics and crime scene investigation, people and tools interact with evidence. An understanding of the interaction, its effects on the evidence, and the ability to articulate the reasonableness of the interaction are what matter. An emergency medical technician will not hesitate to leave footprints in blood around a gunshot victim during life-saving efforts because he will have no difficulty defending the reasonableness of his actions. It may be more challenging for computer forensics investigators to justify subtle changes by their actions; however, the same principles apply.

Taking a closer look at the following real-world rationalizations for collecting raw images of live memory evidence, we see that investigators don't need to work hard to justify the reasonability of their approach:

- Understanding the nature of volatile physical memory that will be lost entirely if not captured
- Displacing a few bits of volatile memory may be worth identifying a password cached in memory
- Displacing a few bits of volatile memory may be worth identifying a rootkit that is running only in memory

Understanding the exact nature of any application code added to memory while extracting the remaining memory is critical to any challenges against the investigators that the evidence gleaned during capture was actually placed there by the collection agent application. If a password was the only evidence gained by the collection of volatile memory, the resulting password will normally lead only to the unlocking of evidence in the system's disk or elsewhere; therefore, the challenge of contamination or evidence spoilage would be diminished. Challenges against the source of compromise could be made if the investigator did not use verifiable steps and applications in the collection process.

Investigators can quickly gain confidence in and justify an approach of collecting raw physical memory captures. Where complications enter into the fray is when an investigator desires to collect more information from the running system, such as current IP connections or running applications. Although compelling reasons to capture such information exist, investigators are faced with a magnified set of challenges. One of the greatest justifications to capturing application and operating system volatile data such as IP connections is that disallowing external log sources, the information will most certainly be lost if the system is shut down or requires heroic efforts to glean from captured raw physical memory. The greatest challenge when collecting application and operating system data is that normally no single application is able to collect the data desired, and each application used in collection increases the investigators' interaction with the system and subsequently causes greater adverse effects on the system. The more interaction an investigator has with a live system, the higher the risk of not recovering critical evidence. Each fragment of information written to a running disk, if flushed from memory, can eliminate the recovery process for user-deleted records. Many investigators may be less comfortable with this type of collection. Comfort can be gained only in a better understanding of the available tools and methodologies, coupled with experience. Investigators who choose to collect this type of information should limit the collection to information that can not be collected in other less-intrusive ways. Some investigators, in their zeal to collect evidence, collect information from a live system that was actually static on disk and could have been collected later if the disk was going to be imaged. Here again, least intrusive is better.

NOTE *If the investigator chooses to collect application and operating system volatile data, he should always remember the possibility that the information he captures may be incomplete or compromised if the system I/O itself is compromised. Remember our earlier rootkit discussion. The captured information should be checked against static artifacts from multiple sources, such as external logs and disk files.*

In the end, loading a small program in memory on a suspect machine may displace small amounts of live memory, but it could be very well worth the information gained, provided the investigator uses a well-understood methodology and tools.

In later chapters we will discuss detailed steps for the collection of volatile memory evidence.

SUMMARY

- Today's investigators are beginning to broaden their focus to include both static and volatile disk data because together they can help tell a complete story.

- When most people refer to volatile data in computer systems in the sense of computer forensics, they are referring only to the information or data contained in the active physical memory, such as RAM (random access memory), rather than volatile disk data.
- As most computer forensics investigators know, even the most secure facility can be compromised, often leaving traces in and affecting volatile memory.
- The latest and perhaps most effective way for hackers to hide is by using a kernel-mode rootkit (or kernel-mode Trojan).
- The second-generation of Windows rootkits that affect volatile memory are called library rootkits (also referred to as DLL injection rootkits).
- Although the kernel-mode rootkit is a major threat to live investigations involving volatile memory, effective network-enabled computer forensics tools to detect them are available.
- In Windows-based operating systems, the simple act of moving the mouse accesses dynamic registry hives.
- Tribble is a hardware expansion card design to reliably acquire the volatile memory of a live system.
- Displacing a few bits of volatile memory may be worth identifying a password cached in memory.

REFERENCES

[Akin01] Akin, Thomas, *Hardening Cisco Routers*, O'Reilly, 2003.

[Carrier01] Carrier, Brian D. and Grand, Joe, "A Hardware-based Memory Acquisition PProcedure for Digital Investigations, *Digital Forensics Investigation Journal*, Volume 1, Issue 1, February 2004.

[Cisco01] *Essential IOS Features Every ISP Should Consider v 2.9*, Cisco Systems, 2004.

[DOD01] *Trusted Computer System Evaluation Criteria (TSEC)—Orange Book*, available online at *www.radium.ncsc.mil/tpep/library/rainbow/*, 1985.

[fcc01] Communications Assistance for Law Enforcement Act (CALEA) Web page, available on line at *www.fcc.gov/wcb/iatd/calea.html*, 2004.

[iDefense01] "TK Worm Still Poses Threat in the Wild," available online at *www.idefense.com/application/poi/display?id=2&type=malicious_code*, 2003.

[NSA01] *Router Security Configuration Guide*, National Security Agency, available online at *http://nsa2.www.conxion.com/cisco*, 2004.

[SecurityFocus01] Poulsen, Kevin, "Windows Root Kits a Stealthy Threat," *SecurityFocus*, available online at *www.securityfocus.com/news/2879*, 2003.

[SecurityFocus02] Poulsen, Kevin, "RPC DCOM Worm Hits the Net,: Security Focus, available online at *www.securityfocus.com/news/6689*, 2003.

[Sysinternals01] Sysinternals Web site, available online at *www.sysinternals.com*, 2004.

[XWays01] X-Ways Software (WinHex Application) Web site, available online at *www.x-ways.net/winhex/index-m.html*, 2004.

Part III

Data Storage Systems and Media

The primary focus of many computer forensics investigations is the extraction of digital evidence on disk; data storage systems and media handling are crucial to these investigations. In Part III, "Data Storage Systems and Media," investigators are given detailed technical information on the physical design specifications as well as access methods for the most common media technologies used to store data. Investigators need to understand how media technologies work at the lowest level to ensure they choose the best approach to collecting digital evidence during an investigation.

7 Physical Disk Technologies

In This Chapter

- Physical Disk Characteristics
- Physical Disk Interfaces and Access Methods
- Logical Disk Addressing and Access
- Disk Features

PHYSICAL DISK CHARACTERISTICS

One of the central tasks the computer forensics investigator will perform is bit-stream imaging and analysis of computer hard disks. This chapter provides background to enable the computer forensics investigator to better understand physical storage disk technologies in use today.

Prior to IBM introducing the first computer with a hard disk in 1956 [CED01], computers used core memory, tape, and drums for data storage. The disk approach to data storage used in the IBM 305 RAMAC ultimately replaced magnetic drums, much like magnetic recording tape replaced the early recording drum systems. The just over 4-MB disk storage system used in the IBM 305 consisted of 50 24-inch disks, which became known as *disk packs.*

The multiplatter open disk pack system of hard disk storage is still used in some older mainframe computers. The second innovation by IBM provided the groundwork for what investigators will most commonly see as personal computer hard drives. In 1973, IBM released the 3040 Winchester hard disk. The 3040 Winchester was significant in being the first sealed hard disk, also known as a head disk assembly (HDA). Note that the acronym used to identify disk devices in the Linux operating system is also HDA. Interestingly, the 3040 Winchester was named after the Winchester 30-30 rifle because of its storage capacity and access time of 30 MB and 30 milliseconds [Wikipedia01]. As PCs became more popular during the 1980s, a great deal of disk manufactures popped up, striving to make their place in the market. Today, after vendor consolidation through mergers and acquisitions, only a handful of disk manufacturers still exist. Some of today's disk manufactures include Seagate®, Maxtor®, Western Digital®, Samsung®, Hitachi®, Fujitsu®, and Toshiba®.

Some of the common terminology used when describing a hard disk's physical characteristics is the platter, track, and sector. Each disk has multiple platters, tracks, and sectors. Today's disk platters usually comprise two materials, the first giving the platter its strength and the second is the magnetic coating. Commonly disk platters are magnetic-coated aluminum. The magnetic coating is where data is stored or represented by the set magnetic impulse. In some cases the magnetic coating is covered with a thin, protective layer of carbon and a final lubricating layer to protect the platter from any contact with the data read heads. Today's platters normally have two sides, with each side divided into concentric rings referred to as tracks. These tracks can be further referenced by their sectors, which are smaller sections of each track that can be visualized as an arc. The sector is normally the smallest individual storage component referenced on a disk drive, and it stores a certain number of bytes of data (normally 512). Figure 7.1 shows a representation of platters, tracks, sectors, and read heads.

Another term investigators should become familiar with is the three-dimensional coordinate of a cylinder. A cylinder is the reference of a stack of tracks from multiple platters on top of each other. To visualize a cylinder, imagine looking down on a stack of disk platters and seeing the tracks of each platter (front and back).

Each side of a platter has its own read/write (R/W) head. In sealed hard disk assemblies, the R/W head actually floats over the surface of the platter whereas a floppy disk's R/W head actually touches the disk's surface. Cylinder number locations are used to identify the position of a disk's read/write head. The complete coordinates of a physical location on disk are referenced as cylinder, head, and sector.

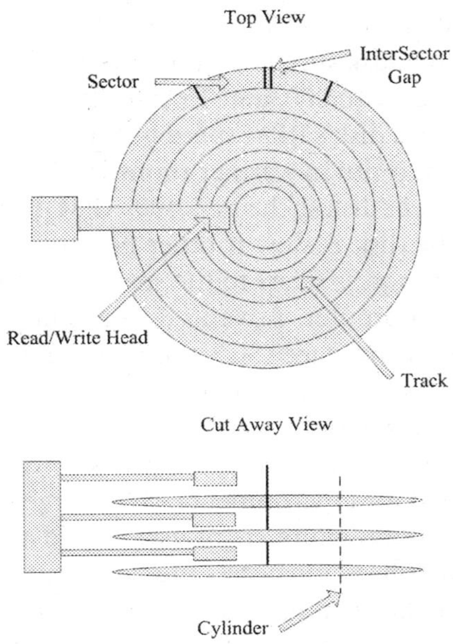

FIGURE 7.1 A cutaway view of a disk.

The capacity of a disk is often referred to as linear bit density, or the number of bits per centimeter stored along a given track. Typically, investigators will see between 50,000 and 100,000 bits/cm. The actual linear bit density depends on factors such as the following:

- Purity of media
- Air quality
- Data-encoding methods

The unformatted capacity disregards low-level components such as preamble, ECC (error correction), and intersector gaps used to electromechanically control the read/write heads. The preamble is written at the beginning of a sector to synchronize the R/W head during disk formatting.

The actual performance of a disk drive is dependant on several characteristics, including the disk R/W head seek time, latency, and external access data rate. Seek time is measured in milliseconds (ms) and is considered to be the greatest performance-determining characteristic of a hard disk. However, all characteristics, including the characteristics of the computer using the disk, are key to overall disk performance. Seek time is simply the amount of time required for a R/W head to move from one sector to another. The latency of a disk is the amount of time required for a disk's R/W head to actually read data once it is positioned at the data's location. The latency of a disk is directly related to the speed at which a disk platter is turning. Today's disk speeds are measured in revolutions per minute (RPM) and include 5,400, 7,200, 10,000, and 15,000 RPM disks. The latency of a disk directly related not only to a disk's RPM speed but also the disk temperature and noise level. Devices designed to run in warmer rooms and quiet environments may intentionally contain a slower disk such as a 5,400-RPM disk. The slower RPM does not necessarily mean the disk is slow if other performance characteristics are high. The external data rate access refers to the speed and method in which the disk is being accessed by the computer. Advanced Technology Attachment (ATA) and Small Computer System Interface (SCSI) are common disk-access methods, but today many more methods are emerging.

Forensics investigators working in large-scale enterprise and the U.S. Department of Defense may run across what is known as a solid-state disk. Solid-state disks were created for environments where large volumes of data needed to be accessed rapidly by large numbers of users. Solid-state disks often provide the same ATA or SCSI interfaces and access methods, but they lack the moving parts (spindle, platters, read head, and so on) that can be found in typical physical disks. The lack of moving parts increases the disk's reliability by reducing the mean time between failures, discussed in Chapter 3, "Evidence Dynamics."

For many years use of solid-state disks had been limited to critical government and military applications such as space and missile programs, due partly to their exorbitant cost. Today's solid-state disks, although still very expensive, are becoming more popular for use in enterprise environments where data access speed and reliability are crucial. Some solid-state disks such as those from BitMicro® [Bitmicro01] offer features that will securely delete all data if power is lost, providing yet another argument in favor of pulling the plug in (see Chapter 3).

Solid-state disks are usually transparent to the operating system and may be bootable with no specialized device driver requirement. The following specifications for the BitMicro 3.5-inch ATA-Flash disk are provided as an example of the dynamic performance seen in this type of physical disk.

- 1,500 to 25,000 IOPS I/O Rate
- 100 to 39 user access time
- 14 to 110 MB/sec sustained R/W Rate
- 16.7 to 133 MB/sec burst R/W Rate
- 1024 MB to 155.6 GB storage capacity
- 1500 Gs operating shock
- MTBF –2 million hours
- –60° to + 95° C (–76° to +203° F) operating temperature range
- 120,000 feet operating altitude

These drives have dramatic specifications, indeed; however, they still lack the storage capacity of today's traditional drives by a factor of 10 or more. Despite the drawbacks of high price and limited storage capacity, they are well suited to many implementation needs. Network security device logging is an area that can benefit greatly from the use of solid-state disks. Logging information, such as CISCO router netflow data, often overwhelms traditional disks because of the rate of information being pushed to disk. In some enterprise systems, solid-state disk area is used as a staging point to provide a cache area for storage and retrieval devices with vastly dissimilar I/O rates. Texas Memory Systems™ [TexasMemory01] and SolidData® [SolidData01] are also manufacturers and distributors of solid-state disk systems.

PHYSICAL DISK INTERFACES AND ACCESS METHODS

As previously stated, the speed characteristics of the access method used to connect to a disk are a key component to the disk's overall performance. The disk-access method and its corresponding physical interface in use are of primary interest to the investigator and will become an important factor in evidence-collection methodology and tools used. Some common specifications that correlate to access method and physical interfaces follow:

- ATA (IDE, EIDE, ATAPI Serial ATA)
- SCSI
- FireWire®/IEEE 1394
- USB
- Fibre Channel

By and large one of the interface and access methods most commonly seen by the forensics investigator will be ATA. The acronym ATA commonly is used to reference several underlying standards or specifications for disk access, much like Ethernet is an umbrella term for several differing network-access methods. Again, as with Ethernet, the ATA standards have improved in performance as technologies have progressed. Rather than referring to the ATA and the standard version number, some people will refer to the access method or interface as Integrated Drive Electronics (IDE), or the follow-on Enhanced IDE (EIDE).

NOTE

Investigators can find ATA specifications and follow developments in the ATA access and interface standards from the T-13 Committee Web site at www.t13.org. T-13 is the technical committee for the International Committee on Information Technology Standards (INCITS) and is responsible for the ATA interface standards. INCITS is accredited by and operates under rules approved by the Ameri-

can National Standards Institute (ANSI). Investigators can find more information on the INCITS at www.incits.org. The T-13 committee comprises many vendor and nonvendor members with an interest in the ATA interface specification.

At the time of this writing the ATA standards were up through drafts of the ATA-8 standard. Not only have there been standards from ATA-1 through ATA-8, there also have been supplemental standards such as the Advanced Technology Attachment Packet Interface (ATAPI). In the ATAPI standard, support was added for devices other than hard disks, including CD-ROM, tape, and other removable media such as Zip® disk and flash memory card readers.

TIP

Investigators should note that devices that are designed to meet a specific standard such as ATA-8 are not required and most likely do not meet all prior standards and supplemental standards. For example, a recently purchased ATA interface card that supports IDE and the newer Series ATA interfaces may not support the connect of ATAPI devices. Investigators will also find that many hardware write blockers are not designed to function with ATAPI devices. Using an IDE hardware write blocker with an ATA/IDE interface ATAPI flash memory device will be problematic if the write blocker does not support ATAPI devices.

Early ATA standards used what was known as programmed input/output (PIO) mode as a disk data access method. This access method proved CPU intensive on the host computer and was later changed to the less CPU-intensive access method of Direct Memory Access (DMA) and follow-on Ultra Direct Memory Access (UDMA). Disks that utilize the IDE interfaces used in ATA devices for years used ribbon cables with 40 wires and 40 pin-block pin connectors. To help support the faster disk access speeds provided in the Ultra DMA-66 standard, 80-wire ribbon cables were created. When using the 80-wire ribbon cables, the same 40-wire block connectors are used because the 40 extra wires are used to provide increased shielding with a groundwire for each signal wire. Ultra DMA-66 is commonly used to describe UDMA Mode 4 because of its speed. Currently the following seven modes of UDMA are available, all of which operate at different speeds:

- Mode 0 operates at 16.7 MB/s
- Mode 1 operates at 25.0 MB/s
- Mode 2 operates at 33.3 MB/s
- Mode 3 operates at 44.4 MB/s
- Mode 4 operates at 66.7 MB/s
- Mode 5 operates at 100.0 MB/s
- Mode 6 operates at 133 MB/s

Most of today's disk drives do not yet support sustained data rates that support Modes Four, Five, and Six.

Many investigators now refer to standard IDE/EIDE ATA as Parallel ATA because of the newer Serial ATA specification for access and physical interfaces.

Computer forensics investigators will often run into issues related to limitations in the ATA specification designs, such as cable length and disk size. Because the ATA specifications were written originally for internal disk connections, the cable limitations can cause problems during the imaging or preview process. The ATA specifications call for maximum cable lengths of 450 to 900 millimeters (18 to 36 inches). With the use of quality cables some investigators have been able to extend cables beyond 900 millimeters (36 inches), but the results on longer cables are unpredictable. Original disk size capacity available in early versions of the ATA specification was small compared to today's disk sizes. Over the course of ATA specification versions, newer addressing schemes were needed to break unpredicted growth in disk sizes. Notable disk-size barriers have been 504 MB, 32 GB, and 137 GB. Although the ATA specifications themselves may have allowed for access to the larger disk when they became available, addressing schemes needed to be supported by computer BIOS, operating systems, and disk-access drivers. An interesting example of operating system support for a large disk can be found in the Windows 2000 operating system. In cases in which a disk (greater than 127 GB) that has *not* been partitioned is added to a Windows-based workstation, the workstation will not show the true size of the disk. To access disks larger than 127 GB with no partition from a Windows 2000 operating system, a new name-value pair must be created in the following Windows registry key:

HKEY_LOCAL_MACHINE\SYSTEM\CurrentControlset\Services\atapi\Parameters

In this key, create the new name-value pair "EnableBigLba" (DWORD key) and set the value to 1. After the computer is restarted, Windows and any forensics software installed will report the disk size correctly. This registry entry can be made only to Windows 2000 systems with Service Pack 3 or later installed.

In single-channel IDE or dual-channel EIDE, each channel supported two devices, one master and one slave. Signaling design makes it advantageous to set slower devices, such as an ATAPI CD-ROM device, as master and faster disks as slaves. Newer disks introduced a new disk setting called *cable select*, which allows the disk to choose which device is master and which is slave. Because wire 28 controls both master and slave, the setting essentially disconnects or cuts wire 28 on 40-wire cables. On an 80-wire UDMA cable, wires 56 and 57 would both be disabled.

The first generation of Serial ATA appeared in 2002. SATA, sometimes written as S-ATA, introduces a completely new physical connector, differing from the 40-

pin connection seen in IDE and EIDE devices. SATA uses seven conductor wires with wafer connectors rather than pins. The new wafer connector is also keyed to prevent a cable from being connected upside down, as is possible in some IDE connector blocks. Although the initial speed advantages of SATA over UDMA are not significant over UDMA mode six, the follow-on SATA II is expected to provide speeds of up to 600 MB/s. Of course internal disks speeds will need to be improved greatly to take advantage of such speeds. SATA II devices should appear on the market in 2005 or 2006. Other than speed, there are many design variations that differ from previous ATA specifications. The most fundamental way in which SATA differs from Standard or Parallel ATA is that access is no longer shared through the same cable. Each SATA device is placed on its own cable and does not need to share cable access with other devices. Forensics investigators can now use longer cables to get to those hard-to-reach drives. The SATA specification allows for cable lengths of up to 1016 millimeters (40 inches) long. The SATA standard also introduced a new power connector, which differs from the current four-pin Molex connector used with IDE disks, but many disk manufactures still offer legacy Molex connectors in addition to the new power connector. The new connector remains the same for use on 3.5-inch desktop hard disk as well as 2.5-inch hard disks used in notebook computers. The SATA specification also begins to provide capabilities normally found in higher-end systems, such as hot swapping of devices found in some SCSI devices. Using the new Serial Attached SCSI, known as SAS interface, SCSI disks and SATA disks can co-exist. SAS is a new generation of SCSI that greatly increases current SCSI speed (3–10 Gbps) and maximum number of devices (16,256), among other improvements. The physical changes to SATA cables and the requirement for new access controllers caused the adoption to be somewhat slow initially; however, all disk manufacturers now make SATA disks, and they are becoming more commonplace.

The SCSI access method for peripheral-device connection is overseen by the T-10 committee, much like the ATA standards are overseen by the T-13 committee. The SCSI T-10 committee Web site, containing published standards and other pertinent information, is located at *www.t10.org*. The original SCSI standard, released in 1986, was made up of the melding of two separate disk-access standards by NCR® and Shugart Associates. Despite having only three official SCSI standards, SCSI-1, 2, and 3, users see SCSI as containing a myriad of standards, connector types, and cables. Much of the confusion associated with SCSI standards stems from independent device manufactures providing slight improvements or variations in the existing standards and thus rebranding the new variation. The complexity of some of the official standards also contributes to the confusion. The SCSI-3 standard alone contains 14 separate standards documents. In simplest terms the three SCSI standards can be described as follows:

SCSI-1: This original specification calls for an 8-bit bus that provides 3.5 MB/s or 5 MB/s, depending on the mode. One of the greatest strengths of this original SCSI standard was the rather lengthy maximum cable length of 6 meters (20 feet), providing a significant improvement over the limitations of the ATA standard.

SCSI-2: This specification, also known as *SCSI Wide* and *SCSI Wide and Fast*, was widely implemented because of its wide device support for tape-backup systems, optical scanners, and CD-ROMs in addition to disks. The now reduced 3-meter (10-feet) maximum cable length coupled with increased numbers of available devices helped make SCSI-2 become the standard for corporate computing systems.

SCSI-3: Performance and speed were focal points of the SCSI-3 standard. SCSI-3 also included new support for SCSI busses over Fibre Channel, which can use 4-pin copper or glass fibre optic cable for device connections.

The creation of a SCSI 4 standards document was not envisioned by the T-10 committee. Instead the committee has adopted a more flexible architectural model referred to as the SCSI Architectural Model (SAM). The original SAM was referred to as SCSI-3 SAM, and the follow-on model was referred to as SCSI-3 SAM-2. From this point forward, the T-10 committee began referring to the model as simply SCSI Architecture Model 2 (SAM-2) and dropped any reference to SCSI-3. Today the current model is SAM-3 revision 14[T1001]. However, a SAM-4 draft document is in progress.

The currently approved SCSI project family is extensive and is managed by other committees such as T-11 for Fibre Channel, private industry in the case of InfiniBand, Internet Engineering Task Force (IETF) in the case of iSCSI, and IEEE in the case of IEEE 1394.

Today's SCSI Architecture Model is more clearly documented within the following high-level categories:

Device Type-Specific Command Sets: This category covers device-specific command types and may include reference commands and behaviors that are common to all SCSI devices. However, it primarily describes the commands used by SCSI Initiator devices to communicate with SCSI target devices such as a physical disk.

Shared Command Sets: This category describes communications command sets used to interact with any device type.

SCSI Transport Protocols: This category sets the requirements for exchanging information between devices.

Interconnect: This category describes the mechanical and electrical signaling requirements needed for devices to connect and communicate.

Within each category numerous documents can be found that outline the category's specific requirements. Current command-set documents include the following:

SCSI-3 Block Commands original and Version 2: Describe the disk drive command set.

Reduced Block Commands and amendment 1: Describe a simplified disk drive command set.

SCSI Stream Commands Versions 1, 2, and 3: Describe first-, second-, and third-generation tape drive command sets.

SCSI Media Changer Commands Versions 1, 2, and 3: Describe first-, second-, and third-generation jukebox command sets.

Multimedia Commands Versions 1, 2, 3, 4, and 5: Describe first-, second-, third-, fourth-, and fifth-generation CD-ROM command sets.

SCSI Controller Commands Version 2: Describe the second-generation RAID controller command set.

SCSI-3 Enclosure Commands Versions 1, amendment to Version 1 and Version 2: Describe the command set used for an enclosure's fans, power supplies, and so on.

Object-based Storage Devices Versions 1 and 2: Describe command sets used for accessing files in disk drives.

Bridge Controller Commands: Describe the command set used for SCSI bridges between protocols.

Automation/Drive Interface Commands Versions 1 and 2: Describe the first- and second-generation command set used in the Automation/Drive interface.

SCSI Primary Commands Versions 1, 2, 3, and 4: Describe first-, second-, third-, and fourth-generation command sets to be supported in all SCSI devices.

Currently defined interconnect and protocol documents include the following:

SCSI Parallel Interface Versions 2, 3, 4, and 5: Version 2 describes the second-generation Ultra2 interface; Version 3 describes the third-generation interface Ultra3, more commonly referred to as Ultra160; Version four describes the fourth-generation Ultra320 interface; and Version five describes the fifth-generation Ultra640 interface.

Automation/Drive Interface Transport Protocol Versions 1 and 2: Describe protocol and transport principally used for first- and second-generation Automation/Drive Commands.

Serial Bus Protocol Versions 1, 2, and 3: Describe first-, second-, and third-generation protocols for transporting SCSI over IEEE 1394 (FireWire).

Fibre Channel Protocol Versions 1, 2, and 3: Describe the first-, second-, and third-generation protocol for transporting SCSI over Fibre Channel.

Serial Storage Architecture (SSA), Transport Layer Versions 1 and 2: Describe the first- and second-generation transport layer protocol for transporting SCSI over SSA.

Serial Storage Architecture (SSA), Physical Layer Versions 1 and 2: Describe the first- and second-generation physical layer protocol used for transporting SCSI over SSA.

Serial Attached SCSI Versions 1 and 1.1: Describe the first-generation plus enhancements to the physical interface for transporting SCSI over serial links.

SCSI/ATA Translation (SAT) Version 1: Describes the software translation layer that maps ATA devices to SCSI controller devices, making them appear to be SCSI devices. This specification is used to create SCSI to IDE bridges used in write-blocking such as the ACARD SCSI-to-IDE Write Blocking Bridge [Microland01].

Investigators can quickly see why some confusion surrounds SCSI specifications and standards. The documents previously mentioned are only a sampling of current specifications and governing technical drafts. Investigators involved in the collection of digital data from businesses will undoubtedly run into a variety of SCSI devices and interfaces requiring an understanding of cables, connectors, and transports. Several SCSI adapter types can be found on the RAM Electronics Web site located at *www.ramelectronics.net/html/scsi_connecters.html* [RAM01]. In many cases the investigator will need to utilize an adapter from one to another SCSI connector for evidence preview, collection, or analysis.

In addition to understanding the variety of adapters used by SCSI devices, investigators investigating larger corporations are likely to find more advanced SCSI technologies implemented, such as Fibre Channel disk storage devices, using complex transport protocols, which can affect evidence collection. Specific challenges and methodologies to collecting evidence from these devices will be covered in Part IV, "Artifact Collection."

NOTE

The Fibre Channel specification [T1002] allows for data transfer rates from 256 Mbits to 10 Gbits per second, point-to-point, fabric switched, and arbitrated loop.

Fibre Channel disk storage was initially designed for utilization in supercomputers, but it has gained popularity for use in corporate storage area networks (SAN). SANs are discussed Chapter 8, "SAN, NAS, and RAID."

FireWire, although not exclusively a disk-access method technology, is commonly used in today's storage devices such as disk and CD-ROM or DVD-ROM drives. FireWire was developed by Apple Computer in 1995 as a digital video serial bus interface and was given the IEEE standards designation of 1394. Given the Apple Computer design focus, FireWire is commonly used and well suited for digital audio and video devices as well as digital storage devices such as disk devices. Each FireWire connector has six pins and can supply each device with up to 45 watts of power, which is a great way to reduce the complexity of a peripheral device power cord snake pit. The FireWire data rates of 400 and 800 MB/s cause it to be well suited for disk storage, too. See Figure 7.2.

FIGURE 7.2 FireWire connectors, both 4 and 6 wire.

NOTE

Sony's implementation of FireWire, called iLink®, uses a different cable connector, with only 4 wires, requiring all external devices to be powered separately. Other venders have now started supporting and providing iLink interfaces, sometimes referred to as "four-wire FireWire."

FireWire is a common interface found in many systems, including digital audio and video equipment such as camcorders. FireWire is often offered as an optional interface to USB in devices such as external disk and CD-ROM/DVD-ROM drives.

USB is in much wider use than FireWire, due partly to licensing fee requirements and cost of implementation. USB uses a connector somewhat similar to FireWire; however, other specifications and access-method protocols differ greatly. USB can provide power (5 volts) to devices through its connections. with limits of 500 volts per draw. Power limits as well as an architecture that supports many devices connected through a hub require most devices, and even hubs, to provide external power sources. USB data rates have changed significantly since its original release in 1995, with USB 1.0 shown in Table 7.1.

TABLE 7.1 USB Data Rates

USB Version	Data Rate	Year Introduced
1.0	1.5 Mbit/s and 12 Mbit/s	Early 1995
1.1 or *USB 2.0 Full Speed*	12 Mbit/s	Late 1995
2.0 or *USB 2.0 High Speed*	480 Mbit/s	2002

Investigators will notice the potentially confusing USB version numbers in Table 7.1. The USB Forum renamed USB 1.1 to USB 2.0 Full Speed and USB 2.0 to USB 2.0 High Speed in an effort to better reflect the difference in speed capabilities. Because of the confusion most people still refer to the two versions as USB 1.1 and USB 2.0.

USB specification allows for up to 127 devices to be connected to a single computer or host, but in reality, users will use many fewer. The proliferation of USB devices has been staggering. Today almost any computer peripheral device one can think of is available with a USB connection: mice, keyboards, printers, scanners, network cards, and yes—storage devices. USB printers have become so successful that USB has all but replaced the parallel printer connection. Investigators looking at Table 7.1 will most likely realize that USB 1.0 and 1.1 provide data rates that are hardly suitable for the disk-imaging process or even the disk preview process for that matter. It was not until the release of USB 2.0 that the access method has become of great use in computer forensics as far as disk evidence collection goes. Computer forensics investigators should ensure that any forensics analysis and acquisition tools they use are USB 2.0 capable. One of the greatest advantages of using USB for storage devices is that the disk becomes *hot-swap* capable when connected via USB. When connecting a disk device to a system via the USB interface rather than providing a native USB-to-USB connection, manufactures will use a converter translating the disk's native ATAPI, ATA, or SCSI interface.

Although a specific access method and physical interface may be in use by the system for standard file system I/O, an investigator may have the option to choose the physical access method by redirecting the disk's I/O to another interface through a device such as a USB-to-IDE adapter, which will convert a disk's native IDE interface to the USB interface. USB-to-IDE conversion is becoming quite common as a way of providing external system backup and auxiliary disk storage. Prior to redirection through an interface such as FireWire or USB, investigators often used redirection through the computer's parallel interface with the assistance of specialized software. Chapter 12, "Imaging Methodologies," which focuses on imaging methodologies, covers specific access methods, interfaces, and tools used in the imaging process.

LOGICAL DISK ADDRESSING AND ACCESS

The logical addressing of data blocks on a hard disk is the method by which the computer system accesses specific data on a hard disk. Two methods of logical addressing used in IBM personal computers are Cylinder-Head-Sector (CHS) and Logical Block Addressing (LBA). CHS was originally designed to address data on a floppy disk and worked quite well referencing the physical location of data. Personal computer BIOS interfaces as well as disk controller interfaces presented limitations on the maximum size of a disk that could be addressed using the CHS addressing method. These limitations brought about the creation of LBA mode, although most of today's ATA drives still power up in CHS mode. LBA mode eliminates lower disk-size limitations by addressing disk sectors using linear numbers, starting with 0. LBA uses either 28-bit- or 48–bit-wide disk addressing, which translates into new disk-size limit of 128 Gigabytes and 128 Petabytes, when using 512 bytes per sector. SCSI controllers have always used LBA mode for disk addressing; however, this does provide commands for identifying the physical locations of data for backwards compatibility with older PC BIOS code.

ATA drives use one of the following three modes of addressing:

- Native CHS mode (older drives only)
- Translated CHS mode
- ATA LBA mode

NOTE

In all personal computer hard disks and floppy disks, a sector is 512 bytes long. This is 512 bytes, excluding preamble, intersector gaps, and error checking. Many investigators will notice a disparity in disk labeling and disk sizes when viewed through different interfaces. The following discussion of "drive math" is intended to help solve the mystery.

A megabyte (MB) or gigabyte (GB) can be properly defined in two different ways:

Decimal Megabyte: 1,000,000 bytes (10 to the 6th power)
Binary Megabyte: 1,048,576 bytes (2 to the 20th power)

Decimal Gigabyte: 1,000,000,000 bytes (10 to the 9th power)
Binary Gigabyte: 1,073,741,824 bytes (2 to the 30th power)

To convert decimal MB to binary MB:

$$\frac{\text{Decimal MB} \times 1{,}000{,}000}{1{,}048{,}576} = \text{binary MB}$$

To convert binary MB to decimal MB:

Binary MB x 1.048576 = decimal MB

When viewed through the DOS application FDISK, older BIOS, and the Windows 3.x file manager, drive capacity is displayed in binary megabytes. When viewed through a newer BIOS or the Windows CHKDSK program, drive capacity is displayed in decimal megabytes. Drive manufacturers report drive capacities in decimal megabytes, but the information may be converted, depending on the method through which it is retrieved, such as directly from firmware, through system BIOS, or using an application.

Specifications call for LBA mode to be requested by the host computer specifically for backwards compatibility, but today's ATA drives larger than 8 GB are always accessed in LBA, because of the 8-GB upper limit imposed by CHS addressing. Older DOS applications often use calls through the system's BIOS Interrupt 13 (Int13) or Extended Interrupt 13 (extInt13) to access the physical hard disk. Investigators should note that BIOS manufacturers use different standards and algorithms to provide the BIOS translations mentioned earlier. These differences can cause a disk to appear different in size or CHS makeup, often referred to as geometry, when imaging or viewing a disk from one make or version of BIOS to another. Investigators should always be cognizant to the access method the operating system and application are using, such as Int13, extInt13, or LBA, and if BIOS CHS translation was being utilized. Although many operating systems' bootstrap code still uses the Int13 interface at boot time, most operating systems access the disk in LBA mode today.

DISK FEATURES

Self-Monitoring, Analysis, and Reporting Technology (S.M.A.R.T.) is a disk-monitoring specification created by Compaq® Corporation and now supported by all leading BIOS, motherboard, and disk manufactures. S.M.A.R.T. provides a set of commands available to the operating system and computer BIOS that allows for the prediction and notification of disk failures. Figure 7.3 shows some of the low-level disk information attributes available via the S.M.A.R.T. command set.

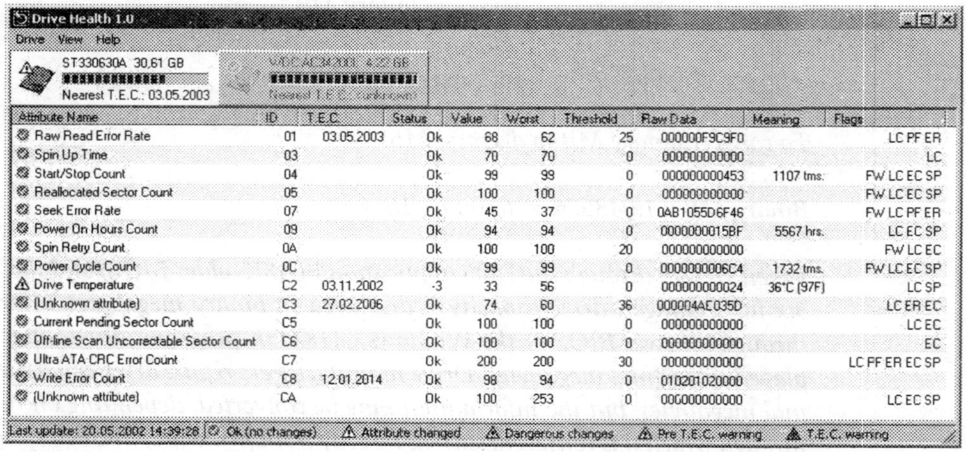

FIGURE 7.3 Low-level disk information seen using the S.M.A.R.T. command set [DriveHealth01].

Utility applications such as those seen in Figure 7.3 allow users to probe varying attributes and collect raw data available from the S.M.A.R.T. interface. Many of today's operating systems, system BIOS, and motherboards also provide disk health checks through the same interfaces.

Device Configuration Overlay (DCO) was originated as a proposal to the T-13 committee from Maxtor Corporation [T1301]. The proposal was presented for addition to the ATA-6 specification in an effort to allow disk manufactures and equipment distributors to buy one device to fit many needs. DCO is of primary interest to investigators because it allows an ATA disk to lie about its true capabilities by modifying information sent from a disk in response to the commands IDENTIFY DEVICE and IDENTIFY PACKET DEVICE. Standard information provided by the IDENTIFY DEVICE and IDENTIFY PACKET DEVICE commands includes command set, mode, capacity, and feature set. The information revealed through the previous commands is altered through the following newly added command sets:

DEVICE CONFIGURATION SET: Allows users to define information provided through the IDENTIFY DEVICE and IDENTIFY PACKET DEVICE commands.

DEVICE CONFIGURATION RESTORE: Disables the *overlay* or settings provided through the DEVICE CONFIGURATION SET command.

DEVICE CONFIGURATION FREEZE/LOCK: Disables further changes to the state of DEVICE CONFIGURATION SET and DEVICE CONFIGURATION RESTORE, requiring a power cycle of the system for future changes.

Specific settings for each command set can be found in the proposed additions found on the T-13 committee Web Site at *www.t13.org/technical/e00140r1.pdf* [T1301]. Today, many disk manufactures support DCO as a means of altering the apparent disk's feature sets available.

A DOS utility application called DRIVEID is available from My Key Technologies (*www.MyKeyTech.com*), which includes the ability to identify if DCO is in effect [MyKey01]. DRIVEID includes other features, such as identifying the suspect drive's electronic serial number, model number, total number of sectors, total number of user-addressable sectors, supported drive features, and status information.

The ATA-4 specification added the "Host Protected Area" as a means for PC distributors to ship diagnostic utilities with PCs. Simply put, the ATA-Protected Area is an area of the hard drive that is not reported to the system BIOS and operating system. Because the Protected Area is not normally seen, many disk forensics imaging tools may not identify or image the area. Initially there was no great concern over the Protected Area by computer forensics investigators, largely because the feature was thought to be used only by PC distributors. There is now a growing level of interest and concern related to user implementation of the Protected Area to hide data, thanks to new utilities marketed for this purpose.

The first such utility was a product called AREA 51, created by StorageSoft, Inc., which has subsequently been purchased by Phoenix Technologies®. Phoenix Technologies took AREA 51 off the market and reintroduced capabilities from the product into their FirstWare® line of products. The FirstWare products are encompassed in what Phoenix Technologies dubbed their Core Management

Environment (CME), for manufactures, distributors, and consumers. Phoenix Technologies has even integrated Protected Area and CME support into their BIOS.

The protected area is outlined in ANSI 346-2001 "Protected Area Runtime Interface Extension Services" (PARITES) [T1302] and is supported on all drives that conform to ANSI NCITS 317-1998 (ATA/ATAPI 4).

Information about the Protected Area is not contained in the expected places, such as the partition table, file allocation tables, and boot record, making the area hard to detect unless you are specifically looking for it. Protected Area information is contained in the Boot Engineering Extension Record (BEER), which is a record stored on the native maximum address (last sector) of the device and contains non-volatile configuration information about the device. Commands outlined in the PARITES specification hide the BEER from the BIOS and operating system.

The specification calls for users to be able to access the Protected Area only at boot time through a modified Master Boot Record (MBR), or a special boot disk.

Today, many computer forensics imaging and analysis tools support, at the very least, identification of the Protected Area's existence, whereas others will allow varying levels of access to the area. No tool is yet known that can recover a password-protected Host Protected Area. Three pioneers in the detection and recovery of the Host Protected Area follow:

My Key Technology: *www.MyKeyTech.com*
Sanderson Forensics: *www.sandersonforensics.co.uk*
Technology Pathways: *www.TechPathways.com*

The Protected Area is beginning to require increased attention due to its availability to the public sector to hide data. Although the Protected Area is fairly easy to detect with good attention to detail and the right tools, detection may become more difficult as new products emerge to use the feature. Computer forensics investigators should become knowledgeable of the ATA Protected Area and how to detect it. Labs are encouraged to add procedures that encompass recovering data from the ATA Protected Area to their standard methodologies.

SUMMARY

- Prior to IBM introducing the first computer with a hard disk in 1956 [CED01], computers used core memory, tape, and drums for data storage.
- The 3040 Winchester was named after the Winchester 30-30 rifle because of its storage capacity and access time of 30 Mb and 30 milliseconds.

- Today's disk platters are normally composed of two materials, the first giving the platter its strength and the second the magnetic coating.
- The unformatted capacity of a disk disregards low-level components such as preamble, ECC (error correction), and Intersector gaps used to electro-mechanically control the R/W heads.
- Today's disk speeds are measured in revolutions per minute (RPM) and include 5,400, 7,200, 10,000, and 15,000 RPM disks.
- The disk-access method and its corresponding physical interface in use are of primary interest to the investigator and will become an important factor in evidence-collection methodology and tools used.
- Today's SCSI Architecture Model (SAM) more clearly documents SCSI specifications with high-level category documents.
- The first generation of Serial ATA appeared in 2002.
- The USB Forum renamed USB 1.1 to USB 2.0 Full Speed and USB 2.0 to USB 2.0 High Speed in an effort to better reflect the difference in speed capabilities.
- Computer forensics investigators should ensure that any forensics analysis and acquisition tools they use are USB 2.0 capable.
- Device Configuration Overlay (DCO) is of primary interest to investigators because it allows an ATA disk to lie about its true capabilities.
- The ATA Host Protected Area is an area of the hard drive that is not reported to the system BIOS and operating system.

REFERENCES

[Bitmicro01] *Bit Micro Web site*, available online at *www.bitmicro.com*, 2004.

[CED01] CED Magic Web site, available online at *www.cedmagic.com/history/ibm-305-ramac.html*, 2004.

[DriveHealth01] Drive Health Application Web site, available online at *www.drivehealth.com*, 2004.

[Microland01] Microland Electronics Web site, available online at *www.microlandusa.com/*, 2004.

[MyKey01] My Key Technologies, Inc. Web site, available online at *www.MyKeyTech.com*, 2004.

[RAM01] RAM Electronics Web site, available online at *www.ramelectronics.net/html/scsi_connecters.html*, 2004.

[SolidData01] SolidData Web site, available online at *www.soliddata.com/*, 2004.

[T1001] *Information Technology—SCSI Architecture Model 3*, T-10 Project 1651-D, September 2004.

[T1002] *Information Technology, Fibre Channel Protocol for SCSI Revision 3c, Third Version*, T-10 Project 1560-D, August 2004.

[T1301] *Drive Configuration Overlay Proposal* E00114R1, Pete McLean, Maxtor Corporation, available online at *www.t13.org/technical/e00140r1.pdf*, September 2000.

[T1302] Host Protected Area Technical Documents, available online at *www.t13.org/technical/*, 2004.

[TexasMemory01] *Texas Memory Systems Web site*, available online at *www.texmemsys.com/*, 2004.

[Wikipedia01] *Wikipedia Free Online Encyclopedia*, "Hard Disks," available online at *http://en.wikipedia.org/wiki/Hard_disk*, 2004.

RESOURCES

[scsifaq01] The SCSI FAQ, available online at [scsita01] The SCSI Trade Association, available online at *www.scsita.org/aboutscsi/*, 2004.

[Wikipedia02] *Wikipedia Free Online Encyclopedia* , "ATA," available online at *http://en.wikipedia.org/wiki/Advanced_Technology_Attachmen*, 2004.

8 SAN, NAS, and RAID

In This Chapter

- Disk Storage Expanded
- Redundant Array of Inexpensive Devices
- Storage Area Networks
- Network Attached Storage
- Storage Service Providers

DISK STORAGE EXPANDED

Every time most people walk into their garage, they are reminded that no matter how big the storage container is, it never seems big enough after some time. This same concept holds true with digital storage devices such as disk drives. In the digital storage realm, this phenomenon is intensified by the continued increase in data processing speed—it seems the faster we can process data, the more we want to process.

NOTE

Moore's law—attributed to the cofounder of Intel, Gordon E. Moore—states that at our rate of technological development and advances in the semiconductor industry, the complexity of integrated circuits doubles every 18 months. Moore's law is commonly referenced by computer scientists when referring to disk storage in addition to integrated circuits.

Consumers have moved from storing simple word-processing, e-mail, and spread sheet documents requiring only a few kilobytes to storing entire audio CD-ROM collections on disk. If you have 200 audio CD-ROMs in your collection, and each CD-ROM takes up around 25 megabytes (compressed), that's 50 gigabytes of storage for the CD-ROM collection alone. In the corporate world, digital storage needs have expanded in much the same way. Customer databases grow, applications become more complex and require more data storage, and digital video presentations have become the norm. Table 8.1 shows some common file types and their storage needs.

TABLE 8.1 Common File Storage

Object	Average Space Required
Single standard character	1 byte
Single extended character (Asian languages)	2 bytes
Single English word	10 bytes
Single-page document	2 kilobytes
Low-resolution graphic file	100 kilobytes
High-resolution graphic file	2 megabytes
CD-ROM	700 megabytes
Pickup truck or minivan full of paper	1 gigabyte
50,000 trees worth of printed paper	1 terabyte
Contents of the U.S. Library of Congress	10 terabytes
Half of all U.S. academic research libraries	1 petabyte
Entire year's worth of production of a hard disk	10 petabytes
All words ever spoken	5 exabytes

Looking at the extensive amount of content that can be stored in a seemingly small measurement (by today's standards) such as 1 gigabyte, it is easy to see why some people may think they'll never need more than an x-gigabyte drive. What may not be clear, however, is the basic human desire to collect and store data far beyond our capability of processing it manually. This characteristic, along with a computer's ability to generate and process large amounts of data automatically, helps push our drive disk storage needs upward.

Table 8.1 does not take into account two forms of measurement—zettabyte and yottabyte. A zettabyte is equal to 1,024 Exabytes, and the yottabyte is equal to 1,024 Zettabytes.

From a computer forensics investigator's standpoint, it can be helpful to look as documents on disk in another way. How many pages of information are in all these documents on disk? This type of question is normally generated by forensics investigators, attorneys, and support staff involved in digital discovery document review. Table 8.2 provides some helpful page-per-document and page-per-gigabyte averages to assist in planning.

TABLE 8.2 Pages in a Gigabyte [Lexis01]

Document Type	Average Pages/Doc	Average Pages/GB
Microsoft Word files	8	64,782
E-mail files	1.5	100,099
Microsoft Excel files	50	165,791
Lotus 1-2-3 files	55	287,317
Microsoft PowerPoint files	14	17,552
text files	20	677,963
image files	1.4	15,477

Computer forensics investigators are cautioned that the information contained in Table 8.2 represents averages only. The actual page counts of documents can vary greatly depending on document format and composition. Table 8.2 should be used as a guide only and cannot replace investigator experience.

Corporations, and even today's small businesses, have business needs other than simple storage space. Devices that offer increased access speed, fault tolerance, and increased availability have become essential. In this chapter, we will present the three most common advanced storage methodologies in use today. Advanced storage systems may lead some computer forensics investigators to believe their use may be employed only in the largest of enterprise environments. Not so: today, advanced storage systems are used in everyday mainstream applications. This mainstreaming of seemingly advanced technologies calls for computer forensics investigators to have a better understanding of their identification, implementation, and use.

REDUNDANT ARRAY OF INEXPENSIVE DEVICES

Redundant Array of Inexpensive Devices (RAID), sometimes referred to as Redundant Array of *Independent* Devices, has been around for more than 15 years and has become one of the most common technologies used to provide increased performance and fault tolerance for information technology data storage. The reason for RAID's popularity is its breadth of implementation possibilities. RAID offers users a number of user levels for implementation-dependant needs. As computer forensics investigators become familiar with the implementations of RAID, the challenges to collecting disk images and evidence collection will become apparent. Whereas RAID 0, 1, and 5 are the most commonly seen implementations of RAID, there are other RAID implementations driven by specialized needs and research. RAID is normally implemented directly by a specialized RAID disk controller card or in a software approach controlled by a network operating system such as Windows or Linux. Let's look at each of the currently accepted RAID implementations, referred to as *levels*.

Level 0

Level 0 is a striped disk array containing no fault tolerance. In a RAID Level 0 implementation, data is spread, or striped, across three or more physical disks to provide increased performance. RAID Level 0 does offer superior performance for read/write operations, but if any one drive from the array fails in an unrecoverable way, all data from the array is lost. Investigators will point out that some data may be recoverable; however, from an operational standpoint, the RAID array will need to be re-created and data restored from backups or low-level data recovery procedures, so therefore, the data is operationally lost.

Level 1

RAID Level 1 is one of the most common and simplest forms of RAID that offers fault tolerance. In RAID Level 1 implementations two physical disks are mirrored, providing a complete backup of the live system while running. If either disk fails, the other can take over, thus providing a fault-tolerant system. Because RAID Level 1 requires twice the read transaction rate of a single disk implementation, some implementations will use a controller card duplexing approach and place two separate disk controller cards in the same computer, with one disk assigned to each controller card. This approach helps increase performance in systems where the RAID array is implemented and controlled by software, such as that of the Windows and Linux software RAID implementations. Because all data is written simultaneously to each disk of the RAID array, any malicious code that generates corruption or destroys data will affect both disks. The safety in RAID Level 1 can be found in mitigating downtime due to disk failure. Some administrators have been known to create a RAID 1 Mirror set and then break the array, thereby maintaining a clean copy of the original installation. Although this method is a dangerous approach to configuration control, it can be effective in providing a clean restore point, and investigators should always be aware of the status of the *active* configuration.

Level 2

RAID Level 2 included error-correcting coding with striped data at the bit level rather than at the block level. This implementation of RAID was an effort to add more fault tolerance to RAID Level 0 and is rarely used today.

Level 3

RAID Level 3 was another effort at providing fault tolerance and better performance by providing bit-interleaved parity. In the RAID Level 3 approach, disks were striped at the byte level, as in RAID Level 0, but a dedicated parity disk was created to provide fault tolerance. Poor performance also caused this level of RAID to be implemented rarely by manufacturers or consumers.

Level 4

RAID Level 4, referred to as Dedicated Parity Drive, was a commonly used implementation of RAID and provided one of the first true improvements over RAID Level 0 with fault tolerance. As in Level 3, Level 4 provides block-level striping and also included a parity disk. Although performance in Level 4 was better, the parity disk can create write bottlenecks, causing it to be implemented less as RAID levels improved.

Level 5

RAID Level 5, Block Interleaved Distributed Parity, provides data striping at the byte level and also stripe error-correction information. By including the striping and parity bits on each disk, a great balance of performance and fault tolerance was achieved. RAID Level 5 is one of the most popular implementations of RAID, so popular that many people refer to RAID Level 5 simply as RAID. Because the performance of RAID Level 5 and the fault tolerance of RAID Level 1 were thought to be best of all the RAID levels, many system administrators install the base operating system to a RAID Level 1 Mirror and place all user-accessible data on a RAID Level 5 array. This implementation was also driven by software implementations of RAID that could not install or expand to a RAID Level 5 array but could create a RAID Level 1 Mirror after the initial operating system was installed.

Level 6

RAID Level 6, Independent Data Disks with Double Parity, was an effort to provide better fault tolerance over RAID Level 5. Level 6 provides block-level striping with parity data distributed across all disks. Whereas RAID Level 6 did improve performance somewhat, most administrators stuck with the widely implemented RAID Level 5.

Level 0+1

As performance needs increased for I/O-intensive applications, manufacturers needed to offer fault tolerance and dramatically increase performance. RAID Level 0+1 was implemented to provide that balance. In Level 0+1, two RAID Level 0 stripes are created, and then the two stripe sets are mirrored using RAID Level 1. This implementation was used by many mail server administrators when implementing high-volume Microsoft Exchange servers. Any transaction-intensive application can benefit by this approach.

Level 10

RAID Level 10 is another approach to the goals of RAID 0+1. In RAID Level 10, a Stripe of Mirrors is created with multiple RAID Level 1 mirrors that are later striped using RAID Level 0. Both RAID Level 0+1 and Level 10 have similar performance ratings and are supported by most of today's hardware RAID controller cards.

Level 7

RAID Level 7 achieves improved performance over RAID Level 5 by adding caching to the basic design of RAID Levels 3 and 4. Level 7 had not been that widely implemented, partially due to its proprietary nature. Level 7 is a trademark of Storage Computer Corporation®.

RAID S

RAID S is EMC® Corporation's proprietary striped parity RAID system used in their Symmetrix® storage systems. Being a proprietary system, RAID S is not publicly documented in great detail, but it can be considered similar to RAID Level 5. RAID S adds improvements to standard RAID Level 5 by adding caching and other improvements.

JBOD

Just a Bunch of Disks (JBOD) is a method of concatenating several disks into a single contiguous disk. When using JBOD, system administrators are able to combine several different sizes of disk into a single volume, providing disk consolidation and a single storage location. Although JBOD is not officially a RAID level, it is supported by many RAID storage controllers and software implementations. Microsoft's extended volumes feature, available for dynamic disk in some versions of Windows 2000 and later, is an example of JBOD capabilities. The concatenation features of JBOD are useful in extending existing storage systems, such as the Network Attached Storage devices discussed later in this chapter.

RAID Levels 0, 1, and 5 are the most commonly found RAID levels. However, an investigator will find that implementations can be quite different. In the early days of RAID implementation, administrators normally used a software approach if cost was of great concern, or a specialized hardware card in situations where the implementation justified the extended cost. Adding a specialized hardware RAID controller is normally an option on server-class systems sold by companies such as Hewlett-Packard® and Dell®. In the earlier implementations only SCSI disk interfaces were supported. Today a wide assortment of cost-effective hardware RAID controller cards support both SCSI and ATA disk interfaces. Even Dell computers sells high-end but cost-effective Fibre Channel RAID controllers. Many of the SATA disk controllers support RAID levels as part of their base configurations. For several years now, small and home office appliance devices such as the Sun Cobalt Qube™ have offered software RAID Level 1 as part of a fault tolerant option.

Forensics investigators should always consider that some method of RAID may be implemented when presented with a system with more than a single disk. Systems found with only two disks could be implementing RAID Level 1 to mirror data. A system with three disks is likely to have RAID Level 5 implemented. Investigators will want to note if RAID has been implemented and controlled by the operating system, often referred to as software RAID, or hardware such as a RAID controller card. If RAID has been implemented with a hardware RAID controller card, the multiple disks will seem to be a single-disk device to the operating system, becoming completely transparent. If the RAID has been implemented by software such as Windows 2000 and XP fault-tolerant dynamic disk, the operating system actually sees each physical disk. These differences become important factors in choosing an imaging process for artifact collections.

The widespread implementation of RAID in all levels of business systems coupled with its low cost and availability for home users in devices such as Network Attached Storage ensure that computer forensics investigators will run across a RAID system eventually—most likely when least expected. In Part IV, "Artifact Collection," we will discuss specific challenges in collecting RAID disk evidence.

STORAGE AREA NETWORKS

RAID was one of the first technologies that allowed data storage to be consolidated beyond the size of a single physical disk by aggregating many disks and presenting a single volume view to the user. Of course, performance and fault tolerance were tremendous benefits and were often the goal of many RAID level designs. As the use of RAID grew, it was not uncommon to find RAID arrays of 16 and 32 disks, which needed to be housed outside a host server and connected via a host bus controller of some type. As the appetite for storage grew past the single large data-storage arrays, system administrators would often install a completely new server platform with yet more RAIDed disks and possibly external large-volume RAID arrays. This approach to disk storage decentralization by happenstance actually benefited some system administrations by allowing for compartmentalized administration of individual storage servers. Unfortunately, the benefits of compartmentalized administration are often outweighed by decreased application performance when accessing data through myriad storage servers across the network. The decrease in performance can be staved off by careful planning when locating data repositories strategically at a point closest to data users and access applications.

Understanding that location is a primary component to data access performance and that the network is another key player in relationship to performance when data storage is decentralized, system administrators and system design engineers often make data storage a focus of network topology design. An example of such design is the creation of a dedicated network backup segment as shown in Figure 8.1. A dedicated network backup segment was, and sometimes still is, implemented in situations where users need access to data continuously and without interruption or degradation in performance. To perform regular data backups in these situations without degradation in performance, each server requires its own backup system assigned to the local SCSI or IDE bus. In situations where more than a few servers require backing up, placing a tape backup system on each system quickly becomes costly and unmanageable. If a single backup server were created with a large-capacity tape backup system that would use the network to back up each server, network performance would slow significantly during backup operations. A common answer to this dilemma is to create a network backup segment, as shown in Figure 8.1.

Essentially, Storage Area Networks (SANs), shown in Figure 8.2, carry the concept of a network backup segment further by attaching a disk (normally a disk array) to a specialized high-speed switch, which allows multiple systems to access the disks. Thus, a SAN solves problems associated with decentralized application and user access in many cases and provides implementation. In reality, a SAN uses specialized switches (normally Fibre Channel), which connect the multiple computers and disks array using specialized Fibre Channel host bus adapters. One of the major advantages of using SANs is that the single-disk array appears to be a directly attached or local disk in many cases. In a SAN, disks are accessed directly and not by means of a network file system, such as Server Message Block (SMB) in Windows or Network File System (NFS) in Unix. The methodology used for disk access by SAN is more commonly referred to as *Block Storage Access*, and it functions similar to the specification provided by ATA and SCSI standards created by the T-13 and T-10 committees, respectively.

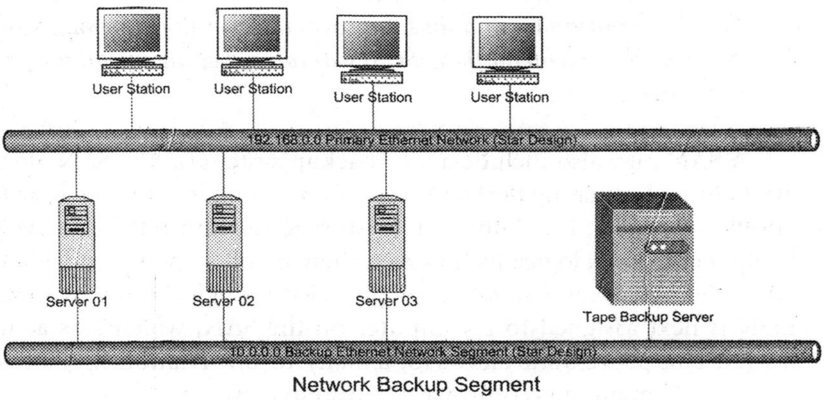

FIGURE 8.1 An example of a network backup segment.

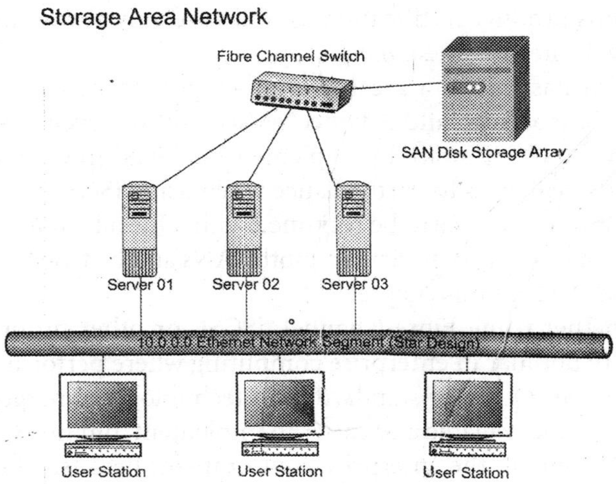

FIGURE 8.2 Storage Area Network (SAN).

NOTE

The relatively new Internet SCSI (iSCSI) standard is gaining ground as a possible replacement to Fibre Channel. iSCSI, which calls for the embedding of SCSI-3 over TCP/IP, performs well on some of today's faster Ethernet standards such as Gigabit Ethernet. Using standard switches and connectors is an obvious advantage over the specialized equipment needed for Fibre Channel installations. There are still challenges to implementing iSCSI over some of the newer and much faster Gigabit or 10 Gigabit Ethernet networks. To mitigate performance issues, iSCSI can be implemented using a network card that contains a TCP Offload Engine (TOE). The TOE in the network card performs TCP header processing, which improves TCP/IP performance and thus improves the overall performance of iSCSI and the iSCSI SAN implementation. iSCSI was ratified as an official standard by the IETF in February 2003.

A SAN may also include a tape backup system on the SAN alongside the disk array, thus eliminating performance issues related to network-based backup operations. In a SAN, the computer-to-storage relationship loses the appearance of being one-to-one; logically, however, there is still a one-to-one relationship. In the SAN, each physical disk device is provided a Logical Unit Number (LUN). The LUN is next assigned to a computer on the SAN, which acts as its initiator, or owner. This process still allows for a many-to-one relationship, but a single system on the SAN maintains control as the resource owner.

There have been many proprietary implementations of SANs over recent years, but standards have recently emerged to promote interoperability. The Storage Networking Industry Association (SNIA) is an international non-vendor-specific organization that promotes standardization within the industry [SNIA01]. The SNIA maintains product certification as well as technical working group documents on their Web site at *www.snia.org.*

iSCSI has gained a great deal of support from industry leaders such as Microsoft, Cisco, Intel, and Adaptec®. Microsoft has even made the latest versions of its software iSCSI aware by implementing iSCSI initiators and drivers. Although there are challenges to performance when using iSCSI over standard Ethernet networks, iSCSI is a force to be reckoned with. One advantage of the iSCSI standard is that it can be used to implement both SANs and Network Attached Storage (NAS), discussed later in this chapter.

Whether using Fibre Channel, iSCSI, or other proprietary implementation, SANs are popular in enterprise computing where performance and fault tolerance are essential. As newer standards and technologies emerge, SAN technologies will become more available and easier to implement, but investigators should expect to see SANs only in the enterprise environment. Because of the proprietary and implementation-specific nature of SANs, investigators can expect each SAN encountered to present its own challenges with respect to evidence collection.

NETWORK ATTACHED STORAGE

The complexity, cost, and proprietary nature of SANs have driven the need for a better, or at least more cost-effective, solution to managing storage growth. Network Attached Storage (NAS) provides a way to simplify storage expansion in a cost-effective manner where lightning-speed performance may not be needed. NAS makes it easier for administrators to add storage by providing a disk storage "appliance" for users to simply plug into the network cable and make available. In this sense NAS could stand for *Network Appliance Storage*, and, in fact, a company emerged in the NAS business named simply Network Appliance® [Netapp01]. The company, often referred to as simply NetApp®, has been a leader in enterprise and corporation implementations of NAS.

As shown in Figure 8.3, NAS in its simplest form is simply a device plugged into the network and made available to users.

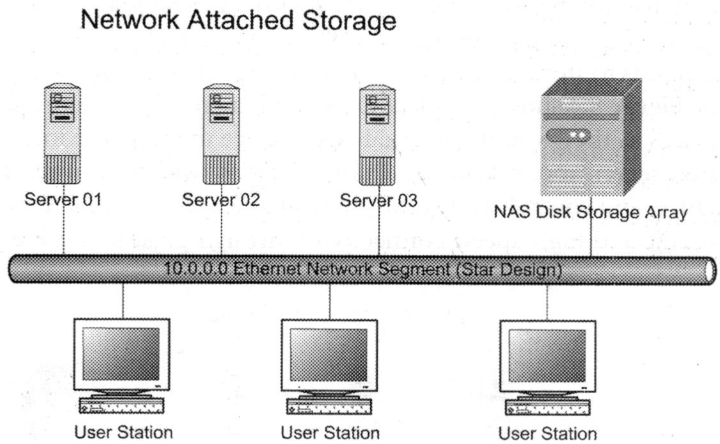

FIGURE 8.3 Network Attached Storage.

NAS in reality is a bit more complex in the corporate enterprise implementation, which can include many levels of RAID support, integrated tapeless backup systems, and multi-operating-system access support. The simplicity of NAS is provided by what is often referred to as the *NAS Head* providing file access to the NAS disks array via standard access protocols, such as SMB in Windows or NFS in Unix. In some of the newer NAS devices the iSCSI protocol for access has been implemented, changing the access method from a standard network access protocol to a Block Storage Access method, such as that used by SANs. Using iSCSI as an access method for NAS greatly increases access performance and provides more flexibility in applications where multiple servers need to access the same resource for high-availability applications.

The more advanced enterprise NAS devices, such as those offered by NetApp, provide additional protocol access for a wide assortment of operating systems. The more advanced NAS Heads may also provide advanced features such as snapshot backups to disk and integration with network operating system directories for file-level security enforcement.

One advantage of NAS is that the device can be plugged into the network at a location close to servers that need to access data or close to users who need access to the data. In situations where a single-server application (and not users) needs access to data on disk, a NAS device could actually be implemented similar to a SAN, where the NAS device is placed on its own fast network segment accessible only by one or more servers. This implementation would be much like creating a dedicated backup segment as shown in Figure 8.1.

Open Storage Networking (OSN) is an initiative created by NetApp to provide flexibility and performance capabilities of both SAN and NAS in one integrated solution. When implementing an OSN solution, system administrators will have several paths to storage, much again like the specialized backup network seen in Figure 8.1. Figure 8.4 shows a typical OSN implementation where users attach to the NAS devices as they would a normal NAS device through the local area network. Dedicated server applications and tape libraries, which require greater speed, performance, and control, access the physical disk similar to the SAN method where there is dedicated high-speed connectivity through gigabit and Fibre Channel switches.

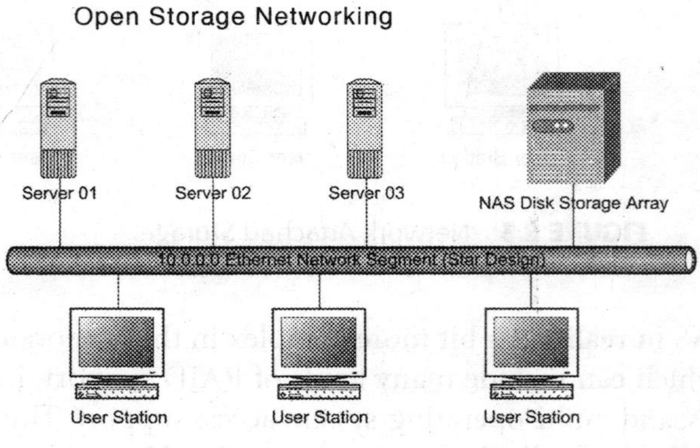

FIGURE 8.4 Open Storage Networking implementation.

Although OSN has received support from IBM, Sun, and other vendors, it has lost some steam because of support for iSCSI, which allows for great flexibility and essentially supports many, if not all, of the goals set forth in the OSN initiative. The true capabilities of advanced disk technologies such as SAN or NAS or hybrids such as OSN are provided by the application layer for control, such as that provided by the NAS Head in NAS or the *initiator* in SAN. Each vendor implementation's application layer will provide vendor-specific capabilities and attributes that should be understood by the investigator.

Although there is certainly a market and wide-scale use for high-end NAS systems, they are becoming pervasive because of the many low-cost systems available. Less than 10 years ago, and in some cases, even today, people consider a terabyte of data to be staggering. Today, home users can purchase a 2 Terabyte RAID-capable NAS device for the price of a good notebook computer [Fastora01]. Where NAS becomes important to computer forensics investigators is its ability to sit virtually unnoticeable on a wireless network. Consider the scenario where investigators enter a home or small office to seize computer systems based on hard evidence that some type of wrongdoing had been performed. When entering, the investigators identify and bag and tag the following items:

- Desktop computer
- Notebook computer (Wi-Fi enabled)
- Wireless access point (connected to DSL line)
- Printer
- Scanner
- Assorted CD-ROMs and floppy disks

Back at the lab investigators find no evidence of the activity on any hard disk image.

For little more than the cost of a single hard disk, our suspect in the scenario could have purchased a Wi-Fi–enabled single-disk NAS device and concealed the NAS on the wireless network. This means that the disk containing evidence of wrongdoing could conceivably have been anywhere within the 802.11 maximum range of around 400 feet. This range can be extended in wireless networks with multiple access points, providing bridging or roaming capabilities. If the suspect had placed the wireless NAS device in a garage, or maybe even the next-door neighbor's house, he could then boot any home computer on the network to a memory resident-only operating system such as Knoppix [Knoppix01]. In this scenario the suspect has access to the data locally while obscuring its presence, providing a seemingly normal network and computer environment for bag and tag. This scenario helps to reinforce the need for a complete understanding of a network environment during the evidence-collection phase of computer forensics investigation.

Whether investigating home networks, small businesses, or enterprise environments, computer forensics investigators can expect to find more advanced disk systems in use. A recent report by TechWeb [Ferrell01] stated: "The shift to Storage Area Networks (SAN) and Network Attached Storage (NAS) is accelerating, with analysts predicting that by 2006 some 70 percent of enterprise information will be spread among Fibre Channel networks or attached storage devices."

STORAGE SERVICE PROVIDERS

Many organizations as well as individual consumers have found application service providers specializing in data storage, dubbed Storage Service Providers (SSP), beneficial. Pervasive and reliable Internet connections coupled with increased reliability of connections has made outsourcing data storage needs not only beneficial but a reasonable addition for data storage.

As with storage technology, SSPs range from high-end enterprise services providing dedicated storage platforms to less complex and capable consumer applications for everyday users.

Enterprise customers may implement remote storage facilities for a variety of reasons, including the following:

- As part of a disaster-recovery/business-continuity plan
- To supplement local storage
- As a means for remotely accessible storage
- All the above

Whereas supplementing local storage sounds like a good idea at first glance, most SSPs have not been able to convince corporations to outsource primary storage. Due partly to equipment cost and partly to customer resistance to outsourcing, many of the SSPs who focused on alternate means of primary storage in the enterprise markets are no longer in business today [Allen01]. Storage Networks, Inc. and StoragePoint, Inc. are two examples of first-generation storage service providers who are no longer in business today.

In most situations corporations are using SSPs as a means of offsite backups as part of their disaster-recovery and business-continuity plans or as a remotely accessible supplemental storage. Although some SSPs have been able to refocus efforts as application service providers who provide outsourced storage management through specialized management software and consulting services [Storability01], off-site backup and recovery remains the most compelling enterprise market. Companies such as IBM and Comdisco® (*www.comdisco.com*) have provided these value-added services along with hot-site and cold-site locations as part of enterprise disaster- and business-continuity planning for many years [Comdisco01].

NOTE

A "hot-site" location is used to identify a location for which data is constantly replicated to online systems capable of providing restoration of business services in a mater of minutes or hours. In many cases a hot site will also provide call-center facilities and other critical corporate capabilities. A "cold site" is similar to a "hot site" but may contain offline systems requiring start-up and some configuration or restoration prior to coming online.

The use of SSPs for hot-site and cold-site locations in disaster-recovery planning is usually limited to large enterprise environments. Smaller companies may find it beneficial to implement SSP capabilities for simple backup and restore services or as a means of long-term weekly or monthly data archives.

Whether a company is using an SSP for full hot-site/cold-site storage or as a method of long-term archiving, computer forensics investigators should be aware of this. In the analytical phase of computer forensics investigations, the recovery of deleted files is often a difficult process. Simply put, the longer the time between a file's deletion and the physical disk's analysis, the less likely the data will be able to be recovered reliably. System backups and, more specifically off-site backups such as those kept at an SSP, are more likely to be forgotten by those attempting to delete data. In addition, archived data backups help to provide snapshots in the history of file systems that can be useful in trend analysis and other forensics analysis processes.

Another common use pointed out for SSPs was universally accessible supplemental storage. In some situations a company's security configuration and architecture does not lend itself to providing business partners and even employees easy remote access to data. Utilizing an SSP as a holding place for files for many users, including external partners, can have its appeal to all sizes of business.

NOTE

The legitimate need to share and remotely access data is a common if not the number-one reason employees will attempt to circumvent corporate security policies. The side effect of legitimate security policy circumvention is often devastating, leaving back doors into corporate networks and compromising corporate data.

The use of SSPs for remotely accessible storage and to share files among groups of interested people has been widely popular among consumers, too. Even with the failure of early SSPs that focused on consumers, such as XDrive, newer companies have been successful. Like many of the consumer-focused SSPs, iBackup® (*www.ibackup.com*) provides low-cost, universally accessible file storage on the Internet [iBackup01]. Consumer-focused SSPs make file storage universally accessible by providing a multitude of client applications from which users can choose. The most common method of access by users is a Web browser such as Internet Explorer, Netscape®, Opera®, or FireFox®. Users can also choose from specific application software to allow access from handheld devices such as phones and PDAs, and can actually map drives on personal computers. Many also provide automated backup software, too.

Unfortunately, consumer use of SSPs for remote access to data storage has become a primary avenue of departure of many corporate secrets and intellectual property. Although many companies' information technology security personnel will try to lock down external access and monitor file transfers, the multitude of access methods makes transfers difficult to identify. Some users involved in questionable activities outside the workplace will also use SSPs as a method of concealing file evidence. Much like the scenario used earlier where data had been located on a NAS device with wireless access, contraband could be stored exclusively on an SSP. Although identification of the existence and use of an SSP or NAS device may occur only during the forensics analysis process, investigators should make every effort to consider and identify such use. By identifying external storage repositories early, investigators have a much better opportunity to collect potential evidence prior to concealment efforts. Identification of such repositories requires crime scene investigative procedures, which can develop a view of the operational environment in which any "apparently" single system is operating. Prior knowledge of the suspect's capabilities and habits in relationship to information technology is also helpful, if not essential.

SUMMARY

- An audio CD-ROM collection consisting of 200 CDs can require up to 50 gigabytes of storage when compressed on disk.
- A zettabyte is equal to 1,024 exabytes.
- A pickup truck or minivan full of paper could require only 1 gigabyte of storage space.
- RAID refers to Redundant Array of Inexpensive Devices, and sometimes Redundant Array of *Independent* Devices.
- RAID is normally implemented directly by a specialized RAID disk controller card or in a software approach controlled by network operating systems such as Windows and Linux.
- Levels 0, 1, and 5 are the most commonly implemented levels of RAID.
- In a Storage Area Network (SAN) the computer-to-storage relationship loses the appearance of being one-to-one; logically, however, there is still a one-to-one relationship.
- Network Attached Storage (NAS) provides a way to simplify storage expansion in a cost-effective manner.

- Advanced NAS Heads may also provide advanced features such as snapshot backups to disk and integration with network operating system directories for file-level security enforcement.
- Where NAS becomes important to computer forensics investigators is its ability to sit virtually unnoticed on a wireless network.
- Today, home users can purchase 2-terabyte RAID-capable NAS devices for the price of a good notebook computer.
- Archived data backups help to provide snapshots in history of file systems, useful in trend analysis and other forensics analysis processes.
- Consumer use of SSPs for remote access to data storage has become a primary avenue of departure of many corporate secrets and intellectual property.
- The most common method of user access to an SSP is a Web browser such as Internet Explorer, Netscape, Opera, or FireFox.
- By identifying external storage repositories early, investigators have a much better opportunity to collect potential evidence prior to concealment efforts.

REFERENCES

[Allen01] Allen, Doug, "Storage Service Providers—By Any Other Name," *Network Magazine*, available online at *www.networkmagazine.com/showArticle.jhtml?articleID=8703339*, May 2002.

[Comdisco01] Comdisco Web site, available online at *www.comdisco.com*, 2004.

[Fastora01] FASTORA Web Site, available online at *www.fastora.com*, 2004.

[Ferrell01] Ferrell, Keith, "Storage Security Gets More Complicated," CMP TechWeb, available online at *www.techweb.com/tech/security/20030813_security*, August 2003.

[iBackup01], ProSoftnet Corporation (iBackup) Web site, available online at *www.ibackup.com*, 2004.

[Knoppix01] Knoppix Linux Distribution Official Web site, available online at *www.knopper.net/knoppix/index-en.html*, 2004.

[Lexis01] "How Many Pages in a Gigabyte—Applied Discovery Fact Sheet", LexisNexis, available online at *www.lexisnexis.com/applieddiscovery*, 2004.

[SNIA01] The Storage Networking Industry Association (SNIA) Web site, available online at *www.snia.org*, 2004.

[Storability01] Storability Web site, available online at *www.storability.com*, 2004.

9 Removable Media

In This Chapter

- Removable, Portable Storage Devices
- Tape Systems
- Optical Discs
- Removable Disks—Floppy and Ridged
- Flash Media

REMOVABLE, PORTABLE STORAGE DEVICES

In Chapter 8, "SAN, NAS, and RAID", users were introduced to advanced fixed-disk storage technologies used in both the enterprise and consumer markets. Chapter 9 introduces computer forensics investigators to the most common types of removable media in use today—the common and almost extinct floppy disk, optical disc, tape backup systems, and the increasingly popular flash media devices.

The expanding capacity of removable media has aided their popularity among all types of users. As investigators become more experienced and develop the "nose" for tracking down digital evidence, they will realize that evidence may not be pervasive throughout the systems they seize or investigate. Evidence may be limited to a small number of documents on a removable disk found at the scene or a single fragment of data on a removable flash drive. Understanding how to identify and process removable media can be critical to many investigations.

> NOTE
> *Flash drives is a generic term for most any type of removable flash storage disk, such as a Secure Digital (SD) disk or USB Flash Disk, sometimes called key drives because they are often affixed to a key chain.*

Removable media was an important component to the prosecution's case when convicting David Westerfield, a 50-year-old engineer, of the murder of seven-year-old Danielle van Dam in San Diego, California [Republic01]. When computer forensics investigators examined the fixed disks of the computers seized in the case, they found catalogs of pornographic Web site addresses (URLs), but no child pornography to help establish a motive. When computer forensics investigators involved in the case processed a handful of removable disks (three Zip disks and three CD-ROMs) found concealed in an envelope on a bookshelf, they hit the jackpot. It was on these pieces of removable media that the child pornography used to help establish motive was found.

Removable media is often the method used for transporting intellectual property out of enterprises by employees. It is not uncommon to find during an intellectual property theft investigation that a stolen customer list or product plans were downloaded from company computer systems to USB key drives. For example, a recent investigation conducted by the author showed clear evidence that an employee suspected of intellectual property theft conducted extensive Internet research of USB key drives prior to purchasing one online. The research was conducted just prior to the employee leaving the company and being hired by a competitor. In the referenced case, a great deal of information was available on the former employee's desktop computer, but not all investigations are this fortunate. This type of scenario happens all too often and highlights the importance of removable media to computer forensics investigators.

TAPE SYSTEMS

Tape systems have been used by corporations and individual users alike to archive data for long-term storage and support the need for data recovery. The archiving habits of users can often be beneficial to forensics investigations. In the civil arena, nightly backups and long-term storage of the tapes (often offsite) can provide historical snapshots of several points in time. The ability to show the evolution of a directory or file's structure over a period of time can be quite useful in identifying specific changes. Consider a scenario where three snapshots in history were provided of a tape backup system. One data set from January shows the contents of a file to be a certain way. The second snapshot, from the February tape backups, shows the fileÕs contents had been changed to present a completely different meaning. Finally, the third snapshot from March shows the contents of the file in question to be changed back to its original meaning. Without the three snapshots in time, an investigator might not be able to show the temporary change to the file in question between January and March.

In the criminal arena, if a suspect has deleted files of evidentiary value, even in a secure manner, the files may still be available on the backup media. Often when people automate a backup process, they forget about the second copy located on tape. Although some users are moving toward using large disk systems as the target device for automated backup systems, the general principle remain the sameÑseveral snapshots in time may still be available.

Physical tape formats, as well as the format of any logical data contained on the tape, can vary and have changed over time. Some physical tape formats can be used for more than digital data storage for computers and may have been designed for something altogether different.

NOTE *The authorÕs first computer was a Radio Shack TRS-80 computer that could use a common cassette recorder to store programs. Of course, CD-ROMs for music and data are another example of physical media being used for two different purposes.*

Table 9.1 shows some of the more common tape formats still seen today and their capacities.

TABLE 9.1 Common Physical Tape Formats

Format	Capacity	Notes
DLT (Digital Liner Tape) III, DLT IV, DLT-1, and Super DLT tapes.	Up to 220 GB	Half-inch-wide tape cartridges; transfer rates of up to 300 MB/minute
LTO (Linear Tape Open) Ultrium and Accelis	Up to 200 GB	Developed jointly by HP, IBM, and Seagate; transfer rates of up to 20 MB per second
4mm DAT (Digital Audio Tape) format DDS, DDS-2, DDS-3, and DDS-4	Up to 40 GB	Transfer rates from 6 MB/minute to 150 MB/minute
Exabyte 8mm, 112m, and 160m tapes and Mammoth (Exabyte 8900)	Up to 40 GB	Transfer rates from 60 MB/minute to 80 MB/minute

→

Format	Capacity	Notes
Seagate AIT (Advanced Intelligent Tape) and AIT-2	Up to 100 GB	Transfer rates up to 360 MB/minute
Travan TR-1, TR-3, TR-4, and TR-5	Up to 20 GB	Transfer rates range from 30 MB/minute to 300 MB/minute
Iomega Ditto (QIC)	Up to 2 GB	Transfer rates range from 30 MB/minute to 300 MB/minute
QIC Mini-Cartridges DC2000-DC2120	Up to 250 MB	Transfer rates range from 30 MB/minute to 300 MB/minute

As with most technology, physical tape formats often enter the marketplace at a fairly high price, then gradually become more affordable as time passes, competition creates price pressures, and new technologies become available. This natural process of technological evolution ensures that forensics investigators will continue to see older technologies for some time to come. Because it is not always cost effective to convert legacy archival data to new systems, investigators will often find archive tapes in two or more physical formats and possibly several different logical tape file formats within organizations.

The logical tape media file format is independent of physical tape characteristics. That is, any given physical tape may contain one of many proprietary backup file formats. The number and types of backup file formats can make the forensic imaging as well as analysis process difficult at best. For this reason all but the largest computer forensics firms will often outsource the data conversion from tape to disk media to a reputable data recovery service that is familiar with the computer forensics process. The following list presents some of the more common tape backup-system file formats:

- Dantz® Retrospect for Macintosh
- Cheyenne/Computer Associates ARCserve for Windows NT® and NetWare
- Microsoft Tape Format (MTF) used in NT Backup and Seagate/VERITAS® BackupExec™ for Windows NT/2000, BackupExec for NetWare
- System Independent Data Format (SIDF) used in Novell Sbackup and Palindrome Backup Director
- Previos/Stac Replica Backup for NT and NetWare
- Legato® NetWorker™

- Unix TAR, CPIO, FBACKUP, FSDUMP, and UFSDUMP
- Compaq/DEC VMS Backup
- Intelliguard/Legato Budtool® used in Unix platforms
- Sytron/Seagate/VERITAS SYTOS & SYTOS Plus used in DOS, NetWare, and OS/2 operating systems

The previous list is only a sampling of the more popular proprietary backup tape formats.

Large and proprietary tape backup systems and the cost of their forensic recovery are not new to the civil discovery arena. In the landmark case *Zubulake v. UBS Warburg* [Zubulake01], the judge ordered UBS to restore five sample backup tapes and submit an affidavit attesting to the cost of the sampling. Because 600 additional e-mails from the sampling were identified as responsive, the judge further ordered that the remaining 77 backup tapes should be restored and reviewed at a cost of over $275,000.00. UBS was ordered to pay 75 percent of the cost to restore the remaining tapes and 100 percent of the cost for attorney review of the resulting e-mails from the tapes.

TIP

eMag Solutions (www.emaglink.com,) the manufacturer of tape backup management and conversion software, is a good reference for archive data-conversion software covering a wide range of logical formats [eMag01].

The archival nature of tape backup systems suggests large volumes of data. With tape format capacities ranging from the tens of gigabytes to only a few hundred gigabytes, multitape systems referred to as tape libraries or autoloaders are a must for organizations with large storage demands. Tape libraries or autoloaders, as the names suggest, are nothing more than robotic systems that manage the automatic loading and unloading of tape media into one or more single tape readers. Even when a single-tape system is used for archiving data, investigators will need to understand the backup methods in use as well as tape rotation schedule. As most investigators recognize, an autoloader can create and manage a complex tape-rotation scheme. A system administrator's approach to backup processes can drastically affect the data available on each tape within a given backup set. Although the following tape-rotation scheme descriptions can vary slightly from vender to vender, these descriptions will help a forensics investigator to better understand what tapes may be needed to obtain the complete digital picture.

Full Backup

A full backup will back up each directory and file identified for backup each time a backup process is scheduled. If a system administrator has scheduled a full backup of a data volume to tape every night, and each night he changes the tape or appends the new data to tape, each backup set contained on the tape will contain a complete set of files and directories from the selected volume. In a full backup, each file's archive bit setting is ignored during the backup process. This type of backup plan is the easiest for an administrator to restore and thus a forensics investigator to restore, but it requires the largest amount of backup tapes.

Incremental Backup

Incremental backup is used when the system administrator desires to back up only files that have changed since the last full backup or last incremental backup. Using this approach, the system administrator can use fewer tapes throughout the week by scheduling a full backup on Friday, then incremental backups during each day of the week. The drawback to this approach is that a restoration to the previous Friday's system state on a Wednesday could require tapes or backup sets from Saturday through Tuesday. In the incremental backup process all files with the archive bit set will be backed up, and the archive bit will be reset to off for all files archived.

Differential Backup

Performing a differential backup is helpful in cutting down the number of tapes or backup sets for a full restoration. When using the differential backup method, all files and directories that have changed since the last full backup are archived. Because every file and directory that has changed since the last full backup is always archived, the system administrator will only ever require two tapes or backup sets to restore the full system; the most recent differential backup and the most recent full backup. In the differential backup process, all files with the archive bit set will be backed up without changing the current bit setting.

CAUTION

Backup systems are intended to provide an archive of file system data, not disk media at the sector level. Because files and directories are normally all that are archived, there is no way to reconstruct or recover information contained in unallocated disk sectors or file slack from the original media when recovering backup data.

In Chapter 4, "Interview, Policy, and Audit," the importance of identifying corporate operational and security policies was highlighted. Understanding the tape rotation and backup plan as well as hardware and software in use can be critical to an investigator's ability to collect the proper media.

OPTICAL DISCS

Optical discs have moved from being an extravagant expense to almost a necessity over the past 10 years. The pervasiveness of writable optical discs and removable flash media discussed later in this chapter has truly meant the death of the floppy in computing today. The widespread ability to write to and save data on optical disc is what makes them of such interest to the forensics investigator.

CD-ROM optical discs differ from CD-R and CD-RW discs in that they do not have an organic dye recording layer between the polycarbonate substrate and the light reflective layer. It's the organic dye recording layer that allows the laser in a CD-R or CD-RW device to be heated and thus create a pit, which is in turn read as digital data. Figure 9.1 shows the physical differences between the two types of optical media.

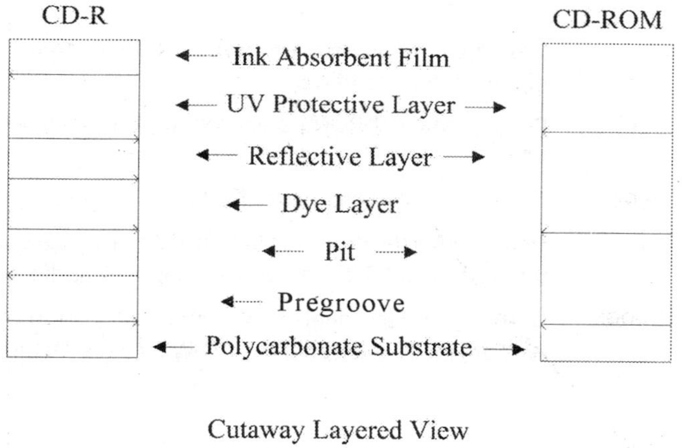

FIGURE 9.1 Differences between a CD-ROM and CD-R.

Investigators will sometimes ask, "Was that a blue CD or a gold CD?" when referring to the quality of a CD-R or CD-RW. The color referenced is the color appearance of the CD-R's underside and a combination of the reflection layer and the dye color. If the investigator saw what appeared to be a "green" CD-R, then the disc most likely contained a blue dye layer and gold reflection layer, causing the appearance of green.

Several types of dye material are used in CD-R and CD-RWs; however, the reflective layer is normally silver or gold. Materials used in the dye layer include the following:

Cyanine: Creates a green or blue/green appearance

Phthalocyanine: Creates a gold appearance
Metallized azo: Creates a dark blue appearance
Advanced phthalocyanine: Creates a gold appearance
Formazan: Creates a green/gold appearance [CDMedia01]

Generally speaking, gold discs provide the highest quality followed by blue, then green.

The physical characteristics of an optical disc described to this point are the basis of storing digital data on disc. To be useful as a data-storage medium, standards need to support common sector layouts and file systems that were not required for audio discs. Audio as well as data-storage standards for optical discs are published in the famous colored books, outlined in Table 9.2.

TABLE 9.2 CD and CD-ROM Colored Books [Deluxe01]

Red book	Describes the physical properties of the compact disc and its digital audio encoding
Yellow book	Provides the CD-ROM specification plus extensions for CD-ROM XA
White book	Defines the Video CD specification
Blue book	Defines specifications for Enhanced Music CD, sometimes referred to as CD Extra, which comprises audio and data sessions
Orange book	Defines CD-Recordable discs with multisession capability; CD-R was originally referred to as CD-WO (Write Once)`

In the yellow book investigators will find two types of sector layouts defined by the CD-ROM specification as Mode 1 and Mode 2. The Mode 1 sector layout is the most commonly used today. In Mode 1, fields are defined as surrounding user data to better support data storage on the CD-ROM data disc. Mode 1 fields include the Sync, Header, ECC, and EDC, as seen in Figure 9.2.

Sync	Header	User Data	EDC	Unused	ECC
12 bytes	4 bytes	2048 bytes	4 bytes	8 bytes	276 bytes

FIGURE 9.2 CD-ROM Mode 1.

The Sync field is used to allow players to identify the start of each sector. The Header file identifies total minutes, seconds, and sectors, and that the sector layout is in Mode 1. The EDC (Error Detection Code) field is used for error detection. The ECC (Error Correction Code) field provides added error protection and recovery.

Yellow book Mode 2 sector layout was designed for use in CD-ROM XA. Mode 2 sector layout is defined as either Form 1 or 2, as seen in Figure 9.3. CD-ROM XA was created to provide support for simultaneous audio and video playback. Although not widely successful in its original design, the CD-ROM XA format was the basis of several other graphics-oriented optical disc formats, including the Photo CD, Video CD, and CD Extra. The subheader in Mode 2 CD-ROMs contains content-related parameters with all other field use maintaining the same format as Mode 1. Because Mode 2 Form 2 CD-ROMs do not provide for ECC, they are useful only for data types that can cover up errors, such as audio or video.

Sync	Header	Subheader	User Data	EDC	ECC
12 bytes	4 bytes	8 bytes	2048 bytes	4 bytes	276 bytes

Mode 2 *Form 1*

Sync	Header	Subheader	User Data	EDC
12 bytes	4 bytes	8 bytes	3234 bytes	4 bytes

Mode 2 *Form 2*

FIGURE 9.3 CD-ROM Mode 2.

NOTE

The Phillips Intellectual Property and Technical Specifications Web site at www.licensing.philips.com is a great reference for optical disc technical specifications [Philips01].

A 76-minute, 30-second CD-ROM contains a total of 336,300 sectors, of which only about 336,100 are available for user data due to overhead, such as the file systems. To identify the total data-storage capability, an investigator would multiply the total sectors available by the bytes available for user data in that mode. Therefore, a Mode 1 CD-ROM could contain 2048 x 336,100 = 688,332,800 bytes.

To be useful for data storage, an optical disc needs a file system readable by the underlying computer's operating system. Although many CD file systems exist today, the most common include ISO 9660, ISO 9660 with Joliet extensions to support long filenames, and HFS (Hierarchical Filing System) for Apple Macintosh support. The M-UDF (Micro Universal Disk Format) had been adopted for use in DVD media because of its ability to support writable, rewritable, and read-only media.

Interestingly, optical discs can contain several file systems similar to magnetic fixed-disk systems. These multifile system discs, referred to as hybrid systems (supporting both PC and Macintosh platforms), contain both the ISO 9660 with Joliet extensions and HFS file systems. In these hybrid discs, the ISO 9660 data is presented first with a pointer to the HFS data in the first 16 sectors.

DVDs were originally referred to as Digital Video Disk but more recently have been dubbed the Digital Versatile Disk. DVDs offer a great improvement in storage capabilities, with 4.7 GB to 17.1 GB, depending on the disk. The technical specifications for DVDs can be found in five different books referenced by their letter designations, A to E, and published by the DVD Forum. The forum can be located on the Web at *www.dvdforum.org [DVD01]*.

The five DVD forum books follow:

Book A: DVD-ROM

Book B: DVD-Video

Book C: DVD-Audio

Book D: DVD-R

Book E: DVD-RAM and RW

Each of the DVD Forum books includes three sections outlining the physical characteristics, supported file systems, and intended application of the disc type.

The sector layout for DVD differs from the standard CD-ROM sector layout as depicted in Figure 9.4.

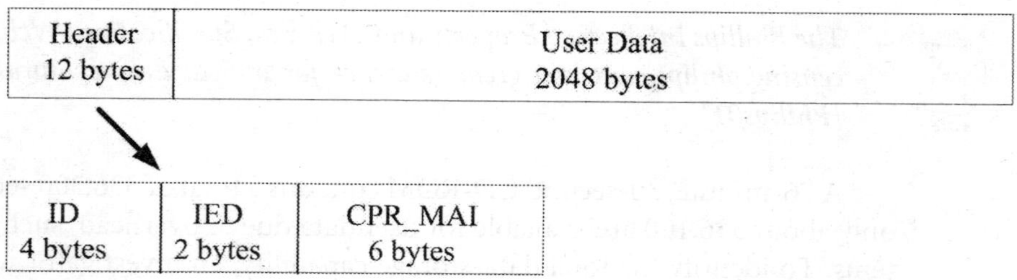

FIGURE 9.4 DVD sector layout.

As seen in Figure 9.4, the 12-byte sector header is divided into three fields: ID, IED, and CPR_MAI. The ID field provides the sector type, data type, layer number, and sector number, whereas the IED holds error-correction code, and the CPR_MAI provides copy protection and region code for use in DVD-Video. Also unique to the DVD is the Burst Cutting Area (BCA), which provides the ability to place a barcode within the disc's hub. The BCA is intended to provide additional information such as serial numbers and other media-tracking information.

Already the standard sizes available to the original DVD specifications are considered less useful, driving the need for yet larger optical discs. To answer this need a group of electronics companies including Hitachi, LG®, Matsushita®, Pioneer®, Philips®, Samsung, Sharp®, Sony®, Thomson®, Mitsubishi®, Dell, and HP joined together in supporting Blu-ray. The new Blu-ray disc specification provides for disk capacity of 27 GB per layer. Though it is hard to say if the Blu-ray standard will be successful, the increased capabilities are encouraging. Other companies such as Toshiba and NEC® have backed formats such as HD DVD, originally called AOD (Advanced Optical Disc). HD DVD allows for differing size capabilities, depending on whether the disc was prewritten, rewritable, or write once. The sizes are 15, 20, and 15 GB, respectively. No matter if one of the two new DVD formats, or some yet unknown format, succeeds, it is clear that newer, larger-capacity optical discs are just around the corner. As with most media these larger-capacity optical discs can be bittersweet for the computer investigator. Larger discs help computer forensics investigators with their own data storage and archiving needs. The same large-capacity discs can also prove time-consuming and challenging when the investigator is processing them as evidence.

REMOVABLE DISKS—FLOPPY AND RIDGED

Over the years removable disks have provided users with security and incremental data storage capabilities. Compartmentalizing information made sense because a user may want to keep certain files in one place and others in another. Of course, the added security of being able to physically secure the removable disk in a locked file cabinet or safe was an easy sell. Although these compelling arguments remain today, the removable optical disc mentioned earlier and flash media mention, discussed later in this chapter, have gained greater favor. Still, investigators can be sure to run across the proverbial floppy or other removable magnetic disk media of some type.

Many proprietary disks exist in many sizes, but the most common floppy disk still in use today is the 3.5-inch floppy. Despite its ridged outer plastic shell, the disk media itself is still pliable, much like the earlier 5.25-inch floppies. Floppy disks use tracks and sectors organized in concentric rings, much like the physical disk media described in Chapter 7, "Physical Disk Technologies." Floppy disks use a thin, plastic base material coated with iron oxide, rather than a rigid platter. The oxide coating is known as a ferromagnetic material, meaning that when a portion of the coating is exposed to a magnetic field, that section of coating is permanently magnetized by the field. Many users attempt to destroy a floppy disk by cutting the disk into pieces to render the disk unreadable. Because the data is actually stored on the magnetic properties of the disk, many cut floppies can still be recovered. Repairing a cut floppy disk can be as simple as taping the disk back together with a thin cellophane tape, which still allows disk track heads to read the magnetic properties.

The pliable nature of floppies has limited their overall data storage capabilities, generating the need for removable disks with greater storage. To answer this need, manufactures created removable rigid disks with larger capacities suitable for graphics, audio, and large file archives that needed to be transported or stored securely. Although many proprietary rigid removable disk systems exist, the most popular included those from Iomega®, Syquest®, and Bernoulli®. Table 9.3 shows some of the more popular removable disk systems (not including optical discs) and their storage capabilities.

TABLE 9.3 Removable Disks

Disk Type	Storage Capability
3.5-inch high-capacity floppy disk—LS-120 and LS-240(SuperDisk) and HIFD-200	120 MB to 240 MB
5.25-inch Bernoulli disk	44 MB, 90 MB, 105 MB, 150 MB, and 230 MB
Iomega Jaz disk	1 GB and 2 GB
Iomega PocketZip (Clik!) disk	40 MB
Iomega Zip disk	100 MB, 250 MB, and 750 MB
Syquest disk cartridge	Ezflyer135 and 230 MB
	SyJet 1.5 GB
	SparQ 1 GB

Although optical discs and flash media have become more popular among users than their magnetic counterparts, investigators will undoubtedly run across removable disks such as those listed in Table 9.3 from time to time.

FLASH MEDIA

Flash memory can be described in two broad categories—memory that requires an electrical charge to maintain its state, such as that used in PDAs and cellular phones; and flash memory media, which maintains its state without an electrical charge. The first type of flash memory used in cellular phones and PDAs allows much faster input and output and is covered in Chapter 6, "Volatile Data." This chapter focuses on the second type of flash memory—flash media cards—which is static in nature.

Although optical media has gained great favor among users for long-term data storage, flash media in its various shapes and sizes is the undisputed leader for temporary data storage and transfer. Many of the early flash memory chips were large in physical form and small in data-storage capabilities. As with many technologies that adhere to Moore's law (see Chapter 8, "SAN, NAS, and RAID"), flash media has grown significantly in storage capacity and reduced in physical size.

Figure 9.5 shows a common early-use flash media card used in cameras and digital audio players. Figure 9.6 shows one of today's smaller flash memory cards.

FIGURE 9.5 An MMC card.

FIGURE 9.6 An xD Picture Card.

One of the greatest factors contributing to the widespread use of flash media is its small size and ease of use. Most computers today provide USB connectors, which can directly accept flash key drives or connect a flash memory adaptor, as shown in Figure 9.7.

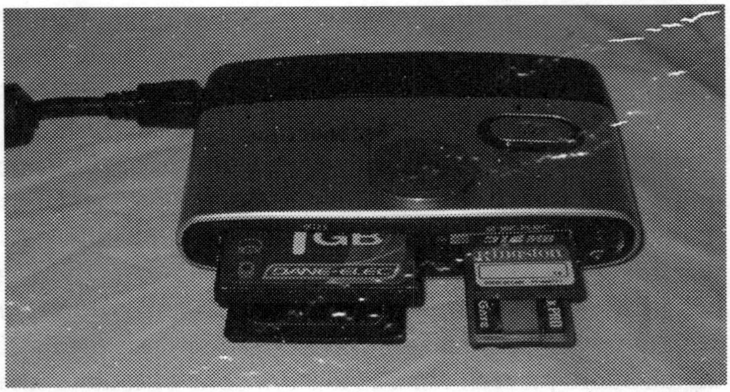

FIGURE 9.7 A flash memory adapter connected to a PC.

Table 9.4 shows some of the flash memory cards in use today and their current capacities. When noting capacity, investigators will remember that Moore's law dictates an almost doubling of capacity over 18 months or more.

TABLE 9.4 Common Flash Memory Cards

Media Type	Current Capacity
Secure Digital (SD)	Up to 2 GB
CompactFlash™ (CF)	Up to 8 GB
SmartMedia™ (SM)	Up to 128 MB
Memory Stick (MS)	Up to 5 GB
MultiMediaCard (MMC) (same physical form as SD Cards)	Up to 256 MB
xD Picture Card (xD)™	Up to 8 GB

The technical specifications can change significantly between flash media cards, but to the user they are all plug-and-play systems. Most operating systems current versions allow for hot-plug and autoconfiguration. The ease of use, small size, and pervasive nature of flash media cards has made these devices a focal point for computer forensics investigators. Flash media cards can hold large amounts of data and be easily concealed by the user either on their person or in common devices such as cellular phones, cameras, audio players, and hybrid devices. Many newer TVs include flash media readers to allow users to display photographs.

One of the best places to hide something is in plain site. Who would expect a flash media card in a camera to actually hold data files containing the designs to a company's latest intellectual property? More and more cellular phones are becoming hybrid devices capable of accepting flash media cards for storage of pictures, audio, and other data. To protect intellectual property many companies have gone so far as to fill USB and FireWire ports in computers with epoxy. Although this may seem like extraordinary efforts, the direct memory access capabilities of FireWire make it a real danger in regard to providing direct access to the computer's peripherals, such as hard disk and physical memory.

Recent developments have fallen outside Moore's law and show staggering storage capabilities when compared to the storage capacities shown in Table 9.4. In December 2004, the Industrial Technology Research Institute of Taiwan announced a new flash media specification for the "μcard," with the capabilities of storing 2 TB—that's 2048 GB of data [Lam01]. As a point of reference, the entire e-mail database for a medium-size company with approximately 400 user accounts will occupy about 50 GB. At the time of this writing, mass production had not yet begun on the μcard; however, working models had been displayed by the MU-Card Alliance, generating a great deal of interest among industry professionals. The specifications were expected to be finalized in February 2005. MU-Card prototypes and initial specification called for 20 pin cards in two physical formats resembling MultiMedia Card and a microsize card measuring 24×18×1.4mm.

SUMMARY

- Evidence may be limited either to a small number of documents on removable disk found at the scene or a single fragment of data on a removable flash drive.
- Understanding how to identify and process removable media can be critical to many investigations.
- Removable media is often the method used by employees for transporting intellectual property out of enterprises.
- The archiving habits of users can often be beneficial to forensics investigations.
- Because it is not always cost-effective to convert legacy archival data to new systems, investigators will often find archive tapes in two or more physical formats and possibly several different logical tape file formats within organizations.
- Generally speaking, gold CD discs provide the highest quality, followed by blue then green.

- CD-ROM optical discs differ from CD-R and CD-RW discs in that they do not have an organic dye recording layer between the polycarbonate substrate and the light-reflective layer.
- Many CD file systems exist today. the most common being ISO 9660, ISO 9660 with Joliet extensions to support long filenames, and HFS (Hierarchical Filing System) for Apple Macintosh support.
- The technical specifications for DVDs can be found in five different books referenced by their letter designations A to E, published by the DVD Forum.
- Some of the most popular rigid disks were those from Iomega, Syquest, and Bernoulli.
- More and more often, cellular phones are becoming hybrid devices capable of accepting flash media cards for storage of pictures, audio, and other data.

REFERENCES

[CDMedia01] CD Media World Web site, available online at *http://cdmedia-world.com/hardware/cdrom/cd_dye.shtml#CD%20Structure*, 2004.

[Deluxe01] Deluxe Global Media Services Ltd. Web site, available online at *www.disctronics.co.uk/technology/cd-rom/cdrom_formats.htm*, 2005.

[Dvd01] The DVD Forum Web site, available online at *www.dvdforum.org*, 2005.

[eMag01] eMag Solutions Company Web site, available online at *www.emaglink.com*, 2005.

[Lam01] Lam, Esther, "Mu-Card Alliance's new 2-terabyte 'μcard' ready to go!," DigiTimes.com, available online at *www.digitimes.com*, December 2004.

[Philips01] Phillips Intellectual Property and Technical Specifications Web site, available online at *www.licensing.philips.com*, 2005.

[Republic01] Balint, Kathryn, "Police Comb Digital Files in Pursuit of Evidence," *Free Republic*, available online at *http://freerepublic.com/focus/news/652576/posts*, March 2002.

[Zubulake01] *Zubulake v. UBS Warburg LLC*, 216 F.R.D. 280 (S.D.N.Y. 2003).

RESOURCES

[DFLLC01] The DVD Format/Logo and Licensing Corporation Web site, available online at *www.dvdfllc.co.jp*, 2005.

[Digitimes01] DigiTimes IT Daily News Web site, available online at *www.digitimes.com/print/a20041231PR204.html*, 2005.

[Leber01] Lebel, Jody, *Windows NT Backup & Restore*, O'Reilly & Associates, 1998.

[StevesDigiCams01] Steve's DigiCams Web site, available online at *www.steves-digicams.com/flash_memory.html*, 2004.

Part IV Artifact Collection

The methods employed for the collection of computer evidence can be one of the most highly scrutinized areas of the computer forensics process. It is essential that investigators use tested and proven methodologies and tools during this task. Part IV, "Artifact Collection," provides detailed procedures for artifact collection as well as a discussion about an array of tools available for digital evidence collection. In Part IV, investigators are shown the importance of collecting volatile data in addition to static data on disk. Single systems and large-scale evidence collection methodologies are discussed.

10 Tools, Preparation, and Documentation

In This Chapter

- Planning
- Boilerplates
- Hardware and Software Tools
- Tool Testing
- Documentation

PLANNING

In this, our final chapter prior to the actual collection of digital evidence, investigators will be introduced to planning and organizational skills to assist in tool selection for each operation. Many time-honored sayings can be attributed to the need for thoughtful planning and preparation. One such saying comes to mind—the seven Ps of planning, which state: "proper prior planning prevents particularly poor performance." The importance of planning in computer forensics operations cannot be overemphasized for many obvious, and not-so-obvious, reasons. Because each computer forensics collection operation can vary so greatly, investigators will need to have a playbook from which to operate, similar to what a sports team coach would use to contain all the plays he intend to use. Another analogy is the IMF Binder (Impossible Mission Taskforce) from the television show *Mission*

Impossible, where a team leader can select the proper people and tools for each job prior to launching the team.

Many computer forensics investigators refer to computer forensics digital-evidence collection operations as *black bag* operations and the collection team as a *flyaway* team. As the IMF Binder analogy suggests, there may be many different black bags and countless possibilities for the flyaway team member composition. No matter what analogy is used, the playbook or IMF Binder will help the team leader select the right bag and proper team composition for each operation.

BOILERPLATES

One of the difficulties in creating boilerplates to guide any type of operation is they must be general enough to be useful in a wide array of situations but detailed enough to be helpful. Many forensics investigators are hesitant to create standard operating procedures (SOP), boilerplates, and other guiding directives because they fear that if they do not follow them, they will be impeached at trial with the ever-painful: "Investigator name, I have here your SOP, which states you should have done X, but you did Y. Can you explain your disregard for procedure?" The solution to this fear, as alluded to earlier, is to generalize the level of detail and to publish guidelines to assist in decision making, not to act as a step-by-step solution when you may not know the problem. Boilerplates, templates, questionnaires, and sometimes even decision trees can be useful in creating the right level of guidelines or playbook for the team. A computer forensics investigator's playbook may include the following:

Introduction: This section describes the book's purpose and use and includes basic principles of evidence collection and handling prescribed by your organization. Examples of such guidelines can be obtained from the International Organization on Computer Evidence (IOCE) [Ioce01], International Association of Computer Investigative Specialists (IACIS) [Iacis01], or High-Tech Crime Investigation Association (HTCIA) [Htcia01].

Flyaway team and equipment decision matrix: This section guides the selection of personnel and equipment based on the type of job from upfront knowledge of the collection environment.

Personnel roster: This section includes contact information, skills, and availability for each team member.

Outside support personnel contact information: In this section are included technical vendor contacts for common hardware and software, consultants, organizational security contacts such as Internet service providers (ISP), and communication carriers such as cellular phones.

Black bag inventories: The inventories in this section allow investigators to quickly determine if any additional equipment will be needed, based on known information prior to the operation. In organizations with several differently configured black bags, investigators will be able to choose the proper bag for the proper operation.

Forms: This section includes the following forms:

- IT procedures questionnaire (See Chapter 4, "Interview, Policy, and Audit")
- Evidence collection inventory
- Original media access log
- Chain of custody forms
- Warrant and consent templates
- IT security audit questionnaire
- Physical security questionnaire
- Blank interview forms

ON THE CD

Sample forms are provided in the appendices and on the accompanying CD-ROM to assist investigators in creating their playbook.

HARDWARE AND SOFTWARE TOOLS

In Chapter 2, "Rules of Evidence, Case Law, and Regulation," investigators learned the importance of tool selection and their relationship to evidence admission in court. Peer review and testing of hardware and software used in the collection of digital evidence are of the highest importance. However, the investigator is still responsible for testing and understanding the tools (software and hardware). Furthermore, information technology innovation advances at a tremendous rate, requiring investigators to be constantly vigilant for new tools, for some of which no peer reviews may exist. Criminals are always coming up with new ways to use technology in crime, which can cause a forensics investigator to repurpose tools for computer forensics needs. This constant change again drives home the need for individual investigators to understand and test their own tools in a controlled environment.

The number of tools, both hardware and software, needed for computer forensics can be endless. This chapter will focus on some of the more common tools in use today. A wider list of tools is provided in Appendix F, "Forensics Tools for Digital Evidence Collection," for further reference.

Much of the hardware used in the computer forensics process today is made up of standard, off-the-shelf components used throughout the information technology industry. The variation of computer systems encountered by forensics investigators requires them to be knowledgeable about many types of architectures. Not only will investigators need to be conversant in the many storage architectures mentioned in previous chapters, they will need connectors, adapters, and cables that allow access to these technologies. Investigators will forever find the need to add yet another adapter for a new disk connector to their black bag. The CS Electronics Web site [Cs01] is a good starting place on the Web for forensics investigators to find many specialized adapters and cables.

Imagers and Write Blocking

Disk or media duplication is at the core of the computer forensics process. One of the driving forces behind the desire to duplicate original evidence disk is the volatile nature of disk data coupled with the destructive potential of examination tools. As previously mentioned, forensics investigators will often need to repurpose software and hardware tools for the forensics process. When attempting to use a file-recovery utility that was not created with the computer forensics concept of preservation in mind, it quickly becomes apparent how useful an extra copy of the original evidence may be. In certain situations, even tools that were created with the computer forensics process in mind may be somewhat destructive. For instance, many software tools that are designed to remove the Host Protected Area hard disk (see Chapter 7, "Physical Disk Technologies,") actually make subtle but permanent changes to the physical media. If an investigator did not expect or could not justify this type of change, it would always be helpful to be able to revert back to the original media, essentially gaining a "do-over." The ability to recover from expected or unexpected tool changes, investigator mistakes, and the general volatile nature of disk media all drive the need for the duplication of original media. Considering the ever-increasing size of data sets being seized, an extra copy or two also allows multiple investigators to work on evidence at the same time. Understanding the benefits of having a duplicate of the original media was only half the battle for early computer forensics investigators. If analysis was to be performed on a copy of the original media, how could the copy be certified to contain the same data as the original? Standard operating system commands and standard "ghosting" would only copy file data. Information in the low-level sectors on disk (allocated to partitions or not) can be valuable in recovering deleted files or, in their own right, making the loss of this information unacceptable. The answer was to create a sector-by-sector copy from the original disk to the target disk, ensuring that any additional sectors on the target disk in excess of the original disk media-sector count would be written with a known data pattern, so as not to contaminate the analysis data. Add in additional considerations for how error recovery is handled during the sector read and sector write, and we have a basis of what is still in use today, commonly referred to as a bit-stream image.

Luckily for forensics investigators, like many of their needs, the need to duplicate a disk was not new to the information technology industry; disk duplicators had been around for some time. There were, however, a few needs associated with disk duplication that were unique to the bit-stream imaging process. In keeping with the iterative preservation phase of the computer forensics process, investigators wanted not only to ensure that no information was written to original evidence media during the imaging process but also to be able to verify that the original evidence was not changed after the imaging process. For this, tool manufactures who had made the standard disk imagers in use by information technology professionals needed to incorporate a disk imager with integrity verification and write blocking. Disk media imaging and write blocking are still the primary hardware tools used by computer forensics professionals today.

CAUTION

Due to the number of components (BIOS, DMA PCI Cards, and so on) that can send write commands to disks prior to an operating system loading, it is considered a best practice to use hardware write blocking when reasonable to prevent any accidental writing to a disk when imaging via a direct connection.

Three leading manufactures of disk-imaging and write-blocking tools are MyKey Technologies [Mykey01], Intelligent Computer Solutions® (ICS) [Ics01], and Logicube® [Logicube01]. Each of these manufactures has been dedicated to providing innovative solutions to computer forensics investigators for some time. In fact, MyKey Technologies makes tools used only in the computer forensics process. Each company provides an array of features and products that many would consider essential tools for the computer forensics investigator. Because of the wide array of disk specification and manufactures, it is advisable to have several tools of different types. Differences in disk media may require a different approach or tool during collection. Investigators will find situations where only one of three similarly purposed tools may get the job done. Notably, each company manufactures hardware disk imagers with write blocking built in and separate hardware write blockers for use when investigators are using another type of imaging process, such as software imaging.

One of the first forensics imagers manufactured by Logicube was the Forensics SF-5000™ imager. A newer version, the Forensics MD5™, is shown in Figure 10.1. Both imagers are designed to be lightweight handheld units that house internally a target IDE evidence disk. When using the Logicube handheld units, the original evidence disk can be connected externally via a direct IDE connection, an IDE-to-USB converter, or a CloneCard™ Pro PCMCIA adapter for capturing notebook computer hard disks. The CloneCard and accompanying boot disk software are particularly useful for imaging notebook computers without cracking the case. One nice feature of the Logicube products when purchased in a kit is rugged, hardened plastic carrying case in which the kit is housed and the variety of accessories that come with it. One of the advantages of the newly introduced Forensic MD5 are its hashing capabilities and removable compact flash disk for storing keyword lists, which allows for live file searching during the imaging process. The Forensics MD5 is also distinguishable from the SF-5000 by its thumb keyboard located on the face-plate, which is used for data entry. One feature Logicube recently added to the Forensics MD5 is also becoming quite common among other handheld disk imagers—the ability to create a Unix-style "dd" image in addition to the standard disk-to-disk image. Logicube, like other computer-forensics-focused hardware manufactures, also makes a variety of standalone hardware write blockers.

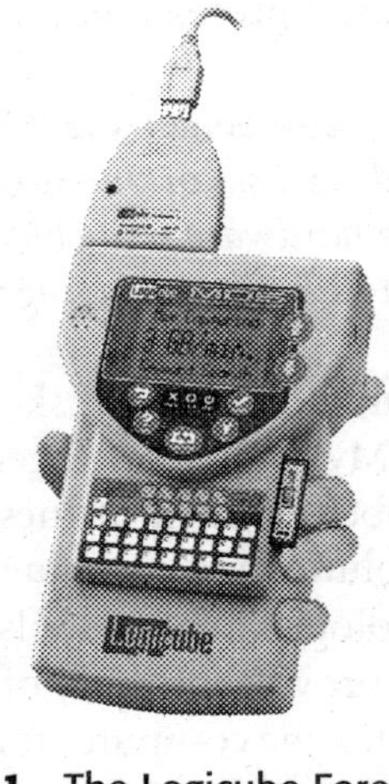

FIGURE 10.1 The Logicube Forensic MD 5.

©Logicube, Inc. 2005.

ICS is another hardware manufacture with a complete computer forensics product line. One of its early products for handheld forensics imaging was the SoloMaster™ Forensics. There are currently three models of the SoloMaster Forensics, with each providing a wide array of features and benefits to the computer forensic practitioner. The original SoloMaster is similar to Logicube's SF-5000, in physical design and abilities, but notably includes the added ability to use an Adaptec SCSI PC card to capture SCSI evidence drives. All target disks are expected to be IDE. The latest ICS handheld imager, the SoloForensics III, shown in Figure 10.2, is a very small form factor imager with the ability to image a single evidence disk to two target disks simultaneously, among other useful features.

FIGURE 10.2 The ICS Solo Forensics III.

As with Logicube, ICS sells a complete line of hardware write blockers, which they call the DriveLock™. ICS is the manufacturer of the Fast Block write blocker for Guidance Software [Guidance01], who manufacture EnCase computer forensics software. In addition to handheld computer forensics imagers and write blockers, ICS also manufactures and sells a wide assortment of disk format converters and adapters useful for the imaging of nonstandard disks, such as those found in proprietary notebook computers. A somewhat recent innovation in computer forensics is the creation of branded portable computer-forensics workstations that provide external native connectors for many different media such as IDE, SCSII, SATA, and flash media. These portable forensics workstations also provide the computing power to allow investigators to perform on-site analysis functions while collecting evidence. The ICS product providing these capabilities is the Road MASSter™ portable forensics workstation.

MyKey Technology is unique in that they manufacture only computer forensics products. The MyKey Technology DriveCopy™ is an easy-to-use standalone drive imager with built-in write blocking designed to provide one-switch imaging. An optional thermal printer is available for the DriveCopy, allowing investigators to print reports containing disks, model number, S/N number, firmware, size, max speed, and configuration as well as the drive's feature set. Reports can be printed for evidence source and target disks. Reports are static and also include the results of the imaging process along with a report of any bad sectors encountered.

As with ICS and Logicube, MyKey Technology also manufactures several write blockers for IDE disks. MyKey Technology was the first manufacturer to create a hardware write blocker specifically created to write-block flash disk media. The use of standard IDE hardware write blockers to protect flash media has been less than successful; flash media devices are ATAPI devices, which require a communications exchange with the media controller. The MyKey Technologies FlashBlock™, seen in Figure 10.3, includes hardware write blocking with a built-in multiformat flash media reader. The NoWrite™, their original write blocker, has several notable features including volatile access to the hardware Protected Area of a disk. NoWrite was designed to be fail-safe, in that all failures prohibit any writes to the evidence drive. MyKey Technology calls this safety mechanism Absolute Write Blocking™.

FIGURE 10.3 The MyKey Technology FlashBlock.

IDE disks are more popular among PC users, and thus, more support exists for the imaging of IDE disks than their corporate counterpart, the SCSI disk. The ICS ImageMASSter line of products offers an SCSI option, but overall there are far fewer dedicated hardware forensics products available that address the needs of SCSI imaging. Corporate Systems Center [Corpsys01] makes a good, low-cost SCSI-to-IDE imaging system for general imaging that includes a forensics mode, allowing for write blocking, logging, and secure disk wiping. Corporate Systems Center also manufactures the Portable Pro Drive™ workstation for service, test, and duplication. The Portable Pro Drive workstation provides many additional features allowing investigators to image, test, and repair a wide assortment of drive combinations.

NOTE

Standalone hardware write blockers are of great use to investigators when using a portable computer forensics workstations (notebook or otherwise). Many computer forensics investigators use these specialized forensics workstations to conduct in-the-field forensics disk preview and imaging using forensics software installed on the workstation.

Two other companies that make standalone hardware write blockers worth noting are ACARD [Acard01] and Digital Intelligence, Inc. [Digitalintel01]. ACARD provides a low-cost method of hardware write blocking called the ACARD SCSI-to-IDE Write Blocking Bridge (AEC7720WP), shown in Figure 10.4. The ACARD SCSI-to-IDE bridge allows investigators who have an SCSI controller built into their computer forensics workstations to add a write-blocked IDE bay. Because the ACARD is an open circuit card, it is best suited for internal uses such as a non-portable forensics workstation. Computer forensics workstations are discussed in detail in Chapter 14, "The Forensics Workstation."

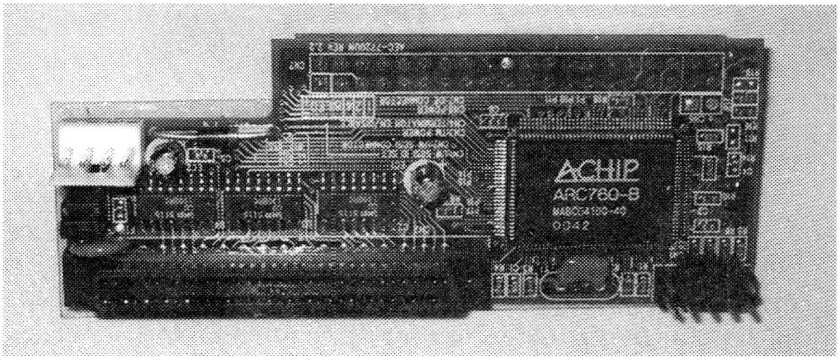

FIGURE 10.4 The ACARD SCSI-to-IDE Write Blocking Bridge.

Digital Intelligence, Inc., who also manufactures a complete line of forensics workstations, makes the FireFly™ write blocker. The FireFly is a compact hardware-based write blocker that allows an IDE hard disk to be connected to system via an IEEE 1394 FireWire-to-IDE converter that has also been write-blocked. Digital Intelligence also markets a kit containing various write blockers, which includes capabilities for SCSI and IDE write blocking.

Many times the challenge of imaging an evidence disk or media is the connection to that media. The USB and FireWire standards discussed in Chapter 9, "Removable Media," have widened the capabilities for connecting to storage media. The approach incorporated in FireFly for integrating a write-blocked FireWire-to-IDE converter has benefited computer users in many ways. Today, computer users everywhere are finding an assortment of FireWire-to-IDE and USB-to-IDE connectors, shown in Figure 10.5, to allow quick, easy connection to, or expansion of, disk media.

CAUTION

When using USB-to-IDE converters to examine or image disk media, investigators should ensure they use USB 2.0-rated devices because the lower USB 1.1 speeds are rarely acceptable for such work.

FIGURE 10.5 USB-to-IDE converter.

A wide array of useful FireWire-to-IDE and USB-to-IDE connectors are available. Some provide the conversion to IDE built into the cable, and others include disk enclosures with or without removable drive bays. It is often helpful to purchase an assortment of these devices for use in forensics image collection, along with independent write blocking devices. A quick Google [Google01] search for "FireWire-to-IDE" or "USB-to-IDE" will surely return many desirable products to help keep an investigator's black bag well stocked.

Software

Software used for the collection and preservation of computer evidence usually falls into one of three broad categories—Forensics Application Suite, Utility, and Other.

Forensics Application Suite

In this category applications are created specifically with computer forensics in mind and usually support all four phases of the computer forensics process: collection, preservation, filtering, and reporting.

Utility

Applications in the Utility category are designed to perform a specific function, such as recover deleted files, remove the Host Protected Area of a disk, or create a disk image. Utility applications used in computer forensics may or may not be created specifically for forensics use. In many situations utilities are repurposed for the forensics process, such as graphic file recovery utilities and hex editors.

Other

The Other category is a catch-all category and often includes full-blown applications used to interpret, represent, or convert data for presentation. Applications in the Other category are often repurposed applications used in the forensics process, such as QuickBooks® being used by a forensics investigator to display a processed view of a QuickBooks data file.

As a forensics investigator may well imagine, there is no end to the applications in the Utilities and Other categories that could be repurposed for the computer forensics process. Indeed, rarely does an investigator completely process a case without needing some new utility or application to display proprietary data. This chapter focuses on providing background on some of the most common forensics application suites and utilities used in computer forensics. The computer forensics investigator will continually be exploring, testing, and adding new utilities and applications to his toolbox.

Forensics Application Suites

As with most broad categories, forensics applications suites can be further defined as Windows-based tools and Unix-based tools. For the purposes of this discussion, Macintosh-based tools can be included with the Unix-based tools because Mac OS X is based on the BSD UNIX variant.

The leaders of the Windows-based computer forensics suites are ProDiscover, EnCase, and the AccessData® FTK® (Forensics Tool Kit). Although all three tools approach the integration of forensics imaging, analysis, and reporting in different ways, they all support full-range computer forensics processes. That is not to say that any one tool, or all three, will be all any computer forensics investigator ever needs. As already mentioned, there is no end to the need for specialized hardware and software tools to get the job done. In addition, each of the tools discussed in this section has its own strengths and weaknesses, which will be evident in different cases processed by investigators.

Notably the Windows-based forensics application suite ILook [Ilook01] was intentionally omitted from this chapter because the tool is available only to law enforcement users. Although ILook was originally developed as a commercial application, the product—intellectual property and all—was purchased by the criminal investigations division of the U.S. Internal Revenue Service. ILook is now maintained and made available only to law enforcement agencies.

NOTE

A concept common to all disk forensics application suites is the ability to create a disk image file in addition to, or instead of, a disk-to-disk image. A disk image file offers several benefits. When an original evidence disk is imaged to a file, the investigator can maintain several evidence images on a single "large" disk. The investigator no longer needs to be concerned about disk-size differences when imaging from disk to disk. Subsequent analysis of a disk image is normally faster than analyzing an image of the original disk. Metadata can be included with the disk image to track elements such as the collection time, the hash value of the original image for integrity-verification purposes, image collection error logging, and so on. Although some imaging tools that write to an image file include this metadata, some do not. The Unix "dd" command for disk imaging, for instance, does not include any metadata surrounding or imbedded in the image. An interesting paper by Mark Scott of the Memphis Technology group titled "Independent Review of Common Forensics Imaging Tools" [Scott01] defines the difference in the two disk-imaging formats as Bit Copy and Bit Copy Plus, where the Bit Copy image does not include any metadata and the Bit Copy Plus does. Both approaches of image-to-file have been widely accepted, but the Unix "dd" format is the most widely accessible from tools today.

ProDiscover [Techpath01], developed by Technology Pathways in late 2001, is available in several different application versions, with features specifically tailored for specific forensics needs. The current ProDiscover product line consists of ProDiscover for Windows, ProDiscover Forensics, ProDiscover Investigator, and ProDiscover Incident Response. One of the most prominent differences between the four current products is that the ProDiscover Investigator and ProDiscover Incident Response versions include the capability to conduct live analysis and imaging of disk or physical memory over TCP/IP networks. The ProDiscover for Windows and ProDiscover Forensics products are designed for forensics workstation use and do not include network capabilities.

All editions of ProDiscover allow the user to collect computer disk evidence in a variety of ways, including disk-to-disk bit-stream images and disk-to-image file-bit-stream images. Users can also directly and in a read-only fashion view directly connected disks. When using ProDiscover Incident Response and Investigator versions, users have the same abilities with remote systems over any TCP/IP network.

The ProDiscover image format is a metaformat (bit copy plus), including a collection of information in the header such as time zone, investigator name, compression, and hash values. An imaging-process error log is provided in a trailer. ProDiscover collects the disk image similar to the Unix "dd" command, then places header information in front of the image with case and investigator information, and places a log file at the end of the image with any I/O errors encountered during collection. Because the ProDiscover image format is similar to the Unix "dd" command, ProDiscover can read images in "dd" format and export its images to "dd" format for use with other tools. ProDiscover can also collect the original image in the "dd" format.

Figure 10.6 shows the ProDiscover Incident Response edition console connected to a remote system with two RAID volumes in a Windows NTFS dynamic disk set. Like the other forensics application suites discussed, ProDiscover allows the investigator to perform an array of common forensic tasks in addition to previewing and imaging, such as searching for keywords, checking for file type extension mismatches, and viewing data in cluster slack space. ProDiscover Forensics edition and later editions allow investigators to use Perl scripting to analyze, export, and report on evidence disks.

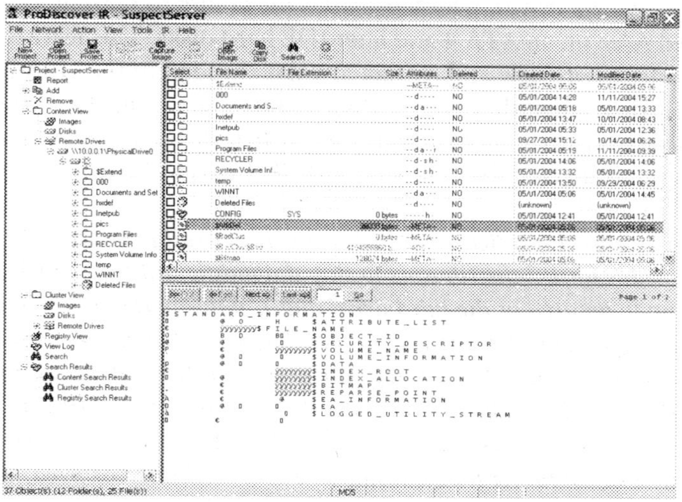

FIGURE 10.6 The ProDiscover Incident Response console.

ProDiscover offers an easy way to perform remote disk imaging and live disk analysis using a remote agent. By placing the remote agent in the CD-ROM, floppy, or USB slot of the target system, an agent will automatically run in memory and allow the investigator to connect via the console over the TCP/IP LAN or WAN. During the connection, all session setup information is passed using 256-bit TwoFish encryption, and globally unique identifiers are set up on both sides of the connection. If any of the connection packets are modified or get out of sync during the communication process, the console and agent are shut down for security reasons. Once the connection is established, the investigator can image the remote disk or add the disk directly to the current project for live analysis, such as hash filtering and keyword searching, all in a standard read-only forensically sound fashion. Because the remote disk is "live" in the earlier examples, some information may change during the imaging or analysis due to the volatility of the remote system. The network-enabled versions of ProDiscover also include a Linux boot CD-ROM that will boot the remote system to a forensically sound environment, allowing the investigator to image or preview the remote disk at rest.

ProDiscover Incident Response edition includes tools used to investigate cyberattacks on live systems. These tools provide the ability to investigate the volatile system state information, such as route tables, connected IP endpoints, running services, processes, and more. ProDiscover IR also includes patent-pending features that provide the ability to find hidden files, create and compare baseline file hashes, and search for suspect files.

A unique, patent-pending feature offered in all versions of ProDiscover is the paremove.sys driver, which provides the ability to temporarily reset the Host Protected Area on an ATA 4 and later IDE hard disks. This feature allows investigators not only to preview and extract any data hidden in the HPA but also to image the entire disk, including the HPA, without changing the original evidence disk. ProDiscover imaging can be accomplished through the Windows interface to any directly connected disk via standard I/O bus, FireWire, USB, or network interface.

NOTE

The Host Protected Area is described in detail in Chapter 7, and was created as a means for PC distributors to ship diagnostic utilities with PCs. The HPA is essentially an area of the hard drive that is not reported to the system BIOS and operating system. Because the protected area is not normally seen, many disk forensics imaging tools will not image the area, or if they do see it and can remove the area they will permanently alter the disk, removing the HPA and leaving all the area from that HPA as unallocated disk slack space. Initially, there was no great concern among computer forensics analysts over the Protected Area, largely because the feature was thought to be used only by PC distributors. The concern has been highlighted by wider use of the HPA among manufactures of PC BIOS and the release of consumer-marketed utilities to implement the Protected Area to protect user data.

Recent developments in the ProDiscover product line include the addition of a Perl scripting engine and extended volatile memory imaging and analysis. Investigators can use Perl scripts to extend ProDiscover's functionality for evidence extraction and reporting of unique disk artifacts. Using ProDiscover's expanded live memory imaging and processed volatile data extraction, investigators can learn more about the target system's interaction within the running environment and find passwords and memory-only resident malware.

The ProDiscover family of products includes analysis support for all current Windows filesystem formats, Unix, and Linux.

EnCase was introduced in the late 1990s by Guidance Software, Inc. EnCase is one of today's most widely used computer forensics application suites. EnCase uses a case methodology in which users create a proprietary case file to work from that contains information about the project for generation of reports. In what has become the standard for tools of this class, users can add and manage multiple directly attached disks or disk images to a case. Within the case, users perform further analysis such as hash filtering, timeline analysis, and reporting. One unique feature of Encase is its image file format. Although EnCase uses a metaimage format (bit copy plus) and, similar to ProDiscover, adds a header and footer to the image of the hard disk, EnCase adds a proprietary CRC value every 32 sectors, or 64 bytes, throughout the image.

EnCase supports a wide assortment of file system formats including NTFS, FAT 12/16/32, EXT 2/3, UFS, FFS, Reiser, CDFS, UDF, JOLIET, ISO9660, HFS, and HFST.

Another unique capability of EnCase is its EnScript, which is a scripting language like the Perl scripting interface in ProDiscover. EnScript allows investigators to automate functions within EnCase, such as file and sector analysis, including extraction and report generation. EnScript is object oriented and looks much like a blending of Visual Basic®, C++, and Java™ from a syntax stance. A collection of prewritten and supported EnScripts can be found on the Guidance Software Web site.

Though the user interfaces provided by ProDiscover and EnCase are similar, the capabilities in each are unique. EnCase includes a DOS boot disk for imaging in addition to allowing imaging through the Windows GUI.

There are two editions of EnCase: EnCase Enterprise Edition (EEE) and EnCase Forensics Edition. The Enterprise Edition consists of three components to perform network-based investigations and forensics, much like ProDiscover Investigator and Incident Response editions but intended to integrate tightly into the enterprise corporate environment. To assist in integration, EnCase EEE requires installation of a SAFE (Secure Authentication For EnCase) Server used to authenticate users, administer access rights, and retain logs. Like the remote agent in ProDiscover network editions, EnCase uses what they call a servlet installed on network workstations and servers to act as a server between the EnCase console and the system being investigated.

Network-enabled disk forensics capabilities provided by products such as ProDiscover and EnCase EEE are of major interest to investigators today. With the growing size and disperse placement of data in today's corporate networks, remote imaging and analysis will certainly play a key role in the future of computer forensics.

FTK [Accessdata01] by Access Data, shown in Figure 10.7, is another well-known forensics application suite for Windows. Like EnCase and ProDiscover, FTK provides an integrated environment that supports collection, analysis, and reporting of computer disk evidence. One of the strengths of FTK is its capability to conduct indexed-based searching. The FTK product incorporates indexed search capabilities by using the software development library provided by dtSearch® [dtSearch01]. By taking the time to create a comprehensive index of the search data up front, an investigator can conduct subsequent searches much faster than nonindexed searches. Considering that a great deal of time spent in the analysis phase of computer forensics is spent by investigators during keyword searching, this approach can be very beneficial. Among other features, FTK implements the ability to search and filter files using the NIST Reference Data Set number 28 hash value databases as well as the National Drug Intelligence Center (NDIC) Hashkeeper database. Another key feature provided by FTK is its tight integration with the Access Data password-cracking tools, Password Recovery Toolkit, and Distributed Network Attack.

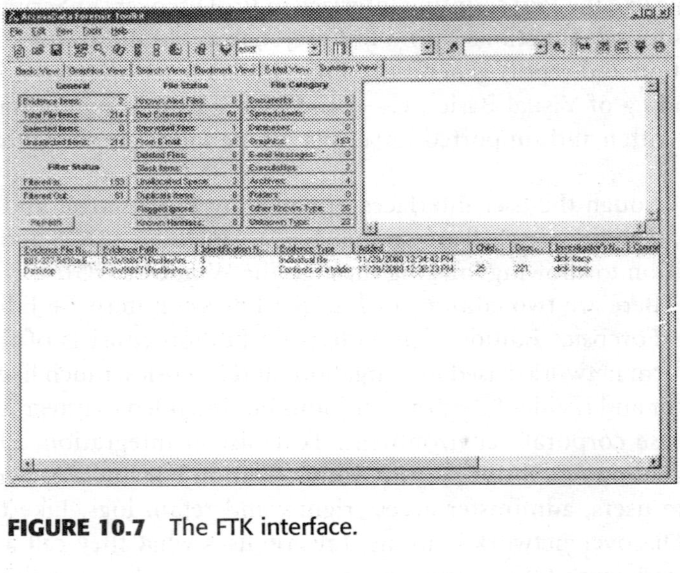

FIGURE 10.7 The FTK interface.

Access Data recently added the ability to read compound files to FTK, including Microsoft e-mail databases, the Windows Registry, and other file formats using the Stellent™ Outside In® Viewer Technology. Access Data has been a long-time computer forensics industry insider, and FTK is easily considered one of the top three integrated computer forensics tools for the Windows platform.

For investigators who wish to work from a Unix platform during collection and analysis, they can choose the Sleuth Kit and Autopsy Forensic Browser [Autopsy01], which are Unix-based investigation tools. Sleuth Kit and Autopsy Forensic Browser allow investigators to collect, analyze, and report on disk evidence from Windows and Unix systems. Autopsy is a HTML-based graphical interface that allows an investigator to examine the files and unallocated areas of disks, file systems, and swap space. The Autopsy HTML interface utilizes command-line tools provided by Sleuth Kit. For investigators who wish to work directly from the command line, Sleuth Kit utilities can also be used individually. Sleuth Kit tools include various NTFS, FAT, UFS, and EXT2FS/EXT3FS filesystem tools; a collection of DOS, Macintosh, Sun, and BSD partition tools; and other tools that help the investigator create and manage hash databases and sort files. Both Autopsy and the Sleuth Kit are open source and free and are maintained by Brian Carrier [Carrier01]. The Autopsy interface to the Sleuth Kit utilities provides the investigator a clean interface in which to interpret the contents of a hard disk or filesystem. At the lowest level, the investigator can view every block or sector in raw, hexadecimal, or ACSII view. The investigator is also provided with tools to examine and organize file data by its underlying metadata. Using the Autopsy Forensics Browser, investigators can view and sort the filesystem's files and directories, including the names of deleted files. Autopsy, shown in Figure 10.8, also provides tools with which to conduct keyword searches and create timelines based on file activity.

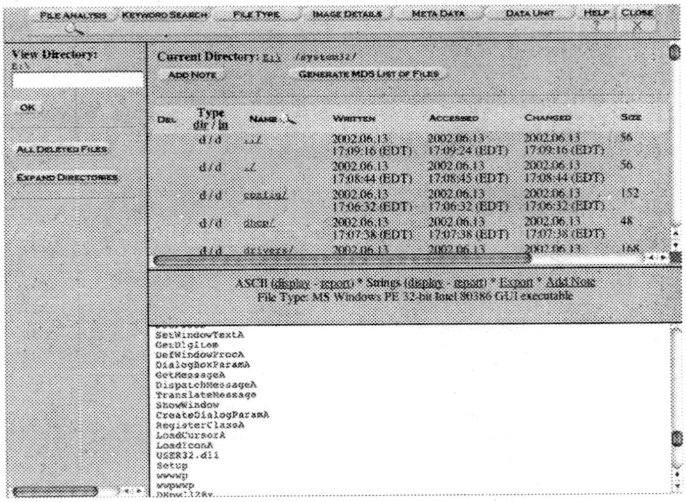

FIGURE 10.8 The Autopsy Forensic browser.

All command-line tools included with the Sleuth Kit are based on tools from the Coroner's Toolkit (TCT) by Dan Farmer and Wietse Venema. Although the individual tools in the Sleuth Kit do allow the investigator to create custom scripts for automation from the Unix command line, these tools are most commonly used in conjunction with an interface, such as Autopsy. Sleuth Kit and the Autopsy Forensics Browser are key components to the freely available Helix boot CD-ROM [efense01] created for forensics and incident-response investigators.

The proverbial last but not least forensics application suite is SMART, manufactured by ASR Data [Asrdata01].

NOTE *Considering the history behind ASR Data and their accomplishments, this may have been a good starting place for computer forensics tool suites. ASR Data originally released the first integrated imaging and analysis platform for Windows in 1992, called Expert Witness. Expert Witness was the basis for what is now sold under the name EnCase by Guidance Software. It eventually became one of the leading forensics analysis suites available for the Windows environment.*

SMART, shown in Figure 10.9, has become one of the top commercial integrated computer forensics environments for the Linux platform. SMART offers investigators a wide assortment of imaging and analysis capabilities, including remote live preview, acquisition, searching, and reporting.

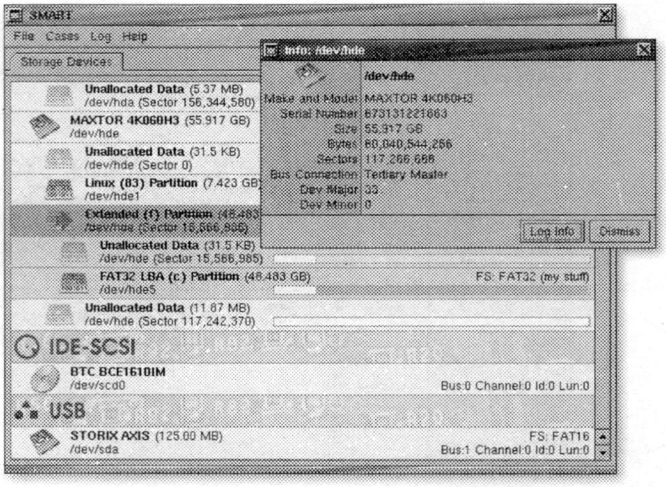

FIGURE 10.9 The SMART interface.

Despite many Unix- and Linux-based tools' power being based in their simplicity and command-line interfaces, one advantage of SMART is its rich user interface. As users navigate the SMART interface, they will find extensive right-click and drill-down capabilities. One unique approach to application extension and customization is how SMART extends application-through-application plug-ins. Using plug-ins, ASR Data can quickly enhance the application in a modular fashion without the need to distribute a completely new application build.

Another notable feature available with SMART is that its network-enabled version is also available on the BeOS platform, which can be run from a bootable CD-ROM.

Utilities and Other Applications

As previously mentioned, there is no end to the utilities and other applications that may be needed by the computer forensics investigator. Although some of these utilities and applications fall more into the analysis phase of computer forensics, which is outside the scope of this book, some cross the line, such as data recovery where a disk may need to be recovered prior to evidence collection. Despite the seemingly endless need for utilities and applications to process and display data, several applications in these categories are worth mentioning. One of the first utilities any computer forensics investigator should consider is not a single utility but a suite of command-line utilities. For occasions where this performance advantage is warranted, Mares and Company [Mares01] sells a comprehensive suite of fast and efficient command-line utilities created specifically for the computer forensics process. The list and feature set of Mares and Company utilities is growing consistently and includes utilities to hash and index large data sets efficiently. Mares' utilities are particularly well suited for scripting an investigator's routine and repetitive tasks via batch files.

X-Ways Software [Xways01] produces a smart, low-cost group of utilities that are increasingly forensically focused. One of the first products gaining widespread use among computer forensics investigators was the WinHex hex editor. WinHex is a standard low-level file system and disk editor with many features that allow investigators to process and view disks. Though WinHex was not originally created as a forensics application, in that it does allow investigators to write to disk and files, these features can be of great use to a forensics investigator. More forensics features are being implemented into WinHex all the time. Because WinHex could be destructive to evidence, it is not recommended for use by inexperienced investigators. Experienced investigators will recognize the need to use a tool like WinHex to accomplish tasks that may change the disk, such as to correct a boot sector corruption issue that may prevent a forensic disk image from booting in the lab. WinHex contains a very useful feature that allows investigators to create templates for what data structures should look like and, thus, identify abnormalities.

Paraben® Software [Paraben01] has been a computer-forensics-focused application vendor for some time. Rather than creating a complete forensics application suite, Paraben has focused on creating specialized feature-rich utility applications. The leading utilities Paraben provides are E-mail Examiner, for the processing of e-mail databases; PDA Seizure, for the processing of PDAs; and Cell Phone Seizure, for the processing of cell phone data. Recently Paraben has also become the U.S. distributor for NetAnalysis, an application for the analysis of Internet history files.

Computer forensics investigators often run across the need to recover data during the collection process. The very nature of computer forensics investigations suggests that someone may have attempted to destroy data prior to the collection. Investigators will want to acquaint themselves with disk-recovery services and utilities to assist in file and disk-level recovery, such as those provided by Ontrack® [Ontrack01] and Data Recovery Software services [DataRecovery01]. The forensics investigator will also find that collecting volatile data can prove crucial to an investigation, as outlined in Chapter 11, "Collecting Volatile Data." A great set of utilities for live-system investigations can be found at the Sysinternals Web site [sysinternals01].

Investigators will continuously find the need for some new tool to assist with collection or maintenance of computer evidence. The tools mentioned thus far provide the core functionality that investigators will use in everyday operations. Investigators should also develop a good network of resources as well as search techniques to help find the tool *de jour*. Always remember that "Google is your friend."

TOOL TESTING

Outside all the recommendations from peers, it only makes sense that computer forensics investigators would test and understand the tools they are using. Several guides can be useful in establishing what a tool should do, such as *NIST Hard Disk Write Block Tool Specification* [Nist02] and NIST *Disk Imaging Tool Specification 3.1.6* [Nist01]. However, an investigator still needs to test and establish that tools perform as advertised or as desired. Pragmatically, these tests are often accomplished over time through real-world use in what could be considered a less-controlled environment; however, controlled test are encouraged. It is recommended that forensics investigators take the following steps in their internal tool-review program:

1. Define what the tool should do in a detailed fashion. Often standards such as those created by NIST [Nist01/02] can be helpful in establishing these capabilities.
2. Create a protocol for testing the tool by outlining the steps and tools to be used during the tests.
3. Outline a controlled test data set. In the case of disk media, this data set would include a standard set of disks or data verifiable by cryptographic hash [Scott01].
4. Conduct the tests in a controlled environment.

5. Validate test results against known and expected results.

As outlined in Chapter 2, peer review can be important when admitting evidence or expert testimony in court. List servers maintained by the International Association of Computer Investigative Specialist (IACIS), High-Technology Criminal Investigation Association (HTCIA), and other such professional organizations can be quite helpful in providing peer review. A specific list server generated with the testing of computer forensics tools is the Computer Forensics Tool Testing Forum (CFTTF), which is self-described by the following caption:

"This group is for discussing and coordinating computer forensics tool testing. Testing methodologies will be discussed as well as the results of testing various tools. The ultimate goal of these tests is to ensure that tools used by computer forensics examiners are providing accurate and complete results. This discussion group is open to all individuals in the field who are interested in participating in the testing of computer forensics tools." [CFTT01]

To learn more about the CFTT group or to subscribe, visit the Web site at *http://groups.yahoo.com/group/cftt.*

Members of the CFTT list server can be quite helpful in providing peer review as well as helping investigators conduct their own tests. Brian Carrier has posted several disk images designed to test specific tool capabilities, such as the ability to recover deleted files, process images, and find keywords through search functions. He keeps these test data sets documented and available at *http://dftt.sourceforge.net/.*

Real-world use, methodical internal tests, and peer review should all be components of a forensics investigator's test plan. Sharing individual results with a community of like-minded individuals through list servers and professional associations helps investigators ensure they are following what can be considered best practices.

DOCUMENTATION

An old Navy saying, "If it wasn't logged, it didn't happen," comes to mind when thinking about documentation and the computer forensics process. Documenting investigators' actions at every step of the computer forensics process cannot be emphasized enough. Investigators in practice take many different approaches to documentation. Some use a collection of preformatted evidence-collection worksheets and chain-of-custody and examination forms to document their collection and examination. Other investigators will also take digital photos of the collection process as well as the examination process to document cable locations and disassembly procedures. Some investigators find it helpful to open a new composition notebook and keep a narrative log of their casework. No matter the approach, it's hard to argue with the sensibility of keeping accurate records of the investigative process.

Many cases that were not intended to go to court (civil or criminal) end up there years later, with the forensics investigator struggling to remember what was done or how he reached a decision. For this reason alone investigators should see that the more chronological detail they have kept, the better off they will be. There is always the argument that if too much detail is kept, something may be used later to impeach the investigator's testimony. Although certainly this could be a risk, the blatant absence of a detailed investigative record could also be damning.

All investigators should consider the following documentation components in assisting in re-creation, testimony, and maintaining chain of custody, thus mitigating authenticity challenges:

- **Keep a photographic record of the collection process or system from which data is being collected:** In many cases law enforcement is limited by warrant to collect only a digital image of the system, leaving original media behind. Photographic records are always helpful in jogging an investigator's memory about the collection scene.
- **If a complete system is being collected, consider placing tamperproof tape [Chief01] with a serial number on the original disk or system being collected:** Consider using a standard number sequence for each case. Something as simple as letter identifiers followed by the date and item number may be helpful. In the case where a single CPU was being collected, tamperproof tape may be placed on the CPU with the serial S-011705-1, showing that this item was the first item collected from the suspect ("S") on January 17, 2005. The tape should be fashioned on the CPU in such a way that the case could not be opened without disturbing the tape. Once back at the lab, if the case was opened to collect a bit-stream image of the original media, the investigator could label the original disk media as "S-011705-1A," noting that this was an incremental component "A" from the original collected item. Any subsequent images could then become B, C, and so on. The specific labeling system used by investigators is not important, but some system should be put in place to manage inventories of complete systems as well as components.
- **For small items, tamperproof evidence collection bags [Chief01] are useful:** If magnetic disk media is being placed in a plastic evidence bag, investigators should consider keeping a collection of static-free bags to place the magnetic media in first, prior to placing them in the plastic evidence bag. Remember Chapter 3, "Evidence Dynamics," and the effects of interaction with the evidence. In this case human and natural forces could be acting on the evidence with static electricity.

- **Large paper bags are useful to keep loose items such as power and miscellaneous cables.**
- **Labeling and documenting cables and their connection points is always a good idea.**
- **A standard college composition notebook (without perforated pages) is helpful to provide a log of investigator notes organized:** Don't forget to date and time the log.
- **Chain of custody forms to document the transfer of individual or groups of items.**
- **Evidence inventory sheets to document the detailed description of computer equipment.**
- **Original media access forms to track any access to a system's original disk media.**
- **Analysis worksheets to manage and track case processing.**

The preceding list is a high-level recommendation for steps toward detailed documentation. Each case is different and may not need one or more of the documentation steps mentioned.

Some investigators have chosen to move away from written records and use a digital equivalent. Certainly a digital log-keeping mechanism can be beneficial and is encouraged. Large-system seizures can be benefited by barcoded tracking and inventory systems. Some investigators like to keep a running digital log with a simple application like Notepad or Microsoft Word. The key when using digital systems to manage case documentation is remembering the number-one attack on digital evidence: authenticity. If investigators are using digital media for logging, they must be prepared for attacks on the log's or documentation's authenticity. The following steps should be considered when protecting digital documentation:

1. Protect file access using an access-control list and operating system security provided by network operating systems.
2. Log all file access (successful and failed).
3. Use digital time stamping and change logging.
4. Establish a secured backup process.
5. Periodically print the case files.

There are business applications created for consultants to manage time and materials that could be customized for the forensics investigator. The area of digitally time-stamping individual record entries is still a weakness for many time-management applications. One simple way some investigators can digitally time-stamp documents is to create a cryptographic hash of the document and use a digital-time-stamping service to certify that the hash value in question, and thus the document, existed in that state at a specific time. A free service to accomplish digital time stamping using PGP can be found at *www.itconsult.co.uk/stamper.htm* [ITConsultancy01]. Surety provides a commercial digital notary service at *www.surety.com/* [Surety01]. Certainly digital records are compelling for many reasons, but investigators will need to ensure they are taking the necessary steps to verify the integrity of any digital records maintained.

SUMMARY

- Because each computer forensics collection operation can vary so greatly, investigators will need to have a playbook from which to operate.
- One of the difficulties when attempting to create boilerplates is to make them general enough to be useful in a wide array of situations but detailed enough to be helpful.
- An investigator's playbook may include black bag inventories and forms.
- In certain situations, even tools that were created with the computer forensics process in mind may be somewhat destructive.
- Three leading manufactures of disk-imaging and write-blocking tools are MyKey Technologies [Mykey01], Intelligent Computer Solutions (ICS) [Ics01], and Logicube [Logicube01].
- Software used for the collection and preservation of computer evidence usually falls in one of three broad categories: Forensics Application Suite, Utility, and Other.
- Standalone hardware write blockers are of great use to investigators when using a portable computer forensics workstations (notebook or otherwise).
- The leaders of the Windows-based computer forensics suites are ProDiscover, EnCase, and FTK (Forensics Tool Kit).
- Expert Witness was the basis for what is now sold under the name EnCase by Guidance Software.
- A computer forensics investigator should test and understand the tools he is using.
- The old Navy saying, "If it wasn't logged, it didn't happen," should come to mind when thinking about documentation and the computer forensics process.
- If a complete system is being collected, consider placing tamper-proof tape [Chief01] with a serial number on the original disk and/or system being collected.
- The key when using digital systems to manage case documentation is remembering the number-one attack on digital evidence: authenticity.

REFERENCES

[Acard01] Microland USA Web site for ACARD SCSI-to-IDE Write Blocking Bridge, available online at *www.microlandusa.com/*, 2004.

[AccessData01] Access Data Web site, available online at *www.accessdata.com*, 2004.

[Asrdata01] ASR Data Web site, available online at *www.asrdata.com/*, 2005.

[Autopsy01] Autopsy and Sleuthkit Web site, available online at *www.sleuthkit.org*, 2004.

[Carrier01] Brian Carrier's Tool Testing Web site, available online at *http://dftt.sourceforge.net/*, 2004.

[CFTT01] Yahoo CFTT List Server Web site, available online at *http://groups.yahoo.com/group/cftt*, 2004.

[Chief01] Chief Supply Web site (evidence bags), available online at *www.chiefsupply.com/fingerprint.phtml*, 2004.

[Corpsys01] Corporate Systems Center Web site, available online at *www.corpsys.com/*, 2004.

[Cs01] CS Electronics Web site, available online at *www.scsi-cables.com/index.htm*, 2004.

[DataRecovery01] Data Recovery Software Web site, available online at *www.datarecoverysoftware.us/index.html*, 2004.

[Digitalintel01] Digital Intelligence, Inc. Web site (F.R.E.D./FireFly), available online at *www.digitalintel.com/*, 2004.

[dtSearch01] dtSearch Web site, available online at *www.dtsearch.com*, 2005.

[efense01] e-Fense Web site, available online at *www.e-fense.com/helix/*, 2005.

[Google01] Google Search Portal Web site, available online at *www.google.com*, 2005.

[Guidance01] Guidance Software Web site, available online at *www.guidance-software.com*, 2004.

[Htcia01] High Technology Crime Investigation Association Web site, available online at *www.htcia.org*, 2005.

[Iacis01] International Association of Computer Investigative Specialist Web site, available online at *www.cops.org*, 2005.

[Ics01] Intelligent Computer Solutions, Inc. Web site, available online at *www.ics-iq.com/*, 2004.

[Ilook01] ILook Investigator Web site, available online at *www.ilook-forensics.org*, 2004.

[Ioce01] International Organization of Computer Forensics Web site, available online at *www.ioce.org*, 2004.

[ITConsultancy01] Free PGP Digital Time-stamping Service Web site, I.T. Consultancy Limited Jersey Channel Islands, available online at *www.itconsult.co.uk/stamper.htm*, 2005.

[Logicube01] Logicube Web site, available online at *www.logicube.com/*, 2004.

[Mares01] Mares and Company Web site, available online at *www.dmares.com*, 2004.

[Mykey01] MyKey Technology, Inc. Web site, available online at *www.mykeytech.com/*, 2004.

[Nist01] NIST *Disk Imaging Tool Specification 3.1.6*, available online at *www.cftt.nist.gov/DI-spec-3-1-6.doc*, 2004.

[Nist02] NIST *Hard Disk Write Block Tool Specification*, available online at *www.cftt.nist.gov/WB-spec-assert-1-may-02.doc*, 2004.

[Ontrack01] Ontrack Data Recovery Web site, available online at *www.ontrack.com/*, 2004.

[Paraben01] Paraben Software Web site, available online at *www.paraben-forensics.com*, 2004.

[Scott01] Scott, Mark, *Independent Review of Common Forensics Imaging Tools*, Memphis Technology Group, available online at *http://mtgroup. com/papers.htm*, 2004.

[Surety01] Surety Digital Notary Service, available online at *www.surety.com/*, 2005.

[sysinternals01] Sysinternals Web site, available online at *www.sysinternals.com*, 2005.

[TechPath01] Technology Pathways, LLC Web site, available online at *www.techpathways.com*, 2005.

[Xways01] X-Ways Software Web site, available online at *www.x-ways.net/winhex/index-m.html*, 2004.

RESOURCES

[Forensicscomputer01] Forensic Computers Web site, available online at *www.forensic-computers.com/products.html*, 2004.

[Nij01] National Institute of Justice—The Computer Forensic Tool Testing Project Web site, available online at *www.ojp.usdoj.gov/nij/topics/ecrime/cftt.htm*, 2004.

ceeds, you will see how easily useful information can be obtained from a raw physical memory image.

As previously stated, the collection of processed volatile physical memory from a live system provides a great deal more useful information to the forensics investigator. What is meant by *processed* is that an application being employed by the investigator and run from the system, a trusted binary CD-ROM, or through network application calls, is issuing operating system programming calls through application programming interfaces (API) to request specific information that may be maintained in physical memory. In some cases the information from these processed calls may be created by extracting information from the computer's physical disk as well as physical memory, and thus, the calls could be somewhat more interactive with the system than evidence collected through a raw physical memory dump. The types of information usually gained from processed API calls to a live system that are useful to an investigation usually includes items such as currently logged-on users, running processes and their dependency libraries, current TCP/IP connections, and listening ports. Often this type of volatile information is available only using applications making API calls to the running operating system, because the system knows its current state. Although the usefulness of processed volatile physical memory is hard to argue with, investigators should always take into account that the information received through these methods may not be complete and could be altered if the system is compromised with a second-generation rootkit or Trojan, as outlined in Chapter 6. Therefore, any time an investigator collects processed volatile physical memory, the collection should be as an adjunct to the collection of raw physical memory.

To streamline the collection of processed volatile physical memory, many incident-response teams created what are commonly referred to as "IR Toolkits," comprising trusted versions of applications for evidence collection. These trusted applications are normally a collection of many small command-line utilities that are scripted to run following a batch process. Examples of early toolkits include Incident Response Collection Report (IRCR) and First Responders Evidence Disk (FRED). Both took different approaches to scripting utility applications for Windows system investigations. In the case of IRCR, which was a compiled Perl application, utilities were included to extract and process information from the event logs and registry in addition to collecting processed volatile physical memory metrics provided by running Microsoft "NET" and "ARP," or address resolution protocol (ARP) resolution, commands. A raw memory dumper was also included. Other toolkits such as FRED included utilities from the Sysinternals Web site [Sysinternals01] to provide a more detailed look at the volatile system state. Many of these toolkits are still in use today; however, investigators are strongly encouraged to conduct comprehensive tests to ensure the toolkit is being as least intrusive as possible for their needs. Many of the early toolkits were created for use prior to incident-response teams' adoption of disk bit-stream imaging techniques. That is, when incident-response teams used the toolkit to collect all information from the live system, including file indexes complete with hash values, they essentially "touched" every file on the remote system. In most situations today, the forensics investigator intends to also collect a bit-stream image of the physical disks, and thus the incident-response utility disk should be modified to collect only volatile data, not data that can be extracted from disk file systems later in a controlled environment.

BUILDING A LIVE COLLECTION DISK

One of the best ways for a computer forensics investigator to ensure he knows how his tools are interacting with evidence is to assemble and test the tools himself. As previously noted, ready-made incident response toolkits may be more intrusive than the forensics investigator desires. In this section you can follow along as a simple batch file for extracting processed volatile data from a running or live Windows-based suspect system is created.

To begin the creation of the volatile extraction tool, which we'll call "VExtract," the forensics investigator will first need to decide what types of processed information from the suspect computer's volatile memory might be of use to an investigation.

NOTE

ON THE CD

The batch files and utilities described in this section for extraction of volatile data are included in the accompanying CD-ROM in the \Volatile Extraction Tool\ folder.

Scenario One

For this first scenario the investigator has decided to use only those commands normally available to users on Windows systems and to be as least intrusive as possible while collecting the information. In keeping with these goals, the investigator decides that he would like to extract information relating to the system's current time, network shares, network connections, user accounts, and routing tables. While researching, our investigator learns the most recent versions of the Windows operating system support a command utility called "NET," which when executed with the proper parameter can return the desired information and more. After executing "NET /?" from the command line, the investigator finds the following list of available parameters:

```
NET [ ACCOUNTS | COMPUTER | CONFIG | CONTINUE | FILE | GROUP | HELP |
       HELPMSG | LOCALGROUP | NAME | PAUSE | PRINT | SEND | SESSION |
       SHARE | START | STATISTICS | STOP | TIME | USE | USER | VIEW ]
```

With "NET" being a command-line utility, our investigator decides that it will be perfect for use in a batch script that can be run to redirect all command output to a log file. Using a text editor to create a file called VExtract.bat, the investigator starts off by setting up the batch script to take a single parameter providing the output log directory while also including basic file information and time settings, as seen in Listing 11.1.

LISTING 11.1 Simple VExtract.bat

```
title Collecting Live Processed Volatile Data
echo off
set OUTPUTDRIVE=%1
set exit=0
if [%1]==[] (echo Syntax: VExtract [Output Drive Letter] Example: VEx-
tract a:
goto :end)
...
@echo. >> %OUTPUTDRIVE%\LiveLog.txt
@echo. >> %OUTPUTDRIVE%\LiveLog.txt
@echo ----------------------------------- >> %OUTPUTDRIVE%\LiveLog.txt
@echo START TIME >> %OUTPUTDRIVE%\LiveLog.txt
@echo ----------------------------------- >> %OUTPUTDRIVE%\LiveLog.txt
time /t >> %OUTPUTDRIVE%\LiveLog.txt
@time /t
date /t >> %OUTPUTDRIVE%\LiveLog.txt
@date /t
@echo. >> %OUTPUTDRIVE%\LiveLog.txt
@echo. >> %OUTPUTDRIVE%\LiveLog.txt
```

After setting up the initial simple batch file the investigator decides to use the following NET commands for extracting useful processed volatile data from physical memory:

NET ACCOUNTS: Provides information about account-policy settings for the specific system, including password-age lockout threshold and computer role.

NET FILE: Displays open files by remote users on the system.

NET SESSION: Displays current remote connections to the local system.

NET SHARE: Displays all local system directory shares accessible from the network.

NET START: Displays all services and their current running status.

NET USE: Displays any remote network shares to which the local system is currently connected.

NET USER: Displays a list of all user accounts on the local system.

NET VIEW: Displays a list of the computers within the local domain.

Comfortable that the preceding NET commands would provide a great deal of useful information about the live status of a Windows system, the investigator adds the commands one by one to the VExtract.bat batch file, as seen in Listing 11.2.

LISTING 11.2 NET User Command Addition

```
...
@echo ------------------------------------ >> %OUTPUTDRIVE%\LiveLog.txt
@echo NET USER >> %OUTPUTDRIVE%\LiveLog.txt
@echo ------------------------------------ >> %OUTPUTDRIVE%\LiveLog.txt
echo on
net user >> %OUTPUTDRIVE%\LiveLog.txt
echo off
...
```

After adding all the NET commands to extract Windows networking information, the investigator decides the following additional commands to extract information about the TCP/IP networking status, as well as scheduled operations for the suspect system:

Route Print: Displays the local system's current route tables used for IP packet routing.

ARP (arp –a): When used with the –a switch, displays the current media access control (MAC) layer address to IP address mapping.

NETSTAT (netstat –anr): Displays all connections and listening ports, with IP addresses and ports in numerical form without DNS resolution, and includes the current routing table.

NBTSTAT (nbtstat –c): Displays the current NetBIOS name cache with remote machine names and IP addresses.

AT: Displays a list of all currently scheduled command scheduler operations.

After adding the preceding commands to the VExtract.bat batch file, the investigator decides that the script is complete and finishes up by creating another call to the Windows `TIME` command to enter the time the batch file finished in the log, as seen in Listing 11.3.

LISTING 11.3 Closing Commands

```
time /t >> %OUTPUTDRIVE%\LiveLog.txt
@time /t
date /t >> %OUTPUTDRIVE%\LiveLog.txt
@date /t
@echo.
@echo.
@echo VExtract is done. >> %OUTPUTDRIVE%\LiveLog.txt
@echo VExtract is done.
```

Now armed with the newly created VExtract.bat batch file, the investigator can run the script from a CD-ROM or USB flash drive on a suspect machine and gain a great deal of information about the system's state.

NOTE

Although the information extracted with VExtract.bat file can be quite useful to an investigation, the information is only as valid as the source. If the system from which the information is being collected has been compromised with a kernel mode or second-generation Trojan that is designed to hide information such as networking connections and services, then the information provided may not be complete. All information gathered from a live system should be weighed by the way in which it was collected and against other information from static sources such as log files and disk artifacts.

Investigators aware of other command-line utilities such as those from the Sysinternals Web site will quickly see ways in which they can enhance the VExtract.bat batch file. Many of the Sysinternals utilities provide low-level operating system process information and include source code for investigators to validate.

Three utilities from the Sysinternals PSTools® Suite that an investigator may find useful to add to his VExtract.bat utility follow:

`PSList:` Lists detailed information about processes.

`PSInfo:` Lists information about a system.

`PSLoggedon:` Lists users logged on locally and via resource sharing.

These three utilities have been added to the Enhanced version of VExtract.bat included on the accompanying CD-ROM in the file \Volatile Extraction Tool\Enhanced\VExtract.bat.

While adding utilities for processed volatile-data extraction from suspect systems, the investigator may want to visit the Foundstone® Web site [mcafee01]. In the site's Resources section under Free Tools, investigators will find two utilities of particular use: `Fport` and `Ntlast`. The `Fport` tool is a Win32 command-line tool that allows investigators to show the specific application associated with open TCP/IP ports. Although the Windows XP operating system included the "-b" switch for the "netstat" command to show associated applications, not all versions of Windows provide this functionality. Ntlast is a security log analyzer that allows investigators to extract security log information processed in many ways, such as the last *x* number of successful logons and the last *x* number of failed logons.

Noting that many investigators want this type of information prior to analyzing the logs found in a static bit-stream disk image collected later, both `Ntlast` and `Fport` have been added to the Enhanced version of VExtract.bat found on the accompanying CD-ROM in the folder \Volatile Extraction Tool\Enhanced\.

Another area of improvement is cryptographic-hash-creation utilities that provide the ability to hash log files for later verification. Incident-response toolkits such as those started with VExtract.bat are limited only by an investigator's imagination and available command-line utilities.

Investigators will always want to evaluate if the processed information they are attempting to extract with a live-response toolkit is indeed volatile data that could be lost if not collected live. Many live-incident response toolkits extract information processed through the live system that is in fact extracted from static disk artifacts, such as log files or registry keys. If the investigator intends to also collect these static artifacts directly or through a complete bit-stream image of the disk, then it may not be reasonable to also collect (and thus, interact) while the system is live. Remember that digital evidence dynamics principles should drive the investigators to understand and limit their interaction with digital evidence to a reasonable minimum.

Processed volatile memory collection is normally collected as an adjunct to raw physical memory collection. Although a raw physical memory image rarely nets the immediate results of volatile information processed by the running operating system, it can be collected with much less system interaction. In addition, it is less likely that the contents of a raw physical memory dump will be compromised by second- or third-generation rootkits.

The Forensics Acquisition Utilities Web site maintained by George M. Garner, Jr., [Garner01] provides a useful collection of utilities ported from the popular Linux platform that are useful not only for disk imaging but also for creating dumps of physical memory.

NOTE *The Forensics Acquisition Web site is available online at http://users.erols.com/gmgarner/forensics/.*

The Web site contains a detailed description outlining the use as well as source code for the following tools:

dd.exe: A modified version of the popular GNU "dd" utility program.

md5lib.dll: A modified version of Ulrich Drepper's MD5 checksum implementation in Windows DLL format.

md5sum.exe: A modified version of Ulrich Drepper's MD5sum utility.

Volume_dump.exe: An original utility to dump volume information.

wipe.exe: An original utility to sterilize media prior to forensic duplication.

zlibU.dll: A modified version of Jean-Loup Gailly and Mark Adler's zlib library based on zlib-1.1.4.

nc.exe: A modified version of the "netcat" utility by Hobbit, allowing users to set up client/server connections in many useful configurations.

getopt.dll: An implementation of the POSIX getopt function in a Windows DLL format.

The listed utilities that are most useful in collecting volatile memory images include dd.exe, nc.exe, and md5sum.exe. By adding these utilities alone to their volatile collection toolkit CD-ROM, the forensics investigator can now capture raw physical memory in addition to the processed volatile data collected by VExtract.bat.

NOTE *Adding the md5sum utility to the enhanced version of the VExtract.bat script allows investigators to create a cryptographic hash of resulting log files for later integrity verification.*

The Forensics Acquisition Utilities have not been added into the VExtract.bat scripts because of the beta nature of the distribution. Extensive documentation for the Forensics Acquisition Utilities is provided on the Web site at *http://users.erols.com/gmgarner/forensics/* but is not included in the download archives, causing many investigators to miss the memory-imaging capabilities of the dd.exe utility. A system's memory can be imaged as simply as issuing the following command:

```
dd if=\\.\PhysicalMemory of=d:\images\PhysicalMemory.img
```

NOTE *Using dd.exe to image physical memory to a local drive would, of course, modify that drive and cannot be considered to be following sound forensics principles in most situations. In most every situation forensics investigators will desire to write the image file to removable media such as a USB or FireWire disk device or possibly across the network.*

Using the NetCat utility "nc.exe," users can pipe the output from "dd" over the network to another station. To accomplish this redirection, investigators need only set up the NetCat utility in a listening mode on the station they wish to receive the memory image and then pipe the output from the "dd" memory image through NetCat, across the network and to the receiving station. Using the following commands on a sending and receiving station, where "a.b.c.d" is the IP address of the receiving station, will send the physical memory image from the sending station to the receiving station over port 3000:

Receiving Station: nc -l -p 3000 | dd of=C:\temp\MemoryImage.img

Sending Station: dd if=\\.\PhysicalMemory | nc a.b.c.d 3000

NOTE *Any time investigators are attempting TCP/IP communications over the network between client and server applications, they must ensure personal firewalling on the host or server system is not blocking communications. Attempting the previous commands between two Windows XP systems with the Service Pack 2 personal firewall enabled will cause the communications between the NetCat components to fail.*

Investigators who feel that the network environment over which they are sending the physical memory image may not be secure and prying eyes could capture their network traffic may wish to use an encrypted channel. Lucky for investigators, a group of computer security professionals at Farm9, Inc. [Farm901] have created a version of NetCat called CryptCat, which encrypts all network traffic. CryptCat is included in the accompanying CD-ROM in the folder \Farm9\. It is also available directly from the Farm9 Web Site at *http://farm9.org/Cryptcat/*. When using CryptCat, investigators would simply change the commands for the sending and receiving stations as follows:

ON THE CD

Receiving Station: cryptcat -l -p 3000 | dd of=C:\temp\MemoryImage.img
Sending Station: dd if=\\.\PhysicalMemory | cryptcat a.b.c.d 3000

By adding CryptCat, NetCat, dd, and Md5Sum, investigators now have a volatile extraction toolkit that will allow them to collect both processed and raw volatile physical data from a suspect system in a least-intrusive manner if the situation warrants.

The Forensics Server Project [Carvey01] is another approach to automate the collection of volatile information from live systems. The Forensics Server Project uses many of the same utilities from Foundstone and Sysinternals but differs in that the utilities are tied together through Perl scripting rather than through Windows batch files. The Forensics Server Project Web site can be found at *http://patriot.net/~carvdawg/fsproj.html.*

Investigators should remember that the tools used to create the volatile extraction toolkit, as well as those found in the Forensics Server Project, are freeware tools from a variety of sources that provide limited to no support. Many of the tools used provide full source code, allowing the investigator to enhance or modify the tool as needed.

COLLECTION SCENARIO USING WINDOWS TOOLS

As with any profession, growth within the computer forensics investigation profession has fueled the advancement of new investigative technology. One particularly exciting area showing recent advancement is the melding of live incident-response collection and investigative technologies with more traditional computer forensics disk-imaging products. Both the makers of EnCase [Guidance01] and ProDiscover [TechPath01] now offer network-enabled versions of their disk forensics products that allow live preview, imaging, and extraction of raw as well as processed data. One of the advantages of the melding of live response and forensics technologies is that first responders can now use forensics-grade tools from the very beginning and thus have a much better understanding of their interaction with evidence.

To outline the use of some of the newer tool capabilities, the following scenario involving the investigation and collection of evidence from a live system uses the ProDiscover Incident Response product.

SCENARIO

In this simple and common scenario, a hacker is suspected of compromising a Windows-based computer system running a Web server within a corporate network. This suspicion could be driven by any number of the normal keying mechanisms such as intrusion-detection systems; firewall logs; hacker extortion, where change management identifies a specific vulnerability; or a simple gut feeling on the part of the information technology security team member.

In our fictitious hacking episode the corporation's forensics investigator identifies the system in question and determines that the initial phases of the investigation should be conducted while the system is live because it is running a Web server that is providing critical functions. In order to maintain the forensics principles, the forensics investigator desires to keep his interaction with the suspect system to a minimum while conducting a least-intrusive live investigation. For the purpose of this scenario, the investigation will include live raw and processed volatile evidence collection and will be followed by a full disk image if suspicions are confirmed.

When questioning the Webmaster responsible for the management of the Web server in question, the investigator is told that the Webmaster had done the following steps based on initial suspicions:

- Browsed through the file system to look for anything unusual, but found nothing.
- Looked at the process manager, but found no unusual processes running.
- Ran the "netstat" command to look for any suspicious listening TCP/IP ports or connections, but again found nothing.

With no overt signs of a compromise on the suspected Web server, the forensics investigator places a CD-ROM with the autostart version of the PDServer remote agent on the suspect server. Once the remote agent is running, the investigator connects to the agent over the network from his forensics workstation running the ProDiscover Incident Response console application, as shown in Figure 11.1.

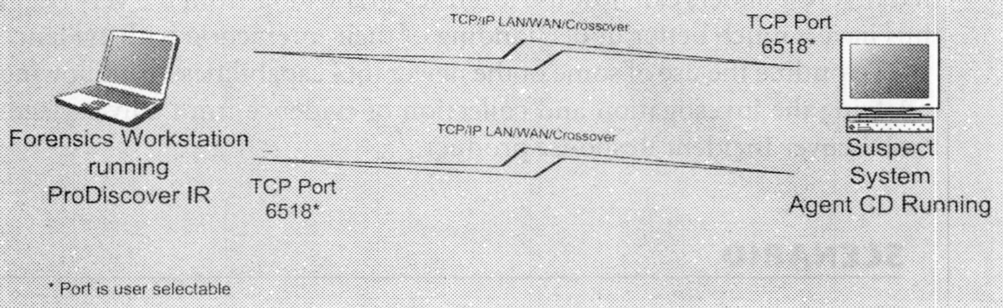

FIGURE 11.1 Remote connection diagram.

After the investigator successfully connects to the remote suspect server, he decides the first thing to do is to capture a raw image of volatile physical memory, as shown in Figure 11.2.

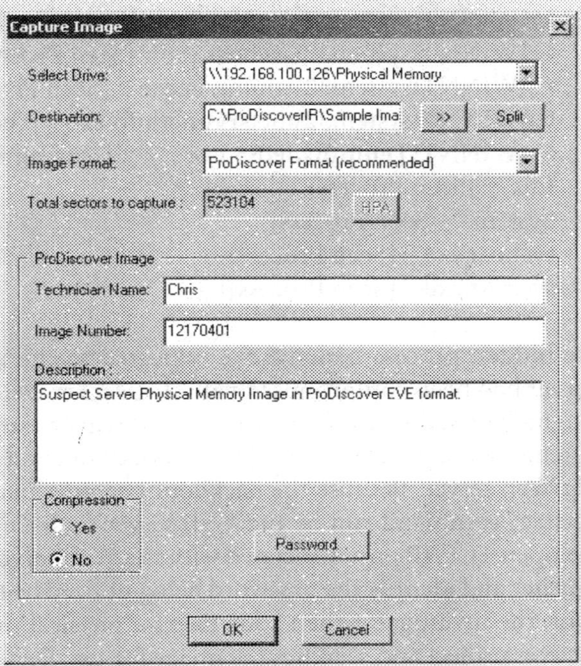

FIGURE 11.2 The ProDiscover Incident Response Capture Image dialog box.

Once the raw physical memory image was complete, the investigator decided to run the ProDiscover Find Unseen Processes function, found in the IR menu, to identify if any unseen processes were running. Confirming suspicions, the report showed the following processes running on the suspect server, one of which was a hidden process:

C:\PDServer\PDServer.exe [Seen Process]
C:\WINNT\explorer.exe [Seen Process]
C:\WINNT\system32\csrss.exe [Seen Process]
C:\WINNT\system32\dfssvc.exe [Seen Process]
C:\WINNT\system32\llssrv.exe [Seen Process]
C:\WINNT\system32\lsass.exe Seen Process]
C:\WINNT\system32\msdtc.exe [Seen Process]
C:\WINNT\system32\mstask.exe [Seen Process]
C:\WINNT\system32\regsvc.exe [Seen Process]
C:\WINNT\system32\services.exe [Seen Process]
C:\WINNT\system32\smss.exe [Seen Process]

```
C:\WINNT\system32\SPOOLSV.EXE   [Seen Process]
C:\WINNT\system32\svchost.exe   [Seen Process]
C:\WINNT\system32\winlogon.exe   [Seen Process]
C:\WINNT\system32\inetsrv\inetinfo.exe   [Seen Process]
C:\WINNT\Temp\hxdefß$.exe   [Unseen Process]
Idle   [Seen Process]
System   [Seen Process]
svchost.exe   [Seen Process]
svchost.exe   [Seen Process]
```

The hidden process hxdefß$.exe indicated to the investigator that the Web server had been compromised with the Hacker Defender rootkit, which is able to hide files, directories, processes, and registry keys. In addition to the ability to hide files, the Hacker Defender rootkit opens a backdoor within the running Web server. Because the backdoor becomes part of the Web server, the "netstat" command run by the Web server's administrator would show only the open TCP/IP port associated with the Web server. To confirm suspicions further and identify the password being utilized by the Hacker Defender backdoor, the investigator then adds the raw physical memory image to the ProDiscover project and searches the image for two keywords. The investigator uses *Password=* as a search term to locate the backdoor password and *HXDEF* to identify fragments of memory that contain code associated with the Hacker Defender rootkit. Figure 11.3 shows the results of the search, including the backdoor password of "owned."

At this point the investigator may decide to add the remote disk to the project and continue a live investigation, as shown in Figure 11.4, or he may decide to collect a disk image over the network and conduct the remaining portions of the investigation offline in the lab. Network-enabled forensics tools that incorporate the capability to perform live volatile data examination and capture greatly enhance the investigator's ability. With today's newer tools investigators can better control their interactions with evidence, be less intrusive to business services, and collect more specific and volatile evidence.

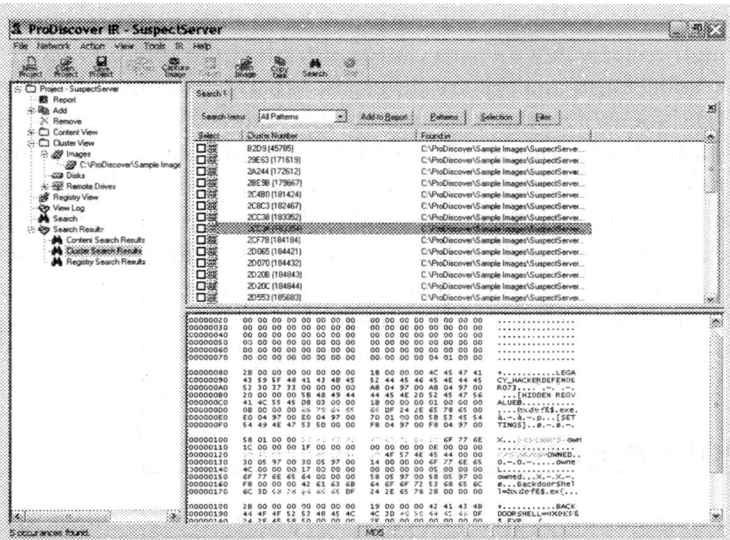

FIGURE 11.3 Raw physical memory search results.

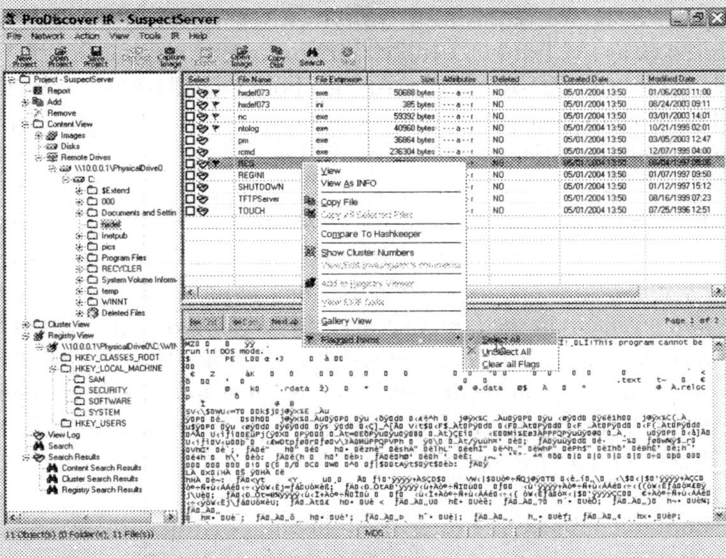

FIGURE 11.4 The Hacker Defender directory.

Another category of tool related to networks and forensics is the Network Forensics Analysis Tool (NFAT). Although the tools discussed to this point do involve the network, they are best referred to as host- or disk-based forensics over the network (DFN/HFN). The reason for the distinction is important, because although conceivably the two classes of tools could meld someday, the types of data they collect and analyze are different. Much like a host-based intrusion detection (HIDS) focuses on the static and volatile state of a host, HFN does, too. NFATs can be more closely compared to the HIDS counterpart, network-based intrusion detection (NIDS), which purely analyzes the network traffic on the wire. NFATs are essentially software/hardware products derived from NIDS and are forensically focused to preserve and analyze network traffic captured from the network. NFATs are beyond the scope of this book; however, three tools that may interest investigators include Niksun® NetDetector® (see *www.niksun.com*), SilentRunner™ (*www.ca.com*), and Sandstorm® NetIntercept® (*www.sandstorm.com*).

LIVE BOOT CD-ROMS

The utility CD-ROMs discussed to this point have two things in common: they require the suspect system to be up and running, and they normally work in a client-server fashion or export data to removable media. In addition, any application running under the local operating system runs the risk of returning faulty data if function calls are made to a compromised system. Bootable disks, commonly referred to as live boot CD-ROMs, are becoming popular in the forensics community. A live boot CD-ROM consists of a bootable CD-ROM (one that adheres to the El Torito Standard [ElTorito01]) complete with its own operating system and preinstalled forensics and security utilities.

NOTE

Bootable disks containing a clean operating system and specialized utilities are not new to the security arena. For some time now information security professionals have used the Trinux [Trinux01] boot floppy disk, which contained a stripped-down version of the Linux kernel and specialized security tools for network monitoring, such as NTOP. Even today the Trinux boot floppy can be useful to boot stripped-down hardware and to monitor traffic patterns when placed on a network. The original Trinux bootable floppy is now available as a bootable CD-ROM with added utilities.

Bootable CD-ROMs offer the following distinct advantages when used in the information security and forensics realms:

- A bootable floppy or CD-ROM can be used to host the base operating system and tools used by an investigator during live investigation in suspect network environments. By using write-protected media, the investigator can keep the base OS and utilities safe from compromise, or at least permanent compromise.

- Bootable floppy or CD-ROMs will often run on systems with fewer resources, providing investigators the choice of several operating environments.
- Bootable floppy or CD-ROMs allow the investigator to reboot a suspect system to the "clean" operating system and utilities, allowing for on-site static bit-stream disk image collection and analysis.

The first two advantages apply to investigators conducting live investigations and collecting volatile data from a suspect system. The third advantage applies specifically to the collection and analysis of static disk data from "dead" systems and will be addressed in Chapter 12, "Imaging Methodologies."

Two live boot CD-ROMs popular among forensics investigators are Helix Bootable Incident Response and Forensics CD [efense01] and Forensics and Incident Response Environment (FIRE) bootable CD-ROM [Fire01], both of which are based on the popular Linux operating system and freely downloadable from their respective Web sites. The Helix live CD-ROM is based on the popular Knoppix [Knopper01] bootable Linux environment created by Linux enthusiasts from Knopper.net. The Knoppix CD-ROM is packed with many applications, games, and utilities with all users in mind. In what has become common these days, e-Fense.com modified the basic Knoppix distribution by stripping out applications and games not needed by investigators and adding forensics-specific tools such as Autopsy and Sleuth Kit. e-Fense.com also made other file system changes to Helix, such as limiting the OS's ability to increment the journal count when mounting journaling file systems, to make it more appealing to the forensics investigator. The Helix environment provides a clean Windows-based graphical environment for investigators to work from within Linux.

NOTE

Because the bootable Knoppix CD-ROM provides users with a full desktop platform and is configured to leave little or no disk artifacts, the platform is of great interest to users conducting criminal activities and misuse.

The FIRE bootable CD-ROM, also based on LINUX, takes the "keep it simple" user interface approach. Rather than launching into a fully configured Windows desktop, FIRE launches into a completely text-based menu system, providing investigators who may not be familiar with Linux or Windows a simple navigation system. The Helix boot CD-ROM seems to be a bit further along as projects go, but FIRE offers a simple user interface and a slew of Windows-based utilities when placed in the cradle of a running Windows system.

Other less-known bootable CD-ROM environments include those customized by users to boot to the Windows PE (Preboot Environment) and the old standby DOS (Disk Operating System). The Windows Preboot Environment is a full but stripped-down version of Windows, much like safe mode with networking capabilities. For investigators who are not members of the Microsoft Developers Network (MDN) and hardcore developers to boot, Bart Lagerweij [Lagerweij01] maintains the definitive Web site called Bart's Preinstalled Environment (BartPE) bootable live windows CD/DVD. This Web site contains a great deal of information, utilities, and links available to assist investigators who wish to create their own bootable Windows or DOS CD-ROMs. The site is available at *www.nu2.nu/pebuilder*.

The BartPE bootable environment can be used by investigators to create a bootable Windows CD-ROM that hosts the VExtract.bat script and supports utilities in a clean, trusted binary environment.

Whether it is professional-grade forensics products, custom-built trusted binary CD-ROMs, live boot CD-ROMs, or simply a collection of utilities and scripts such as VExtract.bat, investigators should always consider collecting volatile data from live systems.

SUMMARY

- Today, forensics investigators may not have the choice of shutting down the computers in question at all or could incur civil liabilities should an improper shutdown destroy data resulting in financial loss.
- If a system is shut down, no matter the method, volatile data in physical memory will be lost.
- Investigators will always need to weigh the benefits against any possible risks and ensure they have the tools and training to access volatile data in a least-intrusive manner.
- Information collected from volatile data in memory can be collected in two ways: raw and processed.
- The simplicity of dumping raw physical memory to a file reduces the ways in which the investigator is interacting with the system.
- The collection of *processed* volatile physical memory should be an adjunct to the collection of *raw* physical memory.
- One of the best ways for a computer forensics investigator to ensure he knows how his tools are interacting with evidence is to assemble and test the tools himself.
- The Forensics Acquisition Utilities Web site maintained by George M. Garner, Jr., [Garner01] provides a useful collection of utilities ported from the popular Linux platform that are useful not only for disk imaging but also for creating dumps of physical memory.
- A system's memory can be imaged as simply as issuing the following command: dd if=\\.\PhysicalMemory of=d:\images\PhysicalMemory.img

- One particularly exciting area showing recent advancement is the melding of live incident-response collection and investigative technologies with more traditional computer forensics disk imaging.
- Another category of tools related to networks and forensics is the Network Forensics Analysis Tool (NFAT).

REFERENCES

[Carrier01] Carrier, Brian D. and Grand, Joe, "A Hardware-based Memory Acquisition Procedure for Digital Investigations," *Digital Forensics Investigation Journal*, Volume 1, Issue 1, February 2004.

[Carvey01] The Forensics Server Project Web site, available online at *http://patriot.net/~carvdawg/fsproj.html*, 2005.

[efense01] Helix Bootable Incident Response and Forensics CD, available online at *www.e-fense.com/helix/*, 2005.

[ElTorito01] *What is the El Torito* CD-ROM Specification, available online at *http://kb.indiana.edu/data/ancc.html?cust=620548.99284.30*, 2005.

[Farm901] Farm9 Web site, available online at *http://farm9.org/Cryptcat/*, 2005.

[Fire01] Forensics and Incident Response Environment Bootable CD-ROM, available online at *http://fire.dmzs.com/*, 2005.

[Garner01] Garner, George M., Jr., Forensics Acquisition Utilities Web site, available online at *http://users.erols.com/gmgarner/forensics/*, 2004.

[Guidance01] Guidance Software Web site, available online at *www.guidance-software.com*, 2004.

[Intel01] *1394 Open Host Controller Interface Specification*, available online at *http://developer.intel.com/technology/1394/download/ohci_11.htm*, 2005.

[Knopper01] Knopper Web site, Knoppix Project, available online at *www.knopper.net*, 2005.

[Lagerweij01] Bart's Preinstalled Environment (BartPE) bootable live windows CD/DVD, available online at *www.nu2.nu/pebuilder/*, 2005.

[mcafee01] Foundstone Web site, available online at *www.foundstone.com/*, 2005.

[Shimokawa01] Hidetoshi Shimokawa Web archive, available online at *http://people.freebsd.org/~simokawa/firewire/*, 2005.

[Sysinternals01] Sysinternals Web site, available online at *www.sysinternals.com*, 2004.

[TechPath01] Technology Pathways, LLC Web site, available online at *www.techpathways.com*, 2005.

[Trinux01] The Trinux Project Web site, available online at *www.trinux.org*, 2005.

[Wilson01] Wilson, Tim, *Taskforce iTconsulting*, available online at *http://cms.nmsalert.com/website-monitoring-articles/downtime-costs-website/view*, October 2004.

RESOURCES

[Frisch01] Frisch, Aeleen, *Windows 2000 Commands—Pocket Reference*, O'Reilly Publishing, March 2001.

[king01] King, Nate King and Weiss, Errol, "Analyze This! Network Forensics Analysis Tools (NFATs) Reveal Insecurities; Turn Sysadmins into Systems Detectives," available online at *http://infosecuritymag.techtarget.com/2002/feb/cover.shtml*, February 2002.

12 Imaging Methodologies

In This Chapter

- Approaches to Collection
- Bit-stream Images
- Local Dead System Collection
- Verification, Testing, and Hashing
- Live and Remote Collection

APPROACHES TO COLLECTION

Disk evidence is easily the cornerstone of computer forensics if for no other reason than digital evidence on disk is as easy to relate to a judge and jury as files in a file cabinet. However, the *completeness and accuracy* of digital evidence collection is often questioned in the legal arena. In an effort to fend off evidentiary challenges relating to the evidence dynamics of disk collection and analysis, computer forensics investigators have for some time placed a major emphasis on careful disk collection and handling.

For a variety of reasons, including the volatility of disk data and potential destructive nature of handling and analysis, computer forensics investigators agree that creating a copy of a disk is a necessary component of disk evidence collection and analysis. Because the term *copy* is such a general term—and one that can indicate that the "copy" is less than complete in the digital realm—investigators have opted for the technical definition of a bit-for-bit clone. An experienced computer user understands that when creating a copy of files from a disk, a great deal of underlying data on the disk, such as metadata and unallocated or unused disk space, is not included in the file copy. However, when a bit-for-bit clone of a disk is created, every bit (pardon the pun) of the original disk information is collected.

NOTE

Terminology differs slightly in the computer forensics field. The National Institute of Standards and Technology (NIST) defines two acceptable forensics-imaging practices: creation of a bit-for-bit copy (unaligned clone) and creation of a bit-stream duplicate (cylinder-aligned clone) of the original disk media. In a bit-stream duplicate, minor changes are allowed to align partitions and cylinder boundaries required to operate the duplicate as a normal filesystem in a computer. The resulting difference being that a bit-for-bit copy is accessed by a tool such as computer forensics software and a bit-stream duplicate is accessed by an operating system. The computer forensics community rarely distinguishes between the two and commonly refers to them as simply a "bit-stream image."

In keeping with the court-acceptable standards of *completeness and accuracy*, computer forensics investigators should create a bit-stream image of original evidence when copying from source media to destination media whenever reasonable.

Disk imaging is such a key component to the evidence collection process that the NIST created the Computer Forensics Tool Testing Project (CFTT) in an effort to standardize technologies in use. The first guidelines published by NIST, *Disk Imaging Tool Specification*, were related to disk imaging [Nist01]. A draft of the follow-on imaging-tool specification was released for public review in October 2004 in *Digital Data Acquisition Tool Specification 4.0 (Draft)* [Nist02], which is available online at *www.cftt.nist.gov/Pub-Draft-1-DDA-Require.pdf*. In the updated specification, NIST defines the disk-imaging process for use in computer forensics and outlines a group of mandatory and optional features for forensics disk-imaging-tool software.

Mandatory computer forensics imaging-tool features outlined by NIST [Nist02] follow:

- The tool shall be able to acquire a digital source using each access interface visible to the tool.
- The tool shall be able to acquire either a clone of a digital source or an image of a digital source, or provide the capability for the user to select and then create either a clone or an image of a digital source.
- The tool shall operate in at least one execution environment and shall be able to acquire digital sources in each execution environment.

- The tool shall completely acquire all visible data sectors from the digital source.
- The tool shall completely acquire all hidden data sectors from the digital source.
- All digital sectors acquired by the tool from the digital source shall be acquired accurately.
- If there are unresolved errors reading from the digital source, then the tool shall notify the user of the error type and location.
- If there are unresolved errors reading from the digital source, then the tool shall use a benign fill-in-the-destination object in place of the inaccessible data.

The NIST imaging-tool specification goes on to identify many key optional features offered by today's computer forensics imaging tools, such as multi-image files and hashing, and how they should perform, if available. Although not regulatory and still in draft format, requirements set forth in the *Digital Data Acquisition Tool Specification 4.0 (Draft)* [Nist02] provide investigators with a valuable guideline for tool selection.

As a computer forensics investigator becomes more experienced, they will notice that not only will their physical tool bag of hardware and software grow to meet the wide array of collection scenarios, so too will their methodological tool bag grow. Investigators need to be prepared to access digital data in a variety of ways. For instance, even while serving a search warrant, law enforcement officers are not always provided the ability to completely seize a computer from which they desire evidence. It is certainly easier to bag and tag the complete computer at the scene and handle any imaging and analysis back at the lab, where time and an array of tools offer greater flexibility. Many judges understand that bit-stream images of evidence disks can often be collected on-site and stipulate such in warrants in an effort to not be overly disruptive in business environments. Today's field investigators need to be cognizant of the many access methods for collecting a source image from many different devices. Investigators increasingly need to possess the tools to support methodologies for collection images from live systems as well as to access media from dead systems quickly and through a variety of approaches.

BIT-STREAM IMAGES

In the field or in the lab, forensics investigators will normally collect one or more bit-stream images of the original evidence media. This image collection allows for subsequent analysis and reporting, leaving the original media (or another image) safely locked away. The method and number of image collection varies greatly by investigator preference and by mitigating factors presented by the case.

When collecting an image, the investigator can use the following high-level approaches:

- Collect a bit-stream image from original media to an evidence file, referred to by NIST as a bit-for-bit copy (unaligned clone) of the original disk media.
- Collect a bit-stream image from original media to an evidence disk, referred to by NIST as a bit-stream duplicate (cylinder-aligned clone) of the original disk media.

When collecting the bit-stream image to file, the investigator will essentially access the data through this method, stream the data sector by sector from the evidence media into a file or group of files residing elsewhere. The format of the resulting file varies, depending on the software used, but it falls into one of two categories: a bit-copy or bit-copy-plus, as defined by Mark Scott of the Memphis Technology Group in his paper "Independent Review of Common Forensics Imaging Tools" [Scott01]. A bit-copy evidence image contains nothing more than the stream of sectors from the original evidence media whereas the bit-copy-plus image contains additional supporting information. In a bit-copy-plus image, additional information may be embedded information in a header or trailer or located throughout the image file at predetermined locations. The embedded information provides information to the forensics application that may be useful in determining integrity, such as a cryptographic hash of original sector/media data. Other embedded information typically included is the investigator's name; the date or time; the original disk serial number, manufacturer, and compression data; and collection error log files. No format standard exists today; however, most computer forensics tools will read a raw disk image with no embedded data, often referred to as a Unix "dd" style image. Some tools such as ProDiscover [TechPath01] will allow the user to choose to collect the original image in "dd" or raw format. ProDiscover provides an additional publicly documented bit-copy-plus image format with header and trailer information. The ProDiscover image file consists of the following five parts:

- Image file header
- Image data header
- Image data
- Array of compressed block sizes
- I/O log errors

The first 16 bytes of each ProDiscover image file contains an image file header, which contains an image signature and version number, as seen in Table 12.1.

TABLE 12.1 Image File Header Structure

Data Type	Size in Bytes	Name of the Data Member	Description
Char	12	m_strSign	Image signature
DWORD	4	m_nVersion	Image Version number

The image file header is followed by a 653-byte image data header, which contains various user-entered information about the image captured, as shown in Table 12.2.

TABLE 12.2 Image Data Header Structure

Data Type	Size in Bytes	Name of the Data Member	Description
Char	20	m_strImageNum	Image number
BOOL	1	m_bCompression	Image compression
Char	24	m_strPassword	Image password
Char	24	m_strTechnicianName	Name of the investigator
Char	400	m_strDescription	Image description
Structure DFTTime	9	m_CapturedTime	Image captured time
Structure DFTTime	9	m_SystemTime	Image system time
BOOL	1	m_bIsPhysical	Is it a physical image
Char	16	m_strSourceDisk	Name of the source disk
Char	25	m_strHardDiskMake	Hard disk make string
LONGLONG size	8	m_nImgDataSize	The original data size/compressed data
DWORD errors	4	NErrInfoSize	Size of the I/O log
BYTE	1	m_chCheckSumType	Type of the checksum (MD5 or SHA1) →

Data Type	Size in Bytes	Name of the Data Member	Description
BYTE	48	m_strCheckSum	The calculated checksum
WORD	2	m_nBytesPerSector	Number of bytes per sector
WORD	2	m_nSectorsPerCluster	Number of sectors per cluster
DWORD	4	m_nStartSectorOf1stCluster	Starting sector number of cluster
DWORD	4	m_nTotalSectors	Total number of sectors
DWORD	4	m_dwATAStartsAt	The starting address of ATA Protected Area; −1 if no protected area exists
DWORD	4	m_nFreeSectors	Total number of free sectors
DWORD	4	m_nBadSectors	Total number of bad sectors
DWORD	4	m_nTotalClusters	Total number of clusters
DWORD	4	m_nFreeClusters	Total number of free clusters
DWORD	4	m_nBadClusters	Total number of bad clusters
Int	4	m_nTimeZoneIndex	The index of the time zone information
BOOL	4	m_bIsDaylightActive	TRUE if summertime is active FALSE if not
Char	12	m_strFileSystemType	File system type
DWORD	4	m_nBlocks	Number of compressed blocks
Char	3	Unused	Unused disk space

The third part of the image file is the image data, which will be a single block or an array of blocks if compressed. Each compressed block corresponds to 1 MB of uncompressed data.

If the image file is not compressed, an array of compressed block sizes will not be available. The image data is immediately followed by an array of LONGs (LONG blockSize [m_nBlocks]). Each LONG corresponds to the compressed size of the block. The size of the array will be the number of compressed blocks.

The last part of the ProDiscover image file contains any I/O errors encountered during image capture. The size of this I/O error log depends on the number of errors that occurred and the type of the error messages. The size of this image file section is described in the image data header.

The EnCase [Guidance01] image file format is another well-known bit-copy-plus format that goes one step further and embeds CRC32 checksum values in every block of 64 sectors (32K) for internal self-checking and validation. By creating a CRC32 checksum for each block of 64 sectors of a disk image, the location of a change within an image can be located when inconsistencies are found. Another proprietary bit-copy-plus image format is the SafeBack™ image format. Although SafeBack is not used nearly as often as it was in the early days of forensics disk imaging, investigators may run across archives and evidence lockers full of SafeBack images. Sanderson Forensics [Sanderson01] manufactures and sells a small utility called SBConvert, which converts SafeBack images to raw disk images. Another handy utility for investigators with archived SafeBack images is SBRecover, also available from Sanderson Forensics.

No matter whether collected as a bit-copy-plus image for use in specialized software or a raw bit-copy such as UNIX "dd," the bit-stream image file is useful to investigators. With the bit-stream image file, an investigator has the flexibility in storage by allowing the creation of a multifile image in many smaller chunks, such as 640 MB for CD-ROMs. With the size of today's hard drives, investigators may want to choose 4.5-GB chunks for DVD-ROMs. Consider that an 80-GB disk divided into 640-MB chunks will leave the investigator with 120 CD-ROMs. Another advantage of the bit-stream image file is that analysis using the specific tool, such as EnCase or ProDiscover, is often faster during searching, hashing, and other disk-intensive operations. The greatest disadvantage of working with a bit-stream image file is that if the tool itself does not offer processing for some type of file, the file in question will need to be extracted from the image to a temporary location that is accessible to the third-party tool for processing. Investigators will find that forensics tools using bit-stream image files often offer the ability to restore an image file back to a disk and process the resulting evidence disk as though it was collected as a disk-to-disk image.

NOTE *When collecting a disk-to-image file, many investigators will forget the file size limitations of the FAT32 file system. No single file in the FAT32 file system can be more than 4 GB, requiring the images to be split into smaller chunks than may be desired. If an investigator desires to collect a disk-to-image file in one contiguous file, he should choose a destination file system such as NTFS.*

When collecting the bit-stream image-to-disk file, the investigator transfers the original evidence media to a forensically clean evidence disk. In the disk-to-disk bit-stream imaging process, only slight alignment changes are allowed to allow possibly varying disk geometry on the target disk.

NOTE *When creating a bit-stream image disk-to-disk, rarely will a source disk and target disk be exactly the same size, causing the target disk to end up being some amount larger than the source disk. A forensically clean evidence disk is a physical disk that has a known or truly random pattern written to the disk, so any extra space on the target will not to be confused as evidence from the original source disk.*

The advantages of creating a disk-to-disk bit stream image instead of a disk-to-file image are that the resulting evidence disk can be mounted with write protection in a forensic workstation and many different tools can be used for evidence analysis. Although the speed of searches may be reduced, depending on the evidence disk's speed and geometry, the ability to work with varying tools without extracting individual artifacts is appreciated by many investigators. Having a second image disk also allows an investigator to boot an evidence workstation and interact with the workstation as a suspect user may have. Of course, multiple disk images also allow multiple investigators to work simultaneously during analysis.

Some investigators prefer to collect disk-to-image images and restore the image file to disk, if needed. Others prefer to collect single or multiple disk-to-disk images, or maybe even a disk-to-disk and disk-to-image file. No matter what an investigator chooses, he should be familiar with both methods because access restrictions may limit the investigator's ability to collect an image in his preferred method.

LOCAL DEAD SYSTEM COLLECTION

As previously mentioned, the investigator has a variety of choices when collecting a disk image. Does he collect a disk-to-disk bit stream, a disk-to-image file bit stream, or possibly both? Often the initial disk-image collection is driven by the tools available and the accessibility of the original evidence-disk media. Whether in the field or back at the lab, accessing the original evidence-disk media can be difficult at best. Accessing evidence-disk media is often one of the most challenging steps in the computer forensics process.

When imaging standard desktop PCs, investigators will often find the disk easily accessible through removable access bays or panels, as shown in Figure 12.1.

FIGURE 12.1 Access a desktop PC disk.

With the PC's internal hard disk easily accessible, the investigator has several options for collecting the disk evidence, regardless of whether he intends to ultimately remove and bag and tag the original evidence disk.

The investigator can use a handheld forensic disk imager, such as the Solo Forensics by ICS [Ics01] or the SF5000 by Logicube [Logicube01] to collect a disk-to-disk bit-stream image. Many handheld forensics disk imagers will also allow a disk-to-image file bit-stream image to be collected.

The investigator may also choose to use a field forensics workstation to connect and image the disk. The advantage of using a field forensics workstation is that the investigator can also perform a preview to the original evidence disk to meet warrant guidelines, if necessary.

Figure 12.2 shows an image being collected using the ImageMASSter Solo Forensics from ICS; Figure 12.3 shows imaging and previewing using a field forensics workstation with ProDiscover forensics software and an external disk enclosure.

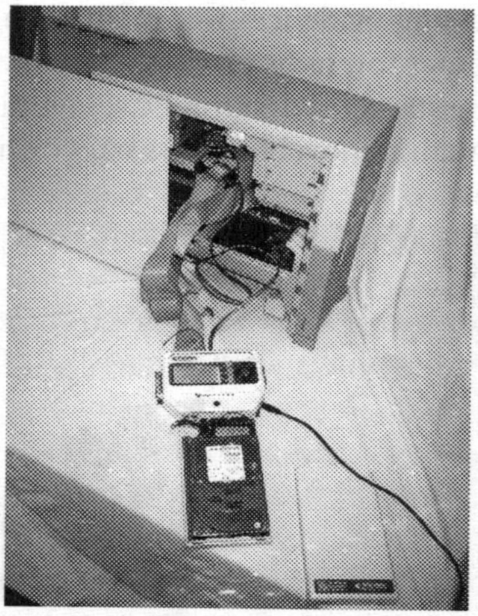

FIGURE 12.2 Handheld imaging using the Solo Forensics ImageMASSter.

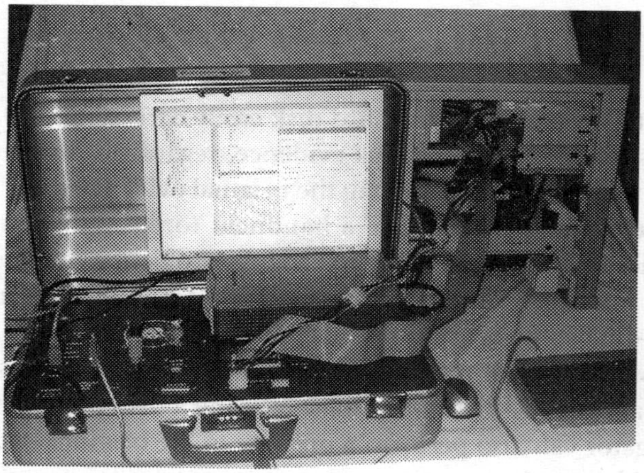

FIGURE 12.3 Workstation imaging using ProDiscover.

NOTE

No matter which initial disk imaging method the forensics investigator chooses, he should start off by initiating good documentation from the very beginning. Documentation in the case log should include information about steps used during the initial capture, including any problems encountered, software and firmware versions, local time, system time settings, tag numbers assigned to the disk, and any other pertinent information.

Although a large number of computer investigators may run across PCs with easily accessible disks, this is not always the case. Notebook computers and specialty desktop PCs often offer a challenge to investigators who want to connect directly to a disk interface connector for imaging. Due to the rise in notebook computer sales, computer forensics investigators will be investigating a growing number of notebook computers. The sale of notebook computers actually surpassed that of desktops in May 2003 [Rto01]. Not all notebook computers have difficult-to-access disks, but many not only offer challenges to disk access but provide newer and smaller proprietary disk interfaces requiring adapters. ICS [Ics01] and MyKey Technologies [Mykey01] both offer specialty disk adapters for forensics imaging. To get around those hard-to-access disks, investigators can use features available in forensics software and handheld forensics imagers to boot the suspect system to a specialized operating system and run software to redirect local disk sectors to some other access interface, such as parallel, USB, FireWire, Network, or PCMCIA card interfaces. Both ICS [Ics01] and Logicube [Logicube01] offer boot software that allows the investigator to boot a suspect system from floppy disk or CD-ROM and redirect disk sectors to a variety of different ports and to the handheld disk imager.

Logicube also provides the CloneCard, which when used with Logicube's boot software, will redirect disk sectors out the CloneCard's PCMCIA-to-IDE interface. Figure 12.4 shows a notebook computer being imaged with the Logicube CloneCard. Network-enabled versions of the ProDiscover [Techpath01] product offer a Linux boot disk that will boot the suspect system to a specialized version of the Linux operating system, bind local network adapters, and run their PDServer remote agent, allowing investigators to image the suspect disk over the network or through a network crossover cable. Figure 12.5 shows a notebook computer being imaged with the ProDiscover Linux boot disk and crossover cable. The EnCase product includes a DOS boot disk that allows investigators to redirect disk sectors from a suspect system through parallel or network interfaces.

Investigators will quickly find that they need to include as many hardware and software tools in their flyaway kits as possible to meet their varied imaging needs. Often investigators will find only one out of three or four tools will work or offer the proper connection method needed to get the job done. Sometimes only one or two tools that offer the same connection methods will work in a specific situation due to incompatibilities. Investigators that choose to work with various boot CD-ROMs that allow imaging notebook computers over a network card and crossover cable should invest in several network cards just in case the suspect notebook computer does not have an installed card. Two network cards that offer interface variety and are known to work with the Knoppix bootable Linux environment [Knopper01] as well as the ProDiscover Linux Boot CD-ROM are:

- D-Link® PC Card 10/100 Card Bus Adapter (Model DFE-690TXD)
- Linksys ® EtherFast 1-/100 Compact USB Network Adapter (Model USB-100M)

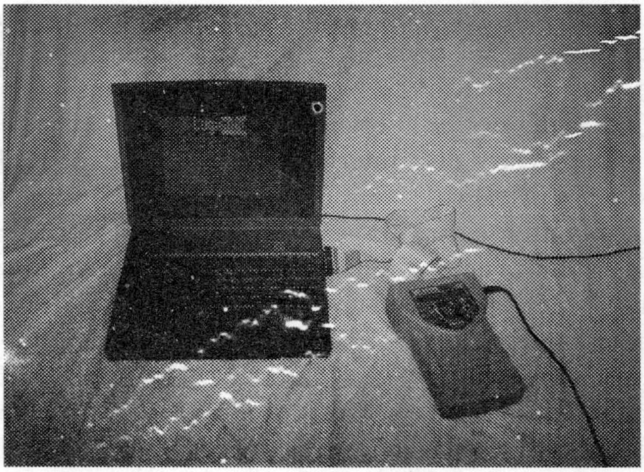

FIGURE 12.4 **Handheld imaging with the Logicube CloneCard.** © Logicube, Inc. 2005

FIGURE 12.5 **Linux boot disk and crossover cable.**

Any time an investigator works with varied equipment, such as during a computer forensics investigation, incompatibilities and interface inconsistencies will present obstacles to accessing the data. The investigator may have the tools that offer many ways to get at the evidence, but he is reduced to only one method due to incompatibilities. Very quickly investigators involved in the imaging process will see the tremendous time commitment consumed by imaging. Performance of the I/O bus, speed of the disk, controller cards, and interfaces can all become bottlenecks to the imaging process. Investigators should always be cognizant of the speed of the interface with which they choose to image. When imaging via a network card crossover cable, the difference between imaging with a 100-megabit half-duplex network card and a 100-megabit full-duplex network card is twice the time requirement. When looking at average speeds of around 20 GB per hour on a 100-megabit full-duplex adapter, that's the difference between 10 hours or 20 hours on one of today's 200-GB drives. The difference outlined for USB in Chapter 7, "Physical Disk Technologies," is even more drastic, at 12 megabits per second for USB 1.1 and 480 megabits per second for USB 2.0. The speed and performance of disks also affect imaging speeds. Even when using a handheld forensic imaging device rated at over 1 GB per second, imaging slower-performing disks, such as from notebooks, investigators may not see speeds greater than 320 megabits per second.

VERIFICATION, TESTING, AND HASHING

As stated throughout the book, peer review and testing as well as an investigator's local testing to ensure his tools are performing as desired is always advisable. To assist investigators in performing their own tests, NIST has posted the forensic software testing support tools and setup documents [Nist03] that they use in tool testing on their public Web site at *www.cftt.nist.gov/disk_imaging.htm.*

In addition to testing tools for performance and accuracy, a key component of the disk-imaging process has been to test the resulting image (disk-to-disk or disk-to-file) for integrity through cryptographic hashing or checksums. Most forensic applications and handheld imagers implement some type of hashing or checksum algorithm to allow investigators to later verify the disk or image integrity.

NOTE

A cryptographic hash is an algorithm used to produce fixed-length character sequences based on input of arbitrary length. Any given input always produces the same output, called a hash. If any input bit changes, the output hash will change significantly and in a random manner. In addition, there is no way the original input can be derived from the hash. Two of the most commonly used hashing algorithms are MD5 and SHA1. Cryptographic hashes have many uses within the cryptography field, but they are normally used in the computer forensics field as a tool to ensure data integrity. To the computer forensics investigator, a cryptographic hash can be considered a digital version of tamper-proof tape.

A cryptographic hashing function or algorithm has the following technical characteristics:

- A hashing algorithm transforms an arbitrarily block of data into a large number called a hash value.
- The value has no correlation to the original data, and nothing about the original data can be inferred from it.
- Small changes in the original data produce large, essentially random changes in the hash value.
- Generated hash values are evenly dispersed throughout the space of possible values (that is, all possible values are equally likely to occur).

The chi-square test [Nist04/Snedecor01] is a mathematical formula used for determining the likelihood that two distributions (hash values) were derived from the same source. The actual formula used in a chi-square test can be found online at *www.itl.nist.gov/div898/handbook/eda/section3/eda35f.htm.*

CAUTION

Cryptographic hashing algorithms were created in part as an effort to provide more crypto-suitable (randomly distributed) signature values than older error-detection algorithms such as CRC-32. Being created as a means of checking data integrity, the CRC-32 algorithm is in wide use for data communications as an efficient mechanism for error detection. Computer forensics investigators should note that although the CRC-32 algorithm is a reasonable algorithm for detecting large data-alteration errors, it may still fail to detect 1 in 227 communications errors [Ieee01]. Not only can CRC-32 miss detecting slight changes in data integrity, there are published algorithms for the creation of new data volumes of input data that will result in identical CRC-32 Checksums [IETF01/02]. Although CRC-32 checksums will identify changes in data integrity, they were not created with the ability to detect the slight changes detectable by cryptographic hashing algorithms. Investigators should resist relying on CRC-32 checksums as a method of attestable integrity.

Table 12.3 shows that the size of the resulting hash value can have great effect on the resulting chances of collision.

TABLE 12.3 Hash Collision Comparison

Hash	Resulting Value Bit Size	Number of Operations	Resulting Chance of Collision
MD5	128	2^64	1 in 18,446,744,073,709,551,616
SHA1	160	2^80	1 in 1,208,925,819,614,629,174,706,176

Hashing algorithms can be used in many ways and are commonly used in cryptography functions to translate variable-length passphrases and passwords into the fixed-length initialization vectors and keys used in symmetric encryption algorithms. In computer forensics, investigators use hashing algorithms to simply identify if a file or volume of data such as a disk drive has changes by creating a hash *signature* for the data at a given point in time and recording the value. Now the investigator, or anyone who suspects that the data may have changes or wants to ensure that it has not changed, can create a new hash signature and compare it against the original to ensure that the signature has indeed not changed. By looking at the third characteristic of a hashing algorithm—"Small changes in the original data produce large, essentially random changes in the hash value"—investigators will see this hashing algorithm is perfect for their intended use. If even one bit has changed on the original disk since the original hash signature was created, any subsequent hash signatures will be significantly different.

Some investigators who follow the cryptographic community have expressed concern over using the MD5 and older SHA-0 hashing algorithm due to reports of forced collisions by researchers. In one of the most recent reports at Crypto 2004 [Crypto01/Rsa01], researchers were able to create two documents that generated the same hash signatures. Although interesting, this type of research has a much greater practical effect on those trying to break encryption keys rather than modifying original evidence and expecting the hash signature to remain the same. MD5 and older hashing algorithms such as MD4 have been known to offer less-than-desirable collision rates for use in cryptography since 1996 [Psu01]. The research is focused solely on the creation of hash collisions (required to break encryption) rather than modifying a document in a specific way, but still returning the same hash signature. In addition, the creation of hash collisions reported at Crypto 2004 was conducted on a specialized system with 256 Intel-Itanium®2 processors and took 80,000 CPU hours.

As a possible solution for concerns about cryptographic collisions, NIST recommends: "*If the risk of applying only one hash value is above accepted levels, multiple hash values may be used to reduce the risk*" [Nist05]. Tools such as the command-line sha_verify.exe application from Mares and Company [Mares01] offer the ability to conduct multiple hash signatures simultaneously. Many forensics investigators now use SHA-1, multiple hashes, or some of the higher-bit algorithms such as SHA-224, SHA-256, SHA-384, and SHA-512 to avoid questions relating to their use of cryptographic hashing algorithms.

Some forensics examiners may create a hash signature of a disk and later find that subsequent hash signatures of that disk have changed. On the surface it may appear that the disk has been altered and is no longer "valid" evidence. Investigators should focus on what the differing hash values really mean, that is, that at least one bit of data on the disk is different than when the original hash signature was created. This difference could be the result of a sector going bad or a sector that could be read the second time and not the first. All the investigator really knows is that one bit is different, and thus the disk has a different hash signature. In another situation the same disk may end up with differing hash values depending on the method in which the disk is accessed. When viewing the disk through Linux and DOS, investigators are often able to reach a small number of sectors from a non-addressable unused disk area that when viewed from Windows will not be visible. The same disk, when imaged from Linux and Windows, will produce two different hash signatures but may contain the same user data. Admissibility is always for the court to decide.

In the end, all investigators should focus on the goal and not the specific technology by ensuring that they implement a process that provides a reasonable level of assurance of the integrity and security of the evidence. This process may include the use of one or more technical methods that allow them to attest to data integrity, but it will most certainly include documentation, attention to detail, physical controls, and personal integrity.

LIVE AND REMOTE COLLECTION

In Chapter 3, "Evidence Dynamics," investigators were introduced to issues relating to shutting down the system. Recently investigators have found a new component to the equation of whether to pull the plug or conduct an orderly system shutdown when collecting disk evidence. That component is the driving force to not shut down the system at all. Besides the loss of volatile data and other technical issues, the following business and operational reasons may compel investigators not to shut down at all:

- For information security investigations, pulling a transaction or Web server offline may severely impact production or revenue.

- Isolating a problem to a specific server in a Web or commerce farm can be difficult; should the investigator take them all down?
- Law enforcement can incur civil liability in the execution of a search warrant on a commercial organization when data or equipment is lost or damaged.
- With disk sizes soaring, the amount of time a system is out of service is skyrocketing (many servers have multiterabytes of storage).
- In cases of internal investigations, secrecy is often paramount, and investigators may not be able to shut down the system of the employee under investigation to perform the investigation.

For these and other similar reasons, investigators may choose to, or be directed by warrant, not to shut down the system at all. To collect disk data from a live system, users would usually use the standard network filesystem allowing access to file data over the network. Accessing files in this way violates several forensic principles—metadata may be altered by excessive interaction, and underlying recoverable sectors of data not currently allocated to files is not visible or collectable. Although collecting file data over a network through standard network file systems may be reasonable in certain large-scale civil discovery cases, advances in forensics-grade tools offers forensics investigators a better and less-intrusive course of action. For some time, command-line utilities for raw disk-level access, such as NetCat and DD [Garner01], have been able to be scripted to allow an investigator to pipe raw sector-read data across the network. Forensics-grade application suites, such as those offered by Technology Pathways [Techpath01] in their ProDiscover Incident Response and Guidance [Guidance01] Software in their EnCase Enterprise Edition, have been network enabled to allow live imagining and analysis [Sealey01/Casey01]. These client/server-enabled applications allow investigators to connect to remote systems over local area networks and wide area networks through the use of a remote server application running on the remote suspect system, which redirects low-level sector data as well as other commands to the forensics workstation for analysis. The investigator can choose from several methods of running the remote server application on the suspect machine, such as preinstallation, scripted push, or local removable media. Understanding that the interaction with the suspect system is different with each of the described remote-server-application run methods, investigators will need to choose a method most suitable for their given situation. When using ProDiscover to image a remote live system, the image created is often referred to as a *smear*. Smears capture the image while disk I/O processes are still taking place, due to other processes running on the system. Although this process may create some internal inconsistencies in large data files, the data in the image is true and accurate at the time of image. Because of possible inconsistencies, some investigators choose to take advantage of live forensics analysis for preview-and-cause justifications or long-term employee investigations and conduct a black bag operation to image a disk locally from a dead system based on the preinvestigation confirmation of suspicions. No matter the choice, it's hard to argue with the advantages of live system forensics for investigation and imaging.

The performance of live forensics analysis is often much more tolerable than imaging due to the network bandwidth available over many wide area networks. Using the average transfer rate of 1.5 hours per gigabyte (with no other users) over a T-1 wide area network link, one of today's 100-GB drives would take well over 155 hours to image over the same link. These bandwidth limitations have caused some investigators who need to be able to react quickly to remote imaging jobs to be creative in their approach by installing remote forensics collection pods within local area network access of each site for which they are responsible. By configuring the remote forensics collection pod with a removable disk bay fitted with a large evidence disk and remote terminal services, the investigator can use the terminal services to collect disk images to the forensics pod remotely. Once the image is completed (at LAN speeds), the investigator can have the evidence disk or entire pod shipped back to the lab for further analysis or storage. Keeping in mind the chain of custody, investigators who utilize the forensics pod approach should ensure the pod is installed in a logically and physically secure location. A placement approach for specific high-interest targets is to place the remote collection pod on a separate backup network segment, as described in Chapter 5, "Networking Topology and Architecture." In cases where no dedicated backup network segment is available, one could be created, essentially creating a forensics collection network segment.

The remote and seemingly disconnected nature of disk forensics over networks adds an increased burden of integrity assurance on the investigator. Security steps to be considered when conducting any type of remote disk forensics over a network include the use of the following elements:

- Encryption to secure the data channel
- Password-protected remote agents
- Write-protected trusted binaries for remote agents
- Digital signatures to attests to remote-agent integrity
- Cryptographic hashing to verify completed images
- Network segment isolation

The live boot CD-ROMs described in Chapter 11, "Collecting Volatile Data," offer both dead and live system imaging capabilities in addition to their capabilities for collecting volatile data. Two popular freeware distributions among forensics investigators are Helix Bootable Incident Response and Forensics CD [efense01] and Forensics and Incident Response Environment Bootable CD-ROM [Fire01]. Both distributions provide forensics investigators the ability to collect images locally through a variety of ports such as USB, FireWire, or the local bus. In addition to local imaging using "dd," investigators can pipe physical disk images over the network using the NetCat utility, as they did with physical memory images in Chapter 11. To accomplish this "redirection," the investigator needs to set up the NetCat utility in a listening mode only on the station that he wants to receive the memory image. He then pipes the output from the "dd" memory image through NetCat, across the network to the receiving station. Using the following commands on a sending and receiving station, where "a.b.c.d" is the IP address of the receiving station, which will send the logical or physical disk image from the sending station to the receiving station over Port 3000:

Receiving Station: nc -l -p 3000 | dd of=C:\temp\PhysicalDiskImage.img

Sending Station: dd if=\\.\PhysicalDisk0 | nc a.b.c.d 3000 (for full physical disk image)dd if=\\.\C: | nc a.b.c.d 3000 (for a partition-only image)

NOTE

The command-line syntax shown is for use of the Windows port of "dd" [Garner01]. Syntax will change slightly for Linux and Unix variants of the tool. Consult the products' main pages for specific syntax on these systems. Garner's tools provide additional command-line options not shown, such as –lock, to lock disk from writes or dismount the disk during the imaging process.

Just as mentioned in Chapter 11, the CryptCat utility can be used with TwoFish encryption in place of the NetCat utility to ensure the data channel is secure.

No matter what the approach, disk forensics over networks is becoming more commonplace. As with any disk-imaging or analysis approach, forensics investigators should always be cognizant of the effects their tools and methodologies have on evidence and ensure they are taking reasonable steps toward providing integrity and authenticity.

SUMMARY

- An experienced computer user understands that when creating a "copy" of files from a disk, a great deal of underlying data on the disk such as metadata and unallocated or unused disk space is not included in the file "copy."
- NIST defines two acceptable forensics imaging practices, which create a bit-for-bit copy (unaligned clone) or bit-stream duplicate (cylinder-aligned clone) of the original disk media.
- Disk imaging is such an important component to the evidence-collection process that the National Institute of Standards and Technology (NIST) created the Computer Forensics Tool Testing Project (CFTT) in an effort to standardize technologies in use.

- Investigators increasingly need to possess the tools to support methodologies for collecting images from live systems as well as accessing media from dead systems quickly and through a variety of approaches.
- When collecting an image the investigator has two high-level approaches:
  1. Collect a bit-stream image, from original media to an evidence file; referred to by NIST as a bit-for-bit copy (unaligned clone) of the original disk media.
  2. Collect a bit-stream image from original media to an evidence disk; referred to by NIST as a bit-stream duplicate (cylinder-aligned clone) of the original disk media.
- The EnCase [Guidance01] image file format is another well-known bit-copy-plus format that embeds CRC32 checksum values in every block of 64 sectors (32K) for internal self-checking and validation.
- No matter which initial disk-imaging method the forensics investigator chooses, he should start off by initiating good documentation from the very beginning.
- As a possible solution for concerns with cryptographic collisions, NIST recommends: "*If the risk of applying only one hash value is above accepted levels, multiple hash values may be used to reduce the risk.*"
- In the end, all investigators should focus on the goal and not the specific technology by ensuring they implement a process that provides a reasonable level of assurance of the integrity and security of the evidence.
- Besides the loss of volatile data and other technical issues, there are various business and operational reasons that may compel investigators not to shut down at all.
- No matter the choice, it's hard to argue with the advantages of live system forensics for investigation and imaging.

REFERENCES

[Casey01] Casey, Eoghan and Stanley, Aaron, "Tool Review: Remote Forensic Preservation and Examination Tools," *Digital Investigations Journal*, Vol. 1 No. 4, December 2004.

[Crypto01] "Collisions in SHA0 and MD5, Crypto 2004, Santa Barbara, August 2004, available online at *www.iacr.org/conferences/crypto2004/index.html*, 2004.

[efense01] Helix Bootable Incident Response and Forensics CD, available online at *www.e-fense.com/helix/*, 2005.

[Fire01] Forensics and Incident Response Environment Bootable CD-ROM, available online at *http://fire.dmzs.com/*, 2005.

[Garner01] Garner, George M. Jr., Forensics Acquisition Utilities Web site, available online at *http://users.erols.com/gmgarner/forensics/*, 2004.

[Guidance01] Guidance Software Web site, available online at *www.guidance-software.com*, 2004.

[Ics01] Intelligent Computer Solutions, Inc. Web site, available online at *www.ics-iq.com/*, 2004.

[Ieee01] IEEE Comments on 802 specifications, available online at *www.ieee802.org/17/documents/presentations/jan2003/ns_crcBitReversa_01l.pdf*, 2004.

[Ietf01] Request for Comment 1624, Internet Engineering Task Force, available online at *www.ietf.org/rfc/rfc1624.txt*, 2004.

[Knopper01] Knopper Web site, Knoppix Project, available online at *www.knopper.net*, 2005.

[Logicube01] Logicube Web site, available online at *www.logicube.com/*, 2004.

[Mares01] Mares and Company Web site, available online at *www.dmares.com/*, 2004.

[Mykey01] MyKey Technology, Inc. Web site, available online at *www.mykeytech.com/*, 2004.

[Nist01] *Disk Imaging Tool Specification 3.1.6*, National Institute of Standards and Technology (NIST), available online at *www.cftt.nist.gov/DI-spec-3-1-6.doc*, 2004

[Nist02] *Digital Data Acquisition Tool Specification 4.0 (Draft)*, NIST, available online at *www.cftt.nist.gov/Pub-Draft-1-DDA-Require.pdf*, October 2004.

[Nist03] Forensic Software Testing Support Tools and Setup Documents, NIST, available online at *www.cftt.nist.gov/disk_imaging.htm*, 2005.

[Nist04] *Engineering Statistics Handbook—Chi-Square Goodness-of-Fit Test*, NIST, available online at *www.itl.nist.gov/div898/handbook/eda/section3/eda35f.htm*, 2005.

[Nist05] *NSRL and Recent Cryptographic News*, available online at *www.nsrl.nist.gov/collision.html*, 2005.

[Psu01] *MD5 Weakness*, Pennsylvania State University, available online at *http://citeseer.ist.psu.edu/68442.html*, 1996.

[Rsa01] Randall, James and Szydlo, Michael, "Collisions for SHA0, MD5, HAVAL, MD4, and RIPEMD, but SHA1 Still Secure," RSA Laboratories, available online at *www.rsasecurity.com/rsalabs/node.asp?id=2738*, August 2004.

[Rto01] "Notebooks Outsell Desktops and LCD Monitors Unit Sales Surpass CRT Monitors in May," RTO Online, available online at *www.rtoonline.com/Content/Article/Jul03/NPDNotebooksOutsellDesktops070303.asp*, 2003.

[Sanderson01] Sanderson Forensics Web site, available online at *www.sanderson forensics.co.uk/products.htm*, 2005.

[Scott01] Scott, Mark, "Independent Review of Common Forensics Imaging Tools," Memphis Technology Group, available online at *http://mtgroup.com/papers.htm*, 2004.

[Sealey01] Sealey, Philip, "Remote Forensics," *Digital Investigations Journal*, Vol. 1 No. 4, available online at *www.compseconline.com/digitalinvestigation*, December 2004.

[Snedecor] Snedecor, George W. and Cochran, William G., *Statistical Methods, Eighth Edition*, Iowa State University Press, 1989.

[TechPath01] Technology Pathways, LLC Web site, available online at *www.techpathways.com*, 2005.

RESOURCES

[Ietf02] Request for Comment 1141, Internet Engineering Task Force, available online at *http://www.ietf.org/rfc/rfc1141.txt*, 2004.

13 Large System Collection

In This Chapter

- Defining a Large Collection
- Large System Imaging Methodologies
- Tying Together Dispersed Systems
- Risk-Sensitive Evidence Collection

DEFINING A LARGE COLLECTION

The definition of *large* is certainly a moving target when it comes to data storage. Twenty years ago, a 10-MB hard disk was considered a costly luxury. Today, users can buy USB key drives with five times that storage capacity for only a few dollars. Large system collection refers not only to single large digital storage repositories but also to large environments with dispersed networks of data. Often corporate networks offer both challenges. As computer systems become more connected, defining a single specific individual digital corpus that contains artifacts of potential evidentiary value becomes more difficult. The growing size of data storage systems only compounds the issue. Even in home and small office networks, forensics investigators can easily encounter multiterabytes of aggregate data storage. After investigators have overcome data volume and dispersion issues, complex technologies such as SAN, NAS, and RAID offer challenges themselves in relation to media access for bit-stream imaging and subsequent analysis.

LARGE SYSTEM IMAGING METHODOLOGIES

One of the first questions asked by investigators entering into a corporate network is, "How do I effectively bit-stream image a RAID array?" Looking back at Chapter 8, "SAN, NAS, and RAID," investigators will recall that RAID technology combines multiple disks (32 or more) and represents them as one or more logical volumes of the attached system. Because the RAID system can be implemented with software by network operating systems such as Windows Server products and Linux or hardware RAID controllers, the reassembly of the RAID disk for analysis could require specialized software or hardware, not to mention all the system downtime caused by removing each disk of a RAID array and imaging one disk at a time. If the RAID is implemented using specialized hardware, the connectors and mounts for each disk are almost certainly proprietary in nature, requiring the investigator to remove the disks from the mount and/or use an interface adapter designed for the specific proprietary adapter. Indeed, using standard disk-by-disk bit-stream imaging methodologies to image a RAID array implemented in software or hardware presents unique challenges. Two critical pieces of information an investigator should collect when faced with RAID array image collection follow:

Define the type of RAID (hardware, software, versions of software, and firmware on the RAID Controller): When a RAID array is implemented by the network operating system (software), rebooting the system to another operating system—DOS, Linux, or Windows Preboot Environment (PE)—will display each physical disk, allowing individual imaging through the boot disk. When RAID is implemented by a hardware RAID array controller, the disk is visible to any operating system as the single or multiple virtual disks that the controller is configured to display, requiring any individual disk imaging to be through offline direct access.

Identify the number, type, and location of each disk within the RAID array: What level of RAID is implemented—0, 1, 5, or otherwise? In a RAID 1 Mirror, two disks of the mirror are completely or almost identical, depending on the implementation. Other factors, such as one disk being marked as "failed" or size mismatches, could also cause disk data differences. In all other forms of RAID, the disk data is spread out over the entire array of disks and each disk is unique. To accurately obtain this information, RAID array management software will need to be accessed on the running system, or the investigator will have to reboot the system and access the hardware BIOS control functions of the RAID array controller. As always, the amount of interaction an investigator has with the system should be weighed to the benefit of the information gathered.

CAUTION

Each implementation of RAID will maintain the integrity data or mechanism to identify if an individual disk is failed. It is imperative that hardware write blockers be utilized to ensure that the original disks are not altered and inadvertently marked as "failed," causing the RAID system to regenerate the RAID array. Causing more than one disk in a RAID array to be marked as "failed" could require heroic efforts on the part of the investigator for recovery. A single disk could be marked as "failed" by its physical removal, even when the system is shut down (many hardware RAID controllers contain an onboard battery for configuration data).

As with most imaging situations, when faced with a RAID array, the investigator may have a variety of imaging methodologies available at his disposal or may be driven by the environment or tools available. When the RAID array is implemented in Windows Server software, disks can easily be imaged as individual disks into image files and analyzed using ProDiscover or EnCase. Both products are capable of regenerating the Windows RAID arrays in their forensic file systems. When other software RAID implementations are used, investigators may be required to image the disks live as a single volume smear (changing in time), which could possibly result in more complex testimony in court. Another option is to image each physical disk via direct access when the system is offline, requiring challenging reconstruction efforts and, again, possibly complex testimony. An imaging option that offers cleaner imaging (however, with possible reconstruction challenges) is to boot the system to a live alternate operating system through the use of DOS, Linux, or Windows Preboot Environment (PE) and image all individual disks at rest (offline) using utilities or an agent that will redirect the sectors out another interface, such as USB or FireWire. ProDiscover, EnCase, SMART, and all the Linux live boot environments offer solutions for this methodology.

NOTE

Some file and data recovery applications such as File Scavenger® from QueTek™ [Quetek01] and Active@Undelete® [Active01] are capable of recovering individual files from or rebuilding damaged RAID arrays.

If the downtime is acceptable, imaging each physical disk from a hardware implementation of RAID can often be rebuilt by the Linux software RAID subsystem for certain hardware controllers. This operation is risky, depending on the controller, because of the tendency of a hardware controller marking removed disks as "failed" or the inability to rebuild the RAID array for analysis. Two excellent online resources for RAID recovery using Linux are:

- *http://software.cfht.hawaii.edu/linuxpc/RAID_recovery.html* [Uh01]
- *www.linux.com/howtos/Software-RAID-0.4x-HOWTO-4.shtml* [Linux01]

Using NetCat or CryptCat [Farm901] and "dd" [Garner01] to conduct images of volatile memory and physical disk images was discussed in Chapter 11, "Collecting Volatile Data," and Chapter 12, "Imaging Methodologies." These same tools can be used from a Linux live boot disk environment such as Helix [efense01]. Using the following commands on a sending and receiving station where "a.b.c.d" is the IP address of the receiving station will send the logical or physical disk image from the sending station to the receiving station over Port 3000.

Receiving Station: nc -l -p 3000 | dd of=C:\temp\RAIDImageDisk0.img

Sending Station: dd if=\\.\PhysicalDisk0 | nc a.b.c.d 3000 (for full physical disk image)

Alternately, or in addition to, a physical disk-by-disk image, the investigator may wish to collect partition images from a live system with the RAID array assembled by the live system. This action will provide a fallback image for analysis should the investigator not be able to reassemble or repair disk-by-disk images taken from an offline system with a boot disk or by direct connection. The following syntax will collect the logical C:\ partition from an active Windows system using NetCat and "dd":

Receiving Station: nc -l -p 3000 | dd of=C:\temp\LogicalRAIDImageC.img
Sending Station: dd if=\\.\C: | nc a.b.c.d 3000 (for a partition only image)

NOTE

The command-line syntax is for use of the Windows port of "dd" [Garner01]. Syntax will change slightly for Linux and Unix variants of the tool. Consult the products' main pages for specific syntax on these systems. Garner's tools provide additional command-line options not shown such as –lock to lock disk from writes or dismount the disk during the imaging process.

Increasingly, imaging live systems is becoming a requirement due to the liability associated with down time. When the investigator is faced with a RAID array, the array's complexity compounds the increased downtime associated with large volumes of data. No matter the choice of tool, investigators will need to formalize their live collection methodologies. NetCat/CryptCat, "dd," and commercial tools such as ProDiscover, EnCase, and SMART all offer the ability to image live systems.

In Chapter 8, investigators were introduced to Network Attached Storage (NAS) and the benefits of its use in corporate as well as home networks. Recall that

NAS is just that—storage attached to a network and shared by users through network file system emulation. The emulation software can often emulate several popular network file systems such as those provided by Microsoft, Apple, and Unix. The more advanced the NAS, the more likely advanced fault-tolerant disk systems such as RAID will be employed, which creates a more complex collection environment for the investigator. Although the same challenges of imaging RAID systems apply to NAS with RAID, NAS offers new challenges. One of the most significant challenges to collecting disk images from NAS is that the proprietary and often firmware-based emulation software may not offer an avenue to boot the system to a live boot CD-ROM such as Helix [efense01]. The same challenge will often also apply to running a live remote agent or servlet offered by ProDiscover and EnCase for imaging, thus leaving the investigator with one choice: taking the NAS offline and imaging the system through direct disk access. The more advanced NAS products offer integrated backup and "snapshot" functionality, which may prove beneficial to an investigator for creating an image but may not create the desired sector-level backup provided by bit-stream imaging. For NAS storage using RAID Level 1 (disk mirroring) in environments unable to tolerate the downtime of a complete imaging process, the investigator could break the mirror and image the single disk from the broken mirror offline while leaving the other disk online to operate as normal (however, in a failed state). While operating in the failed state, the NAS would be vulnerable to further failure and would require RAID regeneration on completion of the offline imaging process. Each collection will provide its unique challenges, requiring the investigator to be creative while adhering to the requirements of completeness and accuracy in evidence collection. Normally, these types of challenges cause the judicial component of "reasonableness" to take the front seat.

Much as with NAS, Storage Area Networks (SAN) may also implement RAID in the underlying system. Also like NAS, SANs offer unique challenges when it comes to imaging. Investigators will recall from Chapter 8, that unlike the proprietary firmware and "sitting on the network" appearance of NAS, SANs are normally directly connected to one or more servers through host-bus-adapters and/or Fibre Channel controllers. This topological approach often gives investigators the impression that a SAN could be imaged easily through a remote agent or servlet on the live system or some other type of redirection local to the server. The challenge created by SANs is that although they are often directly connected to the disk, the SANs are logically mounted locally as though they were remote disks being shared by a network file system. Collecting file-level data as evidence is easy to achieve on a mounted SAN volume, but collecting one or more bit-stream images of the SANs' physical disk may not be. Lucky for investigators, the relatively advanced nature and expense of SANs usually provides advanced file-system management software and firmware. Many SANs offer the ability to create snapshots, backups, and even sector-level management from within the SANs' disk groups. If spare disk bays are available in the SANs' disk housing, the investigator may be able to conduct the imaging process from within the SAN itself.

Whether in criminal or civil matters, investigators need to be prepared to conduct full bit-stream images of numerous workstations. It is common for an investigator to image 30 or 40 individual workstations at a given location. Understanding that with today's hard disk sizes, this task could entail imaging more than three or four terabytes of data, the investigator will need to have a concise imaging plan.

To better understand some of the options available to an investigator while collecting multiple disk images, consider the following scenario where an investigator needs to image 30 workstations containing a 100-GB disk on-site. In preparing to conduct the imaging, the investigator finds out that the workstations in question will be available for imaging beginning at 8:00 P.M. on the collection evening, and all imaging must be completed by 8:00 A.M. the following morning. The investigator is also notified that all workstations are on a 100-Mbps full-duplex Ethernet network using switch technology.

NOTE

On the surface, simply knowing the speed of a network will allow an investigator to quickly determine how fast he will be able to image systems over the network. Knowing the speed of a network is certainly important; however, understanding the network topology in use as well as the actual network's performance is essential for planning. Simply understanding that a network is using 100-Mbps full-duplex Ethernet as opposed to half-duplex can introduce a 100 percent margin of error when calculating the speed at which an investigator can push data across the wire. Access method, protocol, and application overhead will reduce the advertised transfer rates from 10 to 20 percent, depending on the technology. In addition, poorly designed and error-prone networks can operate at a fraction of the advertised data transfer rates less overhead. Any time an investigator is considering disk imaging over the network, whether from live or dead systems, he should draw out a data-flow diagram based on a complete understanding of the topology and performance of the specific network to identify possible performance bottlenecks. Also, the investigator must be cognizant of the effects of the network imaging process to normal users on the network. Transferring huge volumes of data across a network such as that in network bit-stream imaging in an uncontrolled manner can render even the most well-designed networks unusable for normal operations. Some networks implement QoS and other methods of controls, known as "packet shaping," to prevent any one type of connection from monopolizing all available bandwidth.

With these basic metrics the investigator can begin his planning. In the simplest form the investigator has 12 hours to image 30 100-GB disks. The investigator also knows the characteristics of the network, should he decide to conduct any imaging over the network. Three of the most common technical approaches to imaging available to the investigator are:

- Using a handheld forensics disk imager to directly connect and create a disk-to-disk or disk-to-file bit-stream image
- Using a field forensics workstation to directly connect and create a disk-to-disk or disk-to-file bit-stream image
- Using a field forensics workstation to capture a bit-stream disk-to-image file of the workstation over the network or via a network crossover cable

As the investigator begins his planning, initial thoughts surround time and volume calculations. Handheld forensics imagers are generally the fastest means of imaging, with some advertising transfer rates of up to 3 GB per minute under perfect situations. Despite these claims, investigators should not plan on such excessive imaging speeds. For planning purposes investigators should expect speeds of about 1 GB per minute when using a handheld forensics imager on newer desktop IDE disks and even slower speeds on smaller notebook and older desktop disks. Table 13.1 shows the average transfer speeds for various methods.

TABLE 13.1 Average Transfer Speed Matrix

Method	Average Transfer Speed*
Handheld imager	1 GB per minute
Field forensics workstation	600–700 MB per minute
100-MB full-duplex Ethernet	300 MB per minute

*Actual speed can vary greatly, depending on many factors.

If the investigator in our scenario has at his disposal the ability to use any of the three most common imaging practices, he might immediately choose the fastest means: using a handheld forensics imager. The investigator quickly determines that he has 12 hours or 720 minutes to capture a total of 3,000 GB, or three terabytes, of disk images. Referencing Table 13.1, our investigator determines that using the fastest method, he cannot image one disk at a time and complete the job in the allotted time. Dividing the total number of gigabytes to be imaged by the available time (3000/720 = 4.16), the investigator quickly determines that he will need to image four or more workstations at a time to accomplish the task in the allotted time. Noting that the calculations do not take into account any difficulties in physically accessing the disk errors while imaging and setup time, the investigator may want to image five or more workstations simultaneously in this scenario when using handheld forensics imagers. Depending on the number of disk imagers available, the investigator may need to use another one of the common imaging methodologies listed or possibly something more creative. A cost-effective approach to the same problem would be to use a forensics CD-ROM boot environment such as FIRE or Helix, which can create a bit-stream image to a locally attached FireWire or USB port. In this scenario, our investigator would require one boot CD-ROM and FireWire/USB-to-IDE drive enclosure for each system he wants to image simultaneously.

Investigators using USB-to-IDE converters should always ensure that the converter and system to which it is connected support USB 2.0. The lower-speed versions of USB are unsuitable for timely imaging or analysis of directly connected disks.

In the given scenario the investigator can often choose any of the standard imaging approaches desired to get the job done. It is always a good idea to have a backup plan that allows the investigator to use any of the standard approaches should some unknown barrier prevent the use of the method of choice. In some cases, resources may cause the investigator to use multiple approaches to complete the task in the allotted time frame.

No matter what disk or media technology presents itself, research and creativity are key. Investigators should expect the unexpected and be prepared to use alternate and possibly new methodologies in many cases.

TYING TOGETHER DISPERSED SYSTEMS

At the beginning of this chapter, large systems were identified with two critical components: volume size and dispersed nature. Thus, *large* can indicate many smaller volumes of data over a great deal of area or, more simply put, dispersed systems in large networks. Note that a single home computer connected to the Internet can quickly fall into this same category because of the systems and resources it uses when connected. Outside the crime scene investigation, in the challenge of identifying multiple systems containing evidence relating to a collection, the investigator must identify how the dispersed volumes of evidence will be collected.

When collecting evidence from large dispersed networks in civil matters, the discovery process and methodologies used are often driven by cost. In the landmark case *Zubulake v. UBS Warburg* [Zubulake01], a great deal of legal discussion was focused on the cost of large-scale discovery and who should bear the cost. Indeed, the cost and approach to the discovery process will continue to be of great interest to the courts as the volume of data in networks increases. *The Sedona Principles—Best Practices, Recommendations, and Principles for Addressing Electronic Document*

Production [Sedona01], created as a result of the 2003 Sedona Conference Working Group, also places a great deal of emphases on cost. It goes further to discuss that "forensic copies" or bit-stream images of entire evidence volumes, need be required only as an exception based on cost and other justifications. This concept causes a dilemma for many computer forensics investigators who, through their training, desire to provide the most accurate copy of evidence available. It doesn't take too many civil discovery requests involving hundreds or thousands of computers to realize that a compromise must be found to identify and extract the potential evidence from dispersed systems without sacrificing accuracy and completeness, and, thus, reliability. Many investigators may ask, "How can I be complete without collecting the complete bit-stream image?" The answer lies in how well a task is identified. In the case of civil discovery, the discovery request should be specific and identify specific documents, document types, data, and/or specific keywords for which the request is being made. With the scope of the request narrowed down, an investigator can be complete in relation to the highly specific request. In smaller discovery cases involving a limited number of disk data or backup tapes, it is beneficial for the investigator to follow full bit-stream imaging and collection methodologies, thus removing many possible challenges to their methodologies. Cost will often be a driving force in the investigator's collection methodology selection. The investigator must always balance cost with his capability to provide reasonable assertions of completeness, accuracy, and verifiability. Armed with knowledge of the environment from which the evidence is being collected and understanding the cost-balancing needed for collection in a complete, accurate, and verifiable way, the investigator then chooses the methodology for the given situation. Investigators are probably beginning to understand that though there are basic methodologies for bit-stream imaging, data handling, hashing, and documentation, there can be no boilerplate answer to each large-scale collection effort.

The concept of partial "surgical" extraction of evidence from large dispersed networks and volumes of digital data opens up many questions to the most classically trained forensics investigator. Some of the many questions follow:

- How can the investigator identify what will be captured?
- What will be the approach for imaging (capturing) specific file data?
- Are data bases involved? How will they be captured? (Processed queries or the whole database?)
- What software and hardware tools will allow for the identification of evidence in a forensic manner?
- What software and hardware tools will allow for the collection of evidence in a forensic manner?
- How will the evidence be verified?
- What if the evidence is challenged?

The questions can go on and on, but they can be reduced by methodical planning and investigator involvement in the discovery process at the earliest stages. Indeed, what can be considered partial identification and extraction of evidence has been practiced in criminal investigations, too. Consider law enforcement walking into a company where a crime has been committed that is digital in nature or computer evidence is sought. The company's building complex is confirmed to contain more than 10,000 computer workstations, servers, and data-storage devices. Through some form of filtering, the law enforcement agents need to identify which computers relate to the crime in question, even if they intended to collect full bit-stream images. Whereas it is reasonable to expect that a computer virus or worm could essentially touch and place digital evidence on each of the more than 10,000 systems, it would be unreasonable to expect law enforcement to conduct a full bit-stream image of each and every system. In this case a sample may be taken, but no matter what the choice, the key is reasonableness.

Understanding that partial bodies of evidence may be collected in civil, and quite possibly criminal, investigations, the two most important points related to technical collection methodology are

- How to identify the desired evidence
- How to collect and maintain verifiability of the evidence

The key to identifying the desired evidence is not completely technical, but it does involve investigative techniques. Part II, "Information Systems," provided a basic discussion of information systems as well as techniques and questions for personnel interviews in relation to data-storage habits. These items, as well as a basic understanding of crime scene investigation, will help investigators to identify the crime scene or possible locations of evidence. Again, reasonableness will come into play when deciding what to collect. If the only piece of evidence required from a specific server is a single log data base, such as that in a firewall server, does it make sense to bit-stream image the entire server? It may or may not, depending on the situation, but the investigator will need to make the decision based on what is considered reasonable in the specific situation. The other side of the first point is a more technical one, which involves a live search of a network and its data through some technical means. Based on an understanding of the network and its applications and data formats, the investigator may be able to utilize installed line-of-business applications and their inherent capabilities to identify specific files or evidence, such as Microsoft Exchange server's capabilities for administrators to locate specific e-mails. Companies that have implemented intranets, such as with the Microsoft portal server, may have documents indexed in a variety of ways useful to the investigator. If the investigator is looking for a specific set of keywords, he may need to utilize some type of network search application that can *crawl* the network and search inside documents of a specific type. Fortunately, Internet-based Web search engines have advanced software development in this area, and many companies have preexisting indexes of data on the network. dtSearch [dtSearch01] is a Windows-focused product line that is also sold in a network-enabled version for identifying documents throughout a network. Expansion Programs International, Inc. [Thunderstone01], also known as Thunderstone, manufactures several appliance-based information-indexing technologies capable of indexing natural language text, standard data types, geographic information, images, video, audio, and other data. There are many other types of index, search, and retrieval products that could be repurposed for forensics and discovery needs. Although there is no single answer, the identification of desired evidence is almost always a combination of sound investigative principles deriving knowledge for use with identification products such as search and index software.

Collecting and maintaining the verifiability of the evidence is usually the first issue that comes to mind after evidence is identified by whatever means. The easiest answer is to proceed with full bit-stream imaging using methodologies already outlined, but as investigators now know, this action may not be reasonable in large dispersed systems. If the investigator decides that only a log file will be collected from a specific location, he is presented with the question of how to extract the evidence.

Keeping in mind those critical components of completeness, accuracy, and verifiability, the investigator will most likely choose to capture the entire log rather than a specific entry. He will also create a cryptographic hash signature of the log at the time of capture, all the time documenting his steps. Information about the integrity of the server from which the log files came could also be of great importance to verifying the accuracy of the specific log. Of course, we could continue to go down this road until the investigator was back at capturing the entire bit-stream image again. But again, reasonableness in the large-scale environment may have driven the single log capture over the full disk image. To support this single specific artifact (the log file), it is never more crucial that the investigator collect supporting information such as those outlined in the Audit section of Chapter 4, "Interview, Policy, and Audit." An understanding and documentation of the overall security of the environment from which evidence is collected can be as critical to its verifiability as cryptographic hashing.

Network-enabled disk forensics tools such as ProDiscover Investigator and EnCase Enterprise Edition allow forensics investigators to selectively identify, document, create hash signatures, and extract individual artifacts of evidence from live running systems in large networks. Because of the remote nature of these applications, investigators are able to locate, collect, and document evidence over wide area networks in large, dispersed collection efforts. Although simply copying a selective file from a server and then hashing and documenting the process may be acceptable, the forensic nature of tools such as ProDiscover Investigator and EnCase Enterprise Edition provide a higher level of assurance to the investigator that the components of completeness, accuracy, and verifiability were met.

NOTE *What is meant as forensic nature when referring to tools such as ProDiscover Investigator and EnCase Enterprise Edition is that the tool is created with the forensics process in mind. The tool reads disks at the lowest level and conducts all file processing through its own read-only forensic filesystem.*

The larger and more dispersed the system, the more likely an investigator will need to automate his actions. Often the scripting or automation of these collection efforts can become daunting. Many investigators will adhere to the requirements of not taking operational systems offline while collecting evidence live, but they neglect to understand the impact on the network of moving large amounts of data. Understanding the performance characteristics of different network topologies becomes important when collecting evidence from live servers. An investigator can easily prevent normal operations on a network by using an untested script or performing automated evidence collection. Remember that meeting the goal of leaving a server online through live evidence collection is useful only if people can still access and use its services.

Once again investigators have been introduced to new tools including hardware, software, and methodologies, but in the end, integrity is the most important tool an investigator will ever posses. Integrity and documentation are essential when it comes to presenting and defending the evidence down the road.

RISK-SENSITIVE EVIDENCE COLLECTION

The rate at which information technology advances and new developments are unveiled to the mass market can be staggering to any investigator. As outlined throughout this book, data storage continues to be a focal point to the forensics investigator, primarily because the speed at which we can access these new larger volumes of data rarely keeps pace. From a legal perspective, today's legislation and statutory regulation are still struggling to keep up with the fast-paced digital realm. In his paper "Search Warrants in an Era of Digital Evidence" [Kerr01], Orin S. Kerr identifies inconsistencies in Rule 41 of the Federal Rules of Criminal Procedure, which outlines rules for search warrants. The current rule clearly shows that search warrants should be narrow in scope, clearly identifying a specific time and place for the search as well as what evidence is being sought. Whereas the requirements of Rule 41 are generally easy to meet with physical evidence, digital evidence is normally handled a bit differently, in that the entire digital container of evidence is normally seized at the search warrant location and the search of that container (disks) often happens back at the lab and is often complicated by large volume issues. This two-step process opens challenges to the concept of a "specific time and place" for many warrants. In the article, Kerr concludes by offering a series of proposed amendments to Rule 41 of the Federal Rules of Criminal Procedure to update the warrant process for the era of digital evidence.

In their paper "Risk-sensitive Digital Evidence Collection" [Kenneally01], Erin E. Kenneally and Christopher L. T. Brown present arguments and counterarguments as well as a framework for a formalized methodology for partial extraction of evidence from large-volume digital environments. Both articles clearly identify that advances need to continue in both the legal arena and the technical supporting methodologies used in digital investigations.

The early days of capturing every disk in a bit-stream image in an effort to clearly meet the legal system's demands for completeness, accuracy, and verifiability are constantly challenged in today's large digital volumes. To be certain, partial extraction of evidence from large bodies such as server logs and specific business records has been conducted for many years without a formalized methodology. When defining *completeness*, it is easy to establish that a complete bit-stream image of every digital media device at the location is *complete*. However, some may argue that a formalized methodology for collecting selected artifacts identified as evidence along with any required supporting evidence is no less *complete* than taking blood samples from a blood-spattered room rather than completely removing all items in a location that may contain trace evidence, including all wall fixtures. Once again the idea of reasonableness enters the picture. Certainly, in many cases the standard bit-stream everything is a reasonable approach to evidence collection. In other cases, the bit-stream imaging of terabytes, petabytes, or possibly yatabytes may not be. The difficulty in collecting less than "everything" is how to identify what is evidence, and once evidence is identified, determining how should the evidence and any supporting artifacts be collected without omitting exculpatory evidence.

NOTE

Exculpatory evidence is evidence that may prove innocence rather than guilt.

Indeed, although the rapid identification of evidence from large digital bodies of data can be challenging at best, advances in live evidence extraction tools offer great promise. Forensic applications such as ProDiscover Investigator and EnCase Enterprise Edition both offer the ability to conduct evidence search and extraction from live systems over the network. Other offerings are sure to follow.

Outside the legal supporting arguments in their paper "Risk-sensitive Digital Evidence Collection" [Kenneally01], the authors present a methodology framework that not only defines security considerations and mandatory and supporting artifacts to be collected but also calls for the creation of templates that could be used for field automation.

Table 13.2 shows a partial example of types of data that might be desirable for extraction from a Windows 2000 system from which evidence is being collected. Using information from templates created from a formalized and peer-reviewed methodology, investigators could create XML or some other standard language file to automate the extraction of evidence using a support tool for the environment. Much work is still required before methodologies such as RSEC are formalized; however, the need has never been more prevalent.

TABLE 13.2 Partial RSEC Extraction Template for Windows 2000 Systems

Mandatory Artifact	**Default Location**	**Notes**
Master File Table	First Sector of Partition	If volume is formatted, NTFS
Ntuser.dat	\Documents and Settings\<User>	
Supplemental Artifact	**Default Location**	**Notes**
Security Event Log "SecEvent.Evt"	%System%/System32/Config/	
System Event Log "SysEvent.Evt"	%System%/System32/Config/	

Timely court decisions are beginning to emerge supporting disk image evidence, even when the original evidence disk is no longer available. In a recent published decision by the Court of Appeals of Ohio, Ninth District, Wayne County [Ohio01] in *Ohio v. Michael J. Morris*, the court upheld the bit-stream image process after original evidence was no longer available. In the case, after law enforcement personnel had created a bit-stream image of the original evidence disk, the original evidence disk had been completely erased. In the appeal process the defendant claimed that he was denied due process in that the defense was not able to examine the original hard drive evidence to find potentially exculpatory evidence. In the decision the court not only validated the use of the MD-5 hash process but considered forensic disk images to be an exact copy and admissible when the "original" was no longer available.

As with each chapter's suggestion on methodologies and approaches to digital evidence, it is ultimately up to investigators to ensure the methodologies they use provide completeness, accuracy, and verifiability of the digital evidence they present. No amount of peer review can remove the investigator from the responsibility of personally testing the approach they use in digital evidence collection methodologies. In the end, it will be the investigator who stands in front of the court to defend the methodology, tools, and evidence they have collected.

SUMMARY

- Large system collection refers not only to single large digital-storage repositories but also to large environments with dispersed networks of data.
- After investigators have overcome data volume and dispersion issues, complex technologies such as SAN, NAS, and RAID offer challenges themselves in relation to media access for bit-stream imaging and subsequent analysis.
- Two critical steps an investigator should perform when faced with RAID array image collection are defining the type of RAID (hardware, software, versions of software, and firmware on RAID Controller) and identifying the number, type, and location of each disk within the RAID array.
- A single disk could be marked as "failed" by its physical removal, even when the system is shut down (many hardware RAID controllers contain an onboard battery for configuration data).
- ProDiscover, EnCase, SMART, and all the Linux live boot environments offer solutions for a live imaging methodology.
- Understanding that partial bodies of evidence may be collected in civil and, quite possibly, criminal investigations, the two most important questions related to technical collection methodology are how to identify the desired evidence and how to collect and maintain verifiability of the evidence.
- For planning purposes, investigators should expect speeds of about 1 GB per minute when using a handheld forensics imager.
- Transferring huge volumes of data across a network, such as that in network bit-stream imaging, in an uncontrolled manner can render even the most well-designed network unusable for normal operations.
- A cost-effective approach to multidisk imaging is to use forensics CD-ROM boot environment such as FIRE or Helix, which can create a bit-stream image to a locally attached FireWire or USB port.
- dtSearch [dtSearch01] is a Windows-focused product line that is also sold in a network-enabled version for identifying documents throughout a network.

- The current law clearly shows that search warrants should be narrow in scope, clearly identifying a specific time and place for the search as well as what evidence is being sought.
- Exculpatory evidence is evidence that may prove innocence rather than guilt.
- No amount of peer review can remove the investigator's responsibility of personally testing the approach he uses in digital evidence collection methodologies.
- "Risk-sensitive Digital Evidence Collection" is a proposed methodology for identification and partial extraction of digital evidence.
- In the end, integrity is the most important tool the investigator can ever possess.

REFERENCES

[Active01] Active@Undelete Web site, available online at *www.active-undelete.com/*, 2005.

[dtSearch01] dtSearch Web site, available online at *www.dtsearch.com*, 2005.

[efense01] Helix Bootable Incident Response and Forensics CD, available online at *www.e-fense.com/helix/*, 2005.

[farm901] Farm9 Web site, available online at *http://farm9.org/Cryptcat/*, 2005.

[Garner01] George M. Garner, Jr., Forensics Acquisition Utilities Web site, available online at *http://users.erols.com/gmgarner/forensics/*, 2004.

[Kenneally01] Kenneally, Erin E. and Brown, Christopher L. T., "Risk-sensitive Digital Evidence Collection," *Digital Investigations Journal*, Volume 2 Issue 2, available online at *www.compseconline.com/digitalinvestigation/tableofcontents.htm*, 2005.

[Kerr01] Kerr, Orin S., *Search Warrants in an Era of Digital Evidence*, GWU Public Law Research Paper No. 128, available online at *http://papers.ssrn.com/sol3/papers.cfm?abstract_id=665662*, 2005.

[Linux01] *The Linux Software RAID How To Guide*, available online at *www.linux.com/howtos/Software-RAID-0.4x-HOWTO-4.shtml*, 2005.

[Ohio01] *Ohio v. Michael J. Morris*, Court of Appeals of Ohio, Ninth District, Wayne County, No. 04CA0036, Feb. 16, 2005.

[Quetek01]QueTek Web site, available online at *www.quetek.com/prod02.htm*, 2005.

[Sedona01] *The Sedona Principles: Best Practices, Recommendations, and Principles for Addressing Electronic Document Production*, Sedona Conference Working Group, available online at *www.thesedonaconference.org*, March 2003.

[Thunderstone01] Expansion Programs International, Inc. Web site, available online at *www.thunderstone.com*, 2005.

[Uh01] RAID Recovery Web site, available online at *http://software.cfht.hawaii.edu/linuxpc/RAID_recovery.html,* 2005.

[Zubulake01] *Zubulake v. UBS Warburg*, 217 F.R.D. 309 S.D.N.Y., 2003.

RESOURCES

[Guidance01] Guidance Software Web site, available online at *www.guidance-software.com*, 2004.

[TechPath01] Technology Pathways, LLC Web site, available online at *www.techpathways.com*, 2005.

Part V

Archiving and Maintaining Evidence

Once potential computer evidence is collected, it needs to be examined and maintained. In our final section, Part V, "Archiving and Maintaining Evidence," we discuss computer forensics workstations, labs, evidence archival, physical security, and lab certifications/accreditations. Part V closes with a discussion of future trends and directions of the computer forensics field ranging from training and certification to professional associations.

14 The Forensics Workstation

In This Chapter

- The Basics
- Lab Workstations
- Portable Field Workstations
- Configuration Management

THE BASICS

One of the tools central to collecting and investigating computer evidence is a computer itself. When talking to other investigators about what type of computer might be suitable for collecting and investigating computer evidence, the answers received will be as varied as the people to whom the question was asked. Although some components and characteristics can be generalized, it is helpful for the forensics investigator to understand basic PC architecture to eliminate potential performance bottlenecks for his specific needs. The vast volumes of data being processed by the computer forensics investigator in most every case dictate that a great deal of attention should be placed on performance. A 10 percent performance gain on an operation involving 100 hours of processing can net the investigator 10 hours of time savings. To better understand the basic performance characteristics of a standard

PC, it is helpful to review the basic high-level PC architecture. Figure 14.1 displays a high-level view of the basic PC architecture, which has changed only slightly since its introduction in the original IBM personal computer. In its simplest form, any computer program used by a forensics investigator is nothing more than a group of instructions stored in some form of media that is available to the computer for processing through the I/O bus. The computer's CPU executes the instructions provided by the program and follows the logic presented. In the Reduced Instruction Set Computing (RISC) architecture, such as the x86 processor, each instruction takes the CPU about 2.75 processor cycles per instruction on average to complete. The first performance metric enters the scene as the cycle rate of the CPU, measured in megahertz or gigahertz, which relates to millions or billions of cycles per second, respectively. To translate the speed of the CPU effectively to actual instructions executed, the investigator would simply divide the cycles per second by the average cycles per instruction of 2.75. Using this formula the investigator can determine that a 1 GHz processor will on average execute 363,636,363 instructions per second.

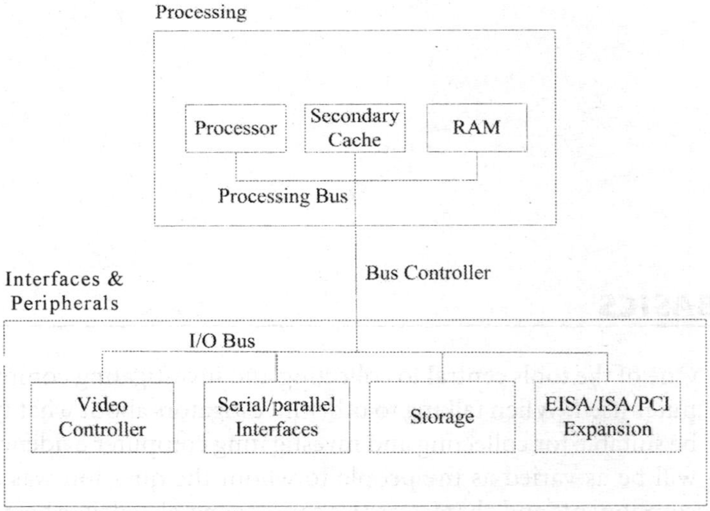

FIGURE 14.1 Block diagram of a basic PC.

The original design of the PC was based heavily on effective use of resources. This is why when executing a program, only portions of larger applications are able to be brought into memory (RAM) in what is referred to as *pages*. By segmenting the amount of data brought into RAM, systems with smaller amounts of RAM, due to its early high cost, could still function effectively. The management of program code loading between physical storage and RAM is referred to as *demand paging*. Operating systems using virtual memory, such as Windows 2000, use *demand paging* and *virtual memory management* to control the flow of program execution code from media, to virtual memory on disk, then physical RAM and all points between.

Once a program or its pages are loaded into RAM, processor control is transferred to the program or the next instruction to be executed. If data is being read from or written to a device on the I/O bus, then once the adapter on the I/O bus is complete, it will send an *interrupt* to the processor. While visualizing this data flow along the processing bus and the I/O bus, recall that these components in the PC architecture are also rated with a speed in MHz or GHz like the processor is. One of the reasons the processor and I/O buses are partitioned is for performance. Most users would not want the CPU to wait for slower I/O data transfers to complete. Although bus speeds are not intended to be a PC bottleneck, they can be sometimes. Particularly in notebook computing, investigators can find two seemingly identical computers with vastly differing performance measurements. When looking closer, the investigator may find that the I/O bus on one notebook computer was rated much lower than the other, with all other primary performance indicators such as RAM, CPU, and disk being the same. This type of low-level discrepancy is often the difference between major manufactures' home and professional line of computers.

When looking at the processing block shown in the Figure 14.1, notice the "Secondary Cache" block. This component is a faster level of memory in which commonly executed instructions are kept, allowing the processor and RAM to maintain their speed when requesting and executing instructions. If the investigator were to delve deeper inside the CPU itself, he would notice that a primary level of cache and bus controller are inside the CPU, allowing instructions to be kept for quicker retrieval and execution.

Another performance enhancement at the lower architectural level is multiprocessor PCs, which implement two or more CPUs, allowing for simultaneous program instruction execution. To take advantage of a multiprocessing PC, the program must be written in a *multithreaded* fashion, allowing for the simultaneous execution and management of program code. Just think what would happen if a CPU, knowing nothing about the order in which instructions needed to be executed, were to give the program back information before it was ready? It is this very issue that requires the program itself be written in a multithreaded fashion. It is important to note that a two-processor computer does not operate twice as fast. When implementing multiprocessor technology, the two CPUs typically share a single set of RAM and coordinate the use and flow of program instructions between the two CPUs. In addition, not all programs or sections of programs are written in a multithreaded fashion. Having said that, if an operating system such as Windows 2000, Linux, or Windows XP is written to be multithreaded, then the overall performance will be better because many OS functions used by applications will perform faster.

To increase performance of individual peripherals on the I/O bus, another low-level capability called DMA, or direct memory access, was created. Using DMA, a peripheral that demands faster transfer of data, such as sound and video, can directly access the memory-transfer capabilities within the processing bus identified in Figure 14.1, and therefore, bypass the slower I/O bus controller. DMA and bus mastering techniques that allow a peripheral to more closely control the I/O bus allow for an overall increased device performance.

As investigators look more closely at the architecture of individual peripheral devices such as SCSI, ATA, and network controllers, they will notice great differences in performance characteristics between brands and models. With each component interacting so closely with the other, it's often difficult to identify performance bottlenecks where the demand has outpaced the component's capabilities. This type of interaction can often be difficult to trace. Consider a networked PC that is suddenly experiencing poor local application performance. Although seemingly the slow performance would be directly related to a local application or the connection to some remote source, it may not be. In situations where the local computer's network card must process large amounts of broadcast traffic, increased drain can be placed on the local system at several levels. This situation is only one example of how a seemingly disconnected factor can affect a local resource. Another example showing the interactive effects within a PC is when a poorly performing disk controller can reduce the effectiveness of a system by taking up too many CPU cycles or depleting RAM. A faster CPU or increased amount of RAM may seem to solve the problem, but the actual bottleneck was in the disk controller. It is precisely this complex interaction that makes tuning the performance of a PC difficult. In our poorly performing disk controller example, the faster CPU or increased RAM only cloaked the actual problem. Often, with any device that caches data in memory, waiting for the device to react results in increased cache buildup and depletion of RAM. Finding a more capable component will clear the bottleneck. With hard disks the performance metrics and cache capabilities of the disk itself can greatly affect performance, even when the system uses the best-performing disk controllers.

From the investigator's standpoint every component in a PC intended for computer forensics investigations is critical. Multiprocessing systems are helpful for processing intensive tasks, such as brute-force password cracking attempts, disk I/O, and memory, and are important to imaging and search functions and processor and I/O bus speeds. In the end the computer forensics investigator may end up with specialized systems for different tasks within the profession, but overall performance of each system will be essential.

LAB WORKSTATIONS

The computer forensics lab workstation is often a workhorse of a computer used for many tasks related to analysis as well as imaging. Computer forensics investigators and system administrators often debate the pros and cons of building their own versus purchasing a prebuilt system. On one hand, nobody knows what you want more than you do; on the other hand, the time required to build a quality system can be extensive. Let's face it—we could all use a few more hours in each day. There is no easy answer, so let's look at some of the benefits on each side of the discussion.

The benefits to building your own workstation follow:

- You know the requirements.
- Specific components of the highest grade can be selected.
- This method is often less expensive than buying a prefabricated system.
- The knowledge gained during assembly is valuable.

The benefits to purchasing a prebuilt workstation follow:

- You save valuable time.
- Individual components are often designed to work well with each other.
- Support for product defects is often better.
- Sometimes higher-quality or specialized components are less expensive in the complete prebuilt package.

It is hard to argue with the ability to save a great deal of time when purchasing prebuilt computer forensics workstations. However, all computer forensics investigators should have the experience of building a small number of computers from the ground up. There is no better place for the investigator to start than with one of his first forensics workstations.

Investigators can find many step-by-step guides on how to build a PC that contain everything from the basics of electrostatic discharge to installing a video controller card. Because the selection of components varies from system to system, most guides generalize to the first critical step. As already discussed, performance is essential when dealing with large volumes of data in computer forensics, and quality is always important. Another area in which the computer forensics workstation stands out is its all-around capabilities. Rather than being tuned to support a specific use, such as graphics processing or database performance, the workstation must be able to support a wide variety of media access. Because of the need for such a wide array of storage media access, computer forensics workstations are normally full-height or extra-height tower cases with many drive bays. It is often difficult to find a computer case that can easily accommodate six or more drive bays and allow for easy routing of the associated cabling. Another unique attribute to the forensics workstation is the investigator's need to be changing the disks constantly. Removable drive bays are a necessary addition to the forensics workstation, even for the operating system boot disk. Many investigators find it useful to change operating systems or possibly reimage the operating system disk. Swapping the physical disk is often easier to manage than managing a multioperating system boot environment.

Disk media I/O controller cards are another element that makes the forensics workstation unique. Rather than choosing between technologies such as ATA, Serial ATA, and SCSI, the forensics workstation will normally support all types of disk access, allowing for analysis and imaging of whatever type of media becomes of interest. Some of today's standard ATA controller cards will offer SATA and standard IDE interfaces in the same card, thus saving valuable resources in expansion slots.

CAUTION

Some ATA/SATA combination cards do not support ATAPI devices, such as CD-ROM drives. If an investigator intends to use an ATAPI CD-ROM drive rather than an SCSI CD-ROM drive, he must ensure that the ATA controller card supports ATAPI devices. Support level for ATAPI devices is not always clearly marked on ATA controller cards.

In providing support for the multitude of disk media, flash card adapters are useful. Although many USB flash card adapters are available to consumers, rarely do they implement write blocking at the controller level. Flash Block from MyKey Technologies [Mykey01] is a multicard reader with built-in write blocking. It attaches to a standard ATA IDE interface. When dealing with SCSI disk media, investigators are challenged by the numerous connector formats available. Chapter 7, "Physical Disk Technologies," discusses some of the many developments to the SCSI standard and connecters used over the years. The investigator could easily need to convert between any of four or more SCSI connector types in disks from a single collection.

Once the forensics investigator has selected all the components for the computer forensics workstation, paying keen attention to quality, he will need to develop a plan for putting it all together.

NOTE

Despite all the planning and design allowing for configuration changes, it is not uncommon for a forensics workstation to live its life with one side of the case open at all times. After opening the side of a forensics workstation a number of times many investigators will simply leave the case open.

Investigators will note that network cards are needed and should be carefully selected for today's forensics workstations. Despite the feeling among many that it is a best practice to not connect a computer forensics workstation to a network, it is hard to imagine not networking any computer forensics lab that contains more than one computer. However, not directly connecting a computer forensics workstation to the Internet is a very good idea. In Chapter 15, "The Forensics Lab," investigators will be introduced to lab design principles that allow for multiple networks to provide security while allowing the lab to function in a networked environment.

Using the following steps, as well as individual component guides, the investigator can commence putting his workstation plan in motion:

1. Identify and collect all required components.
2. Design the case/component layout, noting that some consideration for case layout went into the selection of the case.
3. Prepare the case for installation. Remove the cover, plan for wiring paths, and determine the installation order for the various components. Some cases will require the components be installed in a certain order of component based on accessibility.
4. Configure the motherboard. Adjust the pin settings for CPU speed and motherboard features in accordance with the manual.
5. Install the CPU and heat sink or fan. Many CPUs include a preinstalled heat sink or fan. Proper installation of the CPU's cooling mechanism is critical for this high-heat component.
6. Install the memory. Finding the correct memory type and processor configuration is often challenging for some motherboards. It can be helpful to purchase the motherboard, CPU, and memory together to avoid mismatches.
7. Install the motherboard. When installing the motherboard in the case, be careful to connect all I/O connectors and case options for reset, power, drive activity lights, and so on. Many investigators sidestep these connections thinking they will not be needed, but ultimately, they are.
8. Install the floppy drive. Along with the floppy disk an investigator will want to install other specialty removable disks such as multicard flash readers.
9. Configure the hard drives and CD/DVD-ROM. In configuring the hard drives and CD-ROM drives, determine which devices will be identified on which SCSI channel or which will be primary and which slave. In the forensics workstation it is often a good idea to explicitly select which device is primary and then not use the cable select setting. Don't forget the removable drive bays. Attach an internal write blocker such as an ACard [Acard01] on one drive bay.

10. Mount the hard drive bays and clearly identify which bay is attached to which controller and cable on the outside front of the case.
11. Install the CD/DVD-ROM(s). In some cases an investigator will want more than one optical device; however, in today's environment it is essential that they have a DVD writer. The many CD and DVD formats make it important that investigators research and choose the most widely compatible optical disk available.
12. Connect and run the internal media cables. Floppy drive, hard drive, and optical drive cables can often prove challenging to run, especially when so many are included in the forensics workstation. Good cable management can be harder than it looks. Locking everything down with wire ties in a permanent fashion is not a good idea until you have checked that everything runs accurately.
13. Finish installing any peripheral cards for video or I/O controllers as needed.
14. After you are finished assembling the computer and ready to power up for the first time, recheck all the steps to this point. Double-check all cabling, pin settings, and the security of each device.
15. The initial boot-up is the point at which most investigators consult a higher power or simply cross their fingers. The famous Power-On Self-Test (POST) beep codes can be elusive because they change from BIOS manufacture to manufacture and often from specific model. One thing for certain is that any more than one beep on boot up is often bad news. Table 14.1 shows generic IBM BIOS beep codes. Investigators should consult their specific BIOS implementation for further reference.
16. Configure the BIOS. Each system's BIOS is different, but most will allow for user configuration of details such as boot password, boot device order, time, and specific peripheral settings.
17. Test the System. Some motherboards and peripheral devices include low-level diagnostics that may even include a DOS-like boot disk. Many of these diagnostic disks may not be included with the device but are included in the support section of the companies' Web site for download. Now is the time to stress-test the installation rather than waiting for weeks to go by before noticing some obscure fault-causing errors.
18. Prepare the hard drives. Partitioning and formatting the boot disk as well as other disks can often be accomplished during installation. Sometimes it is helpful to plan and create the boot disk layout prior to installing the operating system, just in case the specific operating system cannot support your desired layout during installation.
19. Choose and install your clean operating system in a nonnetworked or sanitized environment free from Internet connectivity. There is nothing worse

than having a computer system compromised by a worm during installation, just prior to installing that last critical security patch. Fully patch and install desired security software prior to hooking up any network connection.

20. Adjust the installation as necessary. Install desired software utilities and make operating system customizations as desired. Once the investigator's workstation is installed and running, he will benefit from a great deal of inside knowledge of his system, allowing for much quicker troubleshooting should problems appear. By this time the investigator will recognize the time-savings value of purchasing a well-designed prebuilt forensics workstation.

TABLE 14.1 IBM Beep Codes

Number of Beeps	Meaning
1 short beep	Normal POST, computer is OK
2 short beeps	POST error, see screen for details
Continuous beep	Loose card, or short
Repeating short beeps	Loose card, or short
One long and one short beep	Motherboard issue
One long and two short beeps	Video display issue (CGA)
One long and three short beeps	Video display issue (EGA)
Three long beeps	Keyboard error
One Beep, Blank or Incorrect Display	Video display issue

Prebuilt workstations not only save investigators the time and headache of building the system but also save significant time in designing and selecting forensic components. Two leading manufactures of prebuilt systems include:

- Forensic Computers (*www.forensic-computers.com*)
- Digital Intelligence (*www.digitalintelligence.com*)

Both companies have been in the business of exclusively making digital forensics workstations for years and produce quality products.

Figure 14.2 shows the Forensic Recovery of Evidence Device, Modular (FREDM), which is a preassembled workhorse of a forensics workstation manufactured by Digital Intelligence [DigitalIntel01]. The modular design of a prefabricated forensics workstation such as FREDM provides the maximum flexibility for adding additional storage and interface components. Much like Forensic Computers [Forensic-computers01], Digital Intelligence offers a complete line of prebuilt computer forensics workstations designed to suit the varied and specialized needs of the computer forensics investigator.

FIGURE 14.2 The Forensic Recovery of Evidence Device, Modular (FREDM) by Digital Intelligence. ©Digital Intelligence, Inc. 2005.

As the computer forensics investigator becomes more comfortable with his requirements, he may consider creating the workstation design requirements and having the system built by a local PC sales and service centers. Most any PC center that assembles and sells PC systems will be accommodating to fill the specific customer needs of the computer forensics investigator. No matter the approach to design, building, and purchasing a computer forensics workstation, the utmost care must be taken to ensure this core tool is flexible and provides reliable performance.

PORTABLE FIELD WORKSTATIONS

Despite the computer forensics workstation shown in Figure 14.2 being a bit larger than the average workstation, it's safe to say that forensics workstations from the lab are rarely portable. At first glance, the forensics investigator may feel that he can handle imaging workstations on site using a boot CD-ROM or handheld forensics imager and leave all workstations back at the lab. Although this statement is partially true, there are many benefits to bringing one or more forensics workstations on site. One of the first benefits is the ability to use an imaging and analysis suite such as ProDiscover, EnCase, or FTK throughout the case. Having analysis software on site also allows the investigator to perform an on-site preview of potential evidence, thus meeting stringent warrant requirements or possibly ruling out the collection of selected systems. In cases such as probation-compliance visits, the on-site forensics analysis suite is almost a requirement for preview because live inspection was the intended purpose of the visit. Of course, having a forensics workstation capable of imaging is also a great fallback device, just in case other methods of imaging prove unfruitful. No matter how the investigator looks at the situation, it's always useful to have at least one forensics workstation on site. The challenges come in when an investigator takes stock of what capabilities he needs in the now-portable forensics workstation.

The portable forensics workstation, just like its lab-based counterpart, needs to be a workhorse of a machine, providing interfaces to many different types of media and the associated connectors. In the early days of forensics, providing a portable computer forensics workstation meeting the requirements usually translated into *luggable,* rather than *portable.* Today still, there is a struggle for capability and portability, usually ending up in the following two approaches:

- High-end notebook computer with a bag of forensics accessories
- Ruggedized workstation with everything built into the case

The following forensically specialized PC manufacturers all provide an assortment of portable forensics workstations:

- Data Forensics Engineering (*www.dataforensicsengineering.com*)
- Digital Intelligence (*www.digitalintelligence.com*)
- Forensic Computers (*www.forensic-computers.com*)
- Intelligent Computer Solutions, Inc. (*www.ics-iq.com*)

Today's notebooks provide a great deal of capabilities and power over earlier models, but they often lack all the media-connection interfaces needed for forensics purposes. Of course, hardware write blocking and large-volume storage are also important requirements when using a portable workstation. Even when combining all the required storage, interfaces, and hardware write blocking, the ruggedized portable workstation, like the one shown in Figure 14.3, still requires an assortment of tools, cables, and support materials.

FIGURE 14.3 Ruggedized workstation shows the Data Forensics Engineering Guardian portable forensics workstation imaging a notebook commuter via a crossover cable using a portable USB 2.0 drive enclosure for the target image.

These materials, together with the portable forensics workstation, form the forensics field kit, often referred to as a *flyaway kit* or *black bag.* The following contents of a standard forensics field kit are also listed in Appendix D, "Forensics Field Kit":

Forensics workstation: Notebook or specialized portable case system. If a notebook workstation is used, ensure it is FireWire and USB 2.0 capable and that an included CD/DVD-RW drive is present.

Handheld forensic drive imager: Such as those from ICS ImageMASSter and Logicube.

Portable USB 2.0/FireWire drive enclosure: With removable drive bay for target images.

USB 2.0-to-IDE cable: For accessing evidence drives within cases.

Target hard disks: Several large, forensically clean hard disks for target images.

Box of blank CD-ROMs/DVD-ROMs

Adaptec SCSI PC card: If using a notebook forensics workstation.

PC CloneCard IDE converter: Helpful in imaging hard-to-access notebook disks.

Internal disk drive power converter: For powering up evidence drives for imaging when removed from workstations.

Network cables: Include standard cables as well as crossover cables of various lengths.

Various interface adapters: SCSI II (50-pin) to every other type of SCSI, SCA to SCSI III, IDE 40-pin (notebook) to Standard IDE, 1.8-inch to standard IDE, SATA to ATA, and so on.

Software:

- Forensics analysis suites
- Disk recovery software
- Forensics boot CD-ROMs
- Incident response CD with trusted binaries for collecting volatile data
- Other specialized software as needed

Administrative Materials:

- Pens and permanent markers
- Several new composition books for notes
- Tamper-proof evidence bags, labels, and tape

Portable PC tool kit: Screw drivers, ESD (electrostatic discharge) wristbands, and so on. Include specialized star screwdrivers and Macintosh case-access tools, if needed.

Large bag: Or hardened case for transporting equipment.

NOTE

Many of the consumable items contained in the forensics investigator's flyaway kit are heat sensitive and can be damaged if left for extended periods of time in a car trunk or other high-temperature location. Tamperproof tape is especially heat sensitive and should never be left in hot areas for extended periods of time.

Once assembled the kit will need periodic maintenance to ensure software and firmware are kept up to date. Consumable items will need to be replaced when used, and spare cables should always be available. Having a well-constructed and well-maintained flyaway kit is a necessity for any forensics practitioner. Even corporate incident-response teams that outsource forensics analysis and digital discovery should consider assembling a team forensics flyaway kit to ensure they are able to react to any short-fused bag and tag jobs.

CONFIGURATION MANAGEMENT

Configuration management can have several connotations. In software development configuration management often refers to managing the software development life-cycle from build to build and version to version. In relation to the computer forensics workstation, investigators will want to establish some level of operating system configuration management using systems configuration management.

Even within the field of systems configuration management, the concept can mean many things. As with any discipline involving procedures and controls, there is a balance of reasonableness to be obtained in regard to configuration management.

Consider the average home computer user and the approach he might take to managing his personal computer's configuration. The average user may install one or more applications, utilities, and software patches to applications and the operating systems as the week passes. Then one day he can no longer print in color or, worse, connect to the Internet. The difficulty in tracking down what happened to cause a printer or network connection to go bad is that many changes have been recently made, and by now the user doesn't remember what he changed and when throughout the week. In this home user scenario, poor configuration management leads to difficulties in troubleshooting the problem. One of the first questions a user or technical support person might ask when something goes wrong is, "What was the last change you made?" For our home user the last change may be easy to remember, but the other 12 changes may not always be that clear.

Consider an extreme opposite of the home user scenario, where a computer used in nuclear power systems monitoring is being managed by a systems control person. In this case, before any change is made to the computer, it may require logging to a log by a witness, and the same configuration change may need to be validated on a completely separate test system prior to being installed on the production system. Further controls may require that only one change can be made, followed by multiple tests to the system to validate stability prior to any subsequent change. There may even be software controls installed on the monitoring systems to prevent changes without some type of safeguard. Obviously, these and other types of controls provide a high degree of configuration management but offer little flexibility in the system's use. A balance must be met between controls and usability, much like the balance between usability and security controls in information technology security. A reasonable balance between the two extremes can normally be better understood by conducting a risk analysis. In most businesses, conducting risk analysis is complex, but it can be simplified with the following four primary steps:

1. Determine asset value.
2. Estimate potential asset loss.
3. Analyze potential threats to assets.
4. Define an annualized loss expectancy.

The annualized loss expectancy (ALE) can be found by multiplying the Single Loss Expectancy (SLE) by the Annualized Rate of Occurrence (ARO), or SLE × ARO = ALE.

The difficulty in risk analysis is not identifying the quantitative or hard dollar risk but putting a value on the qualitative intangible components, such as loss of reputation or customer confidence.

The results of a formalized risk analysis should include the following:

- Critical asset valuations
- Lists of significant threats
- Likelihood of threat occurrence
- Estimated dollar loss by potential threat occurrence
- Recommendations on actions to either reduce, transfer, or accept each risk.

Reducing the risk usually involves implementing safeguards to mitigate the risk's occurrence. Transferring a risk consists of actions such as purchasing insurance, thus allowing the insurance company to assume risk. Accepting the risk usually occurs when the protection measures were too costly or the likelihood of occurrence was very low. In computer forensics, two prominent risks related to the forensics workstation include

- Compromised forensics workstation through malware or viruses
- Erroneous results or loss of data brought about through unmanaged operating system or application software changes

Although many forensics investigators choose to avoid compromised workstations by never connecting them to a network, certainly compromises can occur through other means. By running a thoughtful risk-analysis process, investigators may find other methods of risk mitigation to provide an acceptable balance between usability and protection. In Chapter 15, "The Forensics Lab," mitigating strategies for this risk will be discussed in more detail.

Interestingly, implementing a comprehensive configuration management program can help mitigate security issues associated with malware and unmanaged system changes. In practice, a balance is normally achieved involving a mixture of many actions or remedies.

Because of the sensitive nature of forensics labs and digital evidence, many forensics investigators will take extreme measures to protect the integrity of each workstation. In the early days of forensics, when investigators analyzed only a few disks at a time, they often took extreme approaches, such as eliminating network cards. In today's climate involving many disks with large volumes of data and forensics labs with 10 or more forensics workstations, it is reasonable to expect that each machine be able to interact and exchange data more easily. Networked computer forensics labs should, however, utilize best practices to prohibit direct Internet and outside-world connectivity.

One of the most useful methods for configuration management that provides security and integrity for systems is to completely reimage the forensics workstation prior to each case. Although this measure could be considered extreme, it can be quite effective, allowing the forensics investigator to carefully manage the configuration of a single image used by many forensics workstations. Of course, maintaining software revisions and patch levels will still need to be accomplished on the baseline image. One interesting approach in supporting the concept of clean imaging workstations is the Data Forensics Engineering Guardian [Dataforensics01] portable forensics workstation, which includes a complete operating system image stored in the Host Protected Area of the hard disk. Each time the forensics investigator wants to refresh the installation, he uses a hot-key approach to resetting the system back to a clean install.

Other methods of operating system configuration management include various software controls that may lock the system from changes or monitor and report on system changes. Simple measures for configuration management on Windows and other systems can include the following:

- Set tightly controlled access-control restrictions on each file. In Windows, this requires the use of the NTFS file system.
- Turn on filesystem auditing for critical directory structures involving the operating system and specific applications. Investigators should note that too much filesystem auditing can cause degradation in performance.
- Periodically audit systems for configuration settings.
- Create cryptographic hash baselines of the file system or specific sections of the file system. Periodically compare the cryptographic hash baseline as part of the audit process. Investigators should note that the use of user mode applications for the creation of a baseline is subject to compromise when performing hash baseline comparisons. See Chapter 6, "Volatile Data," for a discussion of rootkits and Trojans that can affect user mode application operation.
- Test proposed software and operating systems on a test bed system prior to rollout to production forensics workstations.

- Develop and execute a comprehensive test plan with known data values and operating metrics prior to production rollout.

Most investigators will note from these recommendations that setting controls, auditing their status, and reporting on variances are key to configuration management. As with any such time-consuming operation in the information technology arena, there are turn-key packages to allow system administrators and investigators alike to automate the configuration-management process. Larger labs may want to implement automated configuration management through management platforms such as HP OpenView® [Hp01], IBM Tivoli® [Ibm01], or other solutions. Smaller labs will most likely be able to provide a reasonable level of configuration management by setting controls, auditing their status, and monitoring for variances.

SUMMARY

- It is helpful for the forensics investigator to understand basic PC architecture to help in eliminating potential performance bottlenecks for his specific needs.
- A 10 percent performance gain on an operation involving 100 hours of processing can net the investigator 10 hours of time savings.
- In the Reduced Instruction Set Computing (RISC) architecture, such as the x86 processor, each instruction takes the CPU about 2.75 processor cycles per instruction on average to complete.
- To take advantage of a multiprocessing PC, the program must be written in a multithreaded fashion, allowing for the simultaneous execution and management of program code.
- All computer forensics investigators should have built a small number of computers form the ground up.
- Rather than choosing between technologies such as ATA, Serial ATA, and SCSI, the forensics workstation will normally support all types of disk access, allowing for analysis and imaging of whatever type of media becomes of interest.
- Three long beeps during boot up on systems using the IBM BIOS means a keyboard error has occurred.
- Prebuilt workstations can save not only the time and headache of building the system but also significant time in designing and selecting forensic components.
- Having analysis software on site allows the investigator to perform an on-site preview of potential evidence, thus meeting stringent warrant requirements or possibly ruling out the collection of selected systems.
- Some ATA/SATA combination cards do not support ATAPI devices such as CD-ROM drives.

- Having a well-constructed and well-maintained flyaway kit is a necessity for any forensics practitioner.
- The annualized loss expectancy (ALE) can be found by multiplying the Single Loss Expectancy (SLE) by the Annualized Rate of Occurrence (ARO).
- In risk analysis, reducing the risk usually involves implementing safeguards to mitigate the risk's occurrence.

REFERENCES

[Acard01] Microland USA Web site for ACARD SCSI-to-IDE Write Blocking Bridge, available online at *www.microlandusa.com/*, 2004.

[Dataforensics01] Data Forensics Engineering Web site, available online at *www.dataforensicsengineering.com/*, 2005.

[DigitalIntel01] Digital Intelligence Web site, available online at *www.digital-intelligence.com/*, 2005.

[Forensic-computers01] Forensic Computers Web site, available online at *www.forensic-computers.com/*, 2005.

[Hp01] HP RADIA Web site, available online at *www.managementsoftware.hp.com/products/radia_osm/*, 2005.

[Ibm01] IBM Tivoli Web site, available online at *www-306.ibm.com/software/tivoli/*, 2005.

[Mykey01] MyKey Technology, Inc. Web site, available online at *www.mykeytech.com/*, 2004.

RESOURCES

[Blake01] Blake, Russ, *Optimizing Windows NT*, Microsoft Press, 1993.

[Ics01] Intelligent Computer Solutions, Inc. Web site, available online at *www.ics-iq.com/*, 2004.

15 The Forensics Lab

In This Chapter

- Lab and Network Design
- Logical Design, Topology, and Operations
- Storage
- Lab Certifications

LAB AND NETWORK DESIGN

As discussed several times throughout this book, some investigators will simply state that it's best not to have your computer forensics lab or workstation connected to a network. What is normally meant by this statement—and often misunderstood or left out—is that forensics workstations should not be *directly* connected to the Internet. Most users and experienced investigators alike would agree that connecting any computer directly to the Internet, sometimes even with a firewall, can be dangerous. Luckily, investigators don't need to make such a broad choice and can have their cake and eat it, too, so to speak.

Even the smallest computer forensics practice will quickly grow beyond two or more computer forensics workstations and will likely require Network Attached Storage (NAS) or some other large-volume storage devices. By simply separating the operational forensics network from an administrative network that is connected to the Internet, wide area network, or other partner networks, the same risk can be mitigated. Figure 15.1 shows the concept of two distinctly different networks in the same physical location.

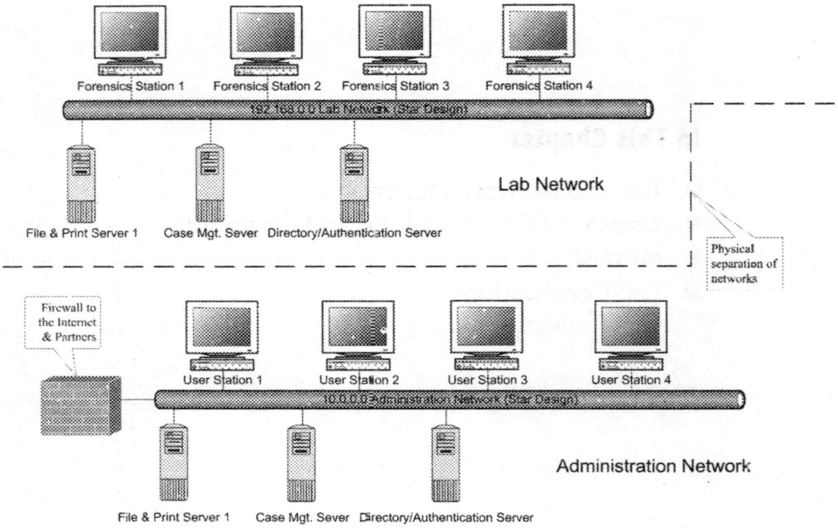

FIGURE 15.1 Segmented lab network.

Before jumping in and designing a forensics network, let's look at some basic network design principles. Any time a network is being designed from the top-down [Oppenheimer01], the engineer should be first analyzing his business goals and constraints and then taking a close look at his technical goals and constraints. As with security—and life in general—there are always trade-offs to be made in the journey toward balance. At first glance the forensics investigator may say, "This is easy; I need the highest possible security and the ability to push and store large volumes of data across the network." Although this statement certainly is true, there are many technical components and constraints within network design. Components of the network design that the forensics investigator should first evaluate follow:

Scalability: The ability for the network to grow and handle more workstations, storage servers, and traffic.

Availability: Should the network be resilient to faults and to what level? For instance, should there be backup paths for network traffic in case a network cable snaps or goes bad? What about servers—should there be redundant servers as well as storage?

Performance: How many users and how much traffic should the network handle? This area should gain much attention due to the large volumes of data that can be expected in the computer forensics field. Rarely does a normal administrative network need to handle as much data as a computer forensics lab's network does.

Security: Again, this area requires a high level of attention for the forensics lab network. A great deal of security protective measures will be provided by segmenting the operational and administrative networks. Other security components will apply, depending on design goals and cost constraints.

Manageability: All networks need some level of manageability. The more network devices you have, the more complex they become to manage. Some may feel that the manageability of individual devices may not be as important in a small computer forensic lab due to the limited number of devices. Though essentially true, many of the manageability features in switches are also a benefit to security configuration, such as the ability to set up a monitoring port in a managed network switch.

Usability: Many networks can sacrifice usability components that allow inexperienced personnel to tap into or change network configuration easily. Often small networks do not implement patch panels and structured wiring, allowing for easy reconfiguration. The usability component will often bleed over into other areas such as adaptability, affordability, and manageability.

Adaptability: Although it might seem that a small computer forensics lab does not need to adapt to changes, this is far from the truth. Computer forensics labs will be in a constant state of change and need the ability to adapt to new technologies and configurations quickly.

Affordability: Cost is always a concern, no matter what the organization. Where would the challenge be without affordability entering the picture to balance out other components?

After reviewing the components of the network design, many forensics investigators will still come back to the basic concept of securely moving large volumes of data from point to point. Moving large volumes of data across a network of computers can be enabled by many technologies, but it will normally involve extensive use of switch technology and high-bandwidth network-access methods such as Gigabit Ethernet. From a network topology standpoint, some security is being provided by segmenting the operational forensics lab network from other networks, but other physical design approaches can help enhance security.

NOTE

Extensive logical security measures should be implemented to support any physical and network topology security measures put in place.

Depending on the cost and other considerations, investigators might wish to implement a computer forensics lab completely with fiber optic cabling. Although tremendous speeds can be achieved with today's copper networks in Gigabit Ethernet, fiber optic cable provides for emanations security known within the military as Tempest [Cryptome01]. Not only are fiber networks secure against electromagnetic emanations eavesdropping, they provide an additional layer of physical security in that they are hard to tap into without being detected. A piece of fiber optic test equipment called an Optical Time Domain Reflectometer (OTDR) [Nettest01] can detect a point of connection for unauthorized fiber network taps. Added security when using fiber cabling is gained by the difficulty introduced for tapping a network with nonstandard optical connections. Wireless, or Wi-Fi, networks have become very popular and many may be considered due to their adaptability. Wi-Fi networks do offer numerous benefits, but they do not offer the speed performance or security requirements of most forensics labs. Other physical security measures associated with the network topology and design include the physical separation of the operational forensics lab and administrative network. As most investigators might expect there are several approaches to the segmentation of both networks. Some may take the stand that the two networks should be so segmented that no equipment from both networks should be in the same rack or room, as seen in Figure 15.1. However, others may say that merely color-coding connection jacks, equipment, and patch panels can provide the necessary segmentation as long as other logical protection measures are put in place. The correct answer can be answered only by going through risk analysis and reviewing the technical constraints previously listed. After conducting the risk analysis, investigators may find they need to back up and consider the physical characteristics of their lab choice. Characteristics that provide for physical security of the lab facility include reinforced doors, security-enhanced venting, and access controls.

Physical controls and a lab's overall physical location are every bit as important to the confidentiality, integrity, and availability of data as logical controls are. Criteria used in the selection of the lab location within a facility should allow complete access control. When implementing physical access controls on doors and storage facilities, investigators should consider the integration of logical monitoring controls. The use of biometric, proximity, and smart card readers for physical access often provides for enhanced access logging.

The use of video monitoring systems is always a dilemma within labs from an investigator's standpoint. Often investigators are concerned that when logging of this type is performed, the information is just something else that will be subpoenaed by the defense. Whether investigators subscribe to video monitoring the lab room or not, video monitoring a lab and evidence locker access is always a good idea.

During the risk analysis, the investigator will undoubtedly consider outsourcing physical controls to commercial alarm companies. In viewing the cost benefit trade-offs of outsourcing, investigators should consider the companies' capabilities to offer not only access control alarming but also enhanced services. Other services may include video monitoring systems and general physical access controls logging. The use of smart cards for forensics workstation access can also be integrated with physical access controls, allowing for centralization of access control, monitoring, and auditing within the facility. Far fewer commercial companies can offer such integration.

Reflecting back on Chapter 3, "Evidence Dynamics," and the forces of nature that can act on digital evidence, investigators will remember that the ideal humidity range for a lab will be between 40 percent and 60 percent. The lab's heating, ventilation, and air-conditioning system (HVAC) should be able to support maintaining this humidity range. By keeping the humidity within this range, data systems are protected from corrosion as well as harm from electrostatic discharge.

Another area surrounding physical control and evidence dynamics relates to the storage of digital evidence. The lab will need to secure digital evidence in such a way that protects physical access but also helps to preserve digital integrity of the evidence. A well-controlled HVAC system will help preserve the naturally rated longevity of media; however, if a fire were to break out, media may need further protections. Long-term digital-evidence storage should be in a fire-rated safe for magnetic media. To protect data on magnetic media from destruction, the internal safe temperature should be kept below 38°C (100°C) and are normally rated below 52°C (93°F).

Most labs will need to provide several levels of storage for digital media: one level of storage that provides quick access for investigators actively working cases, and another level for long-term archiving of case data. The digitally rated fireproof safe is more likely a good choice for long-term archival needs. For near-term storage of digital evidence, locker-room-type lockers work well to provide multiple storage containers that can help compartmentalize case data. By compartmentalizing case data in separate locker storage areas, investigator access can be limited to only the investigators who truly need access to the media. There are several approaches investigators can take toward the use of digital evidence storage lockers, depending on the physical security provided by lab and overall building facility. In some situations where physical security of the facility is high, welded heavy-duty metal lockers alone, such as those provided by Lyon Workspace Products [Lyon01], will be sufficient. In other situations, the investigator may wish to enclose all lockers in a wire-mesh cage or other physical control area. This choice, much like others, will be driven by a comprehensive risk analysis. Most distributors of lockers can modify the locker installation to provide multiple-sized lockers in a single bank, thus allowing for storage of just media or of complete CPU units.

Work surfaces should provide protection measures against electrostatic discharge (ESD) through the use of nonconductive matting and grounding ESD wristband connections. By now investigators are beginning to see that the physical attributes of a good computer forensics lab end up resembling a cross between large carrier-class data centers and an electronics lab.

Because of their resemblance to data centers, investigators building large-scale forensics labs may want to consider consulting with companies experienced with data center design and construction. Companies such as Rancho Santa Fe Technology [Rsft01] have been building and maintaining data centers for many years and can assist in every facet of the lab's construction and design.

The tools, cleanliness, and workspaces of a standard electronics lab allow forensics investigators to perform assembly and disassembly of equipment necessary to access digital media. The security, performance, and structured wiring environment of a carrier-class data center ensure the data's confidentiality integrity and availability are kept intact. The data-availability components found in data centers, comprising battery backup and generators, sometimes seem excessive to investigators for lab use. The need for power fault tolerance will always need to be weighed, but the first time a power outage causes an investigator to lose many hours of work, he will at least consider battery backup systems. In the computer forensics lab, one added layer to the normal structured wiring found in carrier-class data centers is the clear delimitation between two distinct networks. From a physical aspect, investigators should consider the following as a means to identify each network when two networks are available in the same facility:

- Color-coded cables clearly identifying each network
- Color-coded patch panels with segmentation and short cables preventing inadvertent cross connections
- Color-coded connectors with safety covers to prevent improper network connections in rooms with access to both networks
- Clear equipment markings identifying specifically which network the equipment has access to
- Segmented and organized cabinets to prevent inadvertent cross connects

Each forensics lab will differ based on an assessment of the individual investigator's needs and specific risks. Thoughtful designs can allow investigators to take advantage of the benefits provided by a network environment, but small single- and dual-station forensics labs may still choose to work with individual nonnetworked workstations.

LOGICAL DESIGN, TOPOLOGY, AND OPERATIONS

Once the investigator has moved past risk analysis and physical requirements and decides on a dual-network environment, he has several difficult choices for implementing the network infrastructure from a topological standpoint.

When both the administrative network and the operational lab network are separated physically, and are intended to be kept that way, one of the greatest concerns from a security standpoint is cross-connect. In a cross-connect situation, where the investigator has inadvertently connected the forensics lab to a less-protected network environment, the risk of exposure can be considered higher. Logical design implementations, such as configuring specific systems to not accept packets from other networks on the lab network side, packet-level encryption, and IPSec, can all help mitigate the exposure to risk. In addition, if the administrative network to which the cross-connect was established is reasonably protected using firewalls, intrusion detection, antivirus protection, and monitoring, then the exposure may not be that great. Without a full understanding of the actual physical and logical controls in place for both networks and their outside connections, it is hard to say if an inadvertent cross-connect would elevate risk more than a negligible amount.

Networks with differing security requirements have been connected for many years in the corporate world. Even in home networks, multiple networks with clearly differing security requirements are connected—the home network or computers are connected to the Internet. Just as in protecting the inside home network from the outside—but connected—network with a firewall, any two or more connected networks can be protected through firewalling.

NOTE

Firewalls are commonly thought of as a product that is placed in between two networks to protect one from the other. It is best to think of firewalling as a methodology rather than a specific product or technology. The protective measures provided by firewalls were first as simple as packet filtering on routers. A packet filter is nothing more than a set of rules (access-control list) stating which packets can pass and which cannot. As time went on and techniques were created to circumvent simple packet filtering, new features such as stateful packet inspection, monitoring, and reactive rules needed to be added as a means of protection. As more features were added, specialized routers now labeled "firewalls" were introduced with the primary purpose of protecting networks. However, investigators should keep in mind that the individual methodologies that make up a firewall, such as packet filtering and routing, are normally also offered in routers and switches. These firewalling methodologies should be implemented in a layered approach throughout networks, thus providing in-depth defense.

Many corporate networks install complex firewalls between departments that require differing levels of security as well as at the point of demark with partners and the Internet. This same approach can be utilized to connect and protect a lab and administrative network. Figure 15.2 depicts a dual-network environment that has been intentionally cross-connected and contains increased logical and physical controls.

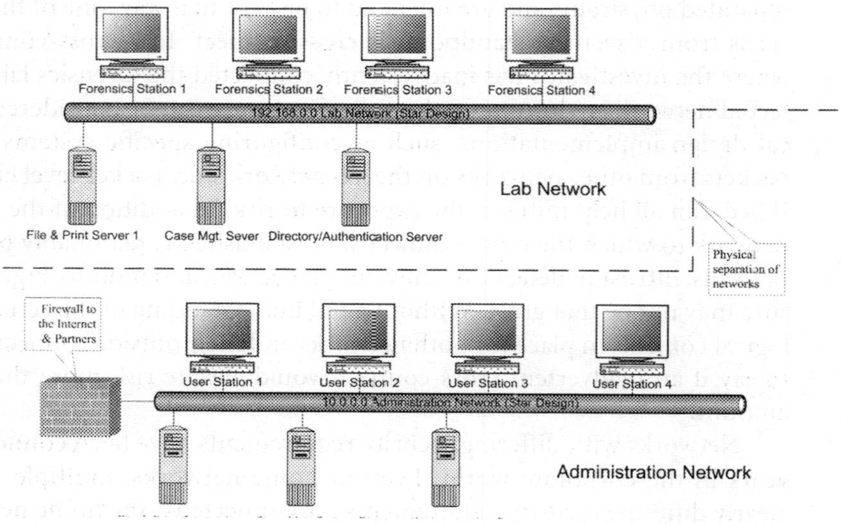

FIGURE 15.2 Connected lab network.

The logical and physical controls necessary to protect connected networks are more involved and will always present a higher risk of exposure than fully segmented networks based on risk analysis. No matter which method is employed, logical protection mechanisms must be put into place to protect the lab network. Some logical protective measures follow:

Port settings: Deactivate network ports not in use on all hubs and switches. Purchasing manageable hubs and switches will be more expensive but it often provides advanced features for locking down ports and setting access lists in addition to simplified group device management.

Access list: Set network access list on routers and switches in addition to packet filtering on firewalls. By providing this in-depth granular level of defense, investigators can ensure that should one logical protective measure fail or become subject to misconfiguration, all protection is not lost. Appendix H, "Investigator's Cisco Router Command Cheat Sheet," provides with basic examples of Cisco access lists. For a comprehensive discussion of Cisco router security features, investigators should see [Akin01], [Cisco01], and [Nsa01].

Outbound filtering: Ensure outbound packet filtering is implemented on routers and firewalls. Outbound packet filtering not only helps prevent the spread of worms but can render many remote-control compromise attempts ineffective.

IP network selection: Using nonroutable networks internally on all networks and routing between internal networks provides a great deal of packet-flow control. RFC 1918 *Address Allocation for Private Internets* [Rfc01] identifies three network groups that, although they will route just fine, are intended for internal private network use. These RFC 1918 networks are often referred to as nonrouteable networks because ISPs will often configure their routers to drop packets sent to any of the address blocks. The RFC private network blocks include the following:

Class A: 10.0.0.0 through 10.255.255.255

Class B: 172.16.0.0 through 172.31.255.255

Class C: 192.168.0.0 through 192.168.255.255

Static routing: By implementing static routing and configuring external routers to explicitly route to null any packets from an internal network, investigators can help eliminate internal traffic from exiting the network unintendedly. In Cisco routers using a route-to-null approach, protection is often less of a resource impact than the equivalent access-control list.

Removal of default gateway: Simply removing the default gateway on workstations within the forensics lab can prevent external communications while allowing local networking to function uninterruptedly.

Packet-level authentication/encryption: The IPSec protocol managed by the Internet Engineering Task Force (IETF) [Ietf01] provides a standards-based approach for both packet-level encryption of network traffic and packet authentication. Investigators can choose to implement fully encrypted network traffic or simply choose to have all packets authenticated by devices individually. IPSec is a widely implemented protocol used by operating systems and network devices in everything from virtual private networking (VPN) to packet authentication for network-level access controls. Many operating systems can accept or reject packets based on their IPSec authentication.

Active monitoring and alerting: Investigators should ensure that a comprehensive plan is put into place for monitoring the network at the lowest possible level. All monitoring systems, which may be dubbed Network Intrusion Detection Systems (NIDS), Network Forensics Analysis (NFA), or Intrusion Prevention Systems (IPS), should include active capabilities that allow the system to automatically react to threats and notify administrations of threats in real time.

Many logical security controls are available to the investigator that directly support networking topology and infrastructure. In many cases these security mechanisms will work hand in hand with the network operating systems used to manage user authentication, file-level access controls, and basic file and print services. The selection of network operating system will often drive other technology choices and how a network is secured. Unix, Windows, and Macintosh operating systems all provide the basic directory services and access controls required in network operating systems. Although many system administrators are zealots for one operating system or another, the choice will often come down to experience at hand, cost, and training. Indeed, the operating system in favor for most administrators is often the one for which they have the most experience. Dual-network environments, such as with the operational lab and administrative networks, will most likely end up with two complete network operating systems and directories of users and services. The capabilities and manageability of access controls should be one of the primary focuses for investigators who are involved in the selection of a network operating system. Remembering that there may be two completely separated systems also plays an important part in the manageability component of selection.

One of the most common ways for a system to be compromised is not by some sophisticated hack involving hours of low-level programming and genius IQ but by obtaining the user name and password of a privileged user on the network. Methods to obtain this information can vary from technical to social engineering, but once someone has the user name and password and has logged in, he is an authorized user with all the capabilities and privileges afforded the user. The other issue closely associated with identity and user authentication is that with a simple user name and password combination, it is hard to confirm that the intended user is actually who is using the credentials.

Because of possible user-credential compromises and the inability to securely attest to the user's identity, it is recommended that enhanced measures be utilized for identity management within forensics lab networks. For some time now, system administrators have implemented enhanced authentication measures for remote users who connect to internal networks from the outside for precisely these reasons. Normally, these enhanced authentication measures involve what is referred to as multifactor authentication. In multifactor authentication a user is required not only to know a user name and password combination but to also possess something else. One of the first "something else's" was a simple RSA [Rsa01] SecureID Authentication key device. With a SecureID card, the user might be challenged with a number that they would enter into a time-synchronized device, which would in turn provide the expected reply for the user. Other options included simply reading the number from a device and entering the number during the logon process. In both of these multifactor authentication schemes, the user not only needs to know the user name and password but also must physically posses a device that is synchronized with the network. Loss of the device or compromise of the user name and password would not allow compromise of the network unless both occurred in tandem. Some people refer to this multifactor authentication scheme as "something you know" and "something you have." In contrast, the use of biometric multifactor authentication is "something you know" and "something you are." With today's public key infrastructure (PKI)-enabled products, including smart cards, the cost of multifactor authentication has never been so low. Multifactor authentication schemes should be considered seriously for all local user authentications on forensic lab networks. By using multifactor authentication in forensic labs, investigators not only gain a higher degree of security against credential compromises but also can better attest to each investigator's identity in user audit logs.

Most network operating systems provide some level of logging and log management. In the forensics lab, maybe even more so than in the administrative network, investigators should focus on the aggregation and security of logs from various sources. The default behavior of many operating systems rarely includes log-file aggregation and increased security at the entry level. Secure Syslog server applications are a good way to aggregate and secure log data from network devices such as routers and firewalls as well as network servers. One such application is the LogLogic™ [Loglogic01] application, which aggregates and archives large volumes of log data for extended periods of time. LogLogic provides a Web-based interface for management and analysis.

The increasing amounts of legislation focused on data integrity and security within the United States have driven increased interest not only in secure audit logging but also in specialized devices for the protection, access control, and auditing of file access. One such device, dubbed an identity-driven access gateway, is manufactured by Caymas Systems® [Caymas01].

STORAGE

Even the smallest computer forensics lab will quickly generate the need for abundant storage of several types. Forensics investigators focused in small desktop systems will accumulate physical disks requiring evidence locker storage for the near term and long term. Even the quickest computer forensics case may require disks to be stored for two or three years before final disposition. For years forensics investigators have been challenged by the need to archive forensics image files for long periods of time. Often the choice has been to break up the images into CD-ROM- or DVD-ROM-sized pieces and archive to the optical media. Still today, many forensics practitioners follow this practice despite the growing challenges of volume. Considering that an image file of a notebook computer today, when broken down into 640-MB fragments can fill 90 or more CD-ROMs, investigators are seeking new solutions. Optical media is gaining in capacity but not at an equivalent rate of growth with magnetic media. The need for large-volume storage is a contributing factor leading many forensics labs to network their labs. By networking the computer forensics lab, investigators can take advantage of the economy of scale provided by technologies such as Storage Area Networks (SAN) and Network Attached Storage (NAS). A fully segmented computer forensics lab incorporating both SAN and NAS is shown in Figure 15.3. By implementing SAN and/or NAS technologies, investigators can provide much better performing near-term archival of disk images for use during the working of cases as well as satisfy some archival needs. Although the implementation of SAN and/or NAS technologies may not completely eliminate the need for optical storage systems for long-term archiving, near-term archival storage and open-case processing access is greatly enhanced. For long-term storage, some forensics investigators continue to implement standard split-image CD-ROMs and DVD-ROMs, but they may choose to use an optical jukebox to automate the storage and retrieval process. Optical jukeboxes with rewrite capabilities help increase the shelf life of long-term storage and can be reused and migrated to active file storage systems as needed.

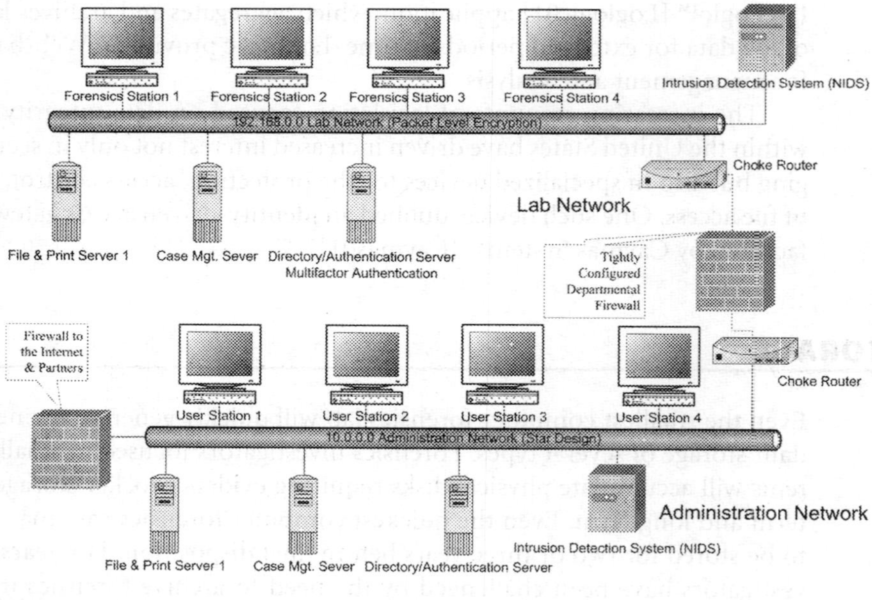

FIGURE 15.3 Lab network with storage.

Depending on the security constraints reflected by risk analysis, investigators may implement the requirement for encrypting all case data at rest. By encrypting all case data resident on storage systems, forensics investigators allow for added protection, despite some levels of compromise—that is, as long as the encryption keys were not compromised along with the data. When implementing any type of encryption, investigators should be cognizant of the performance requirements for encryption and decryption. The encryption and decryption of small files will rarely adversely affect the performance of applications, but the large volumes of data forensics investigators work with almost certainly will. Hardware-based full-disk encryption should be seriously considered when encrypting data at rest in most computer forensics labs.

There comes a time in the life of all data where its need for destruction will arise. Destruction of disks, both optical and magnetic, as well as expungement of case-related data will need to be carefully thought out when designing physical and logical controls as well as implementing lab procedures. Investigators will need to be able to not only completely wipe digital media to Department of Defense standards but selectively wipe case data on a file-by-file basis.

NOTE

The Department of Defense clearing and sanitizing standard, DOD 5220.22-M, outlines procedures for wiping magnetic media containing "unclassified" data for reuse. The standard outlines the procedures for wiping media with random data or known patterns a number of times to ensure the data would not be easily recoverable with magnetic resonance recovery. Software-only recovery methods are limited to the ability of recovering files by reassembly of the file data for which their index has been removed, damaged, or marked for reuse. A single pass writing random or known data to each cluster of a file will render software-only recovery ineffective. Magnetic resonance recovery of file data is achieved by the use of a microscope to view digital shadows left on a disk's surface after deletion. Specialized software used in conjunction with the microscopic view can often recover data from a disk's surface, even when sectors have been overwritten. The Department of Defense clearing and sanitizing standard calls for using three or more passes of disk wiping to help foil magnetic resonance recovery attempts. Investigators should note that DOD requirements for the destruction of magnetic media containing classified data call for physical destruction of the media.

Investigators should be prepared to implement file-level destruction for all lab workstations and servers as well as full disk wiping and physical destruction. Destruction and cross contamination of evidence is another factor leading some forensics investigators to reimage the computer forensics workstation operating system at each case.

When investigators are designing their lab networks, they should reflect on the general principles of the computer forensics process. When running through a risk analysis and identifying the technical components and constraints associated with the forensics lab's network design, the investigator will find that many of the same principles associated with the forensics process also apply. Just as documentation, logging, access controls, and digital tools help ensure the collection of digital evidence meets requirements of completeness, accuracy, and reliability, they also can apply to the lab that analyzes it.

LAB CERTIFICATIONS

The certification of people, their tools, processes, and environments is always a point of discussion in any profession. It can take many years for a profession to mature to the level where a common body of knowledge has passed peer review and is considered acceptable by the masses. The computer forensics profession is in the stages where certifications are beginning to materialize, but they still require a great deal of development. The computer forensics lab certification process, although further along than many other areas within the field, is still under development. As discussed in Chapter, 1 "Computer Forensics Essentials," there are several certification programs or guidelines for labs, but all are based and focused almost exclusively on the basic principles relating to labs of general forensics and scientific principles. As investigators continue to build and become more familiar with the requirements of computer forensics labs, they will most certainly identify unique components over standard scientific disciplines. Although there is much work to be done, the American Society of Crime Laboratory Directors/Laboratory Accreditation Board (ASCLD/LAB) process adopted by the FBI for use by its regional computer forensics labs has provided the certification process a starting point. ASCLD has recently adopted the ISO 17025 lab certification process because of its international focus.

Three interrelated programs of interest to forensics investigators involved in the certification process follow:

ASCLD Forensics Lab Certification and Accreditation Program: This program has been used by various law enforcement organizations for some time and was designed to certify forensic labs in other scientific disciplines such as DNA and Fingerprint. ASCLD now covers digital evidence. Further information on ASCLD can be found on the Web site at *www.ascld-lab.org*.

ISO 17025 Forensics Lab Certification and Accreditation Program: This certification program has the support of the international community, many U.S.

organizations and corporations, and government facilities and law enforcement agencies. ASCLD has adopted ISO 17025 certification process.

NIST Handbook 150 Lab Certification Program: This program is a baseline document that can be used as a foundation for many scientific disciplines such as ASCLD. HB 150 has been used as a foundation to validate various federal government labs.

In 2004, the FBI adopted implementation of the ASCLD certification process in an effort to adapt and mold the certifications to the unique requirements of the computer forensics lab. Because ASCLD and ISO 17025 are so heavily focused on the quality process, much like ISO 9000, they are useful as a basis for certification but require a great deal of additional focus for the unique requirements of computer forensics.

NOTE

The American Academy of Forensic Sciences has not officially recognized digital evidence examination as a forensics science as of this writing. There is much work still to be done in implementing ASCLD and ISO 17025 as a framework for digital evidence lab certifications.

ASCLAD defines the following four items as objectives for their certification and accreditation program in their program overview [Asclad01]:

- To improve the quality of laboratory services
- To develop and maintain standards that may be used by a laboratory to assess its level of performance and to strengthen its operations
- To provide an independent, impartial, and objective system by which laboratories can benefit from a total operational review
- To offer the general public and users of laboratory services a means of identifying those laboratories that have demonstrated they meet established standards

Outside the initial assessment and accreditation fees encountered in the process, the actual certifying agency fees can prove costly. The ASCLAD/LAB Web site at *www.ascld-lab.org* contains a listing of authorized proficiency review organizations for all committee disciplines except the newly formed digital evidence discipline. The following disciplines are currently observed:

- Controlled Substances
- Crime Scene
- Digital Evidence
- Firearms/Toolmarks
- Biology

- Latent Prints
- Questioned Documents
- Toxicology
- Trace Evidence

Investigators will note when reviewing the current forensics science disciplines that Digital Evidence is certainly the newcomer to the scene.

A wide range of PC and networking test equipment and software exist, but they have yet to be scrutinized to the level of lab-test equipment. In standard disciplines, labs, as well as many electronic labs, routinely use calibration and test equipment to ensure equipment meets some level of standardization criteria, which is an important part of the ASCLAD, other lab-certification processes, and equipment calibration labs. Translating this level of control to the computer forensics and digital evidence lab has been difficult partly due to the scope and fast-changing nature of computer forensics hardware and software. Many of the tools used in the analysis, and sometimes collection, of digital evidence are repurposed standard information technology tools, which come and go at the rate of technology itself. By the time a specific set of digital evidence tools, as well as the calibration tools to check their performance, were incorporated into a specific lab certification process, they are likely not to meet the needs of the computer forensics investigator working a case involving the current day's technology. Computer forensics investigators can solve this dilemma by focusing on the quality components of ISO 9000 and 17025. In focusing on the quality process, investigators should develop a set of standardization tests that allow them to quickly and accurately ensure that new tools designed for the computer forensics industry or repurposed information technology tools meet demanding criteria. Any standardization tests must be broad enough to adapt to new technologies and methodologies while still maintaining a standard level of results.

There is not yet a mandate in the United States for computer forensics lab certification, but any lab could benefit from the quality-assurance certification process of ISO 9000 and 17025. Until ASCLD matures to be more focused in digital forensics and specialized addendums are created and accepted for HB 150, mandates will likely be scarce and limited to specific organizations or agencies. Much of HB 150, which is used as a guideline for certification, is focused on scientific equipment calibration, an area that has been difficult to translate to digital data analysis and network engineering.

Certification and accreditation of computer forensics labs will continue to be an area for discussion and growth within the field of computer forensics in the immediate future. Despite their individual stances on certification and accreditation, investigators should ensure labs for which they are responsible meet a high level of quality through official ISO processes or internally developed quality standards. Not only are the lab's equipment and procedures important to quality, so too are the methodologies, training, and integrity of the forensics investigator himself. Ultimately, the forensics investigator should seek accuracy and unimpeachable integrity.

SUMMARY

- Forensics workstations should not be directly connected to the Internet.
- By simply separating the operational forensics network from an administrative network that is connected to the Internet, wide area network, or other partner networks, risks can be mitigated.
- When a network is being designed from the top-down, the engineer should first analyze his business goals and constraints and follow up by taking a close look at his technical goals and constraints.
- How many users and how much traffic should the lab's network be capable of handling? Performance should gain much attention due to the large volumes of data that can be expected in the computer forensics field. Rarely does a normal administrative network need to handle as much data as a computer forensics lab's network.
- Extensive logical security measures should be implemented to support any physical and network topology security measures put in place.
- Long-term digital evidence storage should be in a fire-rated safe for magnetic media.
- Firewalling should be implemented as a methodology to provide in-depth defense.
- Many corporate networks install complex firewalls between departments requiring differing levels of security as well as at the point of demark with partners and the Internet.
- The logical and physical controls necessary to protect connected networks are more involved and will always present a higher risk of exposure than fully segmented networks based on risk analysis.
- Multifactor authentication should be considered even for local authentication in forensics labs.
- By implementing SAN and/or NAS technologies, investigators can provide much better performance for near-term archiving of disk images for use during the working of cases.
- Investigators should be prepared to implement file-level destruction for all lab workstations and servers as well as full disk wiping and physical destruction.
- The American Society of Crime Laboratory Directors/Laboratory Accreditation Board (ASCLD/LAB) process adopted by the FBI for use by its regional

computer forensics labs also incorporates the ISO 17025 quality process into its computer forensics lab certification process.

- Translating stringent certification level of controls to the computer forensics and digital evidence lab has been difficult, partly due to the scope and fast-changing nature of computer forensics hardware and software.
- There is not yet a mandate in the United States for computer forensics lab certification, but any lab could benefit from the quality-assurance certification process of ISO 9000 and 17025.

REFERENCES

[Akin01] Akin, Thomas, *Hardening Cisco Routers*, O'Reilly, 2002.

[Asclad01] ASCLAD/LAB—International Accreditation Program Overview, available online at *www.ascld-lab.org*, March 2004.

[Caymas01] Caymas Systems Web site, available online at *www.caymas.com*, 2005.

[Cisco01] *Essential IOS Features Every ISP Should Consider v. 2.9*, Cisco Systems, 2002.

[Cryptome01] Tempest Timeline Web site, available online at *http://cryptome.org/tempest-time.htm*, 2005.

[Ietf01] The IPSec Security Protocol Web site, available online at *www.ietf.org/proceedings/96dec/charters/ipsec-charter.html*, 2005.

[Loglogic01] LogLogic Web site, available online at *www.loglogic.com*, 2005.

[Lyon01] Lyon Workspace Products Web site, available online at *www.lyonworkspace.com/homepage.asp*, 2005.

[Nettest01] Nettest Web site, available online at *www.nettest.com/Products/Products/CMA,_,4500,_,Optical,_,Time,_,Domain,_,Reflectometer/Overview.aspx*, 2005.

[Nsa01] *National Security Agency Router Security Configuration Guide*, available online at *http://nsa2.www.conxion.com/cisco*, 2002.

[Oppenheimer01] Oppenheimer, Priscilla, *Top-Down Network Design—A Systems Analysis Approach to Enterprise Network Design*, Cisco Press, 1999.

[Rfc01] RFC 1918 *Address Allocation for Private Internets*, Available online at *www.ietf.org/rfc/rfc1918.txt*, 2005.

[Rsa01] RSA Security Web site, available online at *www.rsa.com*, 2005.

[Rsft01] Rancho Santa Fe Technology Web site, available online at *www.rsft.com*, 2005.

16 What's Next

In This Chapter

- Areas of Interest
- Training, Knowledge, and Experience
- Analysis and Reporting
- Methodologies
- Professional Advancement

AREAS OF INTEREST

Throughout this book, the computer forensics investigator has been seen as a single investigator who may be involved in every stage of an investigation from bag and tag, to the lab, and finally in court testimony. Furthermore, because of the similarities, from a technical standpoint, little emphasis has been placed on the differences between criminal investigation and the civil discovery process. Certainly, the computer forensics investigator may be involved in all facets of an investigation in civil discovery as well as in criminal investigation, but as the profession grows, investigators in large organizations will specialize in one or more areas of interest. Investigators will always require training in a broad sense, but they may choose to seek enhanced training to develop their skills in specific areas, including collection, analysis, and discovery, as well as the criminal or corporate environment.

Collection

The first responder often meets with new and challenging collection scenarios. Although the term *bag and tag* implies the simplified collection and transport of evidence, it can offer many challenging situations in the digital realm. Investigators are often presented with new challenges involving the collection of digital evidence from a data-volume or simple-access standpoint. The broad spectrum of equipment coupled with rapid changes in the information technology industry make continued training in new technologies essential for anyone involved in the collection of digital evidence. Investigators who are focused on the collection of digital evidence will seek extended training in the areas of physical disk media, enterprise storage, and imaging methodologies.

Analysis

As indicated in this book's title, this text did not discuss the analysis of digital evidence. Indeed, the analysis of digital evidence is not a single area of interest but can include many specific areas and associated skills. Although the high-level methodologies involved in digital evidence analysis can be generalized to fit most scenarios, many exist. Subspecialties in analysis include investigations involving cyberattack, white-collar crime, and specific platforms such as Windows, Unix, PDAs, and other digital devices that can contain evidence.

Discovery

Investigators involved in the civil discovery process normally adhere to the same basic principles and methodologies used in the overall computer forensics process, described in this book. The unique workflow and slightly differing evidentiary proceedings found in the discovery process does, however, require specific understanding and experience. Many computer forensics investigators find the challenges involved in complex civil disputes rewarding and specialize in the process. By specializing in civil discovery, private sector investigators exclude themselves from stipulations by organizations such as HTCIA, which require them to not perform criminal defense services.

Criminal

Just as many law enforcement members are often driven to service by a higher purpose, so too are many computer forensics investigators. The rewards provided by involvement in the criminal justice system can be plentiful. Computer forensics investigators work in a variety of positions throughout the system, including sworn officer and contract support roles. Investigators focused in criminal investigations will become familiar with rules of civil procedure surrounding individual rights to privacy as they relate to digital-evidence-focused search warrants and criminal case management.

Corporate

Investigators involved in computer forensics for the corporate arena may fall into one or more of several areas. The investigator may find himself focused on incident response for cyberattacks, performing inappropriate-use investigations, supporting digital discovery requests, or all three. Depending on the size of the company and sensitivity of the environment, investigators in the corporate arena may perform only bag and tag operations and then outsource the analysis of evidence, or they may perform all operations internal to the company. Although computer forensics investigation is a growth industry throughout all areas of practice, the corporate use of computer forensics methodologies is a particularly fast-growing area. Legislation, liability, and increased dependence on data systems have forced corporations not only to better protect data but to better prepare to investigate any compromise or complaint of misuse.

No matter how broad or narrow the focus of a computer forensics investigator, he must maintain constant vigilance to refresh his skill set. Not only does technology change at a tremendous rate, the legal system's views of digital evidence are also beginning to change, requiring constant attention. As the profession progresses, computer forensics investigators will need to focus their attention on one or more areas to maintain proficiency, but they should always maintain a good foundation in overall professional knowledge.

TRAINING, KNOWLEDGE, AND EXPERIENCE

In professions supporting the legal system training, knowledge and experience, along with documentation, are usually a point of discussion in qualifying testimony. Whether the testimony involves a computer forensics technician reporting on the facts of a case or an investigator identified as an expert, both professions require training, but experience is key. For many years computer forensics investigators have advised their colleagues to ensure that they fully document their training and experience as a means to show professionalism and develop an *expert* status. Indeed, creating and maintaining a comprehensive training file to document not only official training but on-the-job experience is important. Training files, resumes, and any documentation of experience all help the investigator relay competence to the counsel for which he is working.

Whether for training or simply to find a quick answer for an active case, list servers are a great way for forensics investigators to stay abreast of what's going in the field. By subscribing to forensics list servers, investigators can leverage the knowledge of literally thousands of individuals in the community with varying levels of experience.

NOTE *As within any community of professions, opinions from members of list servers will vary, so investigators should use caution and weigh each answer against personal experience and the overall community consensus.*

There are many online computer security and forensics forums. The following list servers are e-mail-only forums, which can be quite useful to investigators with any level of experience. Several other organizational list servers available only to members, including the HTCIA and IACIS lists.

Computer Forensic Investigators Digest Listserv (CFID)

The CFID is a list designed for discussions in the field of high-technology crime investigations. All subscriptions are managed on an approval basis. Subscription information can be found on the Forensics Web site at *www.forensicsweb.com* or via e-mail to *jnj@infobin.org*.

Computer Forensics Tool Testing (CFTT)

The CFTT is a group for discussing and coordinating computer forensics tool testing. Testing methodologies will be discussed as well as the results of testing various tools. The ultimate goal of these tests is to ensure that tools used by computer forensics examiners provide accurate and complete results. The CFTT group is open to all individuals in the field who are interested in participating in the testing of computer forensics tools. Subscription information can be found on the CFTT Web site at *http://groups.yahoo.com/group/cftt*.

High-Tech Crime Consortium (HTCC)

The High-Tech Crime Consortium (HTCC) list server is restricted to law enforcement personnel, prosecutors, and corporate investigators tasked with the investigation and prosecution of high-technology crime. You must be employed with a federal, state, or local law enforcement agency, or be a senior-level investigator within a corporation to participate in this list.

Investigators who meet the membership requirements can join by completing an application for membership. Application requests should include a business card. Subscription information can be found on the HTCC Web site at *www.hightechcrimecops.org*, or via e-mail to *admin@hightechcrimecops.org*.

Security Focus Forensics

The Security Focus Forensics list server is a discussion mailing list dedicated to technical and process methodologies for the application of computer forensics. Topics of discussion include:

- Audit trail analysis
- General postmortem analysis
- Products and tools for use in this field

Subscription information can be found on the Security Focus Web site at *www.securityfocus.com/archive*.

Other methods of training include self-study through published technical books on the computer forensics process and a wealth of computer forensics sites and resources, some of which can be found in Appendix G, "Agencies, Contacts, and Resources." Many of today's local college extension programs have included training in computer forensics, but some of the best classroom instruction is given by computer-forensics-focused professional associations such as the HTCIA at their international, regional, and local conferences and meetings.

One area of training and experience that has gained an increase of attention over the years is certification. Investigators often desire a way to simplify the process of relaying competence to counsel and juries by pulling our their *certification card*, stating they are indeed certified to perform computer forensics bag and tag, investigations, or whatever component of the computer forensics process in which they are certified. Throughout the early years of the computer forensics profession, one of the difficulties has been, how do you develop a certification process for a practice that does not yet contain a common body of knowledge? Early certifications within the computer forensics profession have been very narrow in scope, focusing on a specific product or segment of the profession, such as certifications provided by the International Association of Computer Investigative Specialists (IACIS) for law enforcement. As the profession has grown over the years, many organizations have attempted to create certifications; however, one of the largest and most respected organizations, the High-Technology Crime Investigation Association (HTCIA), has not yet created or officially endorsed a specific certification. A recent post to the HTCIA list server generated a thread more than 50 messages long. New interest and some agreement among the forensics community may support the creation of a common body of knowledge as a basis for a specific computer forensics certification process.

When stepping back and looking at the big picture, investigators will see that computer forensics, although a profession in its own right, involves a deep understanding of a wide range of technologies. Many of these technologies, including broad categories of information security, have their own certification processes based on accepted common bodies of knowledge. As forensics investigators proceed and seek training in the differing technologies required for investigations, such as operating systems, hardware, and security, they will find many existing certifications to provide a path for gaining a targeted level of knowledge. Some widely accepted, non-computer-forensics-related certifications are described in the next sections.

CISSP

The Certified Information Systems Security Professional (CISSP) is one of the premier vender-neutral security certifications available today. The CISSP is a certification intended for strategist and covers the following topics, what is termed the Ten Domains of Security:

- Security Management Practices
- Access Control Systems
- Telecommunications and Network Security
- Cryptography
- Security Architecture and Models
- Operations Security
- Applications and Systems Development
- Business Continuity Planning and Disaster Recovery Planning
- Law—Investigations and Ethics
- Physical Security

The CISSP is maintained by the nonprofit organization International Information Systems Security Certification Consortium, Inc., or (ISC). Information can be found on their Web site at *www.isc2.org*.

SSCP

The Systems Security Certified Practitioner (SSCP) is a credential intended for information security tacticians and, therefore, is more technically focused than its counterpart, the CISSP. The SSCP is also maintained by (ISC).

GIAC

The Global Information Assurance Certification (GIAC) is a widely respected certification covering a broad area of knowledge, similar to the CISSP. The GIAC certification and training process is managed by the SANS Institute. Information can be found on the SANS GIAC Web site at *www.giac.org*.

CISA

The Certified Information Systems Auditor (CISA) certification is focused on measuring proficiency in the information systems audit, control, and security fields. The CISA certification is managed by the Information Systems Audit and Control Association (ISACA). Information can be found on the ISACA Web site at *www.isaca.org.*

MCSE

The Microsoft Certified Systems Engineer (MCSE) is the top-level certification produced by Microsoft Corporation to certify systems administrations proficiency in the Microsoft Windows operating systems. Information about the MCSE certification can be found on the Microsoft Certified Professional Web site at *www.microsoft.com/mcp.*

MCSD

The Microsoft Certified Solutions Developer (MCSD) is a certification focused on evaluating software development proficiency using the Microsoft platform application programming interfaces and tools. Information about the MCSD certification can be found on the Microsoft Certified Professional Web site at *www.microsoft.com/mcp.*

RHCE

The Red Hat Certified Engineer (RHCE) certification is designed to measure the skills and ability to configure network services and security in Red Hat Linux. The RHCE certification process covers DNS, NFS, Samba, Sendmail, Postfix, Apache, and other key security capabilities in detail. Information about the RHCE certification can be found at the Red Hat Certification Web site at *www.redhat.com/training/certification.*

CCNA

The Cisco-Certified Network Associate is an entry-level certification focused on the ability to configure and manage routers and devices running the Cisco Internet Operating System (IOS). Despite being an entry-level, vendor-focused certification, the CCNA provides a good framework for investigators by requiring an understanding of networking in general. Information about the CCNA certification can be found on the Cisco Career Certifications Web site at *www.cisco.com/en/US/learning/le3/learning_career_certifications_and_learning_paths_home.html.*

CCDA

The Cisco Certified Design Associate is the entry-level CISCO certification focused on understanding basic network design principles. The CCDA certification is based on the Cisco top-down network design philosophy. Information about the CCDA certification can be found on the CISCO Career Certifications Web site at *www.cisco.com/en/US/learning/le3/learning_career_certifications_and_learning_paths_home.html.*

CompTIA

The Computing Technology Industry Association, Inc. (CompTIA) maintains several certifications of interest to computer forensics investigators including Security+, Network+, and A+. Each CompTIA certification is vendor neutral and provides a well-accepted training framework and benchmark of knowledge within a specific area. Information about the various CompTIA certifications can be found on the official Web Site at *www.comptia.com.*

The preceding certifications are only a sample of the core and most widely accepted information technology certifications available today. Specific hardware platform certifications exist for all leading manufactures, including Dell, Sun, IBM, and HP/Compaq. Some of the certifications mentioned are product-specific, whereas others cover more broad categories within the information technology arena. As the computer forensics investigator becomes more experienced, he may seek certifications as a guideline for his training. Opinions of the certification process in general vary greatly; however, most certifications provide a good pathway for those seeking knowledge in specialized areas. In the end, the certification of investigators will only provide another piece of supporting evidence as to his skills. Evaluation of an investigator's training, knowledge, and experience will always go beyond any single certification card.

ANALYSIS AND REPORTING

In the introduction of this book, investigators were introduced to the four phases of computer forensics:

- Collection
- Preservation
- Filtering (Analysis)
- Reporting

Now that investigators have covered basic skills and components of the first two phases, collection and preservation, it only seems fitting that filtering and reporting should be on the "what's next" list. Once the critical stages of identifying, collecting, and preserving the evidence have taken place, it would seem that forensics investigators are free to analyze the evidence at their leisure. Indeed, the ability to recover from mistakes during the analysis phase is one of the benefits afforded by the bit-stream imaging process. Analysis can be a complex stage, requiring a tremendous amount of time to complete, depending on the level of sophistication and concealment implemented by the user.

One area often overlooked by forensics investigators when delving into forensics analysis is the need for an in-depth understanding of recovery techniques for various media types. Either through the natural effects of evidence dynamics or through intentional action from suspects, data recovery is often needed throughout the computer forensics process. Computer forensics investigators seeking education to prepare them for filtering and analysis should start at the bottom and work up by first understanding the media, followed by boot records, the file system, and finally the files and their interrelationships. Highly specialized texts that focus on individual low-level analysis such as *File System Forensic Analysis* [Carrier01] will be of interest to investigators focused on or specializing in forensics analysis.

The simple filtering out and in of artifacts of interest based on hash, keyword, or some other search approach in itself can take days or weeks, depending on the volume. Although filtering or searching comprises a great deal of the analysis performed in the filtering phase, a great deal of low-level volume, file, and data reconstruction also can take place. Other facets of the filtering phase include the migration of data from one format to another—and often from one media type such as magnetic tape to another. The filtering phase is one of the most talked about phases of computer forensics, partly because it is so easy to relate the story of how an investigator found that smoking gun in some chat log or e-mail fragment, and how he had uncovered the evidence that won the case. With a solid foundation in the collection and preservation of evidence, investigators are now ready to enter the world of analysis, where they will quickly find completely new ways of looking at data. No longer will the investigator look at evidence in its printed or digital file format: he will be thinking in terms of inodes, master file tables, sectors, and the clusters of data that make up files within each filesystem. Computer forensics investigators involved in the filtering or analysis of evidence will find a great deal of comfort in their ability to relate to laymen the story of how file slack can be thought of as the unused portion of a one-hour video tape, with a newly recorded 45-minute show recorded over the previous one-hour show. Many of the basic principles found while covering the collection and preservation of evidence will continue to apply as forensics investigators begin to learn the steps of filtering and reporting.

As discussed in the introduction, investigators will find that the preservation phase is, in fact, an iterative process performed throughout all four phases of the computer forensics process. As forensics investigators begin to learn the ins and outs of processing evidence from various operating and filesystems, they will continue to focus on the documentation and verification of each step. Once an investigator enters into the reporting phases of the forensics process, preparing reports for case agents, attorneys, and the court, he will also focus on the completeness, accuracy, and verifiability of the reports and his subsequent testimony.

Court testimony is a specific area within the presentation phase that all computer forensics investigators should seek live classroom training on. Experience through mock trials, in which the computer forensics investigator is questioned on the stand about a fictitious case, can be very enlightening to new investigators. Many of the regional, national, and international conferences held by professional associations include mock trials as part of a comprehensive training program in all phases of the computer forensics process.

As with any profession, training manuals often start with a single manual or book that attempts to cover all concepts. The computer forensics field has been no exception. What was originally covered in a single book is now being treated in segmented topics, like this book does. In time, even more specialized topics will be handled in separate texts.

METHODOLOGIES

Methods driving the interaction between investigators, their tools, and technologies are in as constant a state of change as the data they are analyzing. Even the basic principles of the International Organization of Computer Forensics address the rapid changes within the profession and the need for corresponding methodologies.

NOTE

IOEC Principles [Ioec01]

- *When dealing with digital evidence, all of the general forensic and procedural principles must be applied.*
- *Upon seizing digital evidence, actions taken should not change that evidence.*
- *When it is necessary for a person to access original digital evidence, that person should be trained for the purpose.*

[bullet]All activity relating to the seizure, access, storage, or transfer of digital evidence must be fully documented, preserved, and available for review.

- *An individual is responsible for all actions taken with respect to digital evidence while the digital evidence is in his possession.*
- *Any agency that is responsible for seizing, accessing, storing, or transferring digital evidence is responsible for compliance with these principles.*

New and enhanced methodologies and equipment to support them are on the horizon for this fast-growing field. Computer forensics investigation, though a maturing profession, offers tremendous innovation and growth potential for all practitioners.

Not only do investigators need to keep in step with new methodologies that emerge as technologies change, they should also focus on understanding the variety of methodologies in use for similar situations and technologies. In many cases, the methodology used to capture evidence may be driven by environmental constraints at the scene or possibly the availability of tools and resources. In fact, the investigator should consider each methodology developed or learned as another tool to place in his tool bag for use as needed. Just like one screwdriver might work better than another in a specific situation, so too can one similar technology be more suitable in any given situation.

In Chapter 13, "Large System Collection," the concept of risk-sensitive evidence collection [Kenneally01] was presented as a means of accounting for the large volumes of data residing in corporate and other networks. The issues associated with large-scale digital evidence collection will not go away anytime soon. Even when conducting selective artifact extraction through the use of risk-sensitive evidence collection or some other similar methodology, investigators are presented with tremendous challenges.

One of the greatest technical challenges in the selective extraction of artifacts both primary and supportive is not the extraction itself but the identification of artifacts.

NOTE

A primary artifact can be described as a file or file fragment in a disk. A supportive artifact is an artifact that supports the evidentiary quality of the primary artifact, such as a filesystem's metainformation identifying each cluster on disk from which a file was taken or the access-control list applied to a file from the underlying operating system and filesystem.

Selectively extracting artifacts of interest in an effort to manage resource-exhaustion issues related to data volume is only partially effective if the artifacts cannot be identified quickly and accurately. While research is being conducted, no documented method exists that allows investigators to quickly and accurately identify many artifacts of interest from large volumes of data.

Selective extraction of artifacts is currently the favored approach to solving the resource issues associated with large-volume data collections, but it may not be the only approach. Varying approaches to rapid imaging of large-volume data repositories are continuing to be researched. Much like using a distributed approach to quickly identify artifacts from large volumes of data, the same concept could conceivably be used for imaging large volumes of data. Although no current tool exists to conduct a distributed bit-stream imaging of large volumes of data, several of today's current tools could be adapted quickly. Of course, investigators would still be required to analyze and manage the large volume image.

In the end, no single solution or methodology may end up gaining the most favor, and several may be adopted. The one true constant is the need for innovation on the part of tool manufacturers and investigators to answer challenges as they arise.

PROFESSIONAL ADVANCEMENT

Many would agree that there is plenty of room for advancement in the computer forensics profession. Indeed, many areas for technical advancement are mentioned throughout this book. One appeal of the computer forensics industry is the dynamic nature of the profession and its ripeness for innovation. Two specific areas that have been neglected are the advancement of technologies supporting the needs related to civil discovery and open support groups for professionals practicing computer forensics in support of criminal defense.

Investigators may recall that many professional associations, including the HTCIA, prohibit membership by forensics investigators who provide services for criminal defense. Once or twice a year, a member of the HTCIA challenges this prohibition, reminding his comembers that as members of this professions, they are all merely seeking the truth and that both sides of criminal trial deserve competent forensics services. In rebuttal to this point, some investigators may express their distrust for criminal defense teams. Most investigators can see that this argument becomes personal quickly. In each situation, the constituency is usually successful in bringing the conversation back to the fact that the group was founded by members of law enforcement who enjoyed a close relationship with the criminal prosecution side of our justice system and simply desire to maintain the relationship. In an interesting online article [law01], a gathering of defense attorneys were concerned when finding a prosecutor at their educational event. Certainly everyone deserves a fair trial as well as technical and legal representation; however, professional associations created explicitly for one side of the criminal justice system do not prohibit members from the other side. Generally, the missing component to this conversation is the recognition that there is not yet a professional association dedicated to the computer forensics professional working exclusively for the defense. Something similar to the Computer Forensics Defense Experts Association (CFDEA) is inevitable and would help to shorten the conversation when it arises on either side.

Many forensics investigators will testify that computer forensics principles and methodologies are the same whether used to investigate criminal cases or provide electronic discovery for a civil case. Although in practice many computer forensics investigators do indeed follow a strict forensics collection methodology, no matter the type of case, some do not. Despite the similarities from a technical standpoint, the civil discovery workflow process (sometimes called eDiscovery) and the technical requirements to support the workflow are different. In layman's terms, criminal procedure often calls for warrants or probable cause to seize computer equipment and/or data whereas the eDiscovery process often calls for a production request in the form of interrogatories or preservation of evidence orders. Sometimes the resulting electronic documents will go through several rounds of review in what is known as a responsive process before final determination is made as to the status electronic documents that will finally be produced to the other side. To even further complicate things, a pretrial hearing may occur in which specific procedures for eDiscovery will be identified by the counsel for both sides with the presiding judge. Managing the document workflow is often a difficult process in itself, partially because the actual process differs from case to case and state to state. Civil courts are also quite cost sensitive and have offered decisions focused on cost shifting from party to party during the eDiscovery process [Zubulake01].

The Sedona Conference Working Group Series [Sedona01] assembled a group of attorneys, consultants, academics, and jurists to help establish standardized guidelines or best practices for the handling of eDiscovery. *The Sedona Principles: Best Practices Recommendations and Principles for Addressing Electronic Document Production* was a document published as a result of the working group series in March 2003. In *The Sedona Principles*, which have been posted for public comment, the group recommends a set of recommendations for the handling of eDiscovery that are highly cost sensitive and intended to standardize and reduce the production burden on the courts. Although all experts do not agree with the principles conveyed in the document, its very existence outlines a need for standardization. Documents such as *The Sedona Principles*, *Risk-sensitive Digital Evidence Collection*, and *Search Warrants in an Era of Digital Evidence* [Kerr01] aii intend to promote progressive action in the realm of digital evidence. Many will take the view of a technical solution; others will focus on administration such as statutory and constitutional reform, or procedure. Reform in both the technical and administrative realms is inevitable; however, both should consider the other in their approach. Administrative reform should take into account the projected advancement of technological solutions, and vice versa.

Many tools, utilities, and integrated solutions focused on the collection of digital evidence do not distinguish between civil or criminal procedure. Still more tools exist to assist investigators in managing their cases and evidence. Due partly to the lack of maturation in the field, there has yet to be a comprehensive eDiscovery-focused tool that takes into account the workflow management needs coupled with the initial collection. Technical solutions will need to provide large-scale enterprise searching, identification, and aggregation capabilities coupled with a cradle-to-grave workflow management that is flexible in its methodology.

Other areas for technological advancement include identification and collection of digital evidence from nonstandard devices. The world has become so digitally connected that repositories of digital data are scattered throughout the corporate enterprise, homes, and persons. Enterprise technological advancements are needed to identify and collect evidence from routers, switches, hubs, network appliances, and the network wire itself, in addition to the standard repositories. Although some applications fall into many of these categories, there is a need for advancement in regard to the needs specific to a forensics investigator. Though it is hard to imagine a one-tool-fits-all approach, tools and methodologies that allow for streamlined live investigations are needed.

One recently published and interesting research paper by a University of California at San Diego graduate student [Tkohno01] outlines a proposed method for uniquely identifying computers remotely, much like a fingerprint, and without the fingerprinted device's known cooperation. The paper goes on to identify that the device-fingerprinting methodology is accomplished by exploiting microscopic deviations in device hardware such as system clock skews. It is proposed that investigators could further apply the passive and semipassive techniques, even when the fingerprinted device is behind a NAT or firewall device. Although clearly an academic research paper, similar research is what will eventually lead to technical solutions that benefit the computer forensics investigator.

Some advancement in information technology security features also lend themselves to providing investigators with enhanced forensics support. For more than 10 years, intrusion-detection systems have offered the ability to capture and play back network sessions. As intrusion-detection systems have matured, increased attention by manufacturers has been placed on log integrity. Phoenix Technologies [Phoenix01] has incorporated a line of products aimed at allowing users and technical support personnel to restore systems after compromise or catastrophic system failure. In the recovery software FirstWare, Phoenix Technologies maintains a protected storage area accessible through the system's BIOS in the Host Protected Area [T1301]. The FirstWare line of products is part of an overall Phoenix Technologies strategy to enhance systems security called the Core Management Environment (CME). Data hidden in difficult-to-access areas such as the Host Protected Area should be of keen interest to computer forensics investigators.

Most investigators would expect that Phoenix Technologies is not the only hardware manufacturer interested in providing increased capabilities surrounding systems security and recoverability. Intel recently announced [Krazit01] release of the specifications for Intel Active Management Technology (AMT). Intel's new AMT is a management environment intended to support the ability to manage PCs below the physical-disk and operating-system level. Using AMT, system administrators are intended to be able to react to compromised computer systems, conduct patch management, and restore damaged operating systems remotely and over the network. Many researchers are working on advances like Intel AMT and are often focused on the "sandboxing" of operating systems, memory, and processes as a means of providing protection or recovery from compromise. Computer forensics investigation benefits in two ways from research such as this:

- Research and implementation of solutions focused on the compartmentalization of data often creates new artifacts or enhanced reliability in existing artifacts that may assist in investigations.
- Any research that provides less interactive access to media can allow investigators to more quickly and less intrusively collect evidence.

Many technologies created with IT security and system administration in mind are often repurposed to suit forensics needs. Forensics handheld bit-stream imagers, such as those from ICS and LogiCube, are examples of products that originally had simple imaging purposes for system administrators and PC manufacturers.

Clearly advances from all areas of information technology will directly or indirectly affect the computer forensics investigator or his tools. Forensics investigators should always be on the lookout for new developments and implementations from which they can benefit.

Personal devices are becoming much more sophisticated and pervasive. It is truly difficult to find any person over the age of 12 who does not have at least one digital device at any given time. Whether a cellular phone, digital audio player, or both, the devices can contain vast amounts of data. No longer are cellular phones simple communications devices. Most every phone today is capable of containing personal contact databases and scheduling information. Often the phone will accept some of the many removable digital storage media. In some cases, users will carry a phone, PDA, and a digital media player, or a hybrid device containing the functionality of several devices. The unique challenge to these ultrapersonal devices is the shear number of differing manufactures, models, and capabilities. Another issue that poses challenges to investigators is the technological ability to capture and analyze data from such high turnover devices. Many users will change personal devices every year or two. By the time a solution for capturing and analyzing the specific manufacturer's new product line is available, a new line is on the street. The one current leader in collection and analysis software for personal devices is Paraben Forensics [Paraben01], with their PDA and Cell Phone Seizure products. Other products such as EnCase [Guidance01] have limited PDA imaging and analysis capabilities. Unique devices such as the Blackberry® are often manually collected and analyzed. As with many of the technological areas associated with computer forensics, keeping pace with the fast-moving world of information technology and consumer electronics will continue to provide challenges for the foreseeable future.

No matter if or in what area an investigator intends to specialize, this book has laid the foundation for him to proceed to the filtering and presentation phases of the process. Even the first responder who intends to remain focused on the bag and tag task will need to seek some training and knowledge in the subsequent phases of computer forensics. As the computer forensics investigator moves forward through subsequent phases of the forensics process, he can look back on what he has learned and will recall that preservation is an iterative process throughout all phases, tightly coupled with the investigator's understanding of how he, his tools, and the environment interact with digital evidence through evidence dynamics. Investigators can use this book as a reference for first-responder actions while pursuing the exciting profession of a computer forensics investigator.

SUMMARY

- Because of the similarities from a technical standpoint, little difference has been made between the criminal investigation and the civil discovery process.
- Investigators will always require training in a broad sense, but they may choose to seek enhanced training to develop their skills in specific areas.
- The unique workflow and slightly differing evidentiary proceedings found in the discovery process require specific understanding and experience.
- Analysis of digital evidence is not a single area of interest; it can include many specific areas of interest and associated skills.
- By subscribing to forensics list servers, investigators can leverage the knowledge of thousands of individuals in the community with varying levels of expertise.
- Now that investigators have covered basic skills and components of the first two phases, collection and preservation, it seems only fitting that filtering and reporting should be on the "what's next" list.
- In the end, no single solution to collecting the vast volumes of data may end up gaining the most favor, and several may need to be adopted by the investigator.
- Due partly to the lack of maturation in the field, there has yet to be a comprehensive eDiscovery-focused tool that takes into account the workflow manage-

ment needs coupled with the initial collection.

- As the computer forensics investigator progresses, he will recall that preservation is an iterative process throughout all phases of the computer forensics process.

REFERENCES

[Carrier01] Carrier, Brian, *File System Forensic Analysis*, Addison-Wesley Professional, March 2005.

[Guidance01] Guidance Software Web site, available online at *www.guidance-software.com*, 2004.

[Iacis01] International Association of Computer Investigative Specialists (IACIS) Web site, available online at *www.cops.org*, 2005.

[Ioce01] International Organization of Computer Forensics Web site, available online at *www.ioce.org*, 2004.

[Kenneally01] Kenneally, Erin E. and Brown, Christopher L. T., "Risk-sensitive Digital Evidence Collection," *Digital Investigations Journal*, Volume 2 Issue 2, available online at *www.compseconline.com/digitalinvestigation/tableof-contents.htm*, 2005.

[Kerr01] Kerr, Orin, "Search Warrants in an Era of Digital Evidence," *Mississippi Law Journal*, available online at *lawprofessors.typepad.com/crimprof_blog/2005/02/new_article_spo_6.html*, 2005.

[Krazit01] Krazit, Tom, "Intel Improving Server Performance to a "T"," IDG News Service, available online at *www.nwfusion.com/news/2005/0301iamt.html*, March 2005.

[law01] "How Did He Get In? Asst. DA Unwelcome at Defense-Oriented CLE Event Texas Lawyer", available online at *www.law.com/jsp/article.jsp?id=1109128216335.* February 25, 2005.

[Paraben01] Paraben Forensics Web site, available online at *www.paraben-forensics.com*, 2005.

[Phoenix01] Phoenix Technologies Web site, available online at *www.phoenix.com/en/Home/default.htm*, 2005.

[Sedona01] *The Sedona Principles: Best Practices Recommendations and Principles for Addressing Electronic Document Production*, Sedona Conference Working Group, available online at *www.thesedonaconference.org*, March 2003.

[T1301] Host Protected Area Technical Documents, available online at *www.t13.org/technical/*, 2004.

[Tkohno01] Kohno, Tadayoshi, Broido, Andre, and Claffy, KC, *Remote Physical Device Fingerprinting*, available online at *www.cse.ucsd.edu/users/tkohno/papers/PDF*, 2005.

[Zubulake01] *Zubulake v. UBS Warburg*, 217 F.R.D. 309 S.D.N.Y., 2003.

RESOURC ES

[Htcia01] High-Technology Crime Investigation Association Web site, available online at *www.htcia.org*, 2005.

[Ohio01] *Ohio v. Michael J. Morris*, Court of Appeals of Ohio, Ninth District, Wayne County, No. 04CA0036, Feb. 16, 2005.

Appendix

A Sample Chain of Custody Form

ON THE CD This form is available in electronic format on the companion CD-ROM.

<table>
<tr><td colspan="2">Evidence Custody Form</td><td>1. Case Control Number:</td></tr>
<tr><td colspan="3">Evidence Received From:</td></tr>
<tr><td colspan="2">2. (Full Name):</td><td>3. (Full Address):</td></tr>
<tr><td colspan="2">4. Primary Phone:</td><td>5. Secondary Phone:</td></tr>
<tr><td colspan="2">6. E-mail:</td><td>7. Date/Time:</td></tr>
<tr><td colspan="2">8. Purpose:</td><td>9. Comments</td></tr>
<tr><td>10. Item Number</td><td>11. Tag Number</td><td>12. Description (Include serial and model numbers if itemized):</td></tr>
<tr><td></td><td></td><td></td></tr>
</table>

Releasing Person *(if available)*:	Person Taking Initial Custody:
13. Printed Name:	15. Printed Name:
14. Signature	16. Signature

17. Chain of Custody					
Item #	Tag #	Date/Time	Released By	Received By	Purpose
			Name	Name	
			Organization	Organization	
			Signature	Signature	
			Name	Name	
			Organization	Organization	
			Signature	Signature	
			Name	Name	
			Organization	Organization	
			Signature	Signature	

<table>
<tr><th colspan="6">17. Chain of Custody</th></tr>
<tr><th>Item #</th><th>Tag #</th><th>Date/Time</th><th>Released By</th><th>Received By</th><th>Purpose</th></tr>
<tr><td rowspan="3"></td><td rowspan="3"></td><td rowspan="3"></td><td>Name</td><td>Name</td><td rowspan="3"></td></tr>
<tr><td>Organization</td><td>Organization</td></tr>
<tr><td>Signature</td><td>Signature</td></tr>
<tr><td rowspan="3"></td><td rowspan="3"></td><td rowspan="3"></td><td>Name</td><td>Name</td><td rowspan="3"></td></tr>
<tr><td>Organization</td><td>Organization</td></tr>
<tr><td>Signature</td><td>Signature</td></tr>
<tr><td rowspan="3"></td><td rowspan="3"></td><td rowspan="3"></td><td>Name</td><td>Name</td><td rowspan="3"></td></tr>
<tr><td>Organization</td><td>Organization</td></tr>
<tr><td>Signature</td><td>Signature</td></tr>
<tr><th colspan="6">18. Final Disposition</th></tr>
<tr><td colspan="6">19. Action Taken:</td></tr>
</table>

20. Receiving Person or Destruction Witness	
21. (Full Name):	22. (Full Address):
23. Primary Phone:	24. Secondary Phone:
25. E-mail:	26. Date/Time
27. Comments:	28. Signature:

Appendix

B Evidence Collection Worksheet

This form is available in electronic format on the companion CD-ROM.

ON THE CD

Evidence Collection Worksheet *(Initial Full System Inventory)*	1. Case Control Number:
2. Owner's First Name:	5. Original Location Address:
3. Owner's Last Name:	
4. Owner's Phone Number:	
6. Collection Date:	7. Collection Time:
8. System Room:	9. Placement in Room:
10. Was System Running:	
11. Action Taken For	
12. Shutdown/Startup:	
13. Display Screen (photo/description):	
14. Cabling (photo/description):	
15. Physical Network Connections:	
16. Wi-Fi Sweep Conducted/Results:	
17. Description:	

Tag #	Description	Markings	Manufacturer	Model #	Serial #
18.					
19.					
20.					
21.					
22.					
23.					
24.					
25.					
26. Investigator's Full Name			27. Investigator's Signature (Date/Time):		

Appendix C

Evidence Access Worksheet

ON THE CD This form is available in electronic format on the companion CD-ROM.

Evidence Access Worksheet	1. Case Control Number: 2. Evidence Tag #
3. Media is *(circle one)*: Original / Bit-Stream Image / Other ____________	
4. Collection / Creation Date & Time:	
5. Media Type:	6. Medial Serial Number / ID:
7. Access Date:	8. Access Time:
9. All Hardware Devices in Connection Chain: __________ __________ __________ __________ __________ (Media)	
10. Comments:	
11. Printed Name:	12. Signature:

7. Access Date:	8. Access Time:
9. All Hardware Devices in Connection Chain: __________ __________ __________ __________ __________ (Media)	
10. Comments:	
11. Printed Name:	12. Signature:

7. Access Date:	8. Access Time:
9. All Hardware Devices in Connection Chain: __________ __________ __________ __________ __________ (Media)	
10. Comments:	
11. Printed Name:	12. Signature:

7. Access Date:	8. Access Time:
9. All Hardware Devices in Connection Chain: ________ ________ ________ ________ ________ (Media)	
10. Comments:	
11. Printed Name:	12. Signature:

7. Access Date:	8. Access Time:
9. All Hardware Devices in Connection Chain: ________ ________ ________ ________ ________ (Media)	
10. Comments:	
11. Printed Name:	12. Signature:

<table>
<tr><td>7. Access Date:</td><td>8. Access Time:</td></tr>
<tr><td colspan="2">9. All Hardware Devices in Connection Chain:

________ ________ ________ ________ ________
(Media)</td></tr>
<tr><td colspan="2">10. Comments:</td></tr>
<tr><td>11. Printed Name:</td><td>12. Signature:</td></tr>
</table>

Appendix D
Forensics Field Kit

Forensics workstation: Notebook or specialized portable case system. If a notebook workstation is used, ensure it is FireWire and USB 2.0 capable and includes a CD/DVD-RW drive.

Handheld forensic drive imager: Such as the ICS ImageMASSter, Logicube, and so on. See the following Web sites for more information:

- Intelligent Computer Solutions, Inc. at *www.ics-iq.com*
- Solitaire Forensics by Logicube at *www.logicube.com*

Portable USB 2.0/FireWire drive enclosure: Make sure to have a removable drive bay for target images.

USB 2.0-to-IDE cable: For accessing evidence drives inside cases.

Target hard disks: Several large, forensically clean hard disks for target images.

Box of blank CD-ROMs/DVD-ROMs

Adaptec SCSI PC card: If using a notebook forensics workstation.

PC CloneCard IDE Converter: Helpful for imaging hard-to-access notebook disks. See *www.logicube.com* for more information.

Internal disk drive power converter: For powering up evidence drives for imaging when removed from workstations.

Network cables: Include standard cables as well as crossover cables of various lengths.

Various interface adapters: SCSI II (50-Pin) to every other type of SCSI, SCA to SCSI III, IDE 40-Pin (notebook) to Standard IDE, 1.8 inch to Standard IDE, SATA to ATA, and so on.

Software:

- Forensics analysis suites (ProDiscover, EnCase, FTK)

- Disk recovery software
- Forensics boot CD-ROMs
- Incident response CD-ROM with trusted binaries for collecting volatile data

Administrative materials:

- Pens and permanent markers
- Several new composition books for notes (use one new book per case)
- Tamperproof evidence bags, labels, and tape; see Chief Supply at *www.chiefsupply.com/fingerprint.phtml*

Portable PC toolkit: Screwdrivers, ESD (electrostatic discharge) wristbands, and so on.

Large bag/hardened case: For transporting equipment.

Appendix

E Hexadecimal Flags For Partition Types

0x00 Unknown type or empty
0x01 12-bit FAT
0x02 XENIX root filesystem
0x03 XENIX /usr filesystem (obsolete)
0x04 16-bit FAT, partition <32 MB
0x05 Extended partition or extended volume
0x06 16-bit FAT, partition >=32 MB
0x07 Installable filesystem: HPFS, NTFS
0x07 QNX
0x07 Advanced Unix
0x08 AIX bootable partition
0x08 AIX (Linux)
0x08 Split drive
0x08 OS/2 (through Version 1.3) (Landis)
0x08 Dell partition spanning multiple drives (array) (Landis)
0x08 Commodore DOS (Landis)
0x09 AIX data partition
0x09 AIX bootable (Linux)
0x09 Coherent filesystem
0x09 QNX
0x0A Coherent swap partition
0x0A OPUS
0x0A OS/2 Boot Manager
0x0B 32-bit FAT
0x0C 32-bit FAT, EXT INT 13
0x0E 16-bit FAT >= 32 MB, Ext INT 13
0x0F Extended partition, Ext INT 13
0x10 OPUS
0x11 Hidden 12-bit FAT
0x12 Compaq diagnostics (Landis)

0x14 Hidden 16-bit FAT, partition <32 MB
0x14 Novell DOS 7.0 (result of bug in FDISK?) (Landis)
0x14 AST DOS with logical sectored FAT
0x16 Hidden 16-bit FAT, partition >= 32 MB
0x17 Hidden IFS
0x18 AST Windows swap file
0x19 Willowtech Photon coS
0x1B Hidden 32-bit FAT
0x1C Hidden 32-bit FAT, Ext INT 13
0x1E Hidden 16-bit FAT >32 MB, Ext INT 13 (PowerQuest specific)
0x20 Willowsoft Overture Filesystem (OFS1)
0x21 Officially listed as reserved (HP Volume Expansion, SpeedStor variant)
0x21 Oxygen FSo2
0x22 Oxygen Extended
0x23 Officially listed as reserved (HP Volume Expansion, SpeedStor variant)
0x24 NEC MS-DOS 3.x
0x26 Officially listed as reserved (HP Volume Expansion, SpeedStor variant)
0x31 Officially listed as reserved (HP Volume Expansion, SpeedStor variant)
0x33 Officially listed as reserved (HP Volume Expansion, SpeedStor variant)
0x34 Officially listed as reserved (HP Volume Expansion, SpeedStor variant)
0x36 Officially listed as reserved (HP Volume Expansion, SpeedStor variant)
0x38 Theos
0x3C PowerQuest Files Partition Format
0x3D Hidden NetWare
0x40 VENIX 80286
0x41 Personal RISC Boot (Landis)
0x41 PowerPC boot partition
0x41 PTS-DOS 6.70 and BootWizard: Alternative Linux, Minix, and DR-DOS
0x42 Secure filesystem (Landis)
0x42 Windows 2000 (NT 5): dynamic extended partition
0x42 PTS-DOS 6.70 and BootWizard: alternative Linux swap and DR-DOS
0x43 Alternative Linux native filesystem (EXT2fs)
0x43 PTS-DOS 6.70 and BootWizard: DR-DOS
0x45 Priam
0x45 EUMEL/Elan
0x46 EUMEL/Elan
0x47 EUMEL/Elan
0x48 EUMEL/Elan
0x4A ALFS/THIN lightweight filesystem for DOS
0x4D QNX
0x4E QNX

0x4F QNX
0x4F Oberon boot/data partition
0x50 Ontrack Disk Manager, read-only partition, FAT partition (logical sector size varies)
0x51 Ontrack Disk Manager, read/write partition, FAT partition (logical sector size varies)
0x51 Novell
0x52 CP/M
0x52 Microport System V/386
0x53 Ontrack Disk Manager, write-only (Landis)
0x54 Ontrack Disk Manager 6.0 (DDO)
0x55 EZ-Drive 3.05
0x56 Golden Bow VFeature
0x5C Priam EDISK
0x61 Storage Dimensions SpeedStor
0x63 GNU HURD
0x63 Mach, MtXinu BSD 4.2 on Mach
0x63 Unix Sys V/386, 386/ix
0x64 Novell NetWare 286
0x64 SpeedStor (Landis)
0x65 Novell NetWare (3.11 and 4.1)
0x66 Novell NetWare 386
0x67 Novell NetWare
0x68 Novell NetWare
0x69 Novell NetWare 5+; Novell Storage Services (NSS)
0x70 DiskSecure Multiboot
0x75 IBM PC/IX

NOTE *Codes 7A to 7F are not shown in the IMB or MS lists obtained by Hale Landis.*

0x80 Minix v1.1–1.4a
0x80 Old Minix (Linux)
0x81 Linux/Minix v1.4b+
0x81 Mitac Advanced Disk Manager
0x82 Linux swap partition
0x82 Prime (Landis)
0x82 Solaris (Unix)
0x83 Linux native filesystem (EXT2fs/xiafs)
0x84 OS/2 hiding type 04h partition
0x84 APM hibernation; can be used by Win98
0x86 NT Stripe Set, Volume Set

0x87 NT Stripe Set, Volume Set
0x87 HPFS FT mirrored partition (Landis)
0x93 Amoeba filesystem
0x93 Hidden Linux EXT2 partition (by PowerQuest products)
0x94 Amoeba bad block table
0x99 Mylex EISA SCSI
0x9F BSDI
0xA0 Phoenix NoteBios Power Management "Save to Disk"
0xA0 IBM hibernation
0xA1 HP volume expansion (SpeedStor variant)
0xA3 HP volume expansion (SpeedStor variant)
0xA4 HP volume expansion (SpeedStor variant)
0xA5 FreeBSD/386
0xA6 OpenBSD
0xA6 HP volume expansion (SpeedStor variant)
0xA7 NextStep partition
0xA9 NetBSD
0xAA Olivetti DOS with FAT12
0xB0 BootStar Dummy (part of DriveStar disk image by Star-Tools GmbH)
0xB1 HP volume expansion (SpeedStor variant)
0xB3 HP volume expansion (SpeedStor variant)
0xB4 HP volume expansion (SpeedStor variant)
0xB6 HP volume expansion (SpeedStor variant)
0xB7 BSDI filesystem or secondarily swap
0xB8 BSDI swap partition or secondarily filesystem
0xBB PTS BootWizard
0xBE Solaris boot partition
0xC0 Novell DOS/OpenDOS/DR-OpenDOS/DR-DOS secured partition
0xC0 CTOS (reported by a customer)
0xC1 DR-DOS 6.0 LOGIN.EXE-secured 12-bit FAT partition
0xC2 Reserved for DR-DOS 7+
0xC3 Reserved for DR-DOS 7+
0xC4 DR-DOS 6.0 LOGIN.EXE-secured 16-bit FAT partition
0xC6 DR-DOS 6.0 LOGIN.EXE-secured huge partition
0xC6 Corrupted FAT16 volume/stripe (V/S) set (Windows NT)
0xC7 Syrinx
0xC7 Cyrnix (Landis)
0xC7 HPFS FT disabled mirrored partition (Landis)
0xC7 Corrupted NTFS volume/stripe set
0xC8 Reserved for DR-DOS 7+
0xC9 Reserved for DR-DOS 7+

0xCA Reserved for DR-DOS 7+
0xCB Reserved for DR-DOS secured FAT32
0xCC Reserved for DR-DOS secured FAT32X (LBA)
0xCD Reserved for DR-DOS 7+
0xCE Reserved for DR-DOS secured FAT16X (LBA)
0xCF Reserved for DR-DOS secured extended partition (LBA)
0xD0 Multiuser DOS secured (FAT12)
0xD1 Old multiuser DOS secured FAT12
0xD4 Old multiuser DOS secured FAT16 (<= 32M)
0xD5 Old multiuser DOS secured extended partition
0xD6 Old multiuser DOS secured FAT16 (BIGDOS > 32 Mb)
0xD8 CP/M 86 (Landis)
0xDB CP/M, Concurrent CP/M, Concurrent DOS
0xDB CTOS (Convergent Technologies OS)
0xDE Dell partition
0xDF BootIt EMBRM
0xE1 SpeedStor 12-bit FAT extended partition
0xE1 DOS access (Linux)
0xE2 DOS read-only (Florian Painke's XFDISK 1.0.4)
0xE3 SpeedStor (Norton, Linux says DOS R/O)
0xE4 SpeedStor 16-bit FAT extended partition
0xE5 Tandy DOS with logical sectored FAT
0xE6 Storage dimensions SpeedStor
0xEB BeOS filesystem
0xED Reserved for Matthias Paul's Spryt*x
0xF1 SpeedStor Dimensions (Norton, Landis)
0xF2 DOS 3.3+ second partition
0xF2 Unisys DOS with logical sectored FAT
0xF3 Storage dimensions SpeedStor
0xF4 SpeedStor Storage Dimensions (Norton, Landis)
0xF5 Prologue
0xF6 Storage dimensions SpeedStor
0xFD Reserved for FreeDOS (*www.freedos.org*)
0xFE LANstep
0xFE IBM PS/2 IML (Initial Microcode Load) partition
0xFE Storage Dimensions SpeedStor (> 1024 cylinder)
0xFF Xenix bad-block table

Appendix F
Forensics Tools for Digital Evidence Collection

ProDiscover Forensics, Investigator, and Incident Response

www.techpathways.com
Platforms: (Windows NT/2000/XP/2003)

ProDiscover is a family of disk forensics tools with the capabilities of many utilities available in one simple-to-use yet powerful product with an intuitive user interface. The ProDiscover family of products allows forensics examiners to collect, analyze, manage, and report on computer disk evidence locally or remotely over any TCP/IP network.

SafeBack

www.forensics-intl.com
Platforms: (DOS)

Forensics International offers various command-line computer forensics tools. NTI limits their sale to government agencies, Fortune 1000 corporations, large law firms, large accounting firms, financial institutions, hospitals, and law enforcement agencies.

SnapBack DatArrest

www.cdp.com
Platforms: (DOS)

The developers of the SnapBack software, Columbia Data Products, specifically state in their documentation that SnapBack DatArrest is a "data seizure" product, and they actively advertise it to law enforcement officers as a forensics tool. This application does not support disk-to-disk imaging.

EnCase

www.encase.com
Platforms: (DOS, Windows NT/2000) EnCase provides full-featured Windows-based computer forensics analysis.

Byte Back

www.toolsthatwork.com
Platforms: (DOS)
This is a DOS-based computer forensics and disk editor application.

Ilook

www.ilook-forensics.org
Platforms: (Windows NT/2000)
Developed by a U.K. engineer in 1998 and 1999, this application is very similar to ProDiscover, and EnCase. The application was sold to the U.S. Internal Revenue Service Criminal Investigations Division and is now available only to law enforcement agencies.

Forensics Tool Kit (FTK)—System Analysis Tool

www.accessdata.com
Platforms: (Windows)
Based on dtSearch, FTK offers extensive search capabilities and e-mail analysis with a forensics focus.

The Coroners Toolkit (TCT)

www.porcupine.org/forensics/tct.html
Platforms: (Solaris, FreeBSD, RedHat, BSD/OS, OpenBSD, SunOS)
TCT is a collection of programs by Dan Farmer and Wietse Venema for a post-mortem analysis of a Unix system after a break-in.

MaresWare Suite

www.maresware.com/maresware/forensic1.htm
Platforms (DOS, UNIX)
The MaresWare Suite comprises a large group of command-line forensics utilities.

PDA Seizure by Paraben

www.paraben-forensics.com
This application is a good Palm OS forensics tool.

pdd

www.atstake.com/research/tools
Platforms: Win 95/98/NT/2K (tested with Palm OS v1.0 to v3.5.2)
pdd enables forensic analysis of Palm OS platform devices. Source code is available for research and legal verification purposes.

TCTUTILs

www.atstake.com/research/tools
Platforms: OpenBSD, Linux, Solaris
TCTUTILS is a package of tools that builds on the popular forensics package, The Coroners Toolkit (TCT).

Autopsy Forensic Browser

www.atstake.com/research/tools
Platforms: OpenBSD, Linux, Solaris
Autopsy Forensic Browser with Sleuth Kit is a Unix-based investigation tool. Autopsy Forensic Browser, when used with Sleuth Kit, allows investigators to collect, analyze, and report on disk evidence from Windows and Unix systems. Autopsy is an HTML-based graphical interface that allows an investigator to examine the files and unallocated areas of disks, filesystems, and swap space.

WinHex

www.sf-soft.de/winhex
Platforms: (Windows NT/2000)
WinHex is a disk editor for hard disks, CD-ROMs, DVDs, Zip drives, smart media, compact flash memory cards, and more. FAT12, FAT16, FAT32, NTFS, CDFS.

Various Must-Have Utilities from Sysinternals

www.sysinternals.com
A large assortment of low-level Windows utilities including the following:

Filemon: This monitoring tool lets you see all filesystem activity in real time. It works on all versions of WinNT/2000, Windows 9x/Me, Windows XP 64-bit Edition, and Linux.

Regmon: This monitoring tool lets you see all registry activity in real time. It works on all versions of WinNT/2000 as well as Windows 9x/Me. Full source code is included.

Foundstone

www.foundstone.com/rdlabs/tools.php?category=Forensic

Foundstone provides must-have command-line forensics including a tool for viewing Windows NT/2000 Alternate Data Streams and a very useful TCP port mapper application. These tools were purchased from NTObjectives.

Frank Heyne Software

www.heysoft.de/index.htm

This company produces a few useful Windows NT/2000 event log and registry utilities.

dtSearch Desktop

www.dtsearch.com

dtSearch Desktop is a powerful text-searching tool.

OrionMagic

www.orionsci.com

OrionMagic enables the investigator to organize multiple search parameters into a matrix format, resembling a spreadsheet, and perform massively parallel searches from a single command. This product, as well as most computer forensic tools with advanced search capabilities, is powered by dtSearch.

TRINIX

http://trinux.sourceforge.net

Platforms: Linux

Trinux is a ramdisk-based Linux distribution that boots from a single floppy or CD-ROM, and loads its packages from an HTTP/FTP server, a FAT/NTFS/ISO filesystem, or additional floppies. Trinux contains the latest versions of popular Open Source network security tools.

PLAC—Portable Linux Auditing CD

http://sourceforge.net/projects/plac/

Platforms: Linux

PLAC is a business-card-sized bootable CD-ROM that runs Linux. It has network auditing, disk recovery, and forensic analysis tools. ISO will be available as will scripts to burn your own CD-ROM.

FIRE (originally named Biatchux)

http://fire.dmzs.com/

FIRE is a nice bootable forensics package and well worth the time to take a look.

AccuBurn

www.cdrom-prod.com

A good group of forensically focused CD/DVD burning and repair products. AccuBurn will automatically span disks, if necessary.

Intelligent Computer Solutions, Inc.

www.ics-iq.com/

This company sells many models of drive-imaging solutions specifically for computer forensics.

Solitaire Forensics by Logicube

www.logicube.com

This company offers handheld disk-imaging hardware.

Portable Drive Service/Test/Dup by Corporate Systems

www.corpsys.com

This company offers a good low-cost SCSI/IDE duplication system with forensics mode.

DIBS, Inc.

www.dibsusa.com/home.html?about/about

DIBS offers several hardware and software forensics products.

NoWrite IDE Write Blocker

www.techpathways.com

Tech Pathways provides a very good IDE write blocker designed by long-time industry insiders. This application works with ProDiscover to allow nondestructive analysis of an ATA disk using the Hardware Protected Area.

ACARD SCSI-to-IDE Write Blocking Bridge (AEC7720WP)

www.microlandusa.com/

Platforms: PC

ACARD AEC-7720UW Ultra Wide SCSI-to-IDE Bridge supports IDE devices attached to SCSI bus, with a write blocked function.

CS Electronics

www.scsi-cables.com/index.htm

This Web site offers many drive adapters that you may need.

F.R.E.D. (Forensic Recovery Evidence Device)

www.digitalintel.com/fred.htm

FRED is a highly integrated hardware/software platform that may be used both for the acquisition and analysis of computer-based evidence.

ZERT by Netherlands Forensic Institute

www.forensischinstituut.nl/

ZERT is a hardware tool developed by NFI for recovery of passwords in PDAs.

CGM Security Solutions

www.tamper.com/

CGM is a good, if expensive, source for tamper-proof evidence bags.

Chief Supply

www.chiefsupply.com/fingerprint.phtml

Chief is another good source for tamper-proof evidence bags, tape, labels, and more, all at good prices.

Appendix

G Agencies, Contacts, and Resources

AGENCIES

FBI Computer Analysis Response Team (CART)

FBI Laboratory
935 Pennsylvania Avenue N.W.
Washington, DC 20535
Phone: 202-324-9307
Web site: *www.fbi.gov/hq/lab/org/cart.htm*

Internal Revenue Service

Criminal Investigation Division
Rich Mendrop
Computer Investigative Specialist Program Manager
2433 South Kirkwood Court
Denver, CO 80222
Phone: 303-756-0646
E-mail: richard.mendrop@ci.irs.gov

National Aeronautics and Space Administration

Cheri Carr
Computer Forensic Lab Chief
NASA Office of the Inspector General
Network and Advanced Technology Protections Office
300 E Street S.W.
Washington, DC 20546
Phone: 202-358-4298

Charles Coe
Director of Technical Services
NASA Office of the Inspector General
Network and Advanced Technology Protections Office
300 E Street S.W.
Washington, DC 20546
Phone: 202-358-2573

Steve Nesbitt
Director of Operations
NASA Office of the Inspector General
Network and Advanced Technology Protections Office
300 E Street S.W.
Washington, DC 20546
Phone: 202-358-2576

National Railroad Passenger Corporation (NRPC) (AMTRAK)

Office of Inspector General
Office of Investigations
William D. Purdy

Senior Special Agent
10 G Street NE, Suite 3E-400
Washington, DC 20002
Phone: 202-906-4318
E-mail: oigagent@aol.com

Social Security Administration Office of Inspector General

Electronic Crime Team
4-S-1 Operations Building
6401 Security Boulevard
Baltimore, MD 21235
Phone: 410-965-7421
Fax: 410-965-5705

U.S. Customs Service's Cyber Smuggling Center

11320 Random Hills, Suite 400
Fairfax, VA 22030
Phone: 703-293-8005
Fax: 703-293-9127

U.S. Department of Defense, Computer Forensics Laboratory

911 Elkridge Landing Road, Suite 300
Linthicum, MD 21090
Phone: 410-981-0100 or 877-981-3235

U.S. Department of Defense, Office of Inspector General

Defense Criminal Investigative Service
David E. Trosch
Special Agent
Program Manager, Computer Forensics Program
400 Army Navy Drive
Arlington, VA 22202
Phone: 703-604-8733
E-mail: dtrosch@dodig.osd.mil

U.S. Department of Energy

Office of the Inspector General
Technology Crimes Section
1000 Independence Avenue, 5A-235
Washington, DC 20585
Phone: 202-586-9939
Fax: 202-586-0754
E-mail: tech.crime@hq.doe.gov

U.S. Department of Justice, Computer Crime Intellectual Property Section (CCIPS)

1301 New York Avenue N.W.
Washington, DC 20530
Phone: 202-514-1026

U.S. Department of Justice Drug Enforcement Administration

Michael J. Phelan
Group Supervisor
Computer Forensics
Special Testing and Research Lab
10555 Furnace Road
Lorton, VA 22079
Phone: 703-495-6787
Fax: 703-495-6794
E-mail: mphelan@erols.com

U.S. Department of Transportation

Office of Inspector General
Jacquie Wente
Special Agent
111 North Canal, Suite 677
Chicago, IL 60606
Phone: 312-353-0106
E-mail: wentej@oig.dot.gov

U.S. Department of the Treasury

Bureau of Alcohol, Tobacco, and Firearms
Technical Support Division
Visual Information Branch
Jack L. Hunter, Jr.
Audio and Video Forensic Enhancement Specialist
650 Massachusetts Avenue N.W., Room 3220
Washington, DC 20226-0013
Phone: 202-927-8037
Fax: 202-927-8682
E-mail: jlhunter@atfhq.atf.treas.gov

U.S. Postal Inspection Service

Digital Evidence
22433 Randolph Drive
Dulles, VA 20104-1000
Phone: 703-406-7927

U.S. Secret Service

Electronic Crimes Branch
950 H Street N.W.
Washington, DC 20223
Phone: 202-406-5850
Fax: 202-406-9233

Veterans Affairs

Office of the Inspector General
Robert Friel
Program Director, Computer Crimes and Forensics
801 I Street N.W., Suite 1064
Washington, DC 20001
Phone: 202-565-5701
E-mail: robert.friel@mail.va.gov

TRAINING RESOURCES

Canadian Police College

PO Box 8900
Ottawa, Ontario K1G 3J2
Phone: 613-993-9500
Web site: *www.cpc.gc.ca/*

Champlain College

Computer and Digital Forensics Program
163 South Willard Street
Burlington, VT 05401
Phone: 802-860-2700
Web site: *http://digitalforensics.champlain.edu*

DoD Computer Investigations Training Program

911 Elkridge Landing Road
Airport Square 11 Building, Suite 200
Linthicum, MD 21090
Phone: 410-981-1604
Fax: 410-850-8906
Web site: *www.dcitp.gov/dc3/home.htm*

FBI Academy at Quantico

U.S. Marine Corps Base
Quantico, VA
Phone: 703-640-6131
Web site: *www.fbi.gov/hq/td/academy/ictu/ictu.htm*

Federal Law Enforcement Training Center

Headquarters Facility
Glynco, GA 31524

Phone: 912-267-2100
Web site: *www.fletc.gov/*

Artesia Facility

1300 West Richey Avenue
Artesia, NM 88210
Phone: 505-748-8000
Web site: *www.fletc.gov/*

Charleston Facility

2000 Bainbridge Avenue
Charleston, SC 29405-2607
Phone: 843-743-8858
Web site: *www.fletc.gov/*

Florida Association of Computer Crime Investigators, Inc.

PO Box 1503
Bartow, FL 33831-1503
Phone: 352-357-0500
Web site: *www.facci.org*

Forensic Association of Computer Technologists

Doug Elrick
PO Box 703
Des Moines, IA 50303
Phone: 515-281-7671
Web site: *www.byteoutofcrime. org/*

High-Technology Crime Investigation Association (International)

1474 Freeman Drive
Amissville, VA 20106
Phone: 540-937-5019
Web site: *www.htcia.org*

Institute of Police Technology and Management

University of North Florida
12000 Alumni Drive
Jacksonville, FL 32224-2678
Phone: 904-620-4786
Fax: 904-620-2453
Web site: *www.iptm.org/*

International Association of Computer Investigative Specialists (IACIS)

PO Box 21688
Keizer, OR 97307-1688
Phone: 503-557-1506
Web site: *www.cops.org*

International Organization on Computer Evidence (IOCE)

Web site: *www.ioce.org/*

International System Security Association (ISSA)

7044 South 13th Street
Oak Creek, WI 53154
Phone: 800-370-4772
Web site: *www.issa.org*

Information Security University

149 New Montgomery Street,
Second Floor
San Francisco, CA 94105
Web site: *www.redsiren.com/infosecu/*

National Center for Forensic Science

University of Central Florida
PO Box 162367
Orlando, FL
Phone: 407-823-6469

Web site: *www.ncfs.ucf.edu/home.html*

National Colloquium for Information Systems Security Education (NCISSE)

Web site: *www.ncisse.org/*

National Criminal Justice Computer Laboratory and Training Center

SEARCH Group, Inc.
7311 Greenhaven Drive, Suite 145
Sacramento, CA 95831
Phone: 916-392-2550
Web site: *www.search.org*

National White Collar Crime Center (NW3C)

1000 Technology Drive, Suite 2130
Fairmont, WV 26554
Phone: 877-628-7674
Web site: *www.cybercrime.org/*

New Technologies, Inc.

2075 N.E. Division Street
Gresham, OR 97030
Phone: 503-661-6912
Web site: *www.forensics-intl.com/*

Purdue University–CERIAS (Center for Education and Research in Information and Assurance Security)

Andra C. Short
Recitation Building
Purdue University
West Lafayette, IN 47907-1315
Phone: 765-494-7806
E-mail: acs@cerias.purdue.edu
Web site: *www.cerias.purdue.edu/*

Redlands Community College

Clayton Hoskinson, CFCE
Program Coordinator
Criminal Justice and Forensic Computer Science
1300 South Country Club Road
El Reno, OK 73036-5304
Phone: 405-262-2552, ext. 2517
E-mail: hoskinsonc@redlandscc.net

University of New Haven

School of Public Safety and Professional Studies
300 Orange Avenue
West Haven, CT 06516
Web site: *www.newhaven.edu/*

University of New Haven–California Campus

Forensic Computer Investigation Program
6060 Sunrise Vista Drive
Citrus Heights, CA 95610
Web site: *www.newhaven.edu/*

Utica College–Economic Crime Institute

Economic Crime Programs
1600 Burrstone Road
Utica, NY 13502
Web site: *www.ecii.edu/*

Wisconsin Association of Computer Crime Investigators

PO Box 510212
New Berlin, WI 53151-0212
Web site: *www.wacci.org/*

ASSOCIATIONS

High-Technology Crime Investigation Association (International)

1474 Freeman Drive
Amissville, VA 20106
Phone: 540-937-5019
Web site: *www.htcia.org*

International Association of Computer Investigative Specialists (IACIS)

Web site: *http://cops.org/*

International Information Systems Forensics Association (IISFA)

300 Satellite Boulevard
Suwanee, GA 30024
Phone: 678-835-5267
Web site: *www.iisfa.org*

International System Security Association (ISSA)

7044 South 13th Street
Oak Creek, WI 53154
Phone: 800-370-4772
Web site: *www.issa.org*

High-Tech Crime Consortium

International Headquarters
1506 North Stevens Street
Tacoma, WA 98406-3826
Phone: 253-752-2427
Fax: 253-752-2430
E-mail: admin@hightechcrimecops.org
Web site: *www.hightechcrimecops.org*

Florida Association of Computer Crime Investigators, Inc.

PO Box 1503
Bartow, FL 33831-1503
Phone: 352-357-0500
Web site: *www.facci.org*

Forensic Association of Computer Technologists

Doug Elrick
PO Box 703
Des Moines, IA 50303
Phone: 515-281-7671
Web site: *www.byteoutofcrime.org/*

STATE

Alabama

Alabama Attorney General's Office
11 South Union Street
Montgomery, AL 36130
Phone: 334-242-7345
Alabama Bureau of Investigation
Internet Crimes Against Children Unit
716 Arcadia Circle
Huntsville, AL 35801
Phone: 256-539-4028
Homewood Police Department
1833 29th Avenue South
Homewood, AL 35209
Phone: 205-877-8637
Hoover Police Department
FBI Innocent Images Task Force, Birmingham
100 Municipal Drive
Hoover, AL 35216
Phone: 205-444-7798

Alaska

Alaska State Troopers
White Collar Crime Section
5700 East Tudor Road
Anchorage, AK 99507
Phone: 907-269-5627
Anchorage Police Department
4501 South Bragaw Street
Anchorage, AK 99507-1599
Phone: 907-786-8767/907-786-8778
University of Alaska at Fairbanks
Police Department
Box 755560
Fairbanks, AK 99775
Phone: 907-474-7721

Arizona

Arizona Attorney General's Office
Technology Crimes
1275 West Washington Street
Phoenix, AZ 85007
Phone: 602-542-3881
Fax: 602-542-5997

Arkansas

University of Arkansas at Little Rock Police Department
2801 South University Avenue
Little Rock, AR 72204
Phone: 501-569-8793/501-569-8794

California

Bureau of Medi-Cal Fraud and Elder Abuse
110 West A Street, Suite 1100
San Diego, CA 92101
Phone: 619-645-2432
Fax: 619-645-2455
California Franchise Tax Board
Investigations Bureau
100 North Barranca Street, Suite 600
West Covina, CA 91791-1600
Phone: 626-859-4678
Kern County Sheriff's Department
1350 Norris Road
Bakersfield, CA 93308
Phone: 661-391-7728
Los Angeles Police Department
Computer Crime Unit
150 North Los Angeles Street
Los Angeles, CA 90012
Phone: 213-485-3795
Modesto Police Department
600 10th Street
Modesto, CA 95353
Phone: 209-572-9500, ext. 29119
North Bay High-Technology Evidence Analysis Team (HEAT)
1125 Third Street
Napa, CA 94559
Phone: 707-253-4500
Regional Computer Forensic Laboratory at San Diego
9797 Aero Drive
San Diego, CA 92123-1800
Phone: 858-499-7799
Fax: 858-499-7798
E-mail: rcfl@rcfl.org
Sacramento Valley High-Tech Crimes Task Force
High-Tech Crimes Division
Sacramento County Sheriff's Department
PO Box 988
Sacramento, CA 95812-0998
Phone: 916-874-3030
San Diego High-Technology Crimes
Economic Fraud Division
District Attorney's Office, County of San Diego

Suite 1020
San Diego, CA 92101
Phone: 619-531-3660

Silicon Valley High-Tech Crime Task Force
Rapid Enforcement Allied Computer Team (REACT)
c/o Federal Bureau of Investigation
950 South Bascom Avenue, Suite 3011
San Jose, CA 95128
Phone: 408-494-7161
Pager: 408-994-3264

Southern California High-Technology Crime Task Force
Commercial Crimes Bureau
Los Angeles County Sheriff's Department
11515 South Colima Road, Room M104
Whittier, CA 90604
Phone: 562-946-7942

U.S. Customs Service
Computer Investigative Specialist
3403 10th Street, Suite 600
Riverside, CA 92501
Phone: 906-276-6664, ext. 231

Colorado

Colorado Bureau of Investigation
600 Kipling Street
Denver, CO 80215
Phone: 303-239-4211

Denver District Attorney's Office
303 West Colfax Avenue, Suite 1300
Denver, CO 80204
Phone: 720-913-9000

Connecticut

Connecticut Department of Public Safety
Division of Scientific Services
Forensic Science Laboratory
Computer Crimes and Electronic Evidence Unit
278 Colony Street
Meriden, CT 06451
Phone: 203-639-6492
Fax: 203-630-3760

Connecticut Department of Revenue Services
Special Investigations Section
25 Sigourney Street
Hartford, CT 06106
Phone: 860-297-5877
Fax: 860-297-5625

Yale University Police Department
98–100 Sachem Street
New Haven, CT 06511
Phone: 203-432-7958

Delaware

Delaware State Police
High-Technology Crimes Unit
1575 McKee Road, Suite 204
Dover, DE 19904
Phone: 302-739-2761

New Castle County Police Department
Criminal Investigations Unit
3601 North DuPont Highway
New Castle, DE 19720
Phone: 302-395-8110

University of Delaware Police Department
101 MOB
700 Pilottown Road
Lewes, DE 19958
Phone: 302-645-4334

District of Columbia

Metropolitan Police Department

Special Investigations Division
Computer Crimes and Forensics Unit
300 Indiana Avenue N.W., Room 3019
Washington, DC 20001
Phone: 202-727-4252 or 202-727-1010

Florida

Florida Atlantic University Police Department
777 Glades Road, #49
Boca Raton, FL 33431
Phone: 561-297-2371
Fax: 561-297-3565
Gainsville Police Department
Criminal Investigations/Computer Unit
721 N.W. Sixth Street
Gainsville, FL 32601
Phone: 352-334-2488
High-Technology Crimes
Office of Statewide Prosecution
135 West Central Boulevard, Suite 1000
Orlando, FL 32801
Phone: 407-245-0893
Fax: 407-245-0356
Institute of Police Technology and Management
Computer Forensics Laboratory
University of North Florida
12000 Alumni Drive
Jacksonville, FL 32224-2678
Phone: 904-620-4786
Fax: 904-620-2453
Web site: *www.iptm.org*
Pinellas County Sheriff's Office
10750 Ulmerton Road
Largo, FL 33778

Georgia

Georgia Bureau of Investigation
Financial Investigations Unit
5255 Snapfinger Drive, Suite 150
Decatur, GA 30035
Phone: 770-987-2323
Fax: 770-987-9775

Hawaii

Honolulu Police Department
White Collar Crime Unit
801 South Beretania Street
Honolulu, HI, 96819
Phone: 808-529-3112

Idaho

Ada County Sheriff's Office
7200 Barrister Drive
Boise, ID 83704
Phone: 208-377-6691

Illinois

Illinois State Police
Computer Crimes Investigation Unit
Division of Operations
Operational Services Command
Statewide Special Investigations Bureau
500 Illes Park Place, Suite 104
Springfield, IL 62718
Phone: 217-524-9572
Fax: 217-785-6793
Illinois State Police
Computer Crimes Investigation Unit
9511 West Harrison Street
Des Plaines, IL 60016-1562
Phone: 847-294-4549
Tazewell County State's Attorney CID
342 Court Street, Suite 6
Pekin, IL 61554-3298
Phone: 309-477-2205, ext. 400
Fax: 309-477-2729

Indiana

Evansville Police Department
Fraud Investigations
15 N.W. Martin Luther King, Jr., Boulevard
Evansville IN, 47708
Phone: 812-436-7995/812-436-7994

Indiana State Police
Computer Crime Unit
5811 Ellison Road
Fort Wayne, IN 46750
Phone: 219-432-8661

Indianapolis Police Department
901 North Post Road, Room 115
Indianapolis, IN 46219
Phone: 317-327-3461

Iowa

Iowa Division of Criminal Investigation
502 East Ninth Street
Des Moines, IA 50319
Phone: 515-281-3666
Fax: 515-281-7638

Kansas

Kansas Bureau of Investigation
High-Technology Crime Investigation Unit
1620 S.W. Tyler Street
Topeka, KS 66612-1837
Phone: 785-296-8222
Fax: 785-296-0525

Olathe Police Department
501 East 56 Highway
Olathe, KS 66061
Phone: 913-782-4500

Wichita Police Department
Forensic Computer Crimes Unit
455 North Main, Sixth Floor Lab
Wichita, KS 67202
Phone: 316-268-4102/316-268-4128

Kentucky

Boone County Sheriff
PO Box 198
Burlington, KY 41005
Phone: 859-334-2175

Louisiana

Gonzales Police Department
120 South Irma Boulevard
Gonzales, LA 70737
Phone: 225-647-7511
Fax: 225-647-9544

Louisiana Department of Justice
Criminal Division
High-Technology Crime Unit
PO Box 94095
Baton Rouge, LA 70804
Phone: 225-342-7552
Fax: 225-342-7893

Maine

Maine Computer Crimes Task Force
171 Park Street
Lewiston, ME 04240
Phone: 207-784-6422

Maryland

Anne Arundel County Police Department
Computer Crimes Unit
41 Community Place
Crownsville, MD 21032
Phone: 410-222-3419
Fax: 410-987-7433

Department of Maryland State Police
Computer Crimes Unit

7155-C Columbia Gateway Drive
Columbia, MD 21046
Phone: 410-290-1620
Fax: 410-290-1831
Montgomery County Police
Computer Crime Unit
2350 Research Boulevard
Rockville, MD 20850
Phone: 301-840-2599

Massachusetts

Massachusetts Office of the Attorney General
High-Tech and Computer Crime Division
One Ashburton Place
Boston, MA 02108
Phone: 617-727-2200

Michigan

Michigan Department of Attorney General
High-Tech Crime Unit
18050 Deering
Livonia, MI 48152
Phone: 734-525-4151
Fax: 734-525-4372
Oakland County Sheriff's Department
Computer Crimes Unit
1201 North Telegraph Road
Pontiac, MI 48341
Phone: 248-858-4942
Fax: 248-858-9565

Minnesota

Ramsey County Sheriff's Department
14 West Kellogg Boulevard
St. Paul, MN 55102
Phone: 651-266-2797

Mississippi

Biloxi Police Department
170 Porter Avenue
Biloxi, MS 39530
Phone: 228-432-9382

Missouri

St. Louis Metropolitan Police Department
High-Tech Crimes Unit
1200 Clark
St. Louis, MO 63103
Phone: 314-444-5441

Montana

Montana Division of Criminal Investigation
Computer Crime Unit
303 North Roberts, Room 367
Helena, MT 59620
Phone: 406-444-6681

Nebraska

Lincoln Police Department
575 South 10th Street
Lincoln, NE 68508
Phone: 402-441-7587
Nebraska State Patrol
Internet Crimes Against Children Unit
4411 South 108th Street
Omaha, NE 68137
Phone: 402-595-2410
Fax: 402-697-1409

Nevada

City of Reno, Nevada, Police Department
Computer Crimes Unit

455 East Second Street (street address)
Reno, NV 89502
PO Box 1900 (mailing address)
Reno, NV 89505
Phone: 775-334-2107
Fax: 775-785-4026

Nevada Attorney General's Office
100 North Carson Street
Carson City, NV 89701
Phone: 775-328-2889

New Hampshire

New Hampshire State Police Forensic Laboratory
Computer Crimes Unit
10 Hazen Drive
Concord, NH 03305
Phone: 603-271-0300

New Jersey

New Jersey Division of Criminal Justice
Computer Analysis and Technology Unit (CATU)
25 Market Street
PO Box 085
Trenton, NJ 08625-0085
Phone: 609-984-5256/609-984-6500
Pager: 888-819-1292

Ocean County Prosecutor's Office
Special Investigations Unit/Computer Crimes
PO Box 2191
Toms River, NJ 08753
Phone: 732-929-2027, ext. 4014
Fax: 732-240-3338

New Mexico

New Mexico Gaming Control Board
Information Systems Division
6400 Uptown Boulevard N.E., Suite 100E
Albuquerque, NM 87110
Phone: 505-841-9719

Twelfth Judicial District Attorney's Office
1000 New York Avenue, Room 301
Alamogordo, NM 88310
Phone: 505-437-1313, ext. 110

New York

Erie County Sheriff's Office
Computer Crime Unit
10 Delaware Avenue
Buffalo, NY 14202
Phone: 716-662-6150
Web site: *www.erie.gov/sheriff/CCU*

Nassau County Police Department
Computer Crime Section
970 Brush Hollow Road
Westbury, NY 11590
Phone: 516-573-5275

New York Electronic Crimes Task Force
United States Secret Service
New York, NY 11048
Phone: 212-637-4500

New York Police Department
Computer Investigation and Technology Unit
1 Police Plaza, Room 1110D
New York, NY, 10038
Phone: 212-374-4247
Fax: 212-374-4249

New York State Department of Taxation and Finance
Office of Deputy Inspector General
W.A. Harriman Campus
Building 9, Room 481
Albany, NY 12227
Phone: 518-485-8698

Web site: *www.tax.state.ny.us*
New York State Police
Computer Crime Unit
Forensic Investigation Center
Building 30, State Campus
1220 Washington Avenue
Albany, NY 12226
Phone: 518-457-5712
Fax: 518-402-2773
Rockland County Sheriff's Department
Computer Crime Task Force
55 New Hempstead Road
New City, NY 10956
Phone: 845-708-7860 or 845-638-5836
Fax: 845-708-7821

North Carolina

Raleigh Police Department
110 South McDowell Street
Raleigh, NC 27601
Phone: 919-890-3555

North Dakota

North Dakota Bureau of Criminal Investigation
PO Box 1054
Bismarck, ND 58502-1054
Phone: 701-328-5500

Ohio

Hamilton County Ohio Sheriff's Office
Justice Center
1000 Sycamore Street, Room 110
Cincinnati, OH 45202
Phone: 513-946-6689
Fax: 513-721-3581
Web site: *www.hcso.org*
Ohio Attorney General's Office
Bureau of Criminal Investigation
Computer Crime Unit
1560 State Route 56
London, OH 43140
Phone: 740-845-2410
Riverside Police Department
1791 Harshman Road
Riverside, OH 45424
Phone: 937-904-1425

Oklahoma

Oklahoma Attorney General
4545 North Lincoln Boulevard
Suite 260
Oklahoma City, OK 73105-3498
Phone: 405-521-4274
Oklahoma State Bureau of Investigation
PO Box 968
Stillwater, OK 74076
Phone: 405-742-8329
Fax: 405-742-8284

Oregon

Portland Police Bureau
Computer Crimes Detail
1115 S.W. 2nd Avenue
Portland, OR 97204
Phone: 503-823-0871
Washington County Sheriff's Office
215 S.W. Adams Avenue, MS32
Hillsboro, OR 97123
Phone: 503-846-2573
Fax: 503-846-2637

Pennsylvania

Allegheny County Police Department
High-Tech Crime Unit
400 North Lexington Street
Pittsburgh, PA 15208
Phone: 412-473-1304

Fax: 412-473-1377
Erie County District Attorney's Office
Erie County Courthouse
140 West 6th Street
Erie, PA 16501
Phone: 814-451-6349
Fax: 814-451-6419

Rhode Island

Warwick Police Department
BCI Unit, Detective Division
99 Veterans Memorial Drive
Warwick, RI 02886
Phone: 401-468-4200 (main)

South Carolina

South Carolina Law Enforcement Division (SLED)
PO Box 21398
Columbia, SC 29221-1398
Phone: 803-737-9000
Winthrop University
Department of Public Safety
02 Crawford Building
Rock Hill, SC 29733
Phone: 803-323-3496

Tennessee

Harriman Police Department
130 Pansy Hill Road
Harriman, TN 37748
Phone: 865-882-3383
Fax: 865-882-0700
Knox County Sheriff's Department
400 West Main Avenue
Knoxville, TN 379902
Phone: 865-971-3911
Tennessee Attorney General's Office
425 Fifth Avenue, North
Nashville, TN 37243
Phone: 615-532-9658

Texas

Austin Police Department
715 East 8th Street
Austin, TX 78701
Web site: *www.ci.austin.tx.us/police*
Bexar County District Attorney's Office
300 Dolorosa
San Antonio, TX 78205
Phone: 210-335-2974/210-335-2991
Dallas Police Department
2014 Main Street
Dallas, TX 75201
Web site: *www.ci.dallas.tx.us/dpd*
Federal Bureau of Investigation
Dallas Field Office
1801 North Lamar Street
Dallas, TX 75202-1795
Phone: 214-720-2200
Web site: *www.fbi.gov/contact/fo/dl/dallas.htm*
Houston Police Department
1200 Travis Street
Houston, TX 77002
Web site: *www.ci.houston.tx.us/departme/police*
Portland Police Department
902 Moore Avenue
Portland, TX 78374
Phone: 361-643-2546
Fax: 361-643-5689
Web site: *www.portlandpd.com*
Texas Department of Public Safety
5805 North Lamar Boulevard (street address)
Austin, TX 78752-4422
PO Box 4087 (mailing address)

Austin, TX 78773-0001
Phone: 512-424-2200 or 800-252-5402
Web site: *www.txdps.state.tx.us*

Utah

Utah Department of Public Safety
Criminal Investigations Bureau, Forensic Computer Lab
5272 South College Drive, Suite 200
Murray, UT 84123
Phone: 801-284-6238

Vermont

State of Vermont Department of Public Safety
Bureau of Criminal Investigation
103 South Main Street
Waterbury, VT 05671-2101
Phone: 802-241-5367
Fax: 802-241-5349
VT Internet Crimes Task Force
1 North Avenue
Burlington VT 05401
Phone: 802-857-0092
info@vtinternetcrimes.com
Web site: *www.vtinternetcrimes.com/*

Virginia

Arlington County Police Department
Criminal Investigations Division
Computer Forensics
1425 North Courthouse Road
Arlington, VA 22201
Phone: 703-228-4239
Pager: 703-866-8965
Fairfax County Police Department
Computer Forensics Section
4100 Chain Bridge Road
Fairfax, VA 22030
Phone: 703-246-7800
Fax: 703-246-4253
Web site: *www.co.fairfax.va.us/ps/police/homepage.htm*
Richmond Police Department
Technology Crimes Section
501 North Ninth Street
Richmond, VA 23219
Phone: 804-646-3949
Virginia Beach Police Department
2509 Princess Anne Road
Virginia Beach, VA 23456
Phone: 757-427-1749
Virginia Department of Motor Vehicles
Law Enforcement Section
945 Edwards Ferry Road
Leesburg, VA 20175
Phone: 703-771-4757
Virginia Office of the Attorney General
900 East Main Street
Richmond, VA 23219
Phone: 804-786-6554
Virginia State Police
Richmond, VA 23236
Phone: 804-323-2040

Washington

The Agora
PO Box 99
Seattle, WA 98111-0099
Phone: 253-573-4738
King County Sheriff's Office
Fraud/Computer Forensic Unit
401 Fourth Avenue North, RJC 104
Kent, WA 98032-4429
Phone: 206-296-4280
Lynnwood Police Department
High-Tech Property Crimes
19321 44th Avenue West (street address)
PO Box 5008 (mailing address)

Lynnwood, WA 98046-5008
Phone: 425-744-6916

Tacoma Police Department
930 Tacoma Avenue South
Tacoma, WA 98402
Phone: 253-591-5679

Vancouver Police Department
Computer Forensics Specialist
300 East 13th Street
Vancouver, WA 98660
Phone: 360-735-8887
E-mail: ecrimes@ci.vancouver.wa.us

Washington State Department of Fish and Wildlife
600 Capitol Way North
Olympia, WA 98501
Phone: 360-902-2210

Washington State Patrol
Computer Forensics Unit
Airdustrial Way, Building 17
Olympia, WA 98507-2347
Phone: 360-753-3277

West Virginia

National White-Collar Crime Center
1000 Technology Drive, Suite 2130
Fairmont, WV 26554
Phone: 877-628-7674
Web site: *www.cybercrime.org*

Wisconsin

Green Bay Police Department
307 South Adams Street
Green Bay, WI 54301

Wisconsin Department of Justice
PO Box 7857
Madison, WI 53707-7851
Phone: 608-266-1221
Web site: *www.doj.state.wi.us*

Wood County Sheriff's Department
400 Market Street
Wis Rapids, WI 54495
Phone: 715-421-8700

Wyoming

Casper Police Department
210 North David
Casper, WY 82601
Phone: 307-235-8489

Gillette Police Department
201 East Fifth Street
Gillette, WY 82716
Phone: 307-682-5109

Green River Police Department
50 East 2nd North
Green River, WY 82935
Phone: 307-872-0555

Wyoming Division of Criminal Investigation
316 West 22nd Street
Cheyenne, WY 82002
Phone: 307-777-7183
Fax: 307-777-7252

GENERAL

Computer Crime and Intellectual Property Section (CCIPS)

Searching and seizing computers and related electronic evidence.
Web site: *www.cybercrime.gov/searching.html#FED_GUID*

Criminal Justice Resources—Michigan State University Libraries

An excellent Web site containing numerous well-organized links related to criminal justice.
Web site: *www.lib.msu.edu/harris23/ crimjust/crimjust.htm*

High-Technology NewsBits

High-Tech "NewsBits" is an e-mail distribution newsletter produced each weekday by Chief Ron Levine that provides news clippings and pointers to open-source news related to high-technology and crime.
Web site: *www.newsbits.net/*

InfoSec News

InfoSec News is a privately run, medium-traffic list that caters to the distribution of information security news articles. These articles will come from newspapers, magazines, online resources, and more.
Web site: *www.c4i.org/isn.html*

Discussion List Servers

Computer Forensic Investigators Digest Listserv (CFID)

The CFID is a list designed for discussions in the field of high-technology crime investigations. All subscriptions are managed on an approval basis. Subscription information can be found on the Forensics Web site at *www.forensicsweb.com* or via e-mail to jnj@infobin.org.

Computer Forensics Tool Testing (CFTT)

The CFTT is a group for discussing and coordinating computer forensics tool testing. Testing methodologies as well as the results of testing various tools will be discussed. The ultimate goal of these tests is to ensure that tools used by computer forensics examiners are providing accurate and complete results. The CFTT group is open to all individuals in the field who are interested in participating in the testing of computer forensics tools. Subscription information can be found on the CFTT Web site at *http://groups.yahoo.com/group/cftt.*

High-Tech Crime Consortium (HTCC)

The High-Tech Crime Consortium listserv is restricted to law enforcement personnel, prosecutors, and corporate investigators tasked with the investigation and prosecution of high-technology crime. You must be employed with a federal, state, or local law enforcement agency or be a senior-level investigator within a corporation to join the group.

Investigators who meet the membership requirements can join by completing an application for membership. Application request should include a business card. Subscription information can be found on the HTCC Web site at *www.hightechcrimecops.org* or via e-mail to admin@hightechcrimecops.org.

Security Focus Forensics

The Security Focus Forensics list server is a discussion mailing list dedicated to technical and process methodologies for the application of computer forensics. Topics of discussion follow:

- Audit trail analysis
- General postmortem analysis
- Products and tools for use in this field

Subscription information can be found on the Security Focus Web site at *www.securityfocus.com/ cgi-bin/forums.pl.*

Appendix

H

Investigator's Cisco Router Command Cheat Sheet

There are two basic levels of login:

- Standard Read Mode (prompt looks like "router-name>")
- Enable Mode (prompt looks like "router-name#")

You only ever need to type enough of the command to distinguish it from other commands.

You can always press the Tab key to finish the command you start typing.

If you are locked up by router output, enter **<ctrl><shift><6><x>**.

"?" is the universal help command.

To see what commands are available beyond an initial command enter **Initial command ?** (for example, **show ?**).

To save configuration changes, enter **copy running-config startup-config.**

To save a configuration to a TFTP Server enter **copy running-config tftp**, then follow the prompts.

Some good Show commands to utilize follow:

- Show Dial
- Show IP Route
- Show IP Protocol
- Show Version

To see debug output from a telnet session you must first enter **Terminal monitor.**

To reboot the router enter reload.

Always remember where you are by the router prompt, as follows:

```
                         router>
             |
             router#
             |
             router(config)#
               / | \
     router(config-if)          # router(config-line)#      router(config-
router)#
```

USING THE CISCO WILDCARD MASK

Cisco wildcard mask for an entire subnet:

```
  255.255.255.255
 – 255.255.192.0
 _______________
  0.  0. 63.255
```

Cisco wildcard mask to match range:

100.1.16.0 - 100.1.31.255

```
  100.1.31.255
– 100.1.16.0
 _______________
  0.0.15.255
```

Take the broadcast and subtract from the network.

PACKET FILTERING ON CISCO ROUTERS

Cisco routers implement packet filters as access control lists (ACLs), not to be confused with Windows NT ACLs. Basically, you create sets of ACLs and then apply them to the desired router interface as access groups.

A sample configuration follows. The first set of ACLs describes the connections allowed into the network from the outside.

List 101

```
access-list 101 deny ip 192.168.100.0 0.0.0.255 any
```

Anti Spoofing—This statement will not allow any connections from IP address within the internal network number.

```
access-list 101 permit tcp any any established
```
#Allow any TCP connections to ports that were established from the inside.

```
access-list 101 permit tcp  192.168.200.0 0.0.0.255 any eq telnet
```
#Allow telnet connections from the specific class C network 192.168.200.0.

```
access-list 101 permit tcp any any eq ftp
```
#Allow FTP connections.

```
access-list 101 permit tcp any any eq ftp-data
```
#Allow FTP-Data connections.

```
access-list 101 permit tcp any any eq domain
access-list 101 permit udp any any eq domain
```
#Allow DNS connections.

```
access-list 101 permit tcp any any eq pop3
```
#Allow POP3 connections for retrieving mail.

```
access-list 101 permit tcp any any eq smtp
```
#Allow SMTP for mail servers to transfer mail.

```
access-list 101 permit tcp any any eq www
```
#Allow connections to Web servers.

```
access-list 101 permit tcp any any eq 443
access-list 101 permit udp any any eq 443
```
#Allow connections to SSL for HTTPS.

```
access-list 101 permit udp any any eq 1723
access-list 101 permit tcp any any eq 1723
```
#Allow connections to port 1723 for Point-to-Point Tunneling Protocol.

```
access-list 101 permit icmp any any
```
#Allow all ICMP messages for flow control, ping, error messages, and so on.

#Note: To protect from smurf attacks and ping flooding, you may need to deny ICMP Echo and Echo-#Request.

```
access-list 101 permit 47 any any
```
#Allow all General Encapsulation Protocol number 47 for VPNs and PPTP.

You don't see it, or need to enter it, but there is always an implicit Deny all Else as the last statement in each ACL.

List 102

```
access-list 102 permit ip any any
```
#Allow all IP connections.

```
access-list 102 permit icmp any any
```
#Allow all ICMP connections.

```
access-list 102 permit 47 any any
```
#Allow all General Encapsulation Protocol number 47 for VPNs and PPTP.

You don't see it, or need to enter it, but there is always an implicit Deny all Else as the last statement in each ACL.

Once these access lists are entered, they can be applied to the desired interfaces to provide protection. This is a point of confusion for many people. The best rule to remember the proper assignment of ACLs to router interfaces is OUT means out of the router interface and IN means into the router interface. Keeping this in mind, consider the following configuration:

A T-1 connection to the Internet is connected to the router Serial 0 interface, and the internal network is connected to router Ethernet 0 Interface.

To apply the most restrictive ACLs described, you could assign access list 101 to Ethernet interface 0 out by

```
Interface ethernet 0
ip access-group 101 out
```

These directives invoke access list 101 directives for all packets, leaving the router destined for the network on Ethernet interface 0.

To apply the least-restrictive ACLs described, you could assign access list 102 to Ethernet interface 0 in for connections leaving your internal network.

```
Interface ethernet 0
ip access-group 101 in
```

These directives invoke access list 102 directives for all packets entering the router destined for anywhere.

Access list can be tricky. Some key points to remember follow:

- Access lists are evaluated from the top down; once a rule is met, the packet is dealt with accordingly.
- There is always an implicit "deny all else" at the end of each ACL.
- It is best to construct and invoke an access list from the terminal rather than a telnet session because you could quite easily implement an access list that would terminate your connection.
- Test your access list completely.

Appendix

I About the CD-ROM

The accompanying CD-ROM has an alphabetically organized directory structure and includes sample batch files, forms, and demo and freeware software applications. Please visit the company Web sites listed for further information and the latest demo versions available.

SYSTEM REQUIREMENTS

The overall minimum hardware requirements follow:

- CPU: Pentium class or later
- Memory: 128 MB
- Available disk space: 128 MB for raw files prior to installation
- CD-ROM or DVD-ROM drive
- VGA monitor or high-resolution monitor
- Keyboard and mouse, or compatible pointing device

The minimum software requirements follow:

- Operating system: Windows 98SE/NT/2000/XP/2003
- Other software: Web browser

Some Web pages included on this CD-ROM contain links to external pages, requiring an Internet connection for viewing.

CD-ROM FOLDERS

Drive Health

This folder contains a demo version of Drive Health IDE disk-monitoring application. This tool allows you to predict possible HDD failure, better understand the drive's actual performance through S.M.A.R.T. Technology, and prevent loss of critical data. S.M.A.R.T. is reliability prediction technology created for both ATA/IDE and SCSI environments. S.M.A.R.T. is under continued development by the top drive manufacturers, including Seagate Technology, Inc., IBM, Conner Peripherals, Inc., Western Digital Corporation, and Quantum Corporation. Drive Health requires a S.M.A.R.T-enabled disk drive and Windows operating system with the baseline operating system requirements. Drive Health is manufactured by Helexis Software Development, which maintains a company Web site at *www.drivehealth.com.*

Farm 9

This folder contains the freeware application CryptCat to create secure TCP/IP data channels. Cryptcat is based on the simple Unix utility NetCat, which reads and writes data across network connections using the TCP or UDP protocol. CryptCat enhances NetCat by adding the TwoFish encryption algorithm to create a secure data channel for the data being transmitted. CryptCat is a Win32 command-line application useful for many batch file programming and utility operations. The CryptCat utility runs on all baseline Win32 operating systems with minimal system impact. CryptCat was created by farm9.com, Inc., who maintains a company Web site at *http://farm9.org/Cryptcat.*

Figures

This folder contains JPEG versions of all the book's figures organized by chapter.

Forms

This folder contains digital copies of the sample chain of custody form and worksheets found in Appendices A, B, and C.

Maresware

This folder contains demo utilities from Mares and Company, LLC, which are useful for scripting large-batch forensic operations. Most of the software will work only on a minimal number of files or on a floppy disk drive until fully licensed. However, all the options and capabilities are fully functional as best as could be obtained in an evaluation setting.

Some of the software from the Maresware freeware Web site is fully functional and may be used or copied as the user requires. These "free" programs will be evident by the fact that they are fully functional and require no registration process. HTML-formatted help files, where available, have been included with the utilities. The utilities included in the Maresware directory are only a sampling of the

Maresware library. For more information and the latest versions, see the company Web site at *www.maresware.com.*

Neon

This folder contains a demo version of LANsurveyor by Neon Software. LANsurveyor allows users to quickly and easily map networks through various automatic discovery methods.

To use LANsurveyor, you must have the following:

- A Pentium-class computer with 256 MB memory
- Windows 2000, XP, or 2003 (Professional, workstation, or Server editions)
- A connection to an IP-based network

In addition, some LANsurveyor features require the following:

- Neon Responder client software installed on nodes for reports and client management
- Nodes that understand SNMP (called "SNMP Agents") and the community string (or password) for SNMP devices on which you wish to report. The SNMP Agents used by LANsurveyor are:

    1. MIB-II SNMP agents that exist on nearly all IP routers and many IP devices
    2. Printer MIB SNMP agents that exist on some IP printers
    3. Bridge MIB SNMP agents to determine switch port connectivity
    4. Repeater MIB SNMP agents to determine hub port connectivity

For more information and the latest product demo see the company Web site at *www.neon.com.*

ProDiscover/

This folder contains a demo version of ProDiscover Forensics Edition disk-imaging and analysis suite. The ProDiscover demo included on the CD-ROM is fully functional for five program runs. Its use can be extended by contacting the Technology Pathways sales department.

The minimum hardware requirements follow:

- CPU: 800 Mhz Pentium III or later
- Memory: 256 MB or greater (512 MB recommended)
- Available disk space: 100 MB (a large amount of temporary space is recommended for viewing and hashing evidence files)

- CD-ROM or DVD-ROM drive
- VGA monitor or high-resolution monitor
- Keyboard and mouse, or compatible pointing device

The minimum software requirements follow:

- Operating System: Windows 98SE/NT/2000/XP/2003 (Windows 2000 Professional preferred)

For more information and the latest demo version, see the Technology Pathways Web site at *www.techpathways.com.*

Sysinternals

This folder contains three freeware utility applications useful in batch file volatile data collection including PSList, PSInfo, and PSLoggedon. These utilities, as well as many more, were written by Mark Russinovich and Bryce Cogswell of Winternals and are available from the SysInternals Web site. All PS Utilities included are designed to work on baseline installations of Windows NT, Windows 2000, Windows XP, and Windows Server 2003. More information and the latest utility versions can be found on the company Web site at *www.sysinternals.com.*

Volatile Extraction Tool

This folder contains several versions of the Volatile Extraction Tool batch file and supporting applications described in Chapter 11, "Collecting Volatile Data."

XWays

This folder contains a demo version of the popular WinHex raw file and disk editor. The WinHex utility is an extremely useful hexadecimal editor, particularly helpful in computer forensics for data recovery and other low-level data processing. The WinHex application is manufactured by X-Ways Software Technology Aktiengesellschaft in Germany. WinHex is designed to run on Windows 9x, Me, NT, and 2000. For more information and the latest demo version of WinHex see the company Web site at *www.x-ways.net.*

Index

S